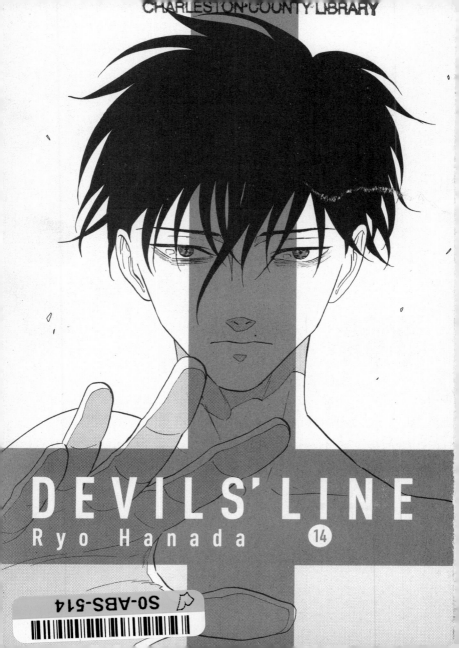

DEVILS' LINE

Ryo Hanada

14

Character and Relationship Diagram

(based on relationships up to the last volume)

TAKESHI MAKIMURA
(Zero Six)

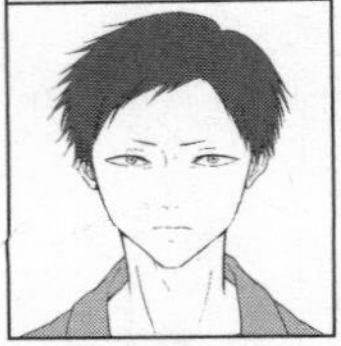

Came into contact with the CCC for an undercover investigation. Currently working with Mayu Sumimori.

NAOYA USHIO
(Zero Five)

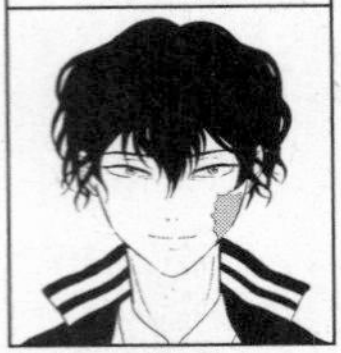

Former CCC member. He took the chance to escape police custody and is currently on the run.

KIRIO KIKUHARA
(Zero Two)

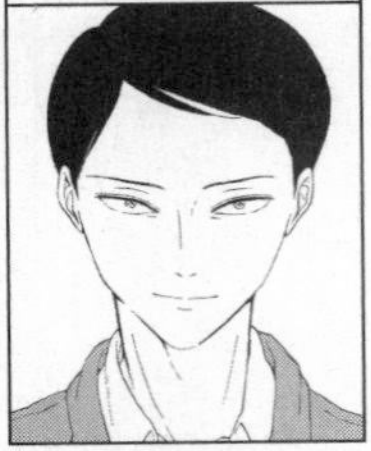

He was the leader of Public Safety Division 5's A Squad, but he was also secretly the commander of the CCC. Someone put a bomb in his car.

YUUKI ANZAI

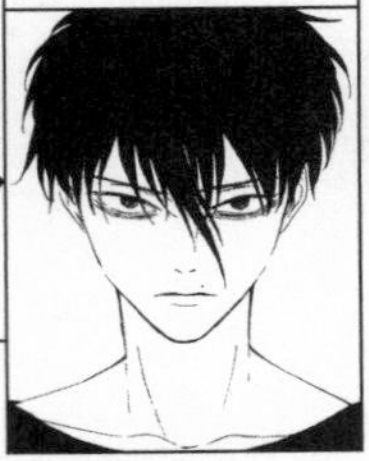

Half-devil, half-human. He was with the police's Public Safety Division 5, but now works for East Bay Security.

MEGUMI ISHIMARU
(Jason)

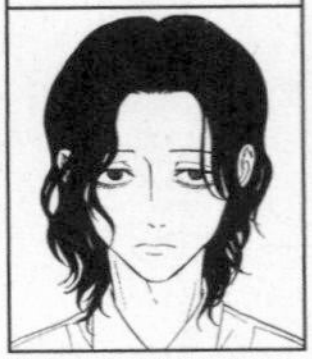

Worked with Division 5 for an undercover investigation. Transferred back to Public Safety General Affairs.

AKIHITO KANZAKI
(Queen)

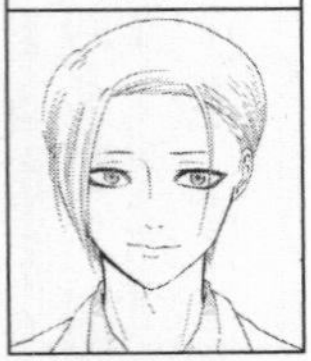

A doctor attached to the CCC. Runs an elite squad of armed guards.

KANAME SHIRASE
(Zero One)

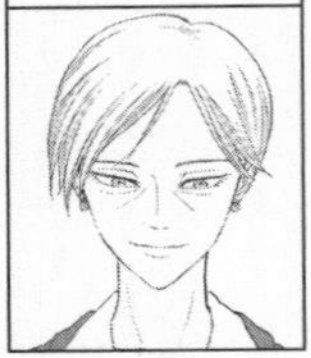

Parliamentary Secretary of Health, Labor and Welfare. Secretly a major player in the CCC.

YANG WEI SHEN

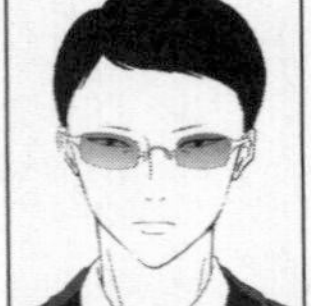

Anzai's boss at East Bay Security. Works in tandem with Anzai on patrols.

JULIANA LLOYD

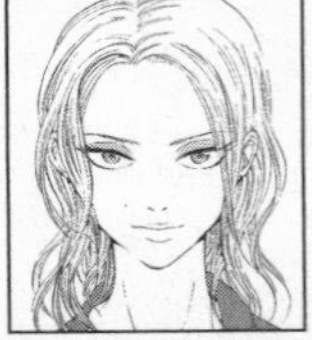

Former devil police officer. Currently employed by East Bay Security along with Anzai.

TAKASHI SAWAZAKI

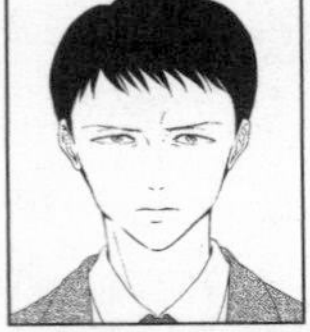

Senior police officer with Public Safety Division 5. Transferred to the General Admin department.

YOUSUKE ASAMI

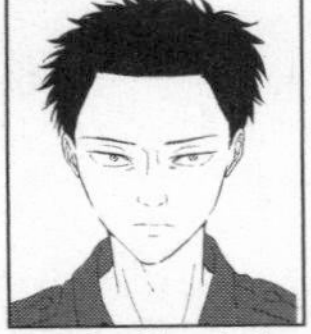

A member of Investigation Division 1, he was assigned to Public Safety Division 5 temporarily.

FORMER CCC MEMBERS

KEN'ICHI YOSHII
(Zero Nine)

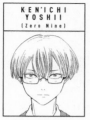

A hacker for the CCC.
In love with Zero Seven.

NANAKO TENJO
(Zero Seven)

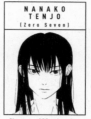

She was a CCC sniper, but has deserted the group. Was on the run alone, but is now under Ishimaru's protection.

MAYU SUMIMORI
(Eleven)

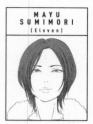

She was responsible for accounting and intel gathering. Makimura's quick thinking saved her life.

DEVIL'S LINE

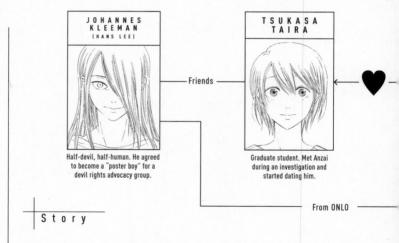

JOHANNES KLEEMAN
(HANS LEE)

Half-devil, half-human. He agreed to become a "poster boy" for a devil rights advocacy group.

Friends

TSUKASA TAIRA

Graduate student. Met Anzai during an investigation and started dating him.

From ONLO

Story

The existence of devils becomes known to the world at large, dramatically changing society. In the midst of this upheaval, Anzai was fatally wounded in a fierce battle with the CCC, and Tsukasa's blood saved his life. The weight of his actions heavy on his mind, Anzai decides to take leave of the police force as well as break up with Tsukasa for the time being, in order to confront his own devil self. Tsukasa accepts his decision and resolves to also move forward. After many twists and turns, they are reunited in Obihiro, and they strengthen their bond by undergoing intercourse training. Meanwhile, as public opinion towards devils grew more antagonistic, Queen's troops took over the Prime Minister's residence. The interim PM risked his life to become a whistleblower, and the attempted terror attack was suppressed. The debate over the fate of devils has only just begun...

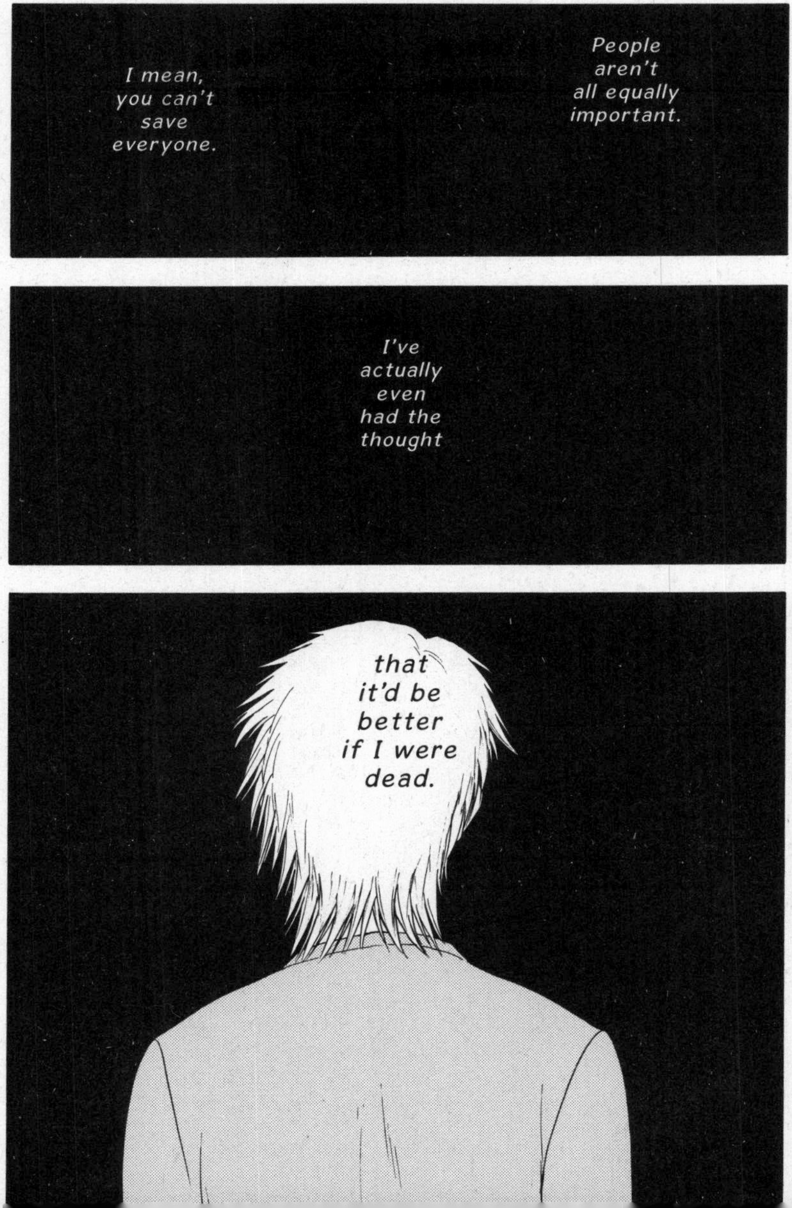
People aren't all equally important.
I mean, you can't save everyone.
I've actually even had the thought
that it'd be better if I were dead.

Line 1.5

Shouta Akimura

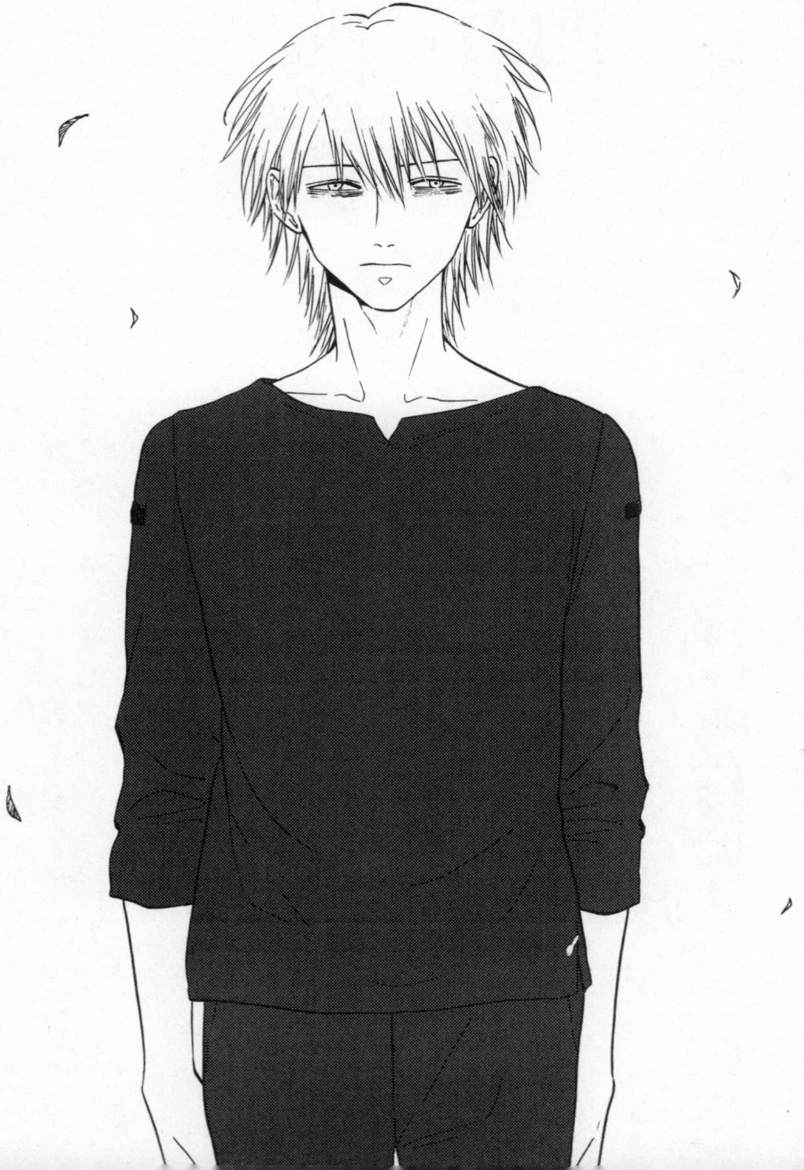

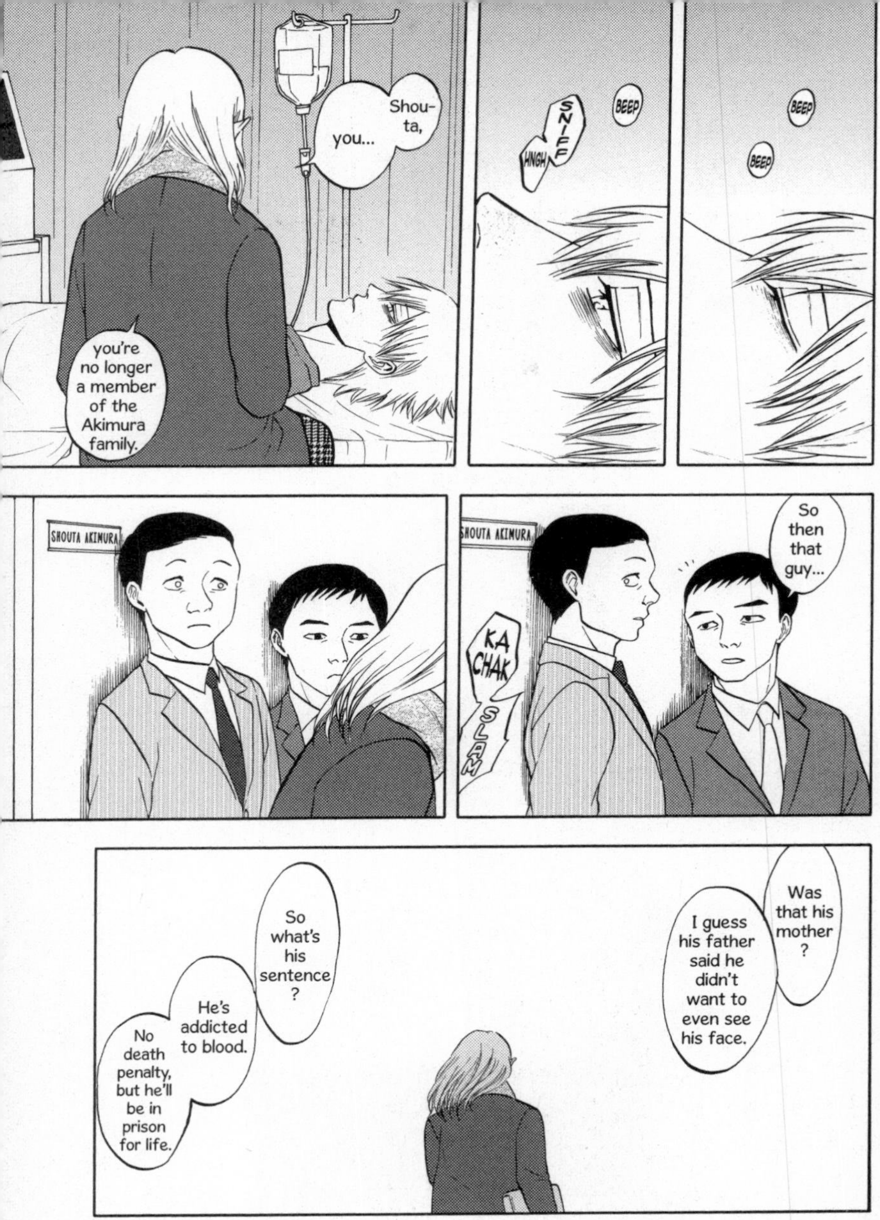
BEEP
BEEP
BEEP
SNIFF
HNGH
Shou-ta, you...
you're no longer a member of the Akimura family.
SHOUTA AKIMURA
So then that guy...
KA CHAK
SLAM
SHOUTA AKIMURA
Was that his mother?
I guess his father said he didn't want to even see his face.
So what's his sentence?
He's addicted to blood.
No death penalty, but he'll be in prison for life.

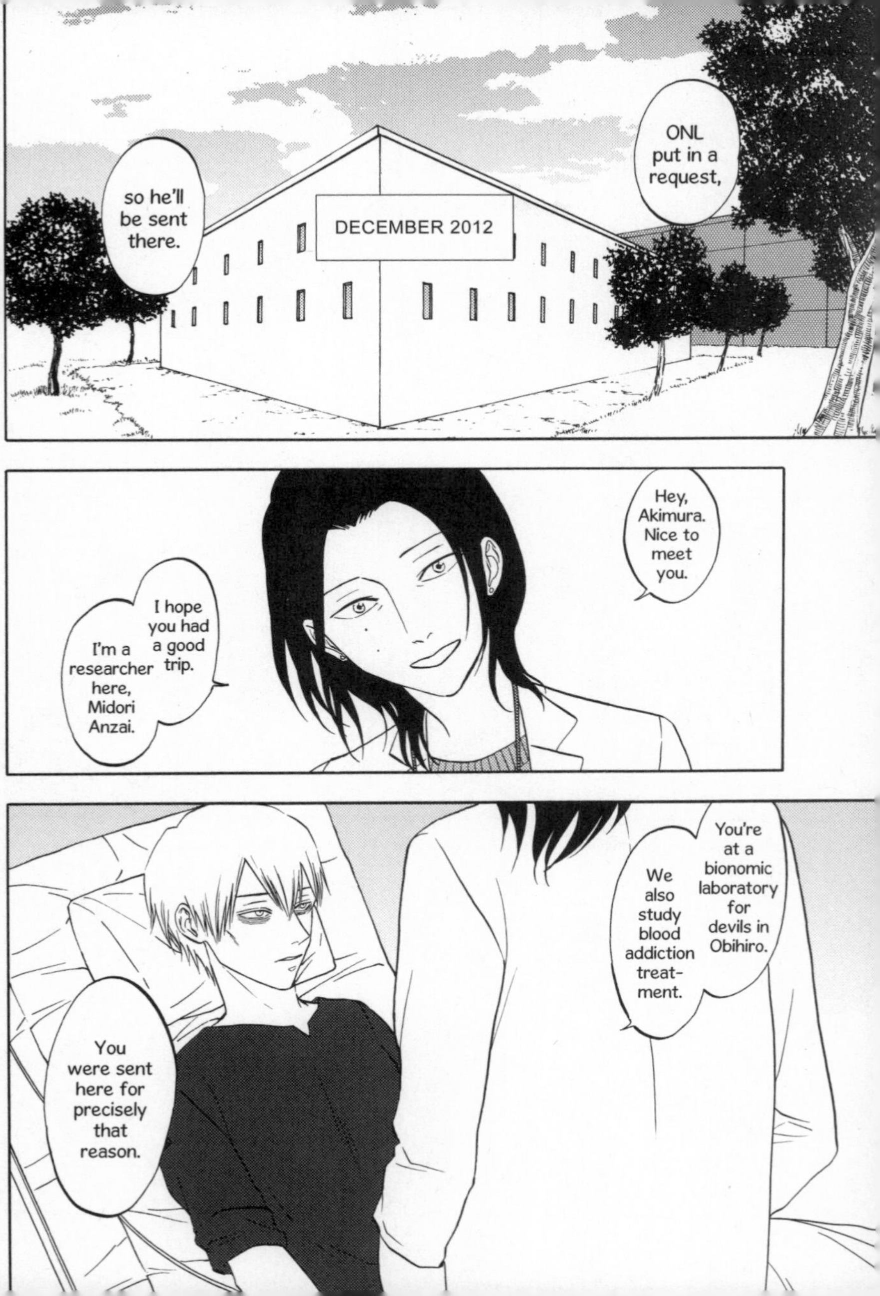
ONL put in a request,
DECEMBER 2012
so he'll be sent there.
Hey, Akimura. Nice to meet you.
I hope you had a good trip.
I'm a researcher here, Midori Anzai.
You're at a bionomic laboratory for devils in Obihiro.
We also study blood addiction treatment.
You were sent here for precisely that reason.

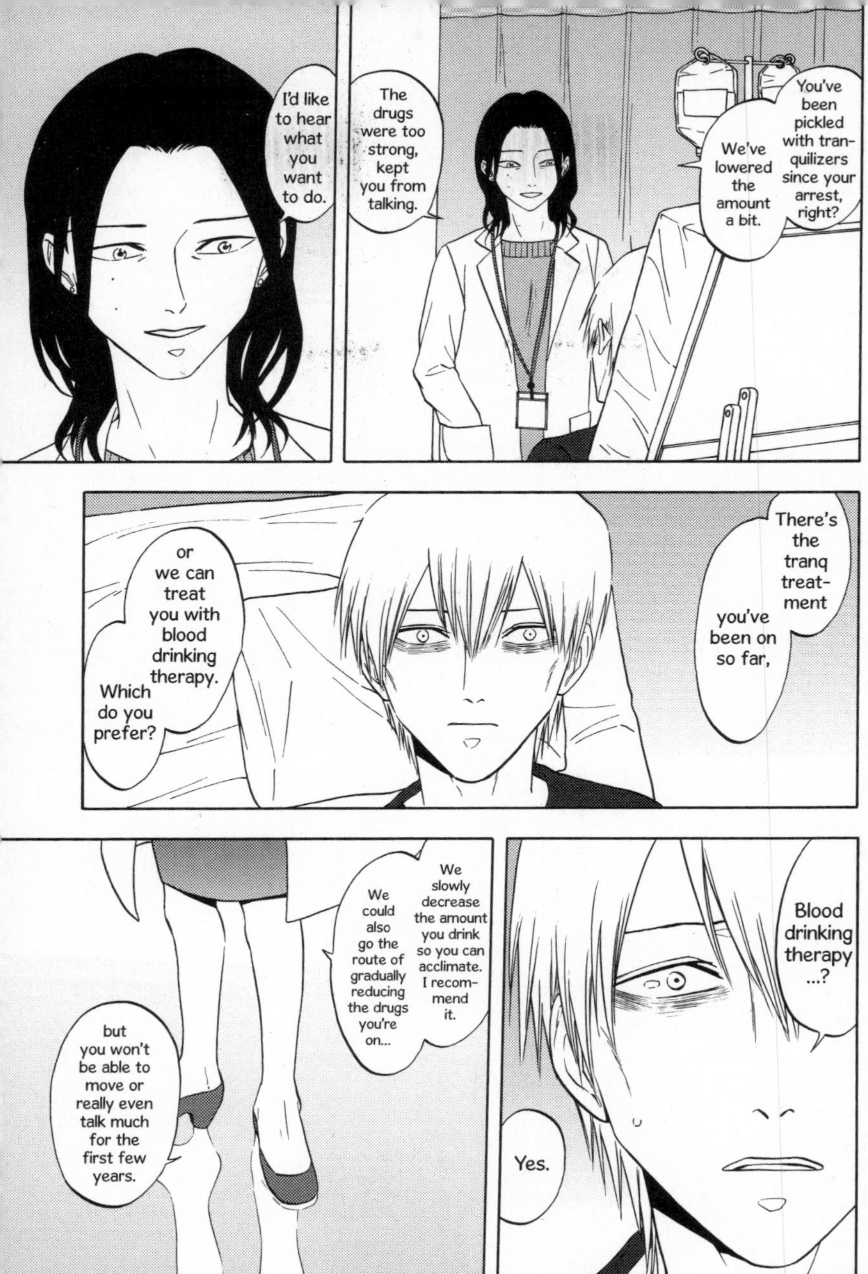

You've been pickled with tran-quilizers since your arrest, right?
We've lowered the amount a bit.
The drugs were too strong, kept you from talking.
I'd like to hear what you want to do.
There's the tranq treat-ment
you've been on so far,
or we can treat you with blood drinking therapy.
Which do you prefer?
Blood drinking therapy ...?
Yes.
We slowly decrease the amount you drink so you can acclimate. I recom-mend it.
We could also go the route of gradually reducing the drugs you're on...
but you won't be able to move or really even talk much for the first few years.

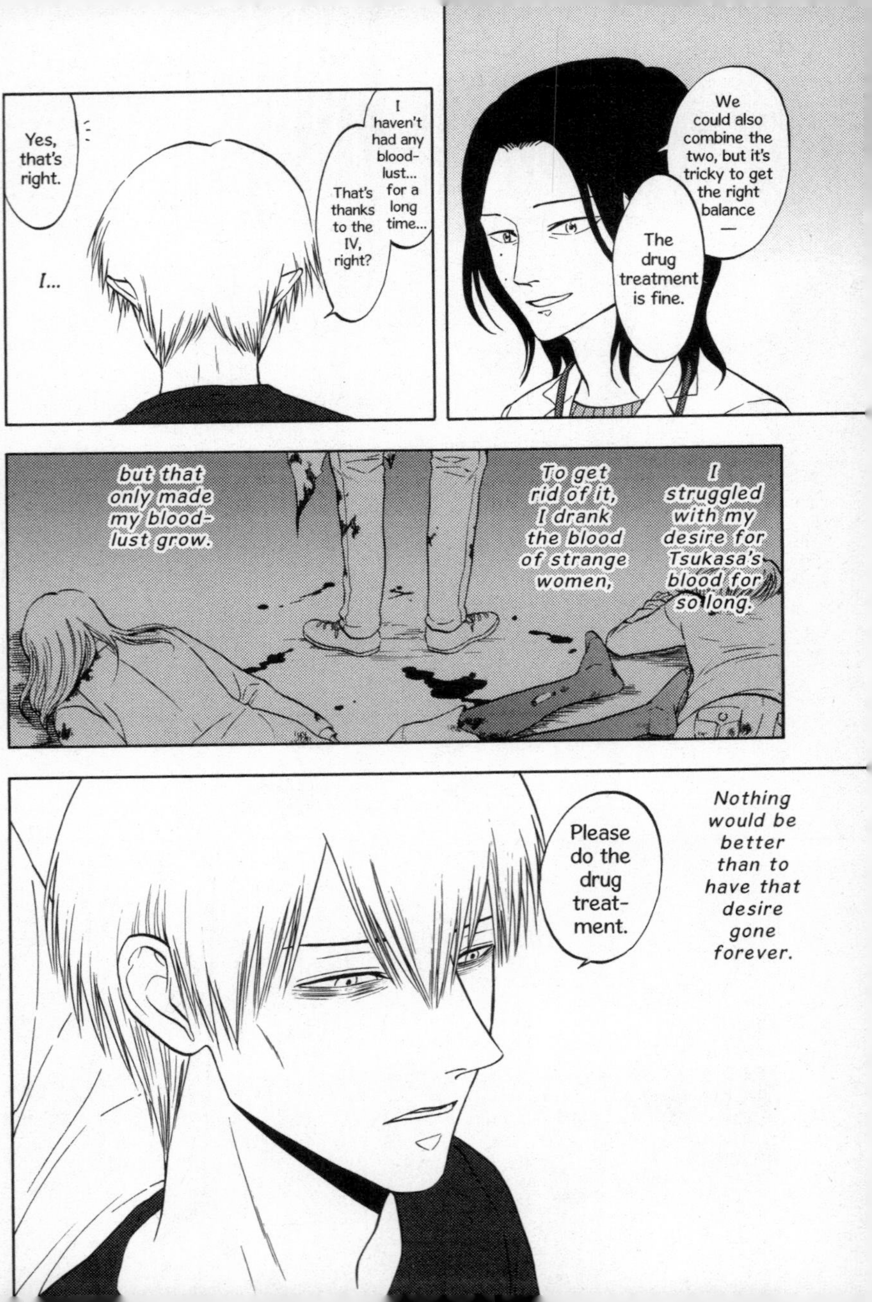
We could also combine the two, but it's tricky to get the right balance —
The drug treatment is fine.
I haven't had any blood-lust... for a long time...
That's thanks to the IV, right?
Yes, that's right.
I...
I struggled with my desire for Tsukasa's blood for so long.
To get rid of it, I drank the blood of strange women,
but that only made my blood-lust grow.
Nothing would be better than to have that desire gone forever.
Please do the drug treatment.

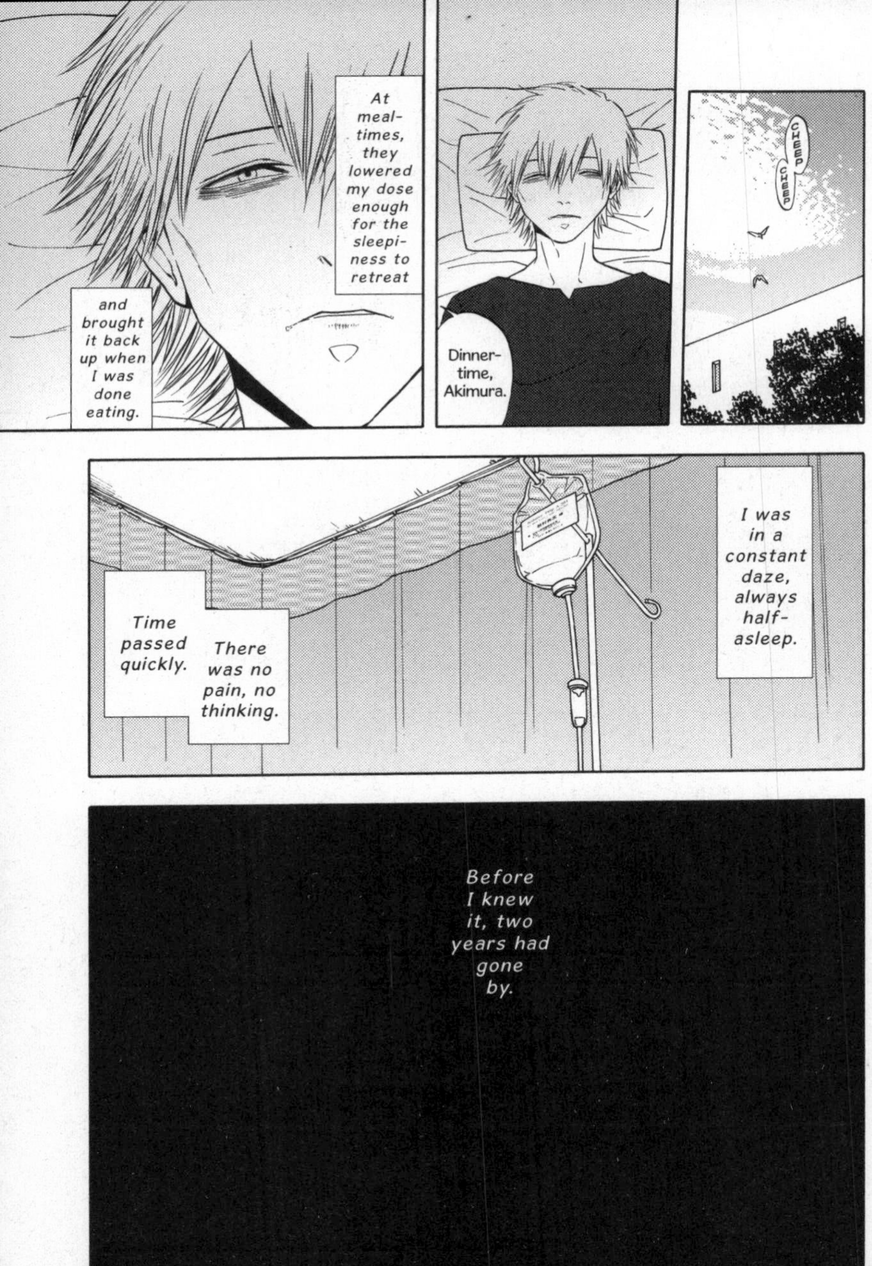
CHEEP
CHEEP
Dinner-time, Akimura.
At meal-times, they lowered my dose enough for the sleepi-ness to retreat
and brought it back up when I was done eating.
I was in a constant daze, always half-asleep.
Time passed quickly.
There was no pain, no thinking.
Before I knew it, two years had gone by.

Then they gradually reduced the dosage.
At the same time, I started therapy and working on getting out of bed.
I still remembered Tsukasa.
Having the dose reduced was rough.
I was put back to sleep again.
Another two years passed.
SEPTEMBER 2016
OATH
To participate in the 20th Hybrid Birth Project carried out by Obihiro National Laboratory Bionomic Research Division, you must swear here to strictly follow the rules hereunder.
MEMORANDUM
1. HANDLING OF CONFIDENTIAL INFORMATION
I do hereby swear not to reveal without the permission of Obihiro National Laboratory Bionomic Research Division any information obtained over the course of participation in the Project (hereafter "Confidential Information").
2. OWNERSHIP OF CONFIDENTIAL INFORMATION
I understand that Confidential Information is owned by Obihiro National Laboratory Bionomic Research Division, and I will assert no rights to Confidential Information, regardless of whether or not it involves my own personal information.
3. CONFIDENTIALITY AFTER PROJECT COMPLETION
I do hereby swear not to disclose Confidential Information even after the end of the project and the termination of the participant contract.
4.
URES
is incurred due to
ision, there may be legal
DAY
OATH NO.:
NAME

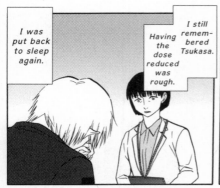

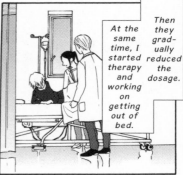

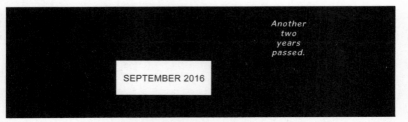

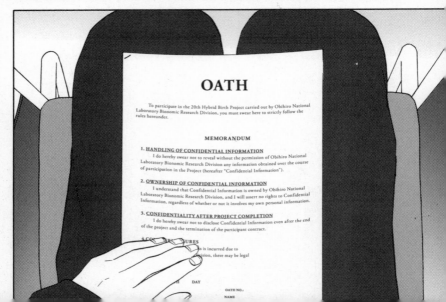

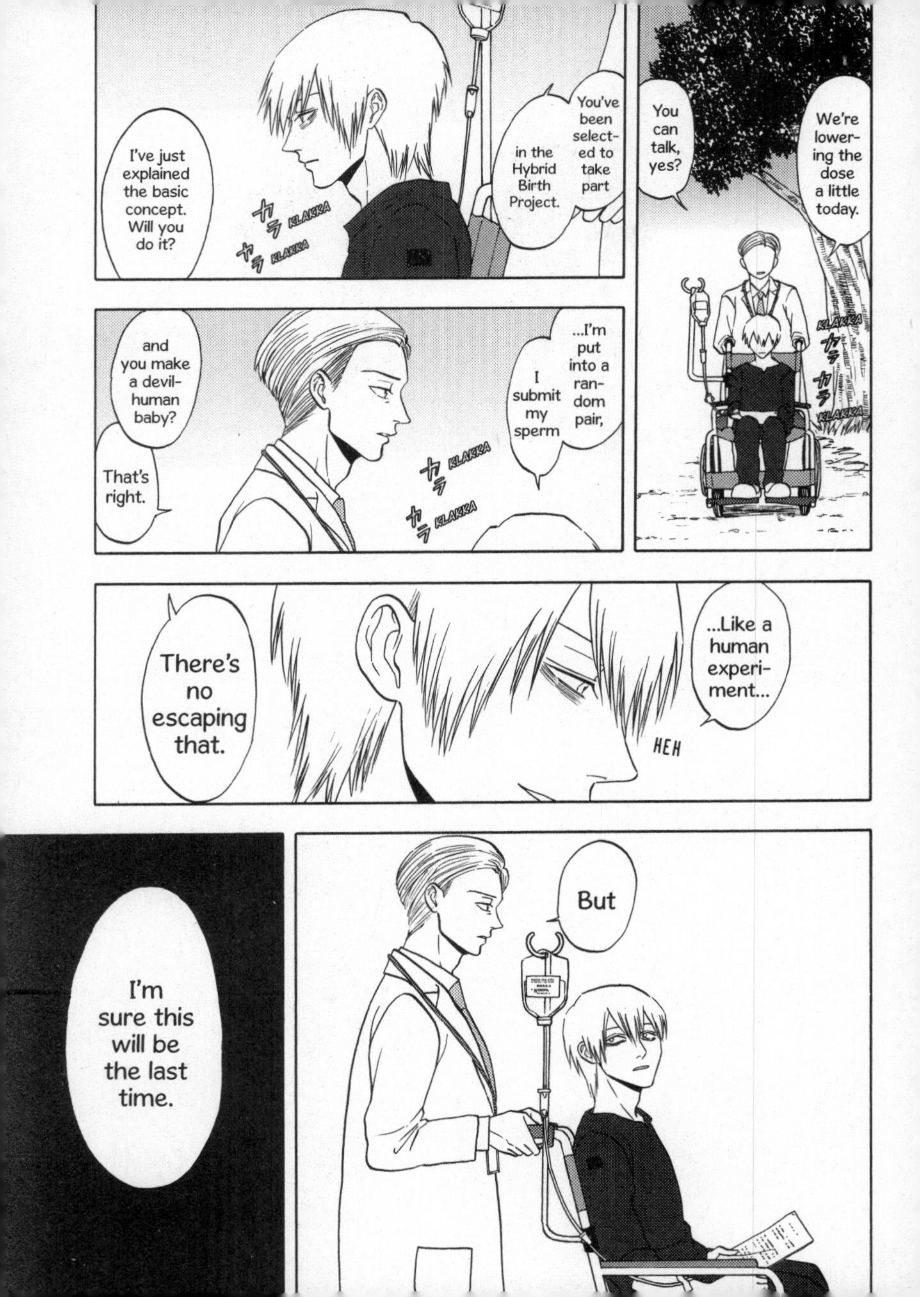
We're lowering the dose a little today.
You can talk, yes?
カラ KLAKKA
カラ KLAKKA
You've been selected to take part
in the Hybrid Birth Project.
I've just explained the basic concept. Will you do it?
カラ KLAKKA
カラ KLAKKA
...I'm put into a random pair,
I submit my sperm
and you make a devil-human baby?
That's right.
カラ KLAKKA
カラ KLAKKA
...Like a human experiment...
HEH
There's no escaping that.
But
I'm sure this will be the last time.

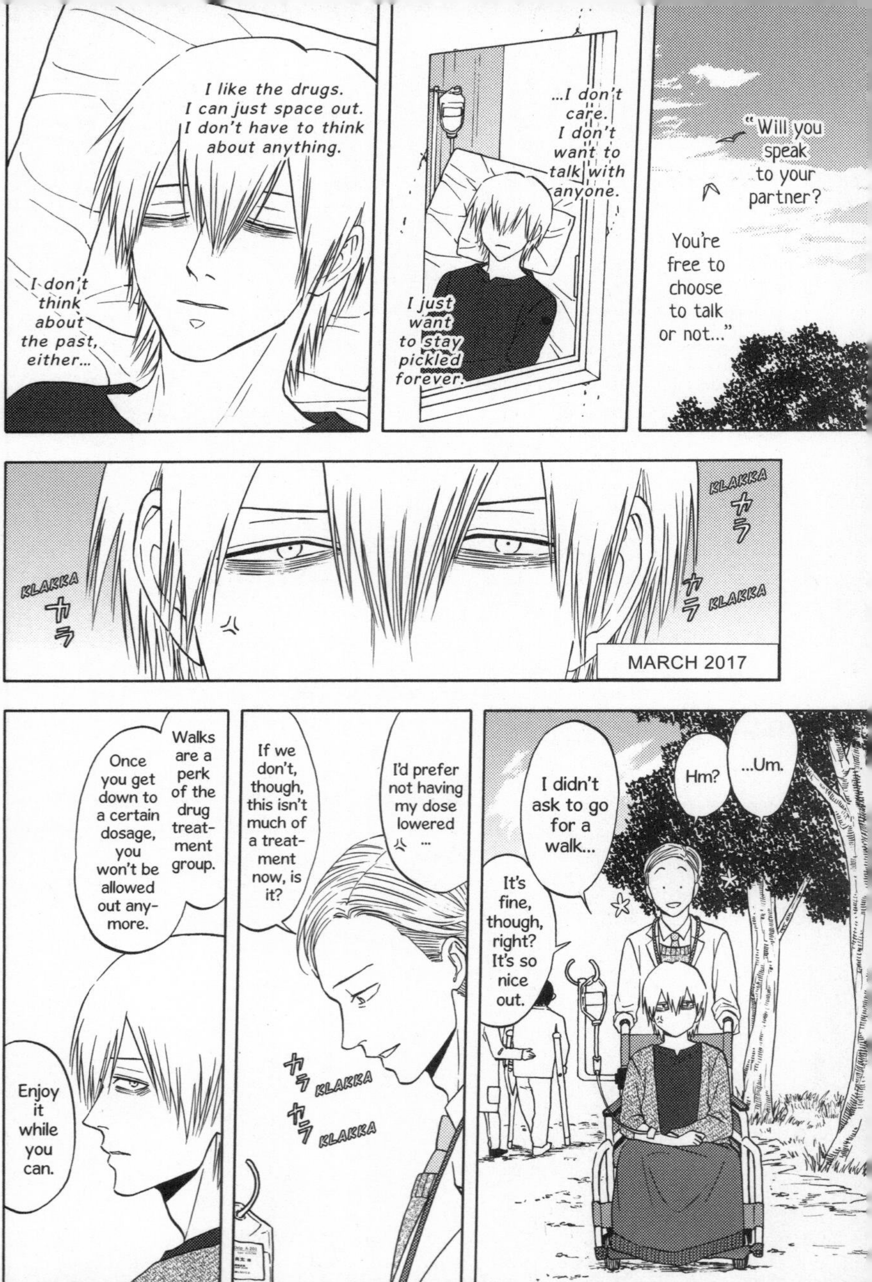
"Will you speak to your partner?
You're free to choose to talk or not..."
...I don't care. I don't want to talk with anyone.
I just want to stay pickled forever.
I like the drugs. I can just space out. I don't have to think about anything.
I don't think about the past, either...
KLAKKA
カラ
カラ
KLAKKA
KLAKKA
カラ
MARCH 2017
...Um.
Hm?
I didn't ask to go for a walk...
It's fine, though, right? It's so nice out.
I'd prefer not having my dose lowered...
If we don't, though, this isn't much of a treatment group now, is it?
カラ
KLAKKA
カラ
KLAKKA
Walks are a perk of the drug treatment group.
Once you get down to a certain dosage, you won't be allowed out anymore.
Enjoy it while you can.

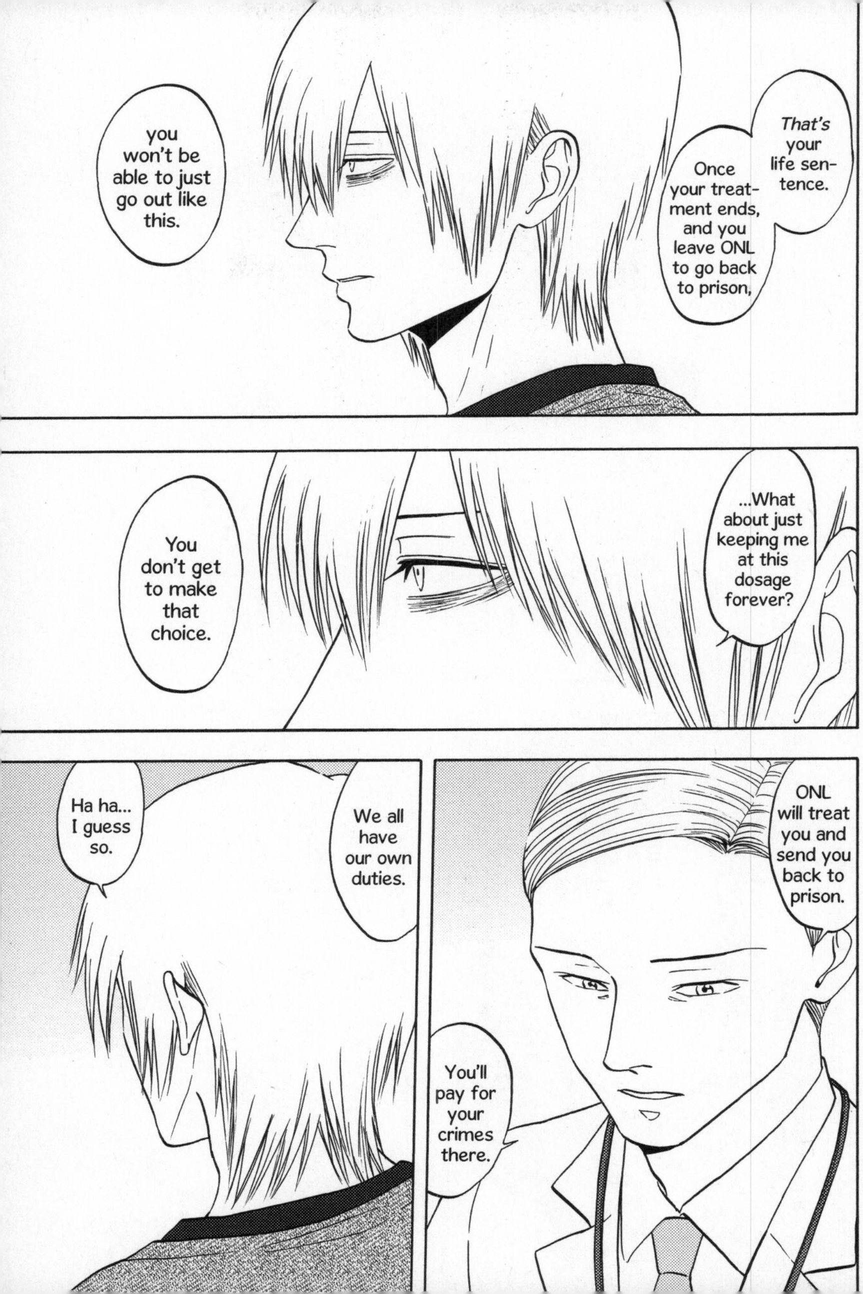
That's your life sentence.
Once your treatment ends, and you leave ONL to go back to prison,
you won't be able to just go out like this.
...What about just keeping me at this dosage forever?
You don't get to make that choice.
ONL will treat you and send you back to prison.
You'll pay for your crimes there.
We all have our own duties.
Ha ha... I guess so.

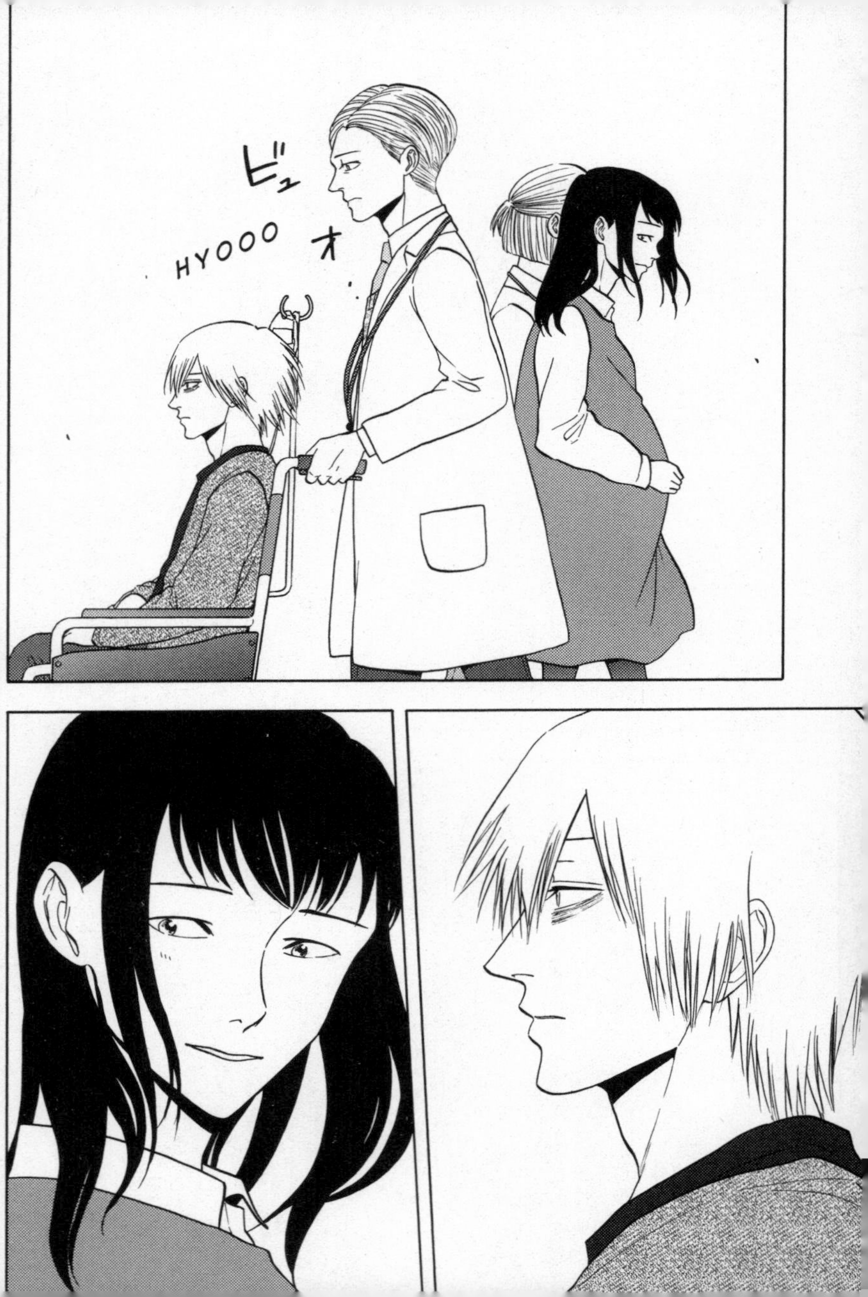
ビュオ
HYOOO

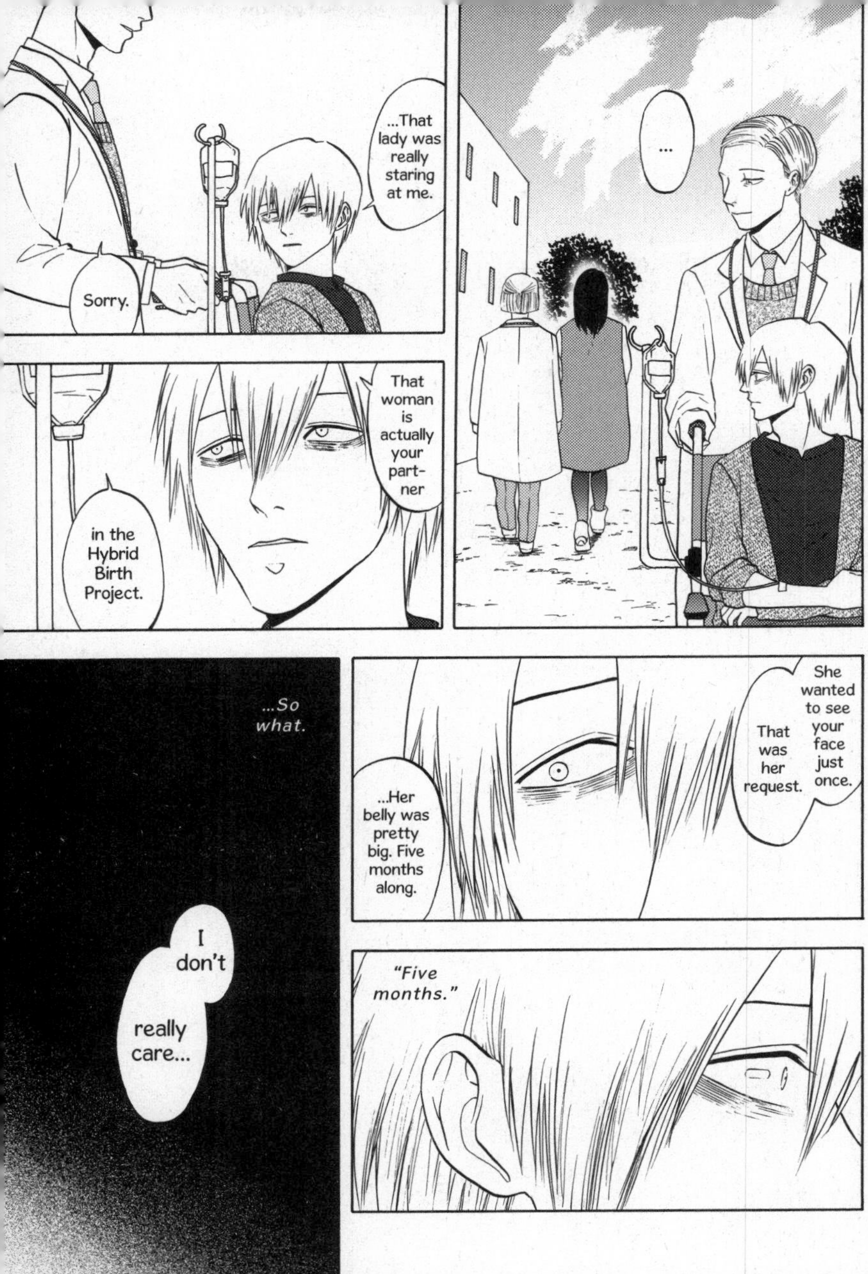
...
...That lady was really staring at me.
Sorry.
That woman is actually your partner
in the Hybrid Birth Project.
She wanted to see your face just once.
That was her request.
...Her belly was pretty big. Five months along.
“Five months.”
...So what.
I don’t really care...

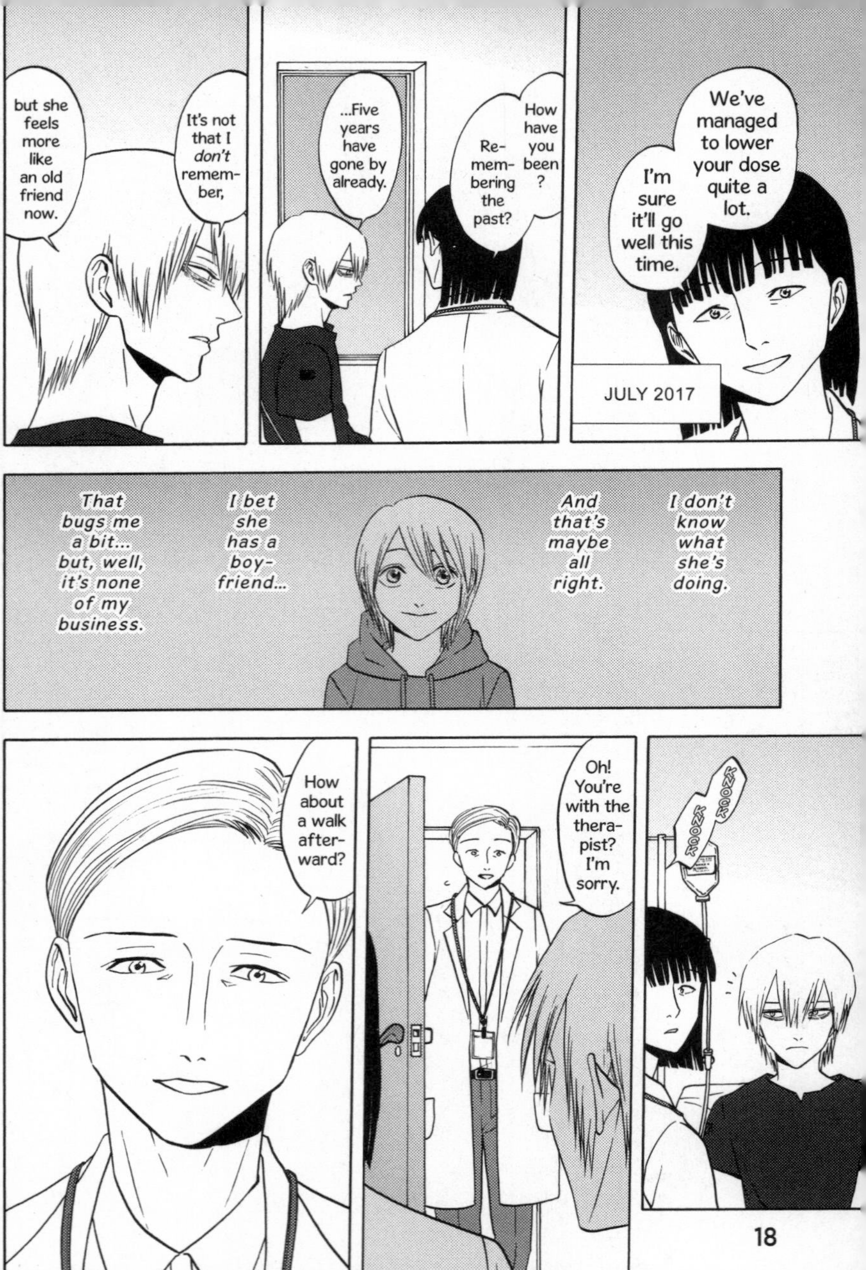
We've managed to lower your dose quite a lot.
I'm sure it'll go well this time.
JULY 2017
How have you been?
Remembering the past?
...Five years have gone by already.
It's not that I *don't* remember,
but she feels more like an old friend now.
I don't know what she's doing.
And that's maybe all right.
I bet she has a boyfriend...
That bugs me a bit... but, well, it's none of my business.
KNOCK
KNOCK
Oh! You're with the therapist? I'm sorry.
How about a walk afterward?

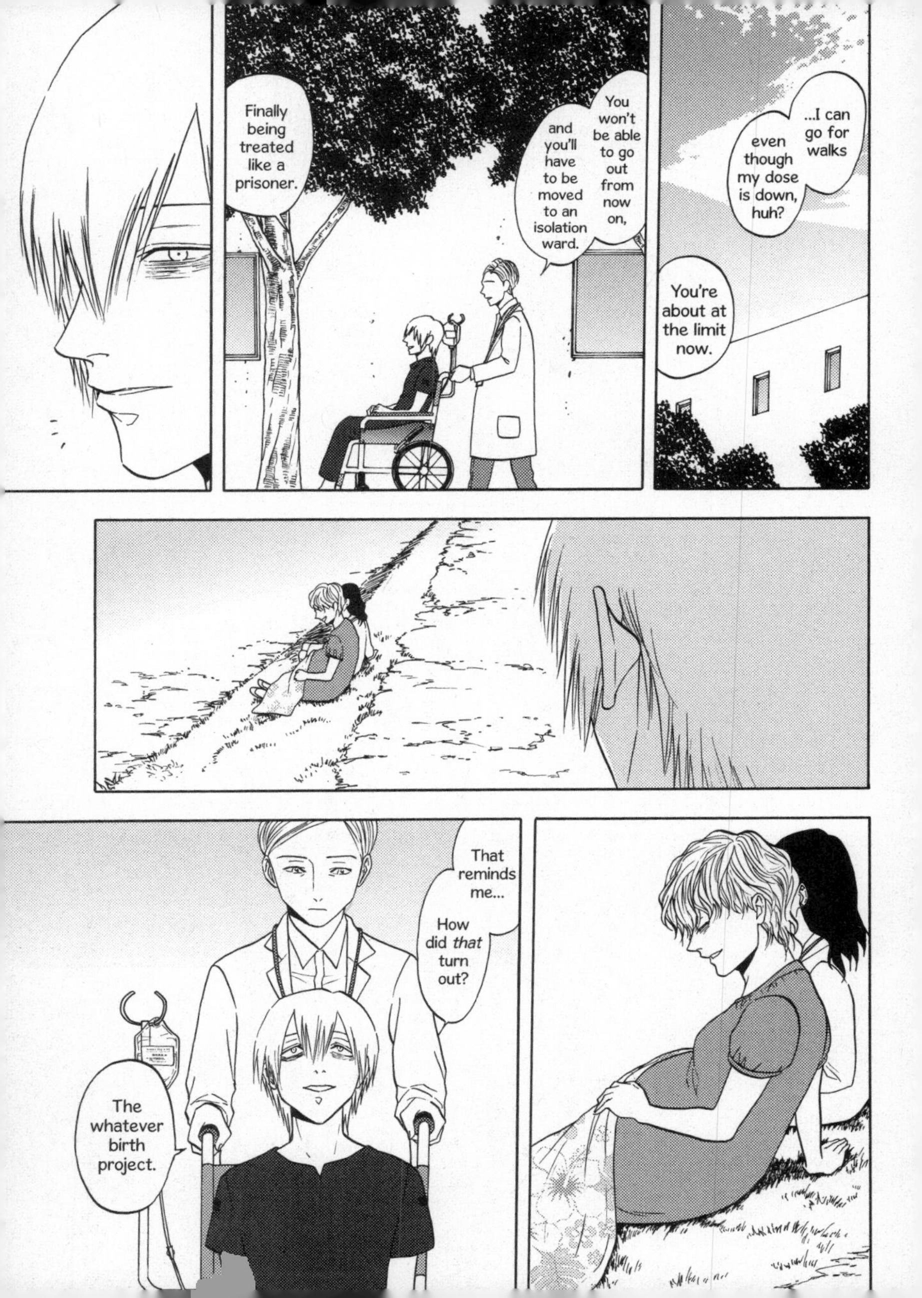
...I can go for walks even though my dose is down, huh?
You're about at the limit now.
You won't be able to go out from now on,
and you'll have to be moved to an isolation ward.
Finally being treated like a prisoner.
That reminds me...
How did *that* turn out?
The whatever birth project.

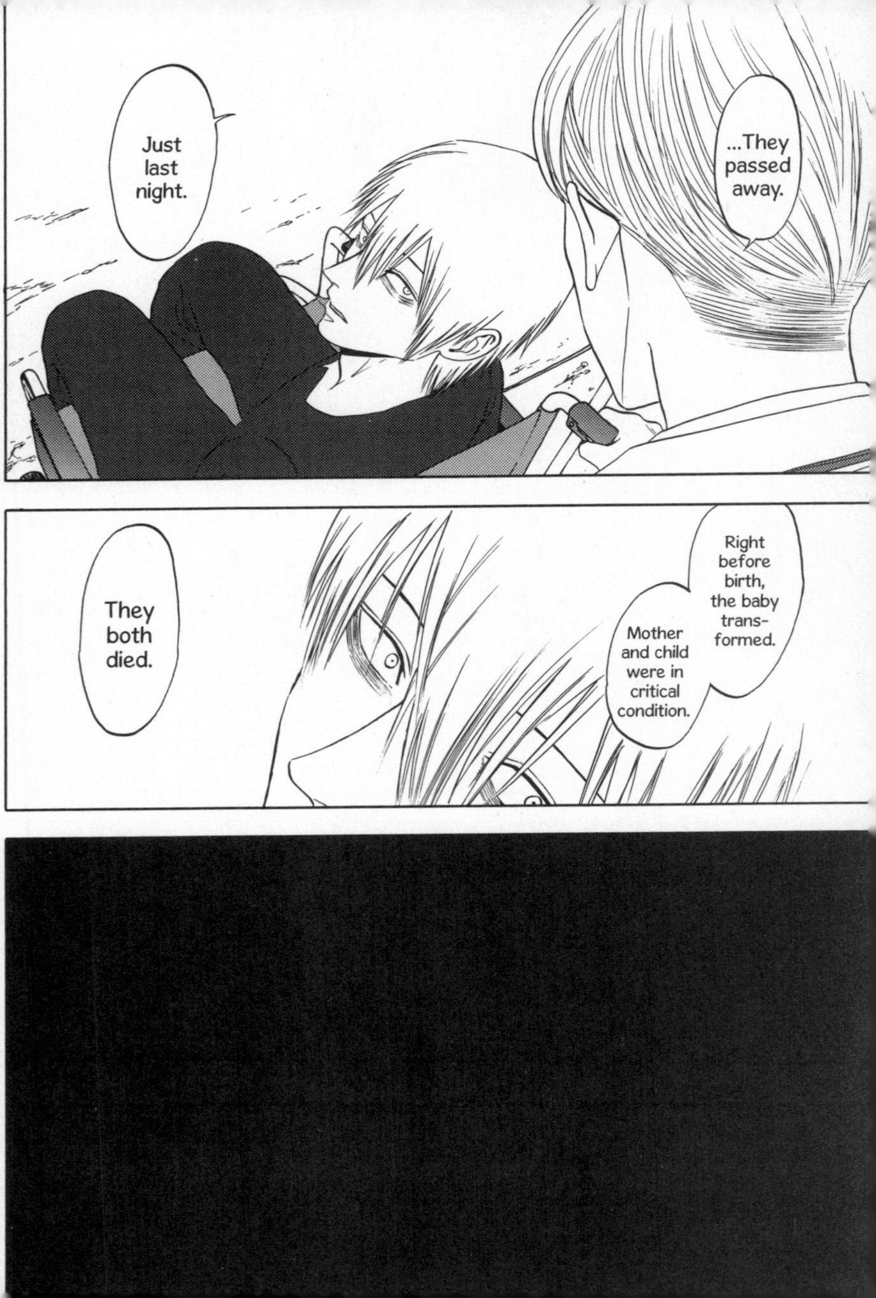
...They passed away.
Just last night.
Right before birth, the baby trans- formed.
Mother and child were in critical condition.
They both died.

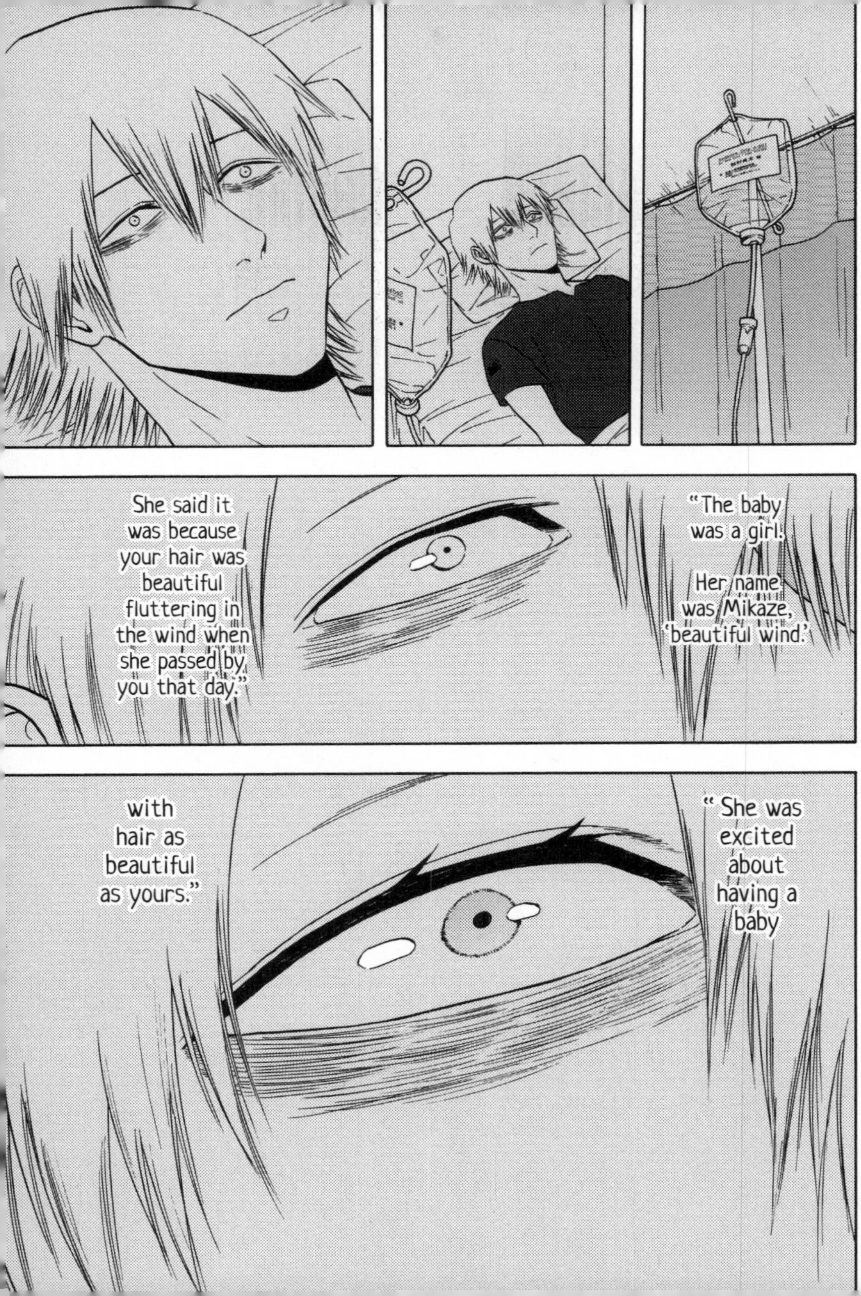
"The baby was a girl.
Her name was Mikaze, 'beautiful wind.'
She said it was because your hair was beautiful fluttering in the wind when she passed by you that day."
"She was excited about having a baby
with hair as beautiful as yours."

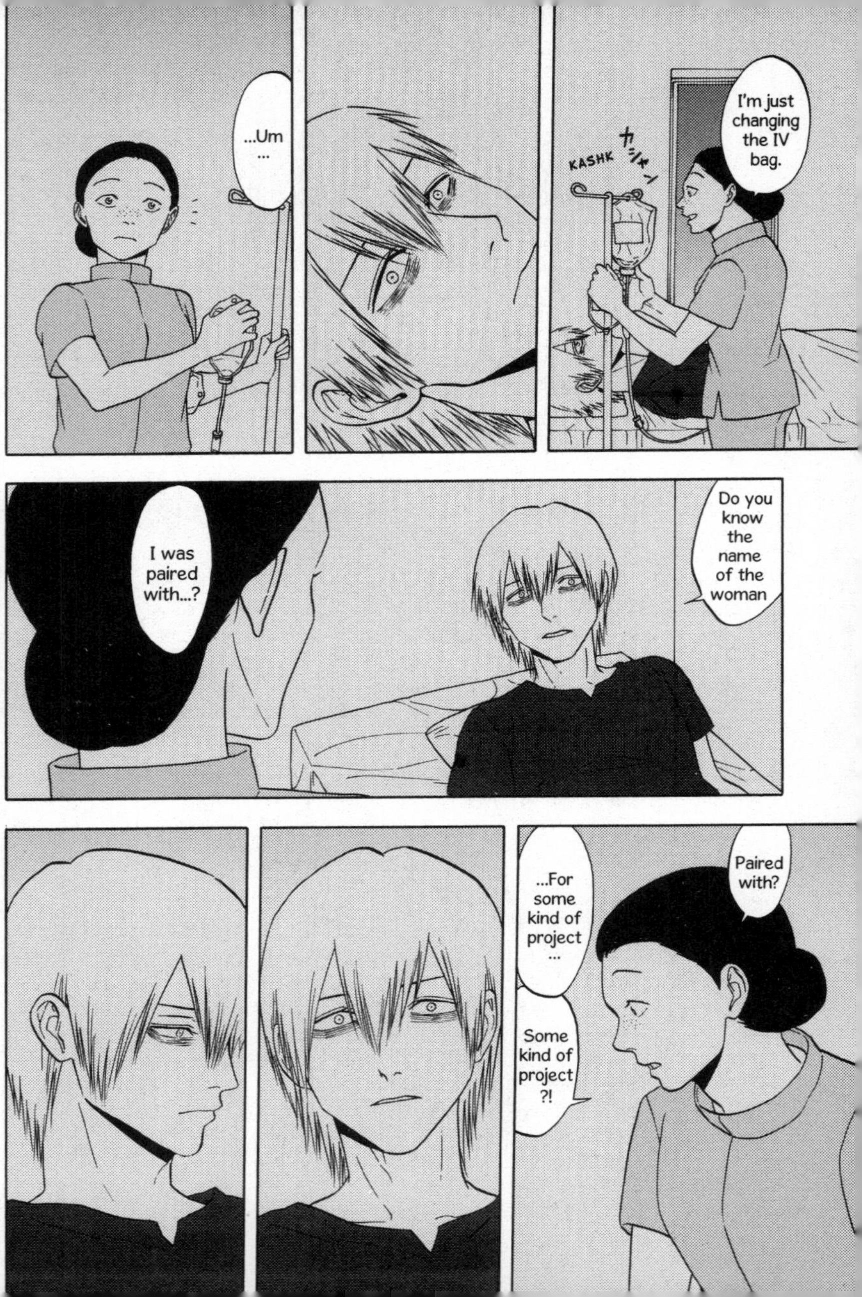
I'm just changing the IV bag.
KASHK
カシャン
...Um ...
Do you know the name of the woman
I was paired with...?
Paired with?
...For some kind of project ...
Some kind of project ?!

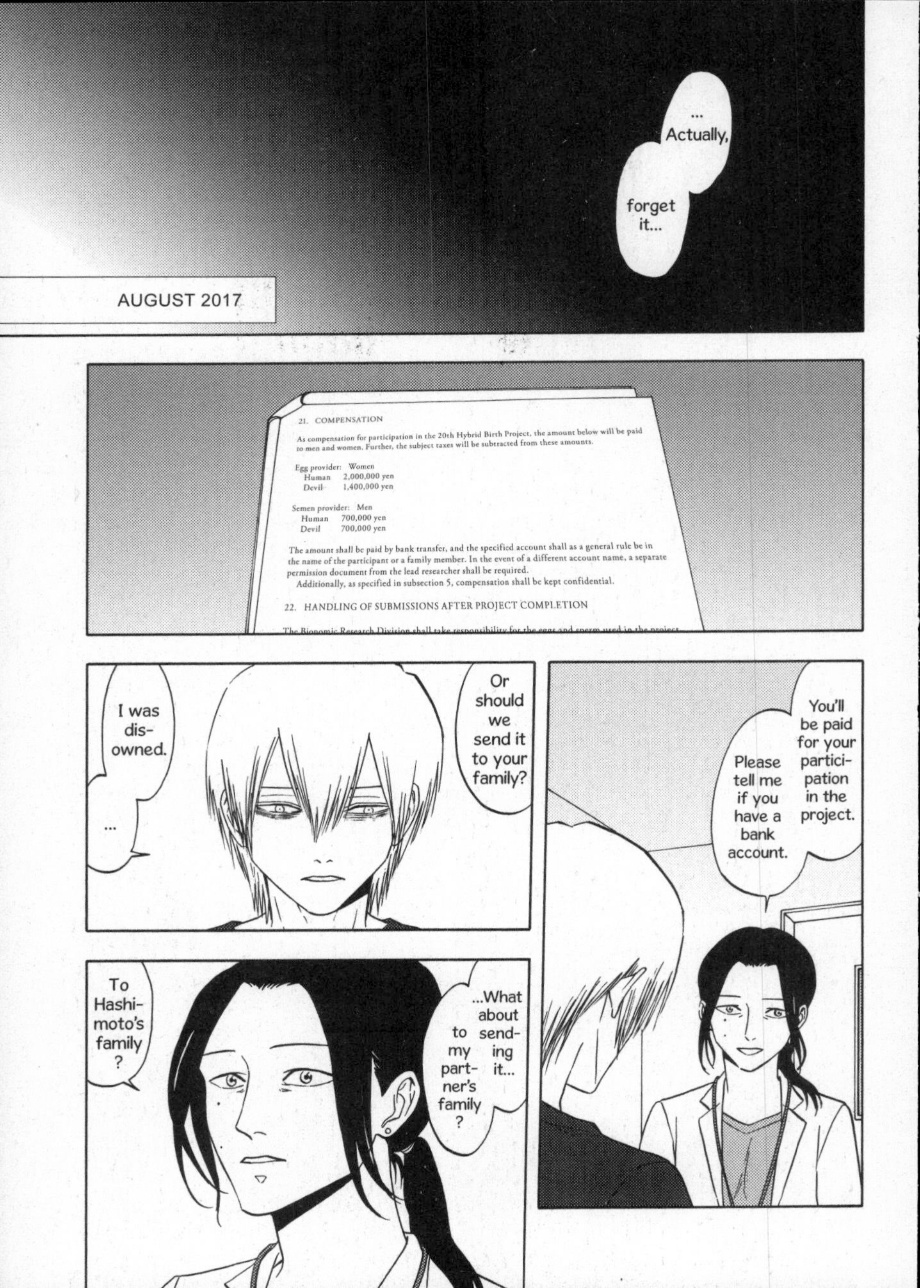
... Actually,
forget it...
AUGUST 2017
21. COMPENSATION
As compensation for participation in the 20th Hybrid Birth Project, the amount below will be paid to men and women. Further, the subject taxes will be subtracted from these amounts.
Egg provider: Women
Human 2,000,000 yen
Devil 1,400,000 yen
Semen provider: Men
Human 700,000 yen
Devil 700,000 yen
The amount shall be paid by bank transfer, and the specified account shall as a general rule be in the name of the participant or a family member. In the event of a different account name, a separate permission document from the lead researcher shall be required.
Additionally, as specified in subsection 5, compensation shall be kept confidential.
22. HANDLING OF SUBMISSIONS AFTER PROJECT COMPLETION
You'll be paid for your participation in the project.
Please tell me if you have a bank account.
Or should we send it to your family?
I was disowned.
...
...What about sending it...
to my partner's family?
To Hashimoto's family?

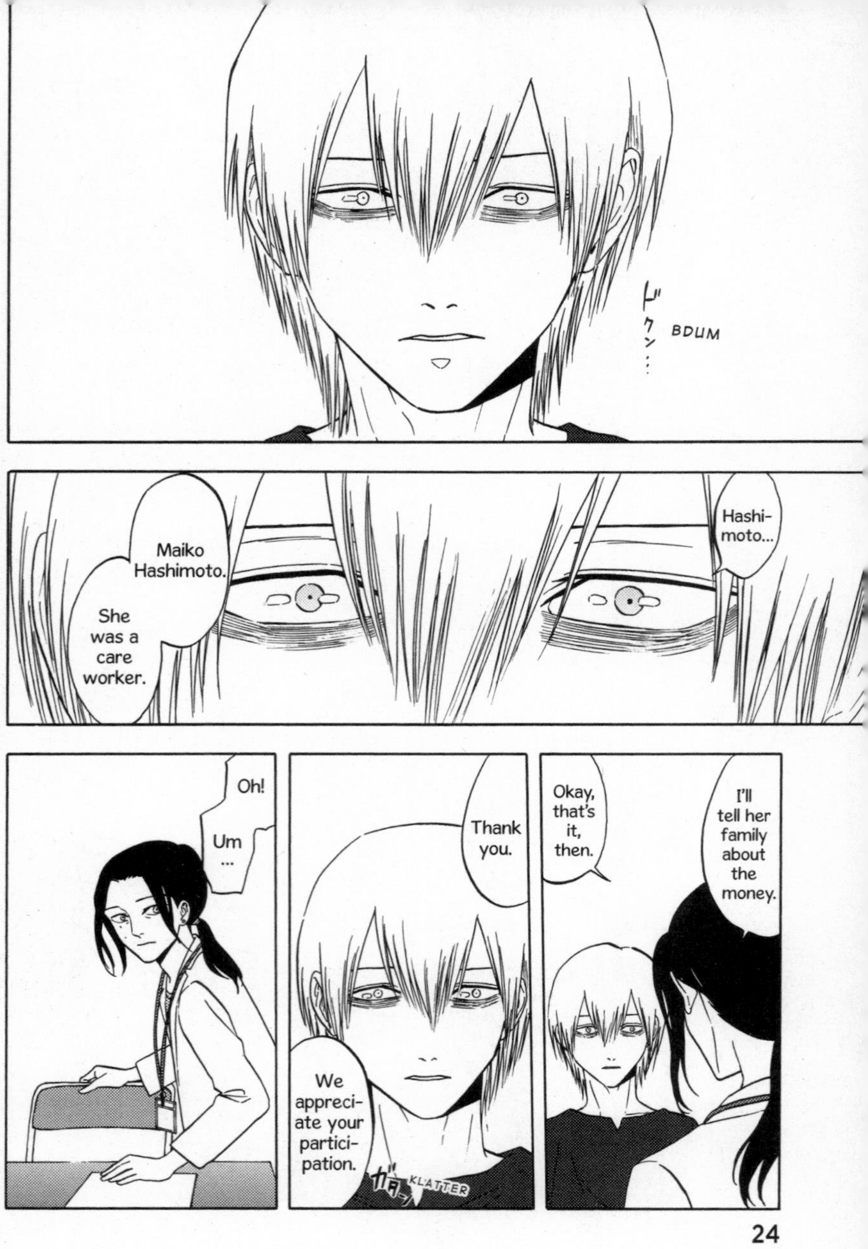
ドクン…
BDUM
Hashi-moto...
Maiko Hashimoto.
She was a care worker.
I'll tell her family about the money.
Okay, that's it, then.
Thank you.
We appreci-ate your partici-pation.
KLATTER
Oh!
Um ...

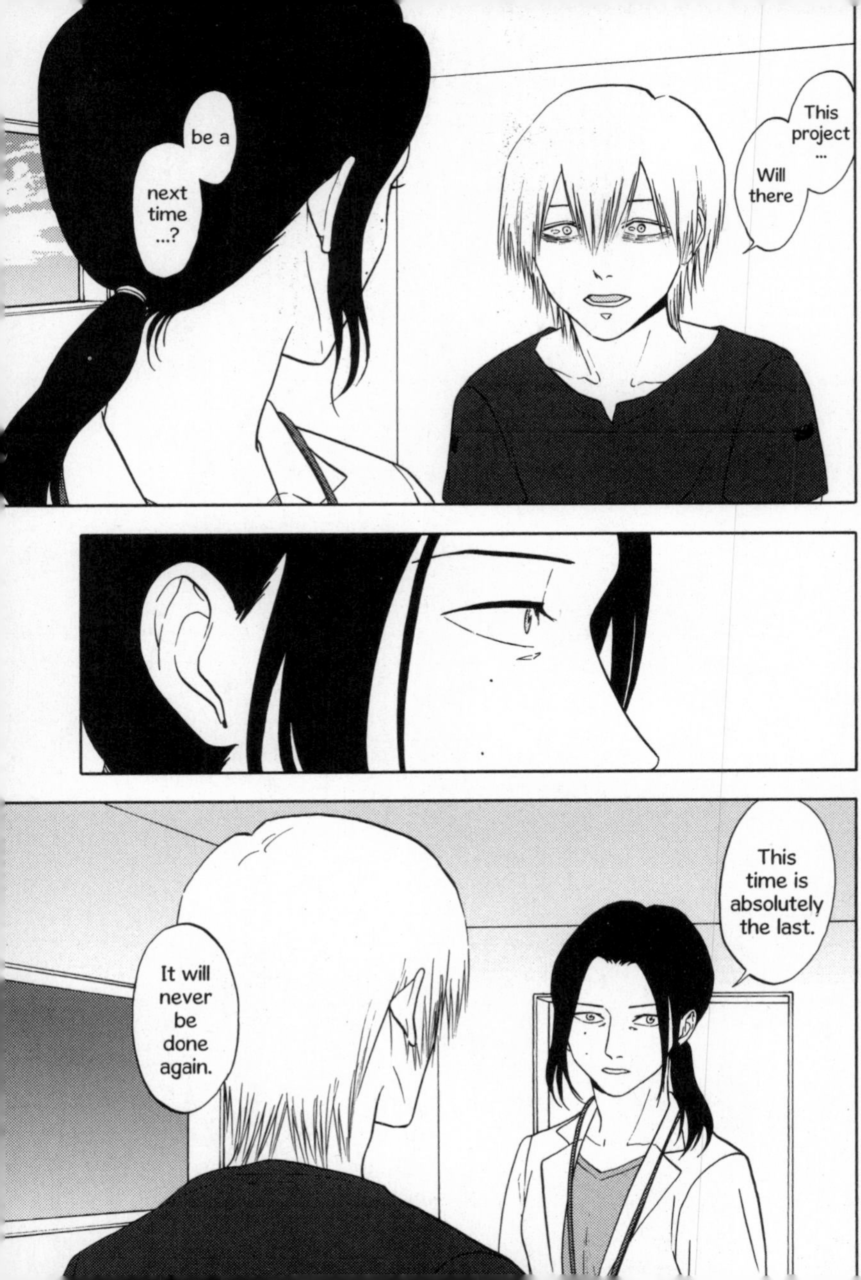
This project ...
Will there
be a next time ...?
This time is absolutely the last.
It will never be done again.

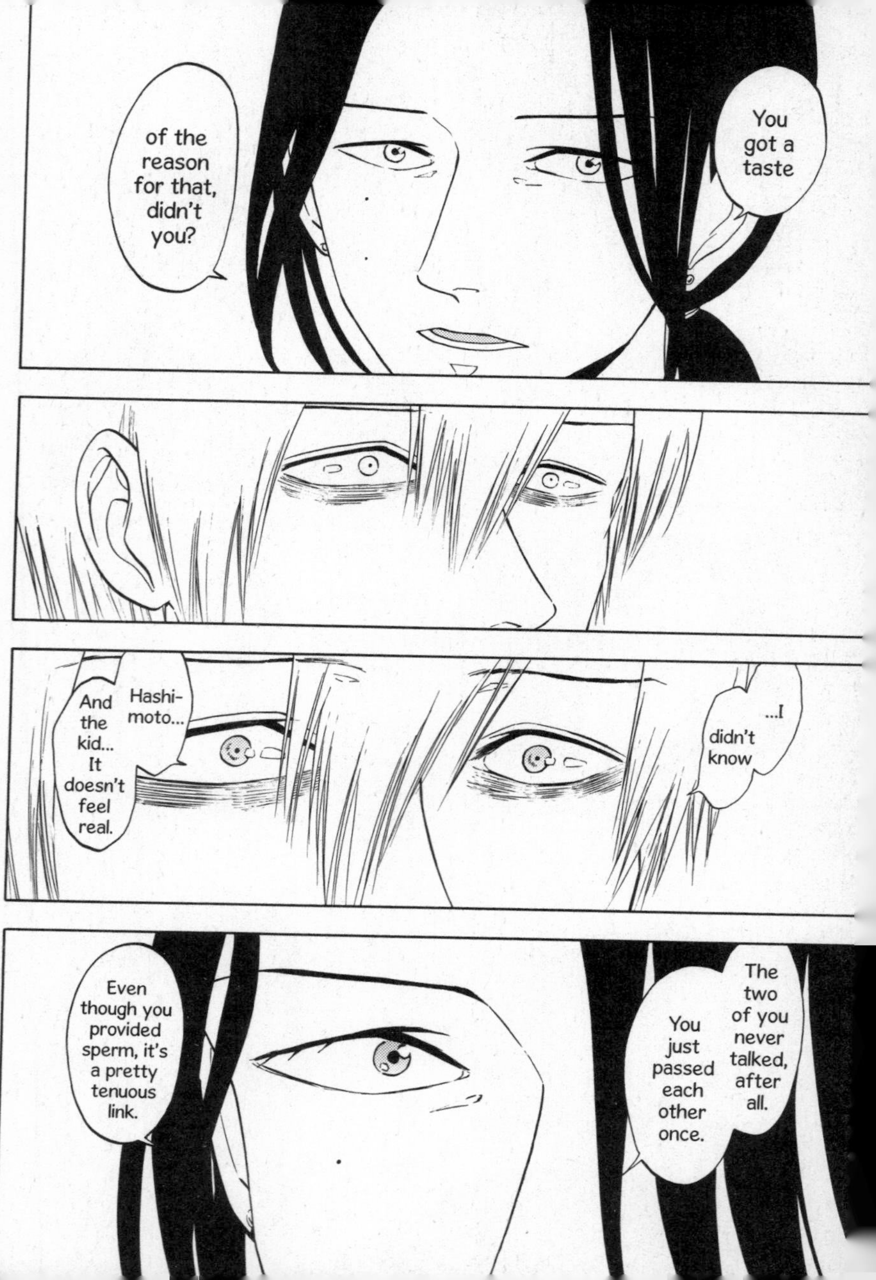
You got a taste
of the reason for that, didn't you?
...I didn't know
Hashi-moto... And the kid... It doesn't feel real.
The two of you never talked, after all.
You just passed each other once.
Even though you provided sperm, it's a pretty tenuous link.

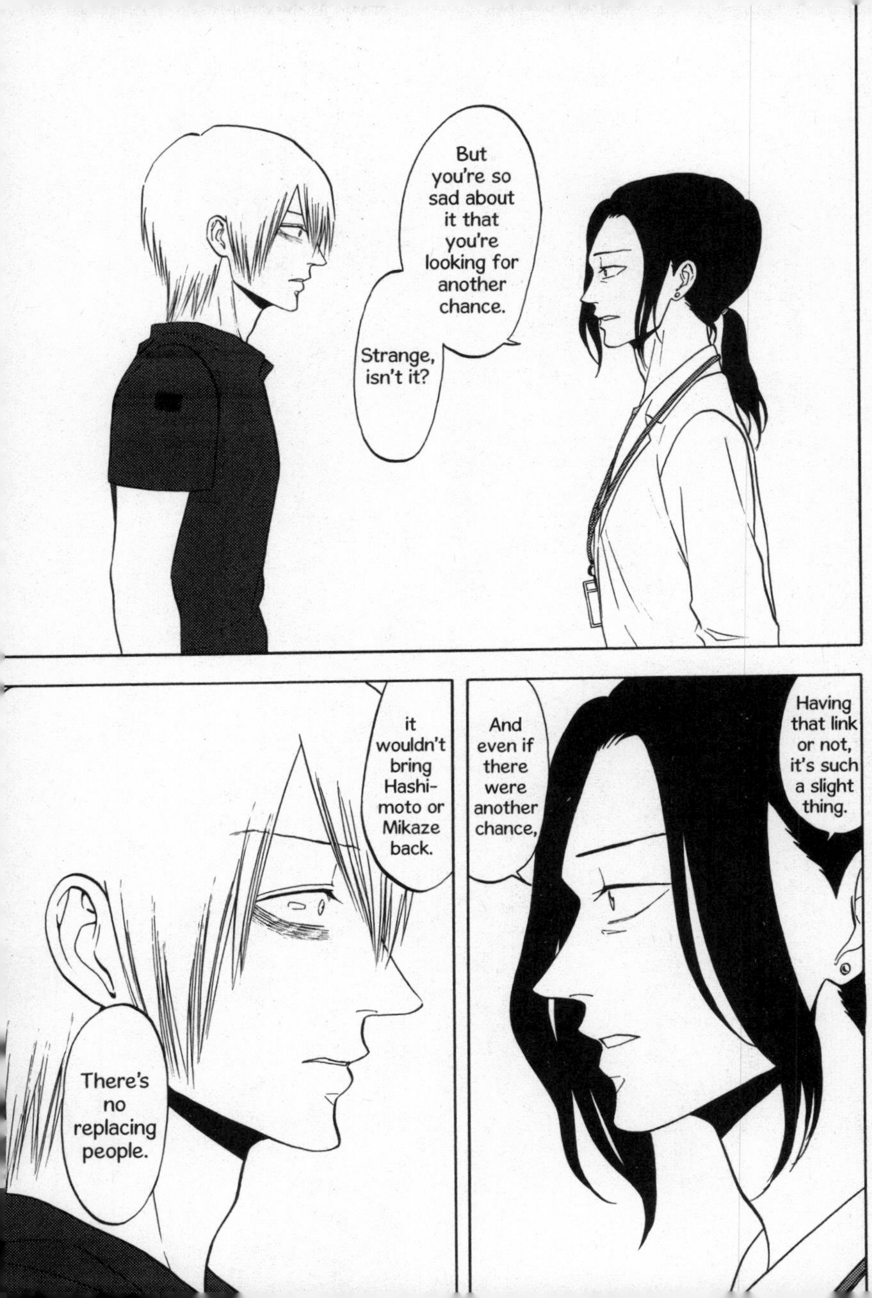
But you're so sad about it that you're looking for another chance.
Strange, isn't it?
Having that link or not, it's such a slight thing.
And even if there were another chance,
it wouldn't bring Hashi-moto or Mikaze back.
There's no replacing people.

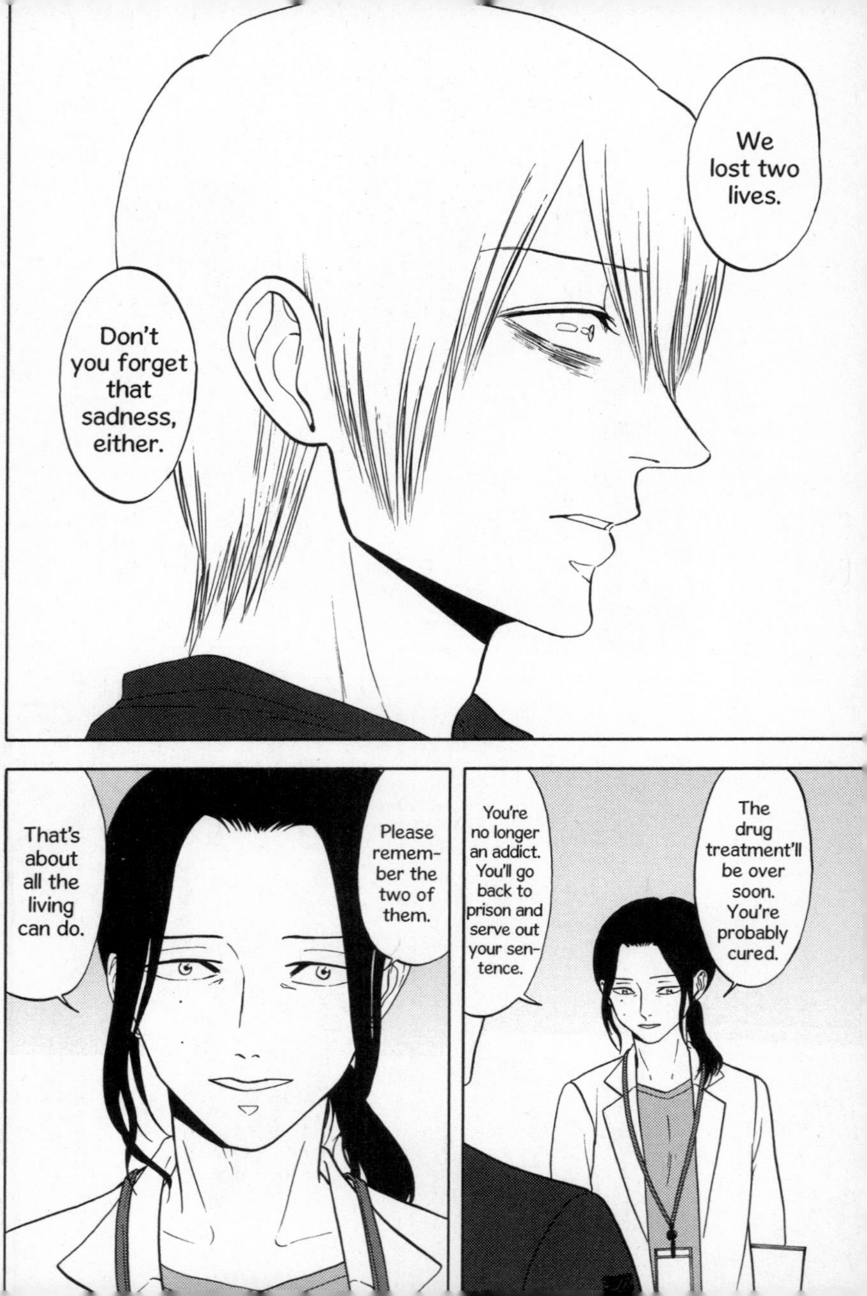
We lost two lives.
Don't you forget that sadness, either.
The drug treatment'll be over soon. You're probably cured.
You're no longer an addict. You'll go back to prison and serve out your sentence.
Please remem-ber the two of them.
That's about all the living can do.

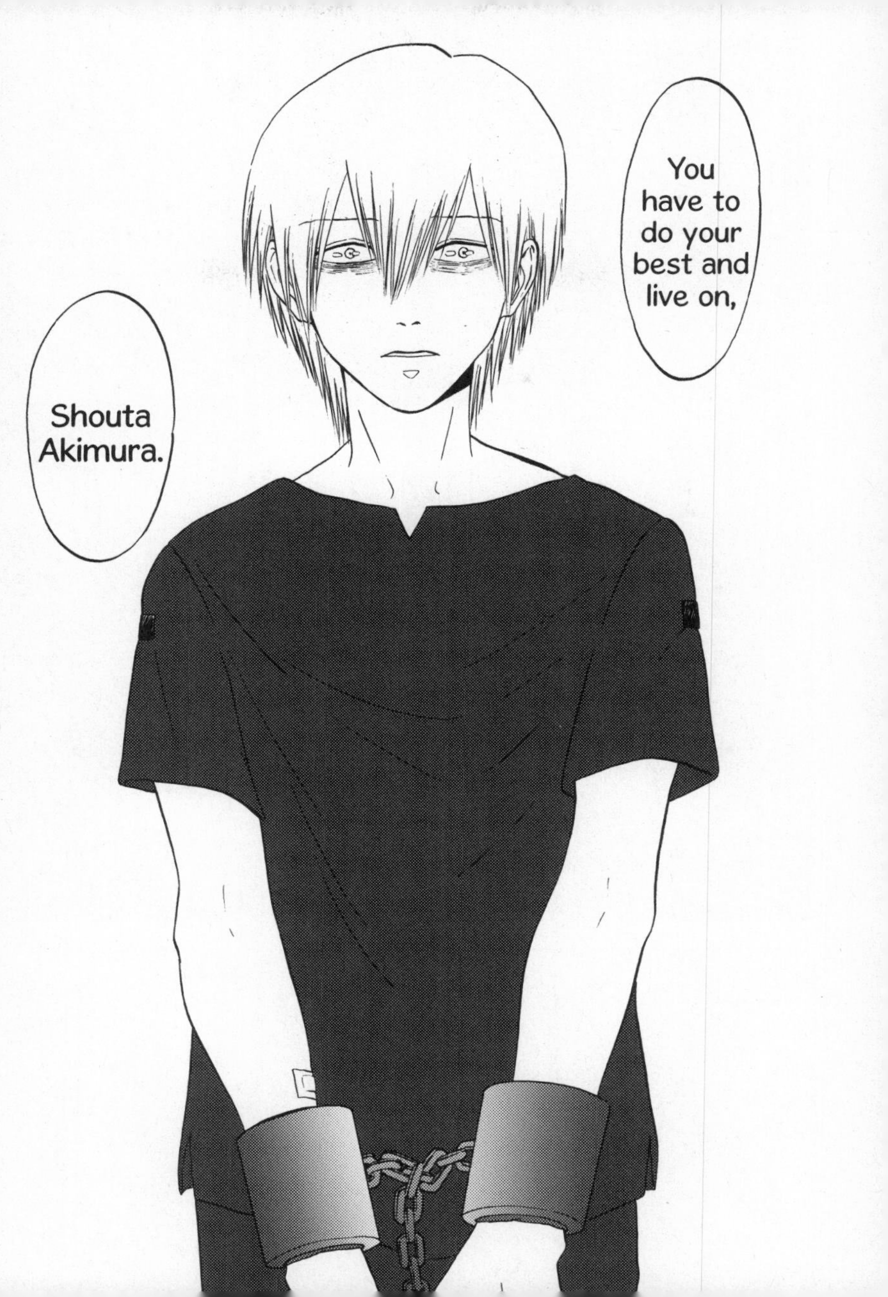
You have to do your best and live on,
Shouta Akimura.

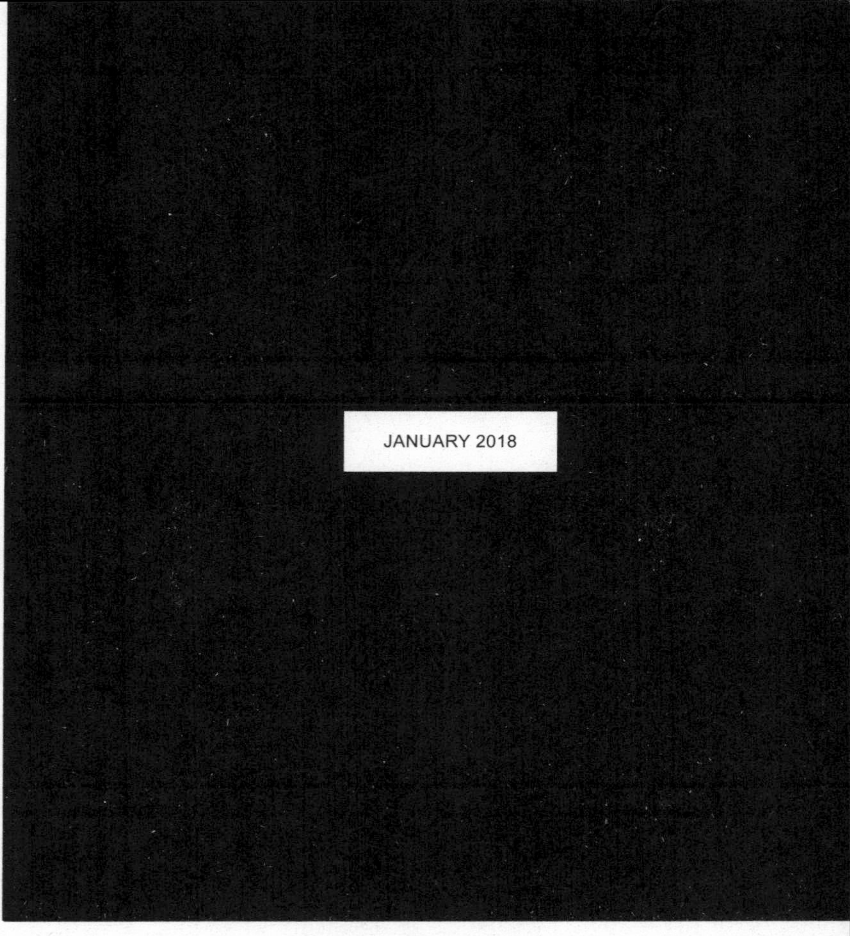
JANUARY 2018

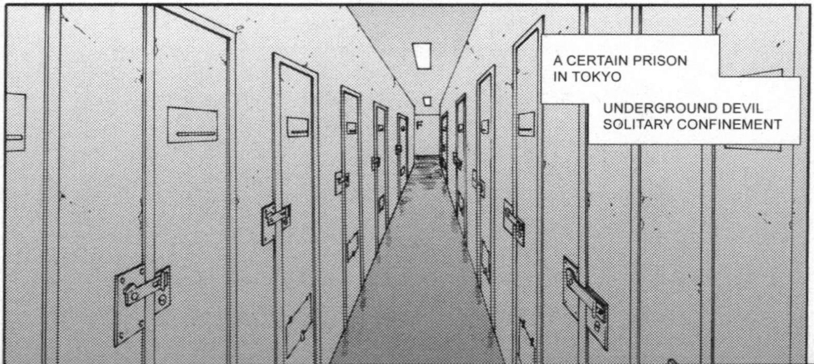
A CERTAIN PRISON
IN TOKYO
UNDERGROUND DEVIL
SOLITARY CONFINEMENT

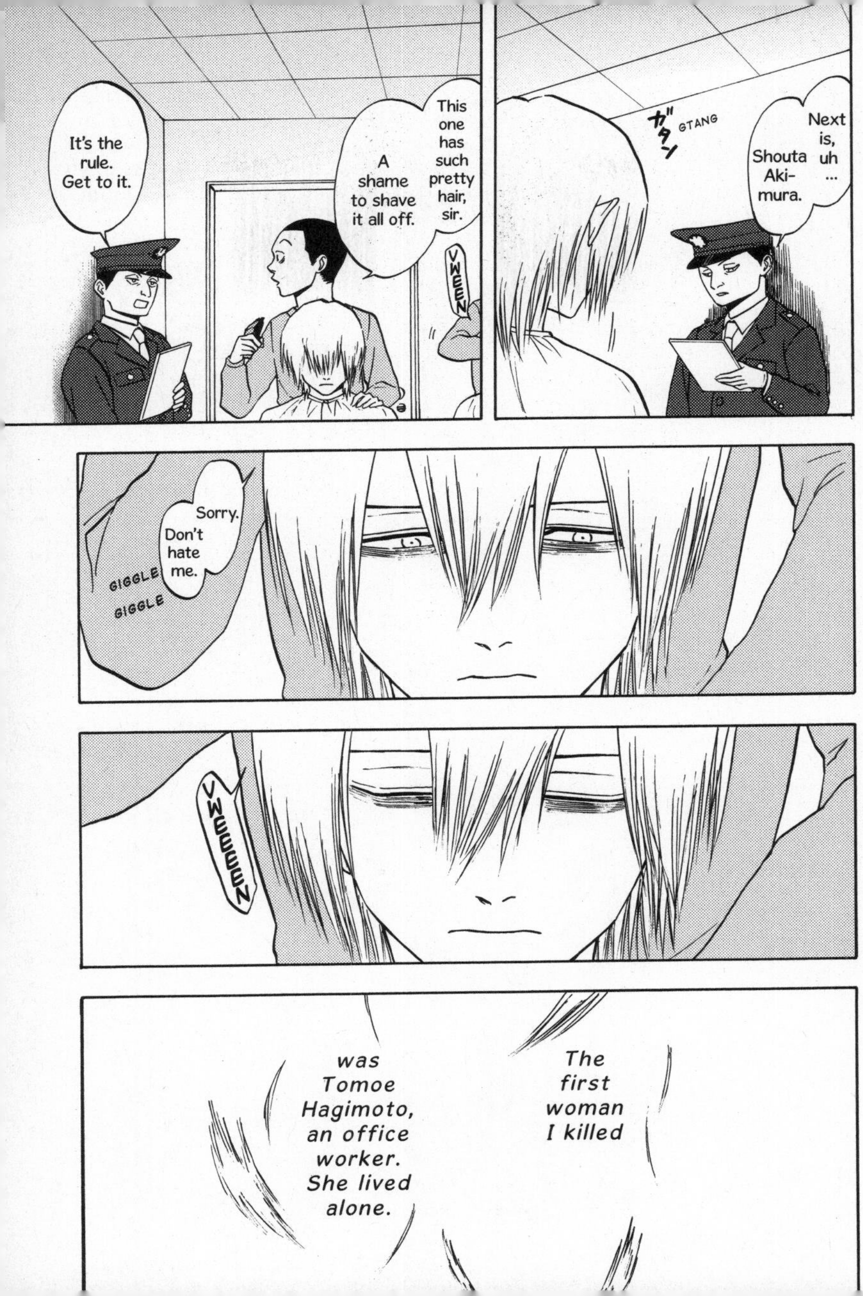
ガタン
GTANG
Next is, uh ... Shouta Akimura.
This one has such pretty hair, sir.
A shame to shave it all off.
VWEEN
It's the rule. Get to it.
Sorry. Don't hate me.
GIGGLE GIGGLE
VWEEEEEN
The first woman I killed
was Tomoe Hagimoto, an office worker. She lived alone.

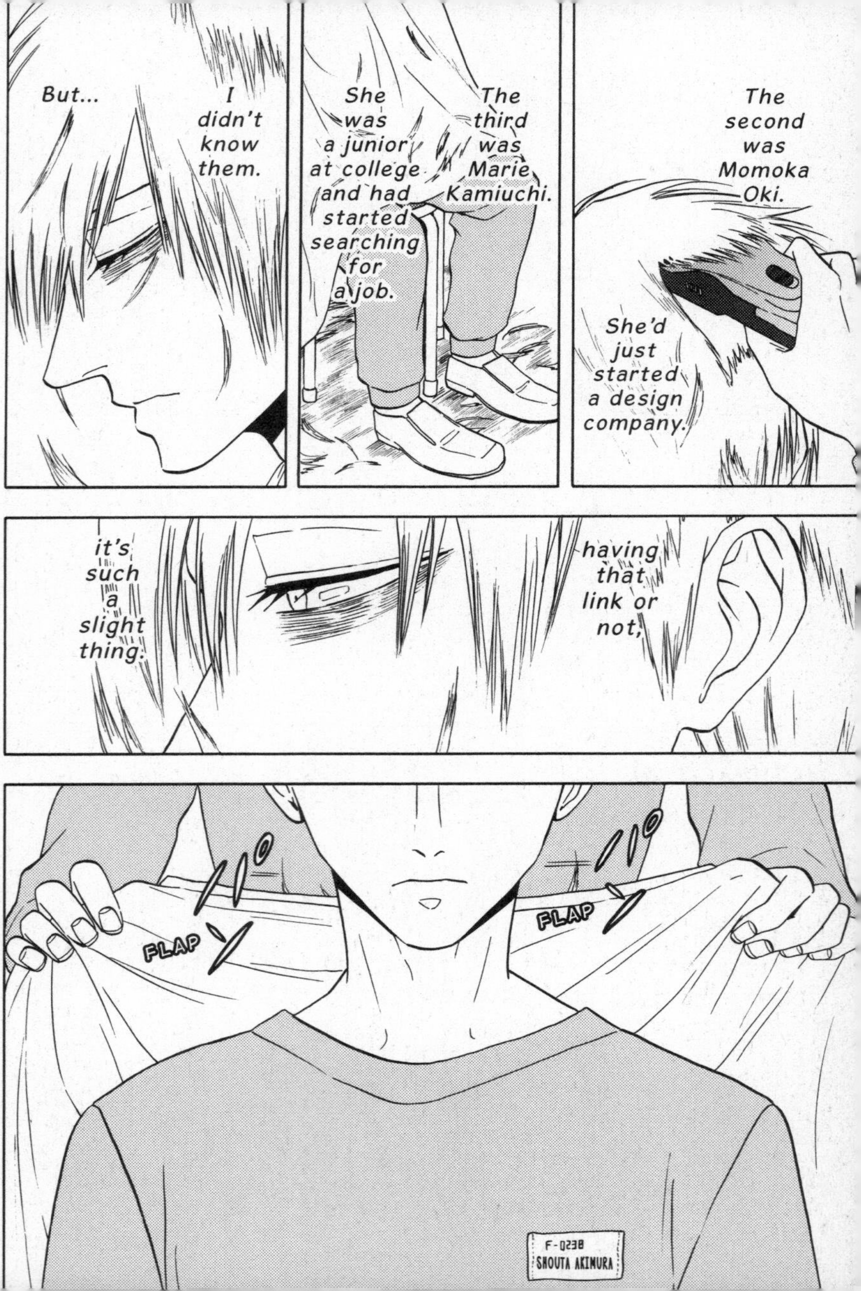
The second was Momoka Oki.
She'd just started a design company.
The third was Marie Kamiuchi.
She was a junior at college and had started searching for a job.
I didn't know them.
But...
having that link or not,
it's such a slight thing.
FLAP
FLAP
F-0238
SHOUTA AKIMURA

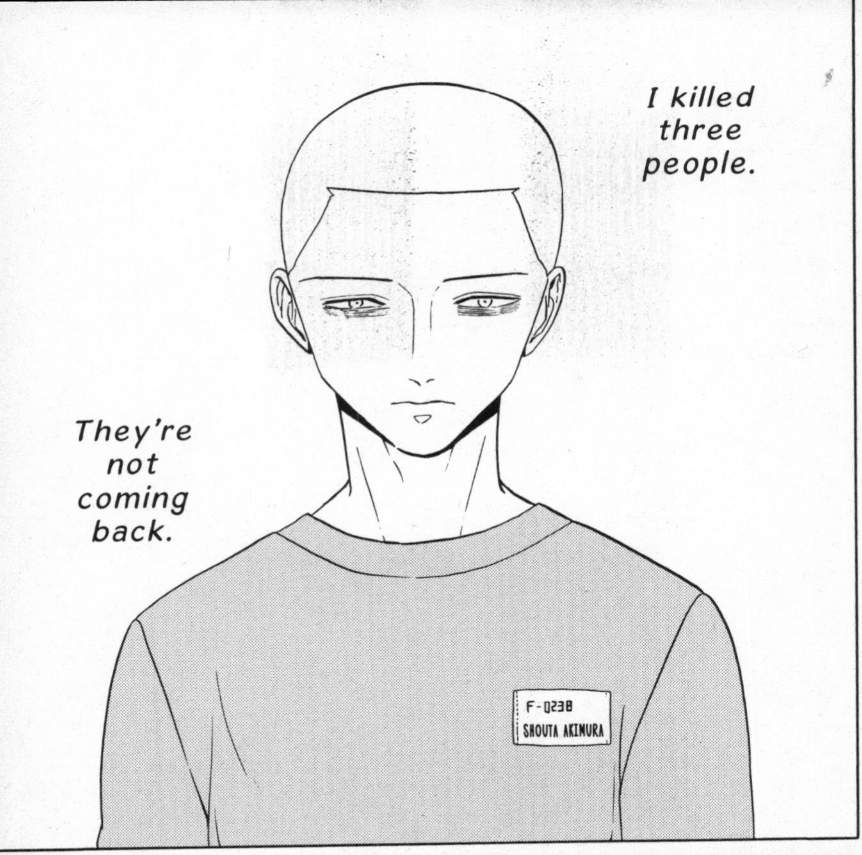
I killed three people.
They're not coming back.
F-0238
SHOUTA AKIMURA
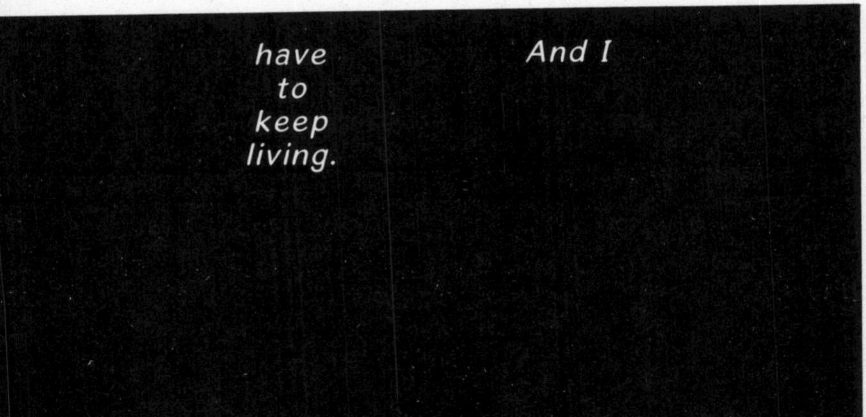
And I
have to keep living.

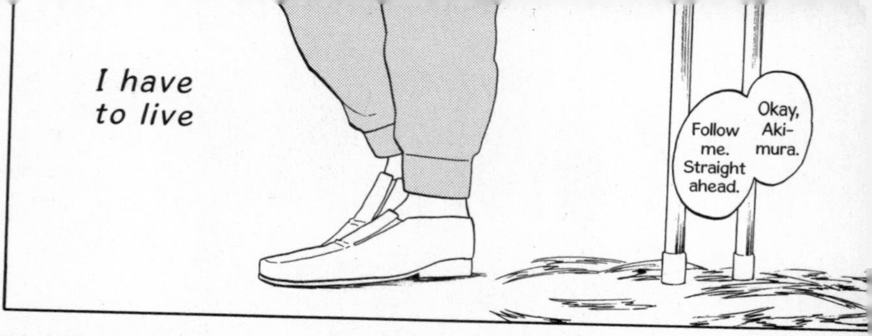
Okay, Aki-mura.
Follow me. Straight ahead.
I have to live
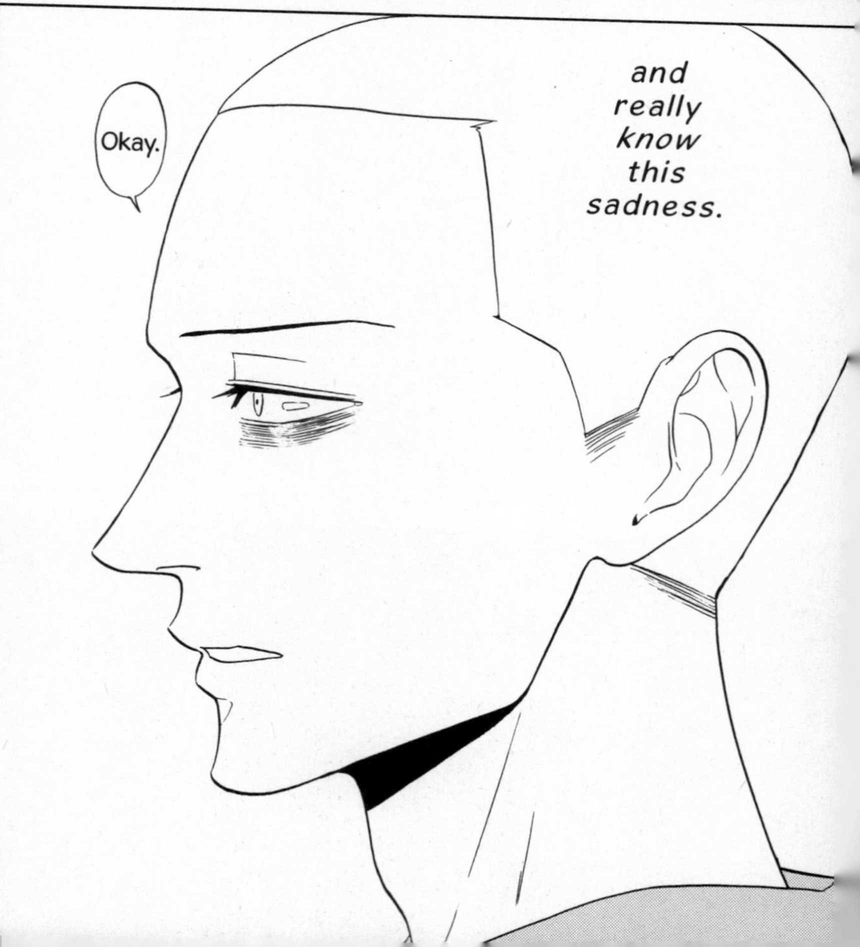
and really know this sadness.
Okay.

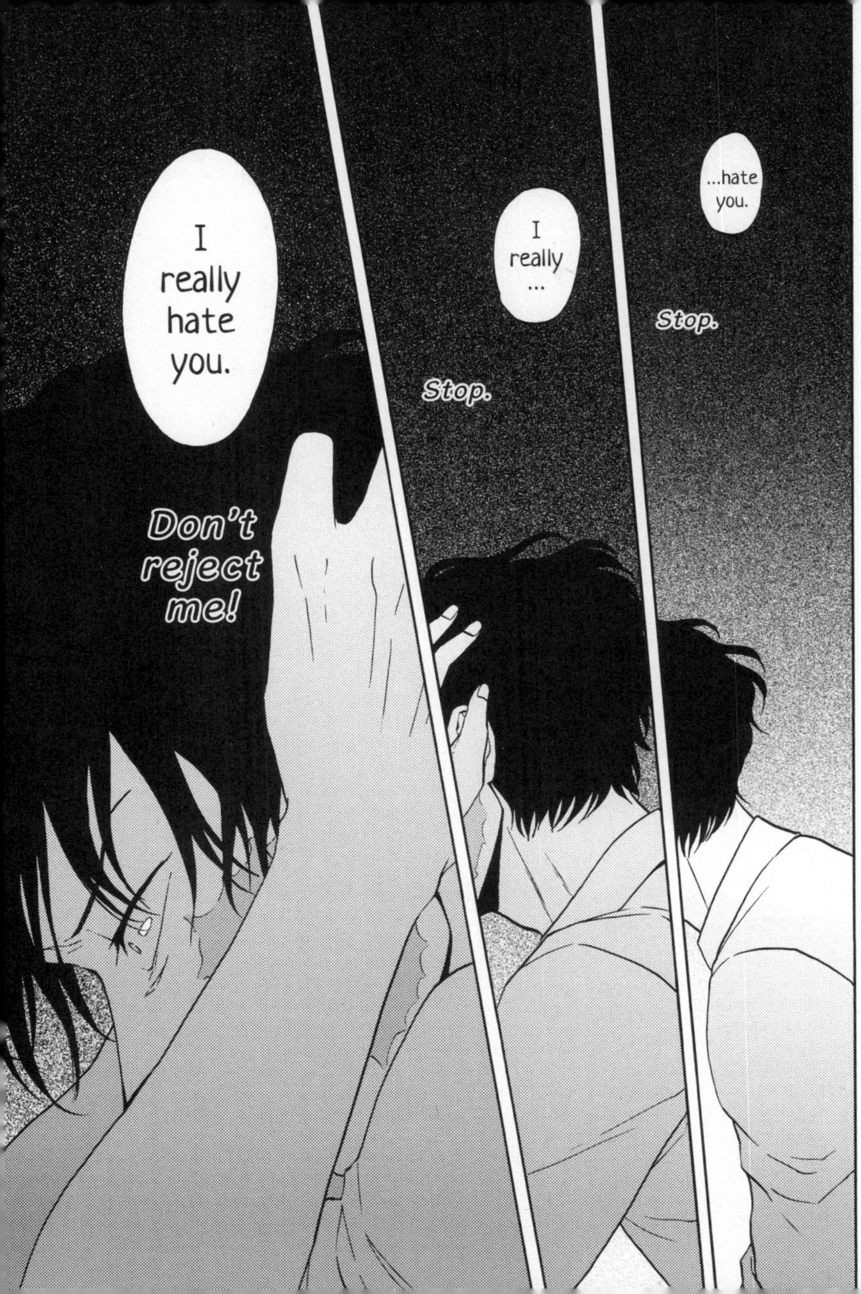
...hate you.
Stop.
I really ...
Stop.
I really hate you.
Don't reject me!

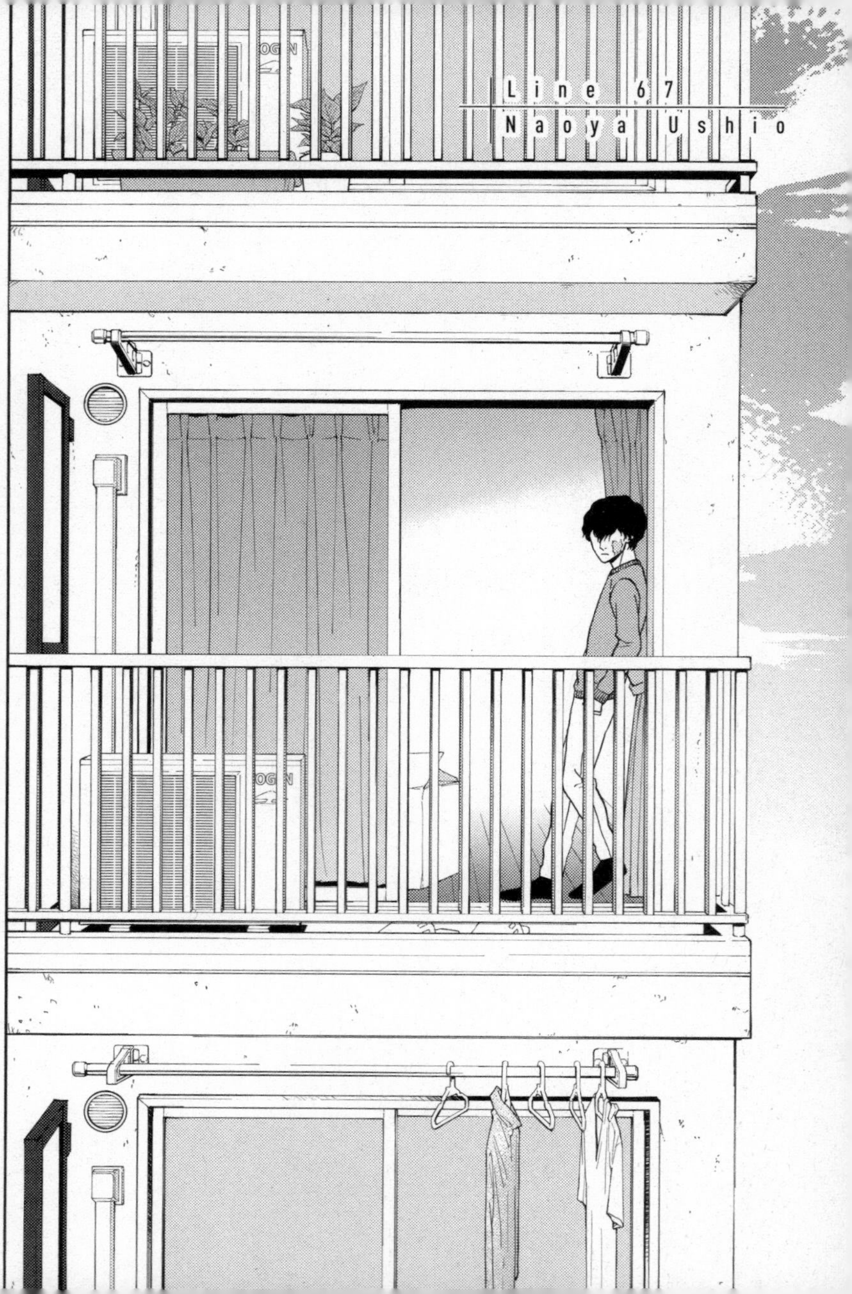
Line 67
Naoya Ushio

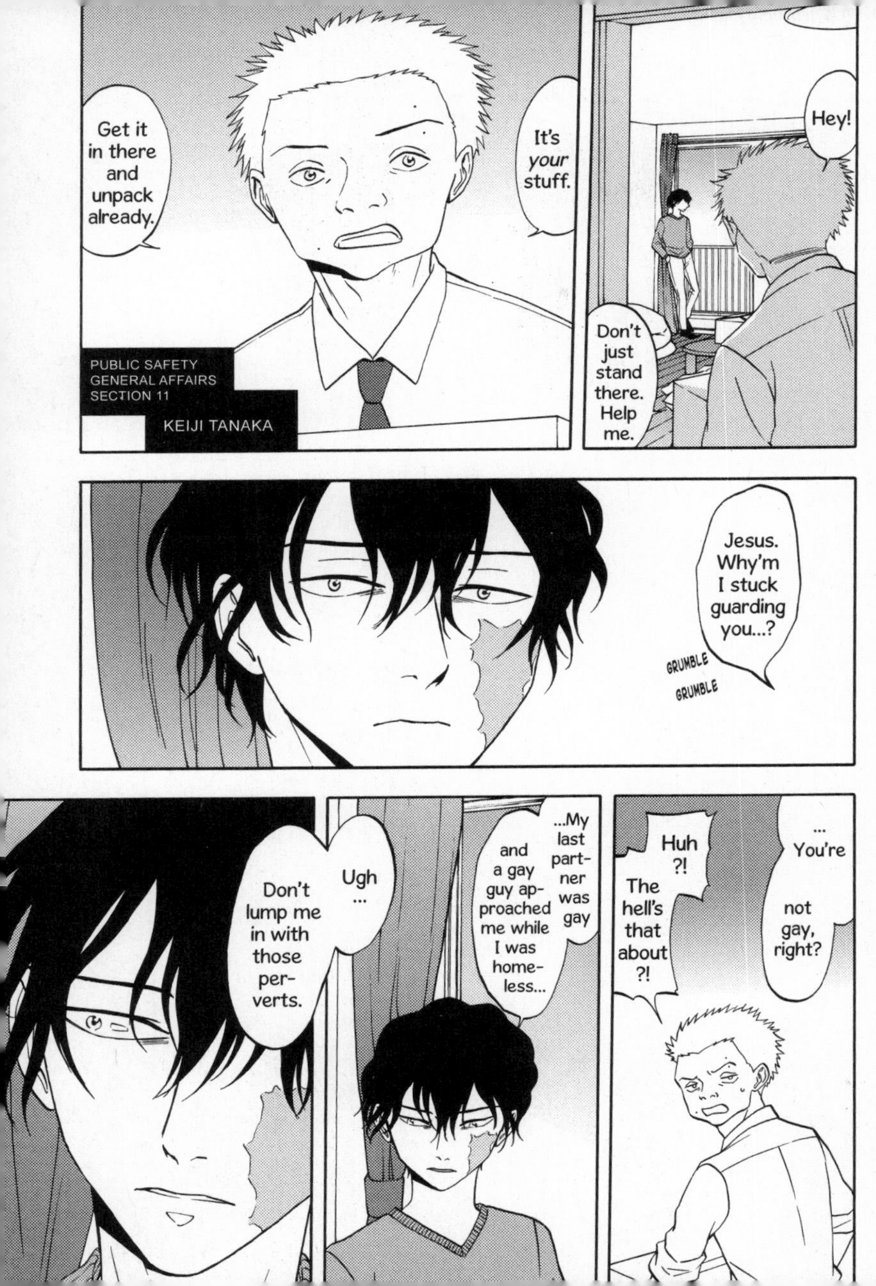
Hey!
Don't just stand there. Help me.
It's *your* stuff.
Get it in there and unpack already.
PUBLIC SAFETY GENERAL AFFAIRS SECTION 11
KEIJI TANAKA
Jesus. Why'm I stuck guarding you...?
GRUMBLE GRUMBLE
... You're not gay, right?
Huh?! The hell's that about?!
...My last partner was gay
and a gay guy approached me while I was homeless...
Ugh...
Don't lump me in with those perverts.

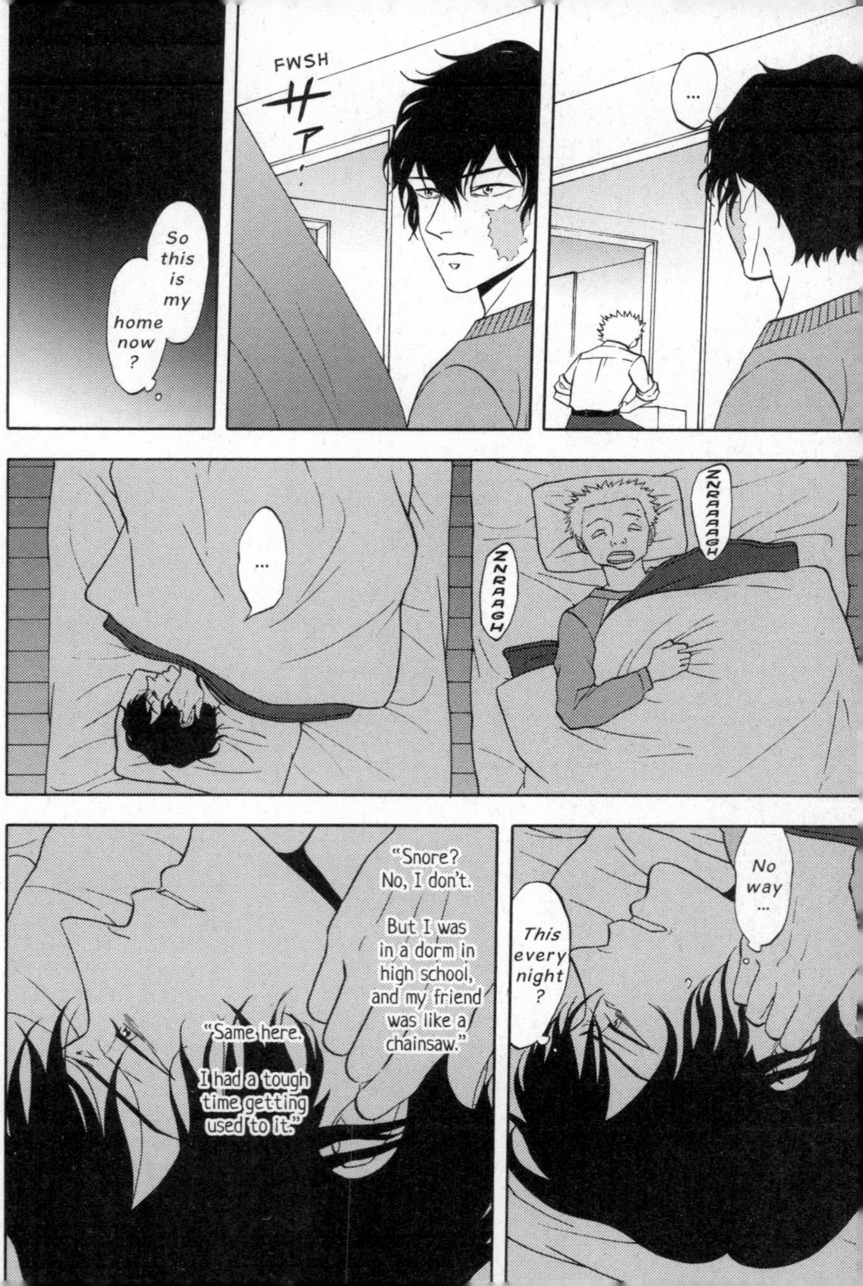
...
FWSH
So this is my home now?
ZNRAAAAGH
ZNRAAGH
...
No way...
This every night?
"Snore? No, I don't.
But I was in a dorm in high school, and my friend was like a chainsaw."
"Same here.
I had a tough time getting used to it."

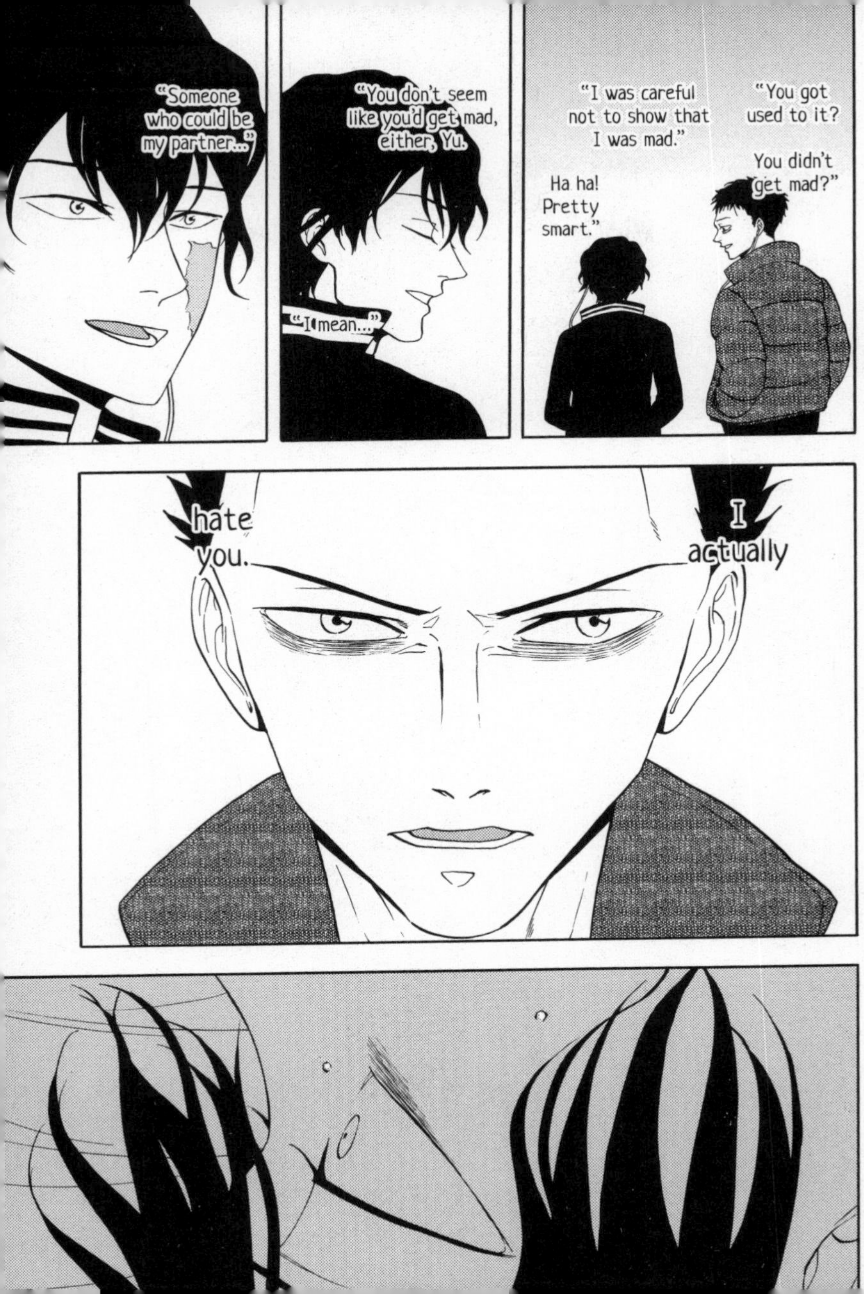
"You got used to it? You didn't get mad?"
"I was careful not to show that I was mad."
Ha ha! Pretty smart."
"You don't seem like you'd get mad, either, Yu.
"I mean..."
"Someone who could be my partner..."
I actually
hate you.

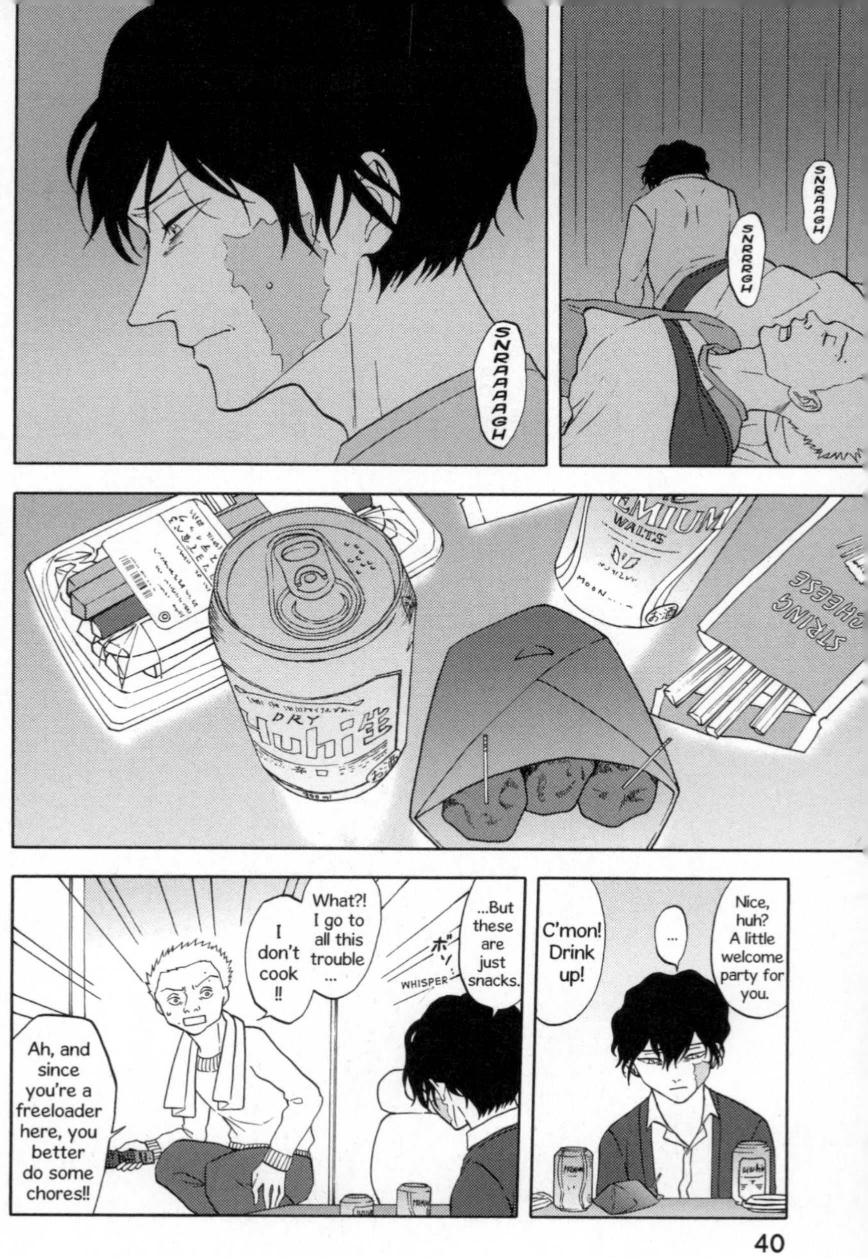
SNRAAAGH
SNRRRGH
SNRAAAAAGH
DRY
Huhi生
STRING CHEESE
Nice, huh? A little welcome party for you.
...
C'mon! Drink up!
...But these are just snacks.
WHISPER
What?! I go to all this trouble ...
I don't cook !!
Ah, and since you're a freeloader here, you better do some chores!!

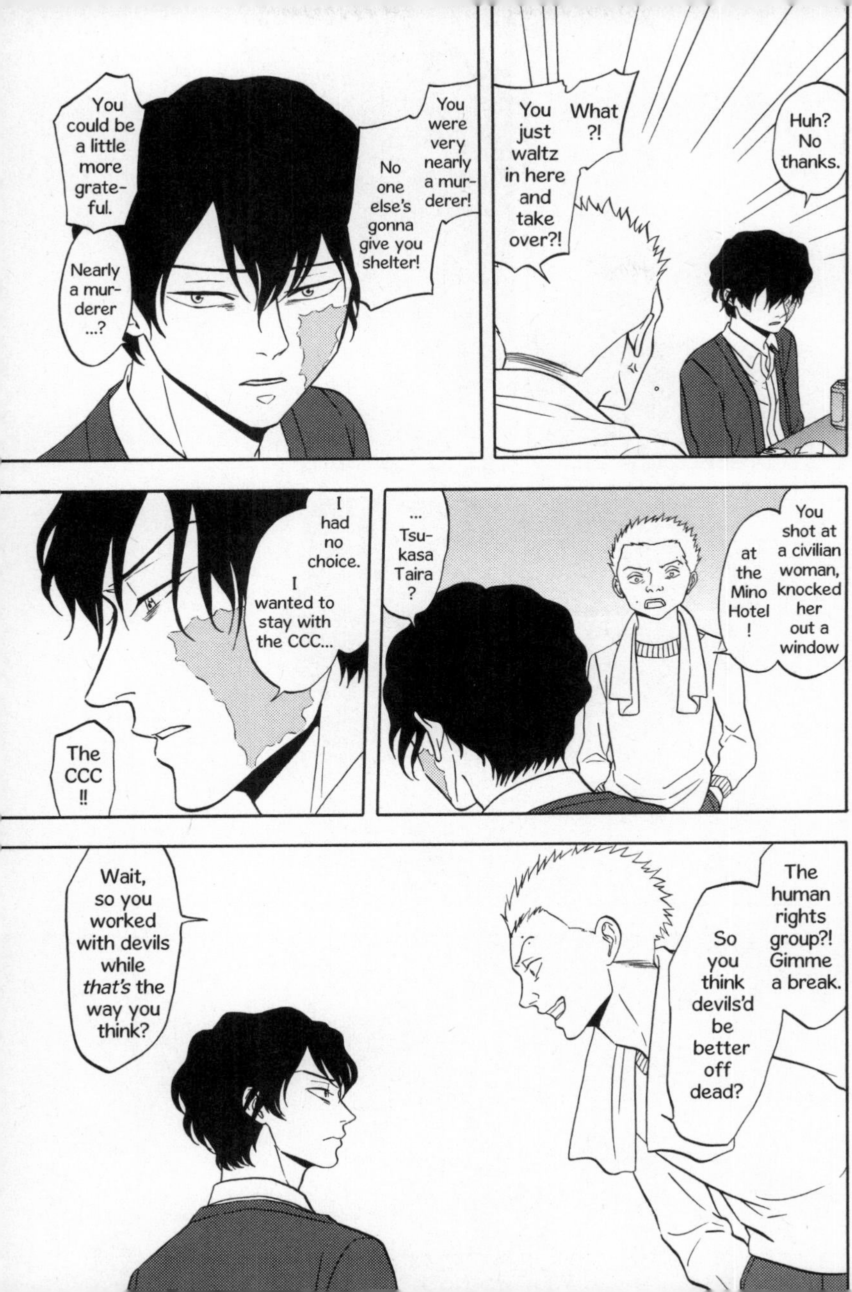
Huh? No thanks.
What?! You just waltz in here and take over?!
You were very nearly a murderer! No one else's gonna give you shelter!
You could be a little more grateful.
Nearly a murderer ...?
You shot at a civilian woman, knocked her out a window at the Mino Hotel!
... Tsukasa Taira?
I had no choice. I wanted to stay with the CCC...
The CCC!!
The human rights group?! Gimme a break. So you think devils'd be better off dead?
Wait, so you worked with devils while *that's* the way you think?

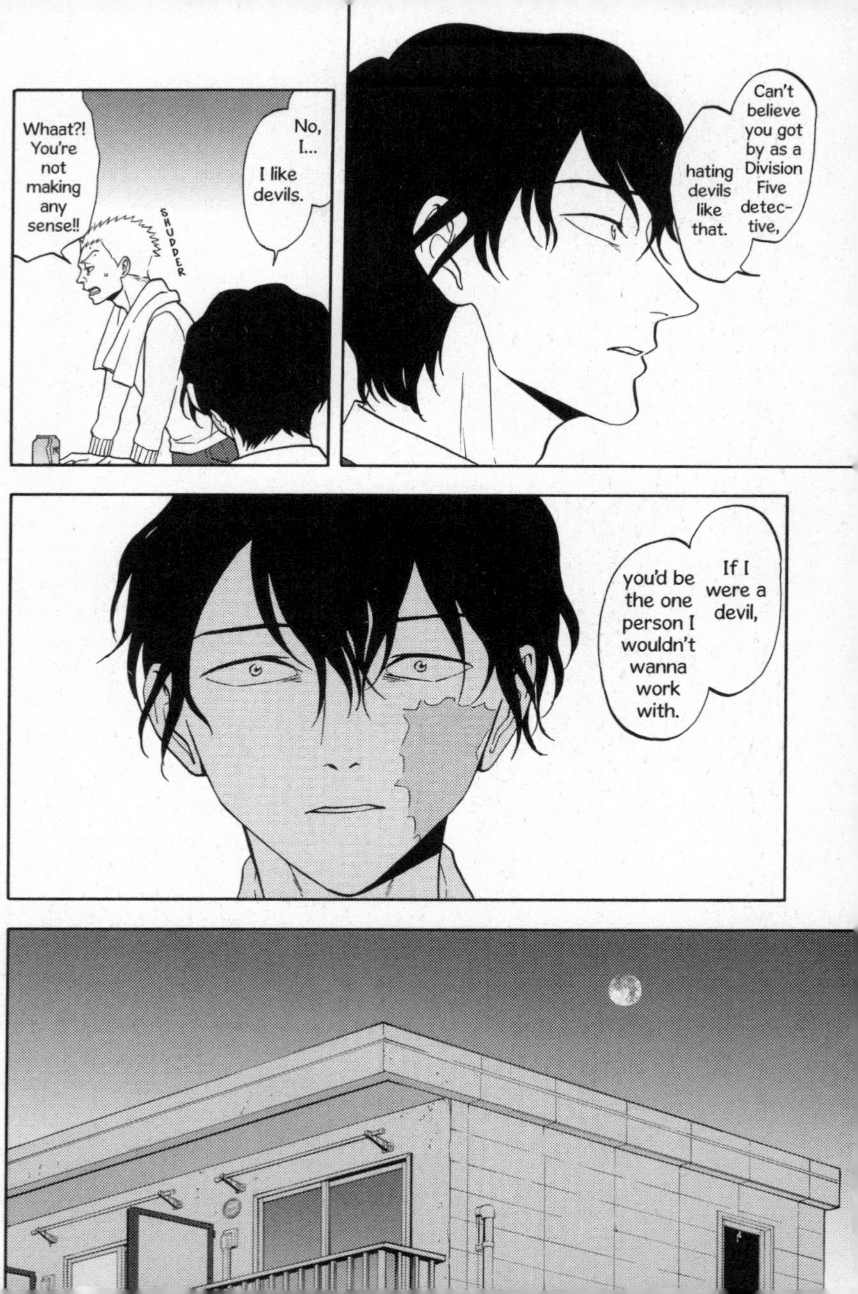
Can't believe you got by as a Division Five detective,
hating devils like that.
No, I... I like devils.
SHUDDER
Whaat?! You're not making any sense!!
If I were a devil,
you'd be the one person I wouldn't wanna work with.

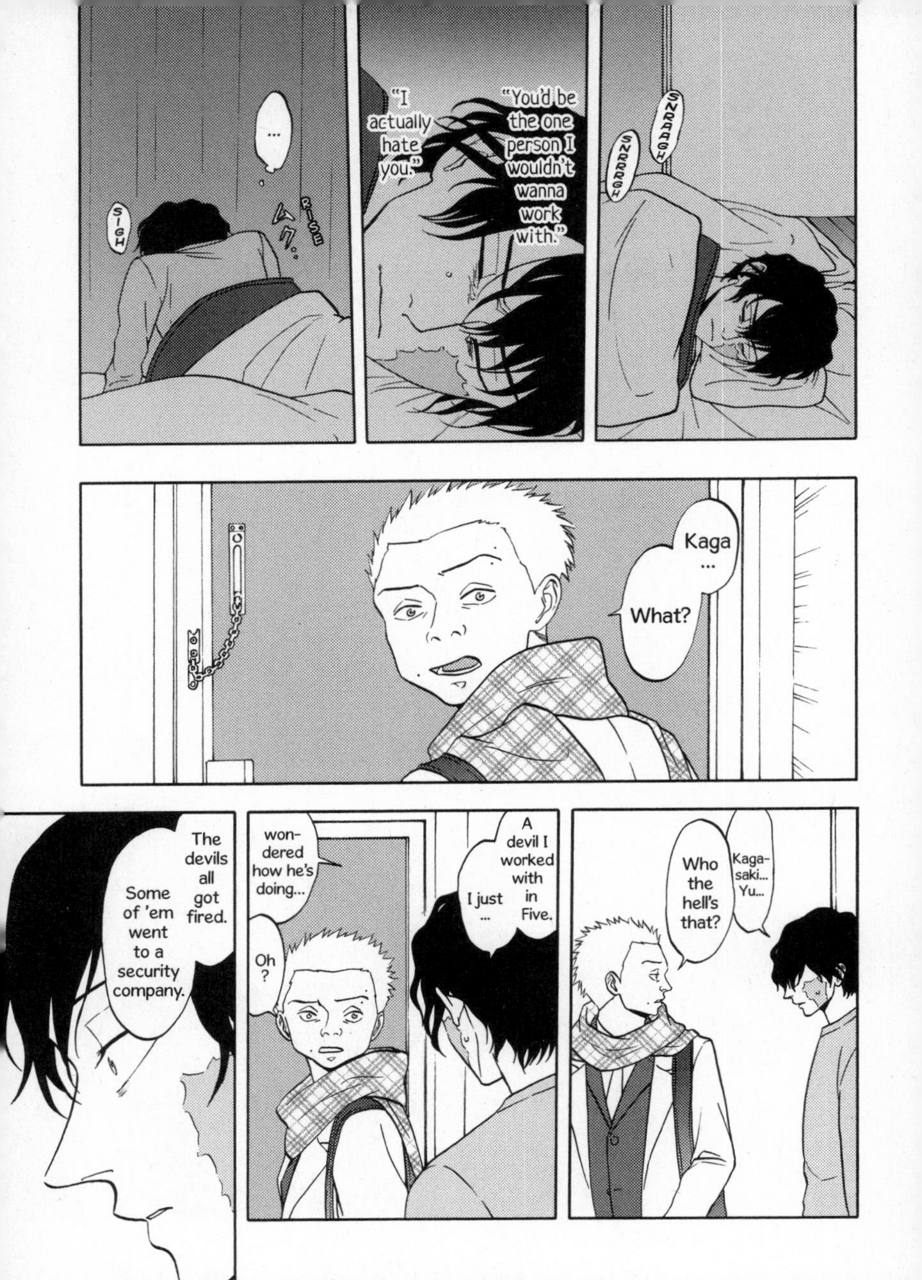
SNRAAGH
SNRRRGH
"You'd be the one person I wouldn't wanna work with."
"I actually hate you."
…
RISE
SIGH
Kaga …
What?
Kaga-saki... Yu...
Who the hell's that?
A devil I worked with in Five.
I just …
wondered how he's doing...
Oh?
The devils all got fired.
Some of 'em went to a security company.

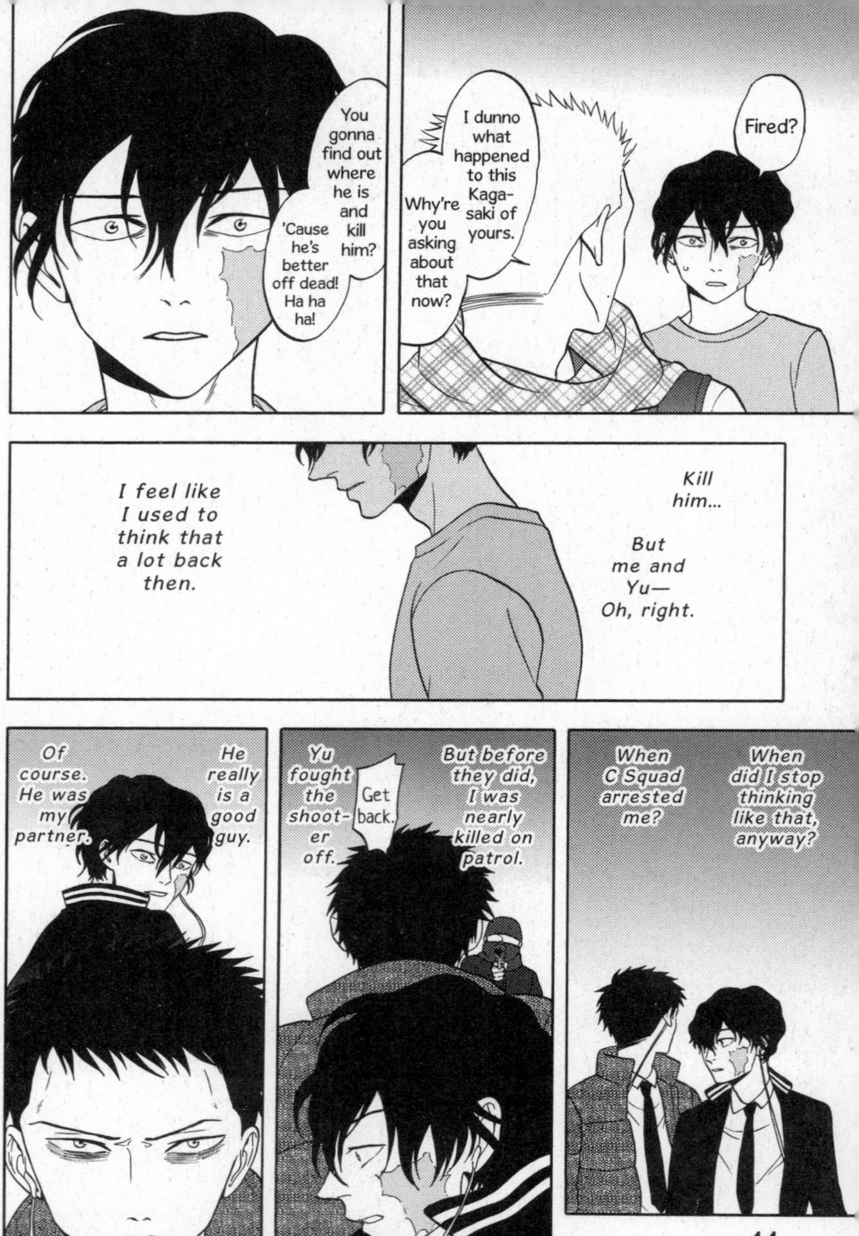
Fired?
I dunno what happened to this Kaga-saki of yours.
Why're you asking about that now?
You gonna find out where he is and kill him?
'Cause he's better off dead! Ha ha ha!
Kill him...
But me and Yu—
Oh, right.
I feel like I used to think that a lot back then.
When did I stop thinking like that, anyway?
When C Squad arrested me?
But before they did, I was nearly killed on patrol.
Get back.
Yu fought the shoot-er off.
He really is a good guy.
Of course. He was my partner.

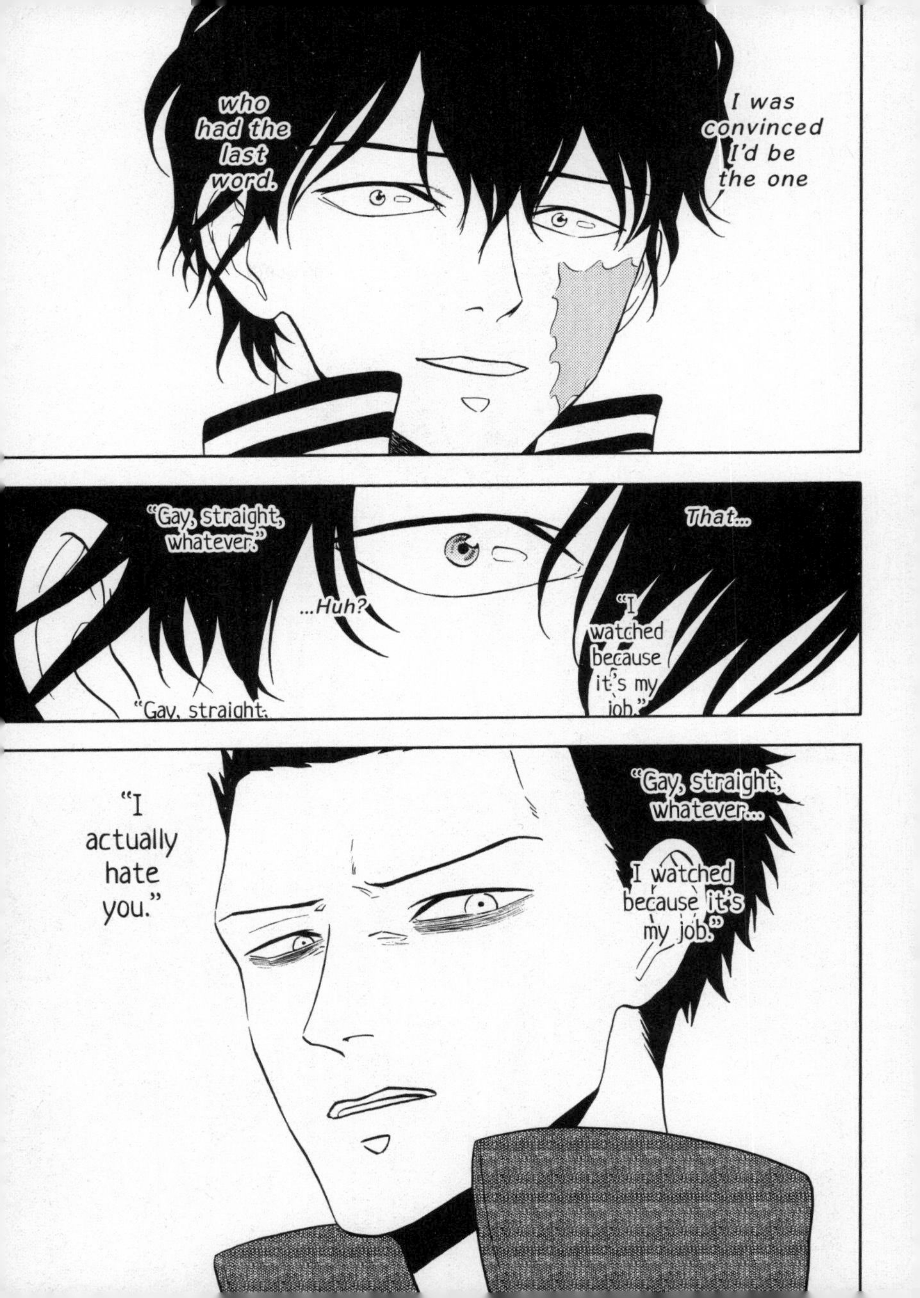
I was convinced I'd be the one
who had the last word.
That...
"I watched because it's my job."
"Gay, straight, whatever."
...Huh?
"Gay, straight,
"Gay, straight, whatever...
I watched because it's my job."
"I actually hate you."

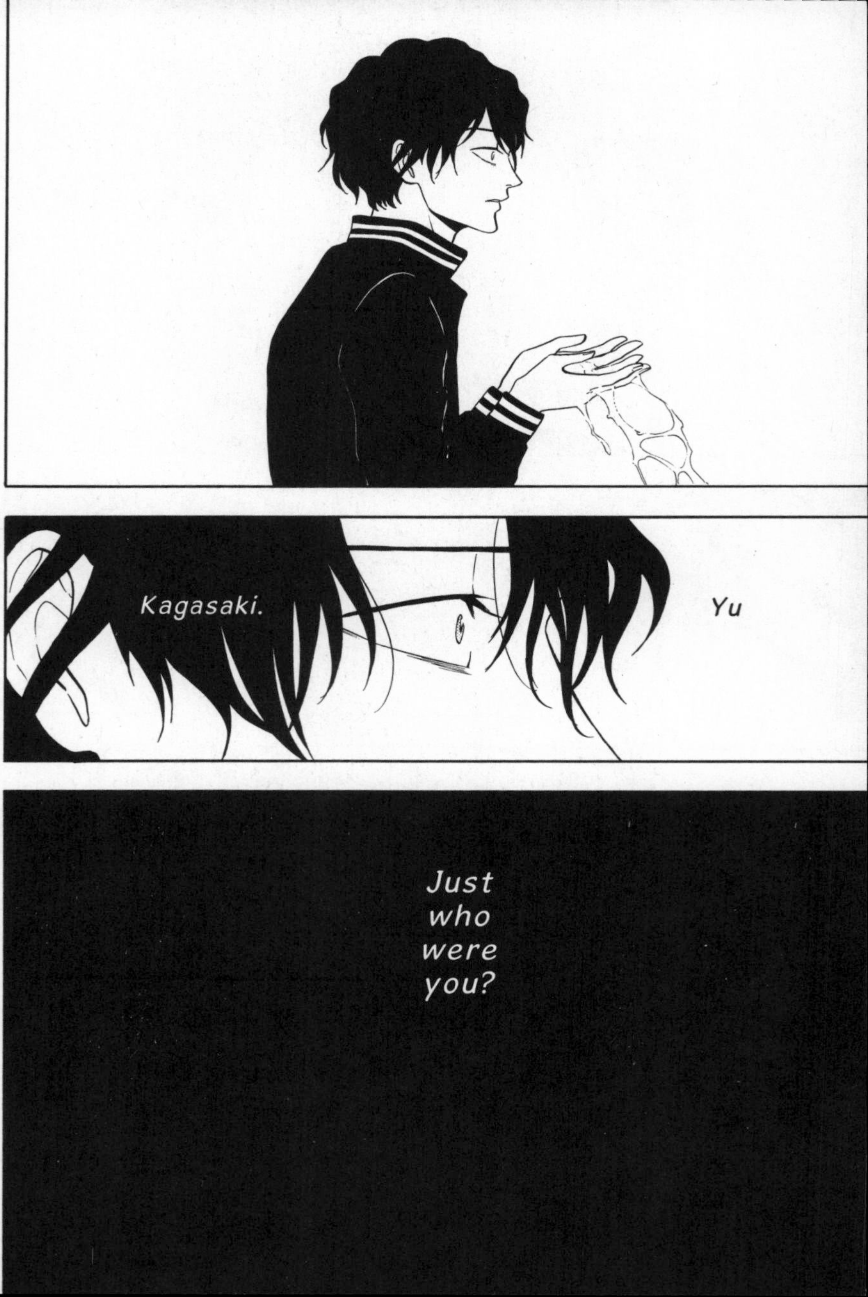
Yu
Kagasaki.
Just who were you?

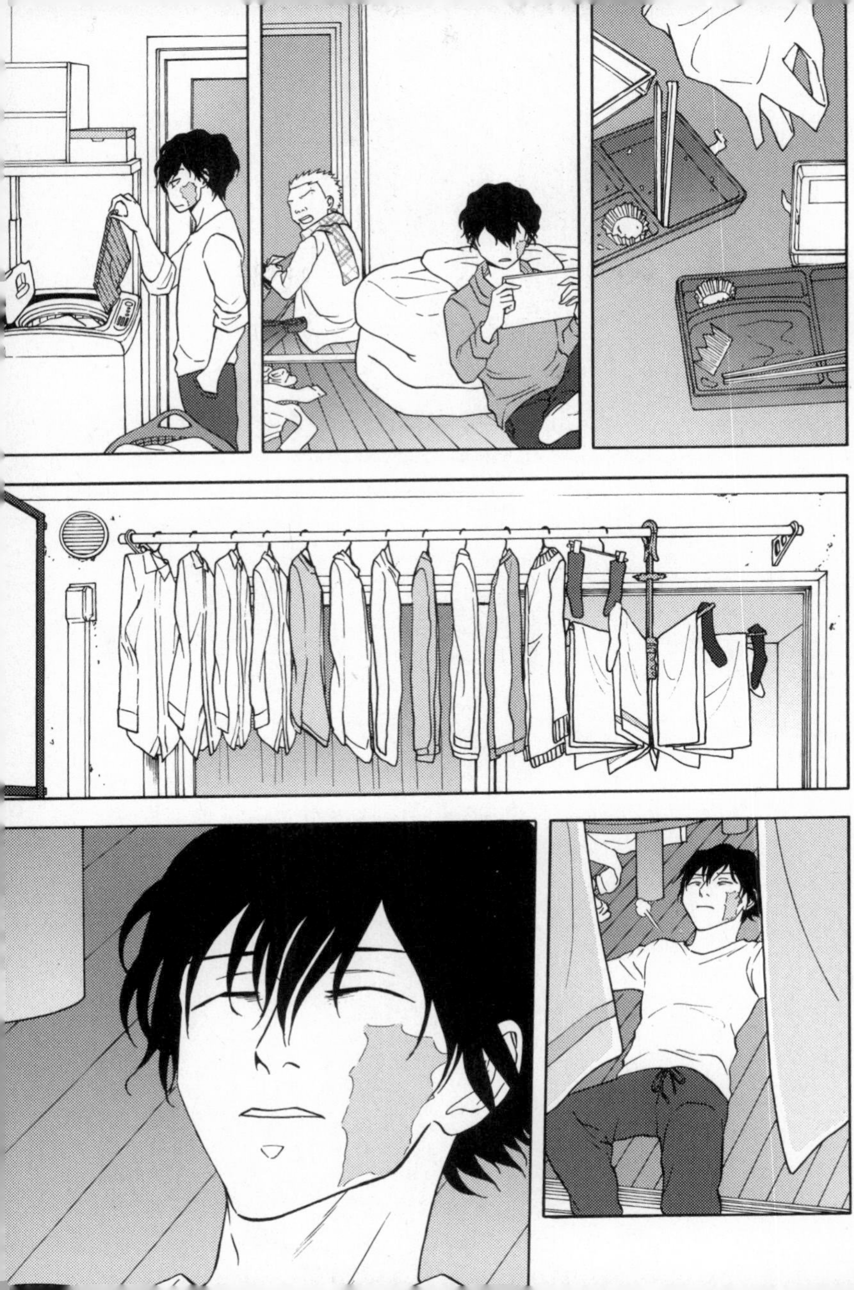

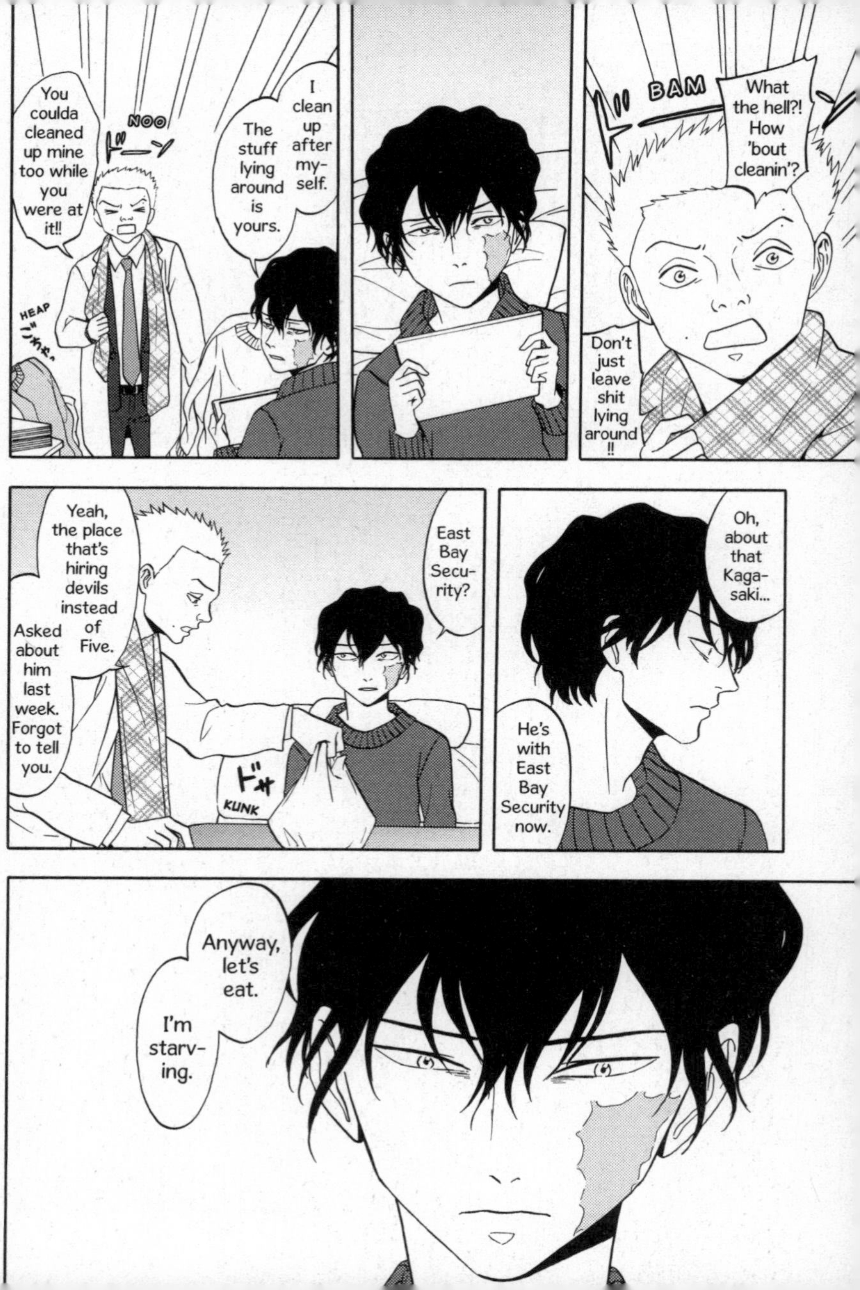
BAM
What the hell?! How 'bout cleanin'?
Don't just leave shit lying around!!
I clean up after myself.
The stuff lying around is yours.
NOO
You coulda cleaned up mine too while you were at it!!
HEAP
Oh, about that Kaga-saki...
He's with East Bay Security now.
East Bay Secu-rity?
Yeah, the place that's hiring devils instead of Five.
Asked about him last week. Forgot to tell you.
KUNK
Anyway, let's eat.
I'm starv-ing.

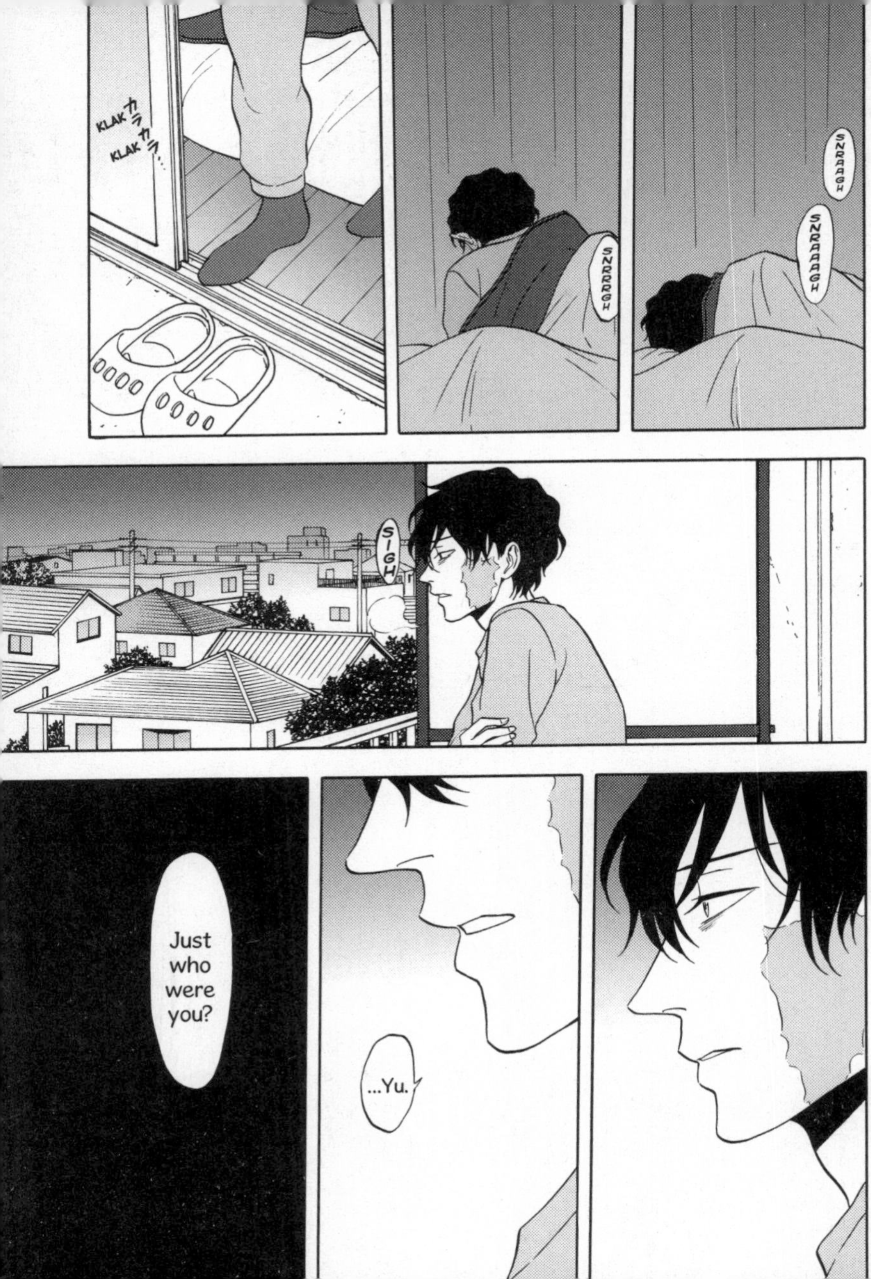
SNRAAGH
SNRAAAGH
SNRRRGH
KLAK カラ
KLAK カラ…
SIGH
...Yu.
Just who were you?

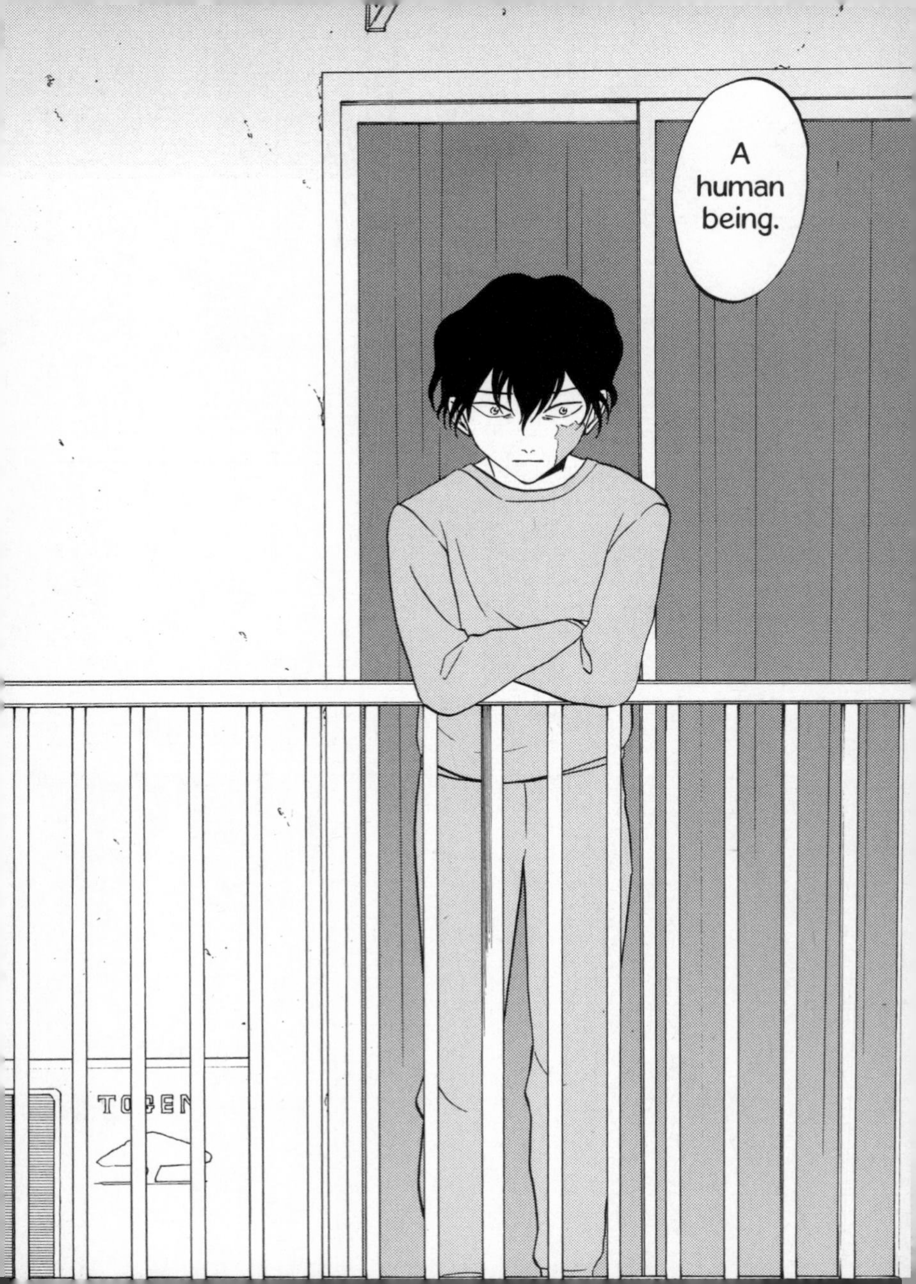
A human being.

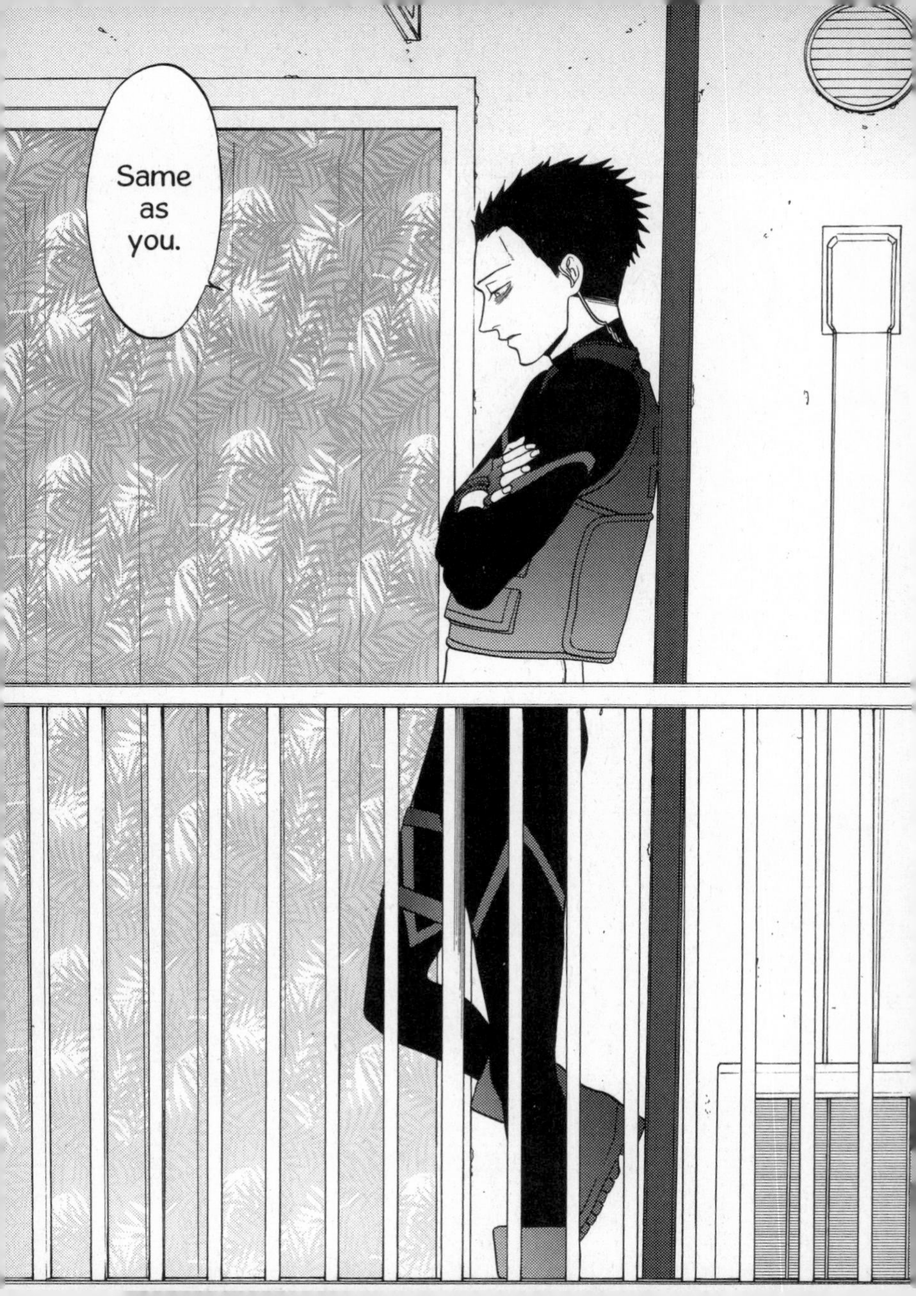
Same as you.

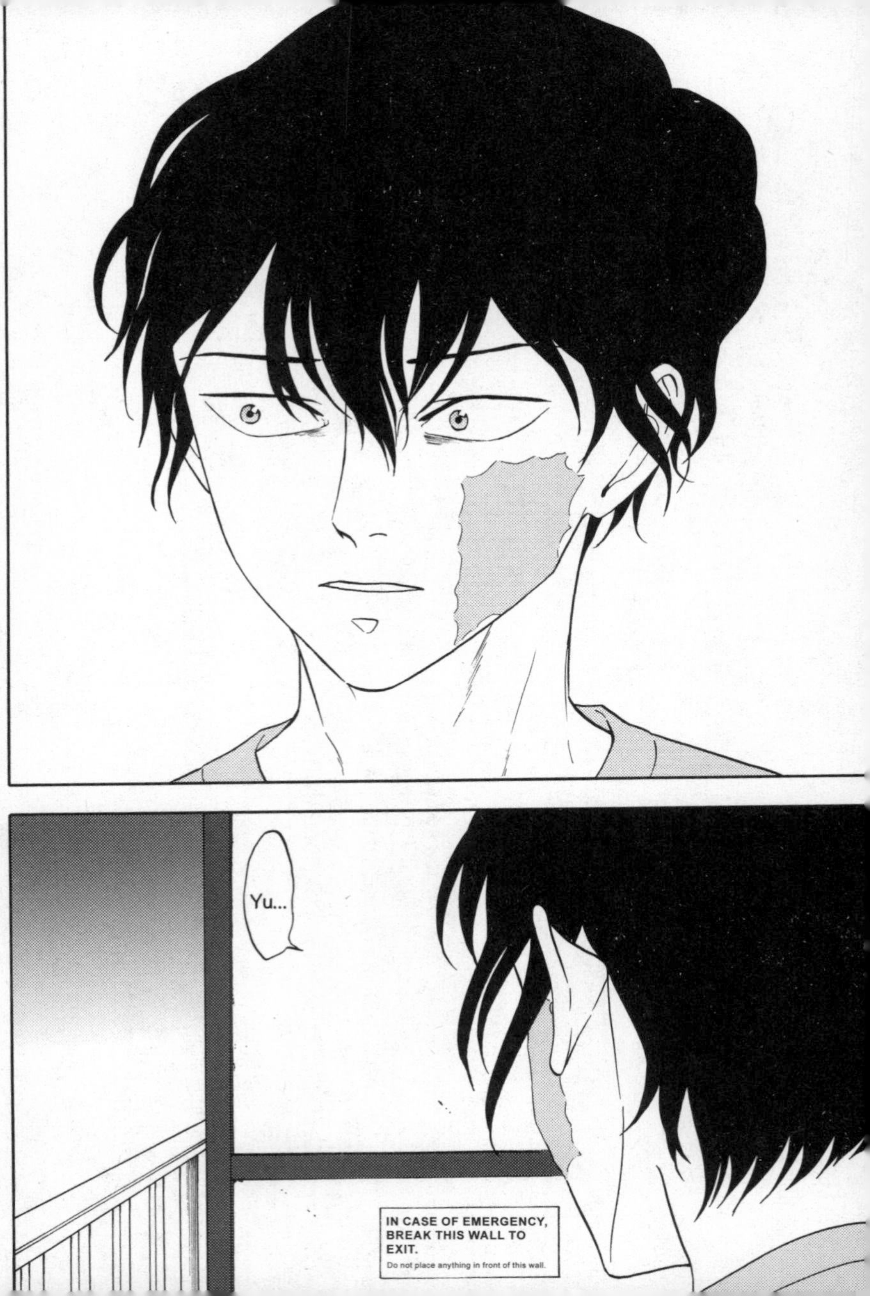
Yu...
IN CASE OF EMERGENCY, BREAK THIS WALL TO EXIT.
Do not place anything in front of this wall.

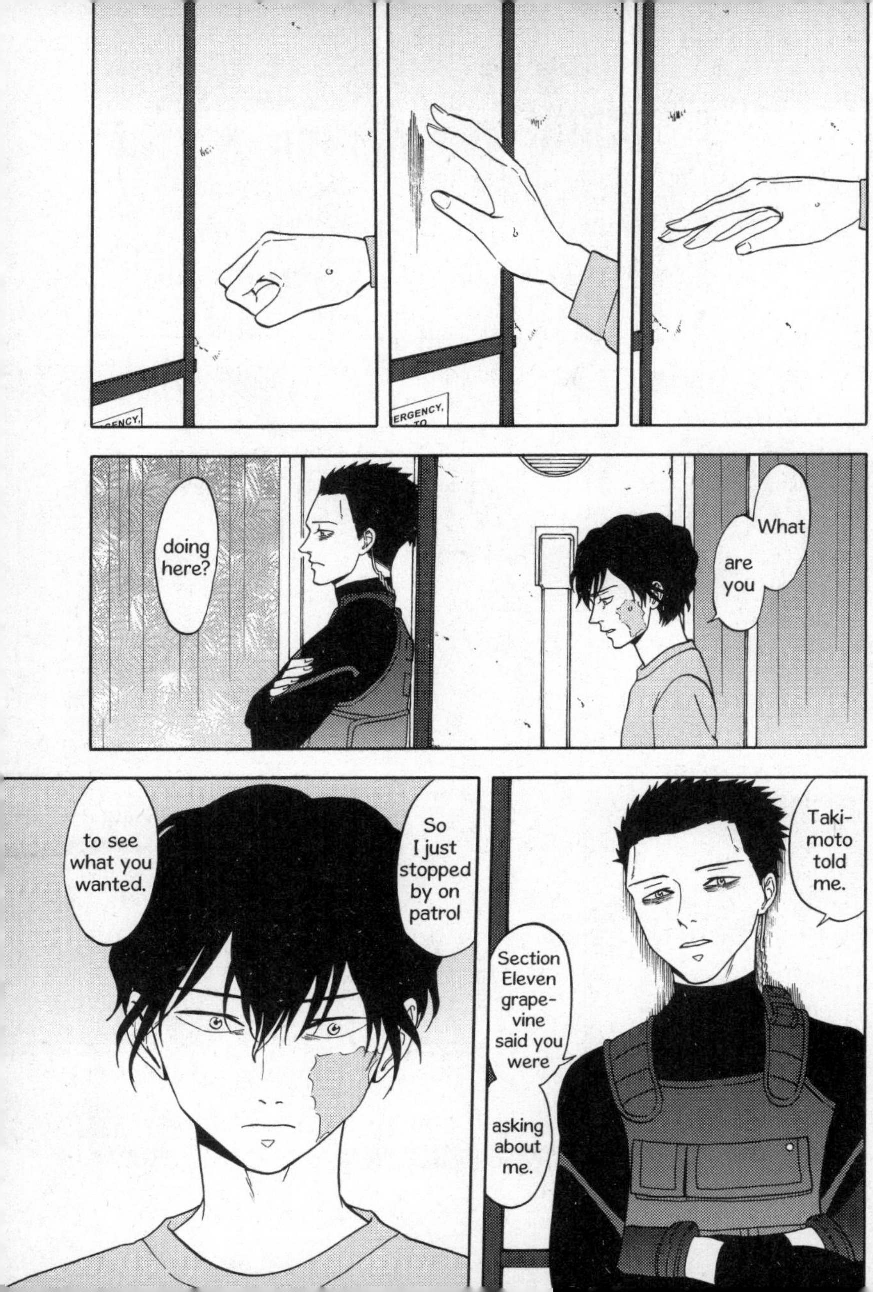
ERGENCY,
TO
GENCY,
What are you
doing here?
Taki-moto told me.
Section Eleven grape-vine said you were
asking about me.
So I just stopped by on patrol
to see what you wanted.

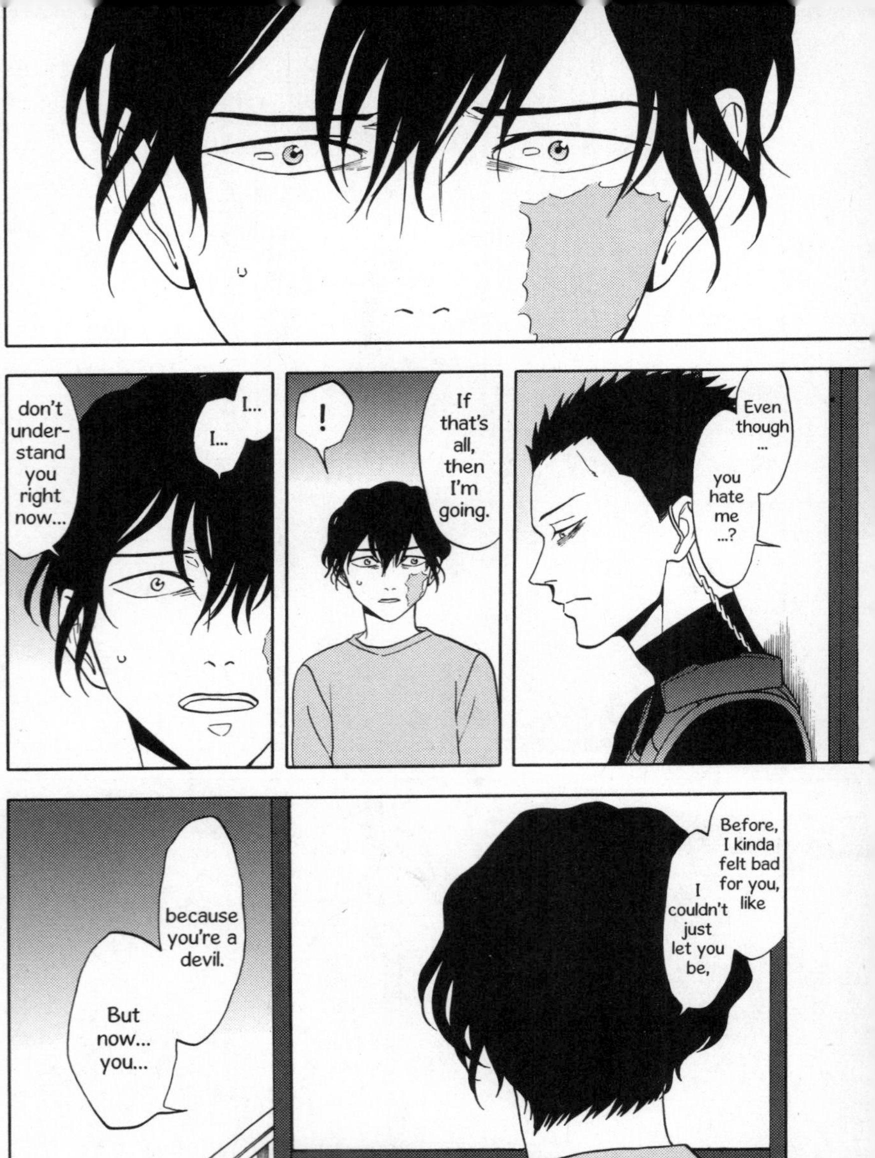
Even though ...
you hate me ...?
If that's all, then I'm going.
!
I...
I...
don't under-stand you right now...
Before, I kinda felt bad for you, like
I couldn't just let you be,
because you're a devil.
But now... you...

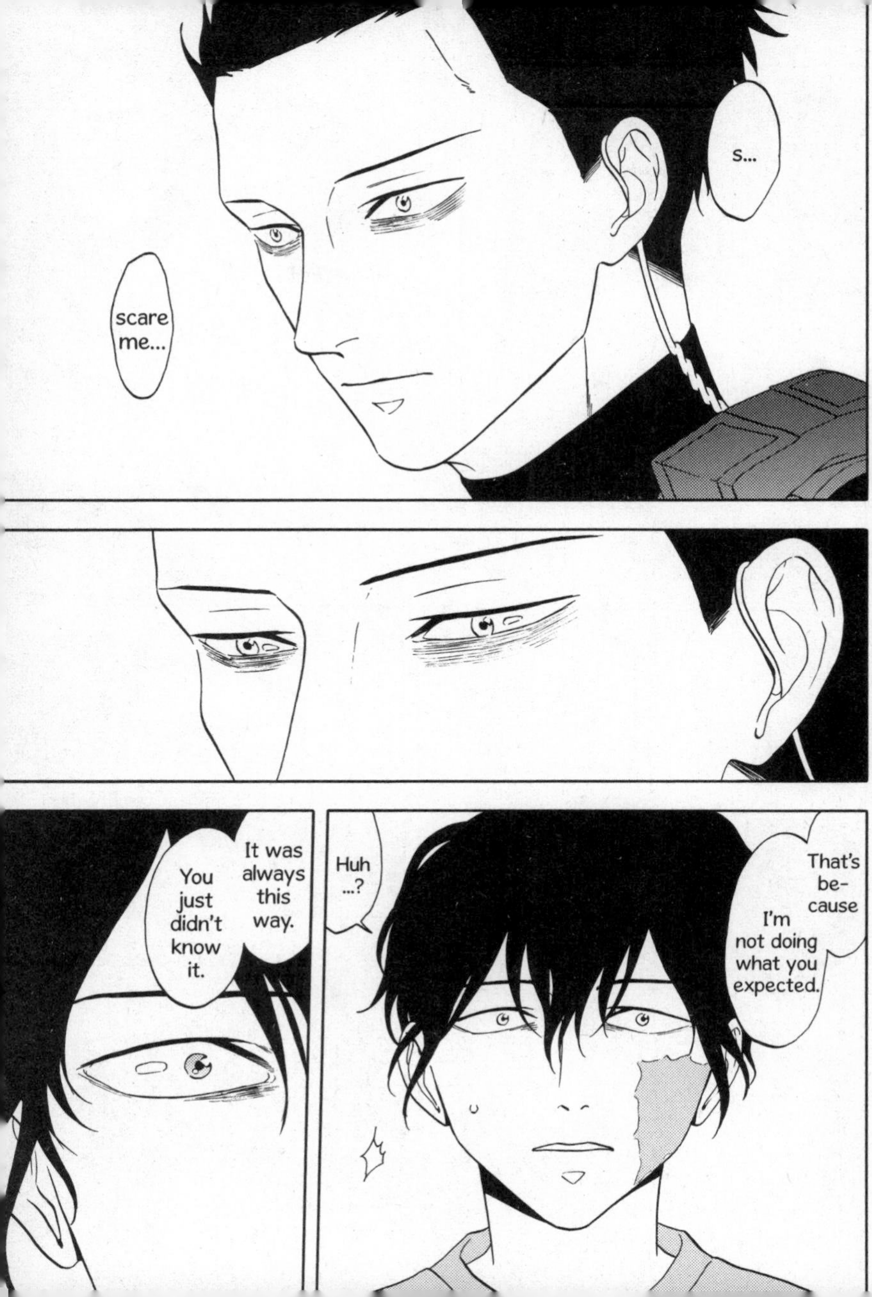
S...
scare me...
That's be- cause I'm not doing what you expected.
Huh ...?
It was always this way.
You just didn't know it.

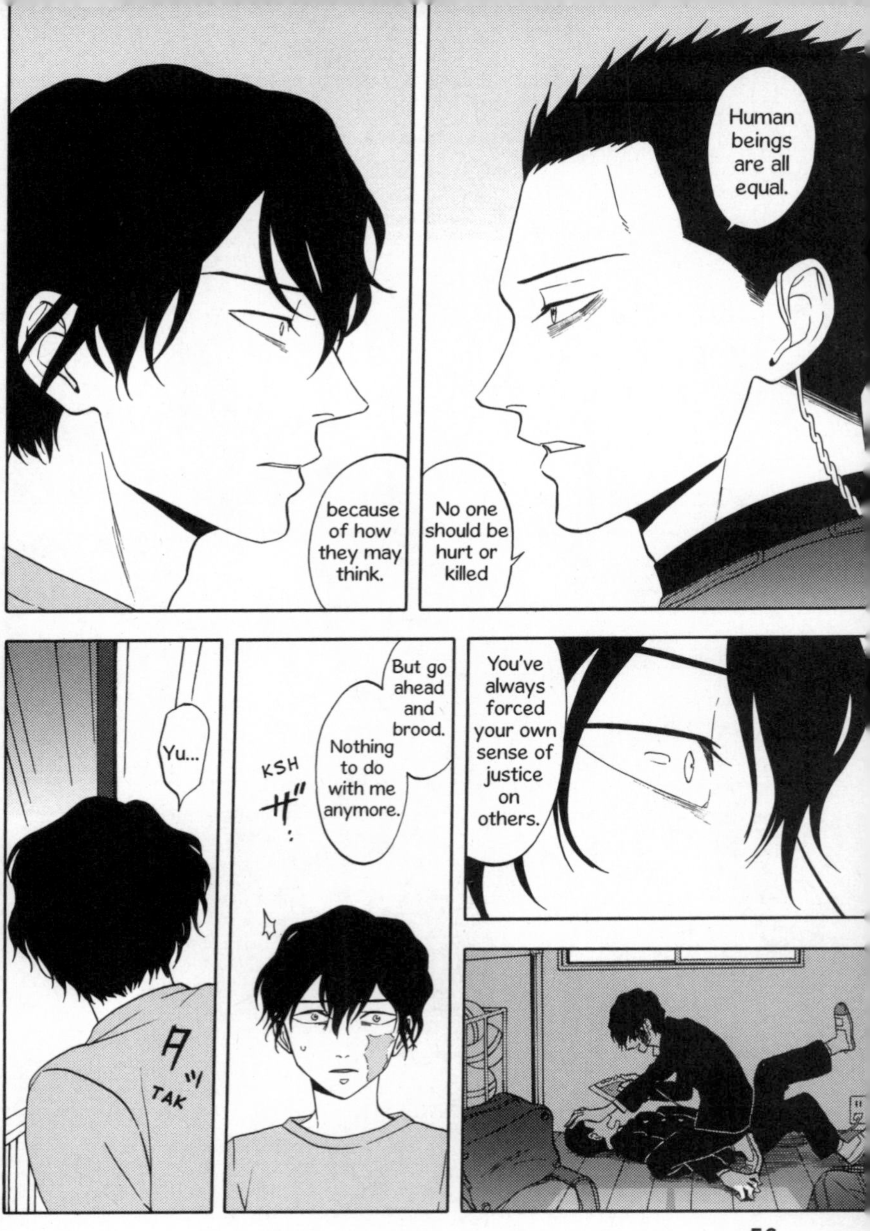

Human beings are all equal.
No one should be hurt or killed
because of how they may think.
You've always forced your own sense of justice on others.
But go ahead and brood.
Nothing to do with me anymore.
KSH
Yu...
TAK

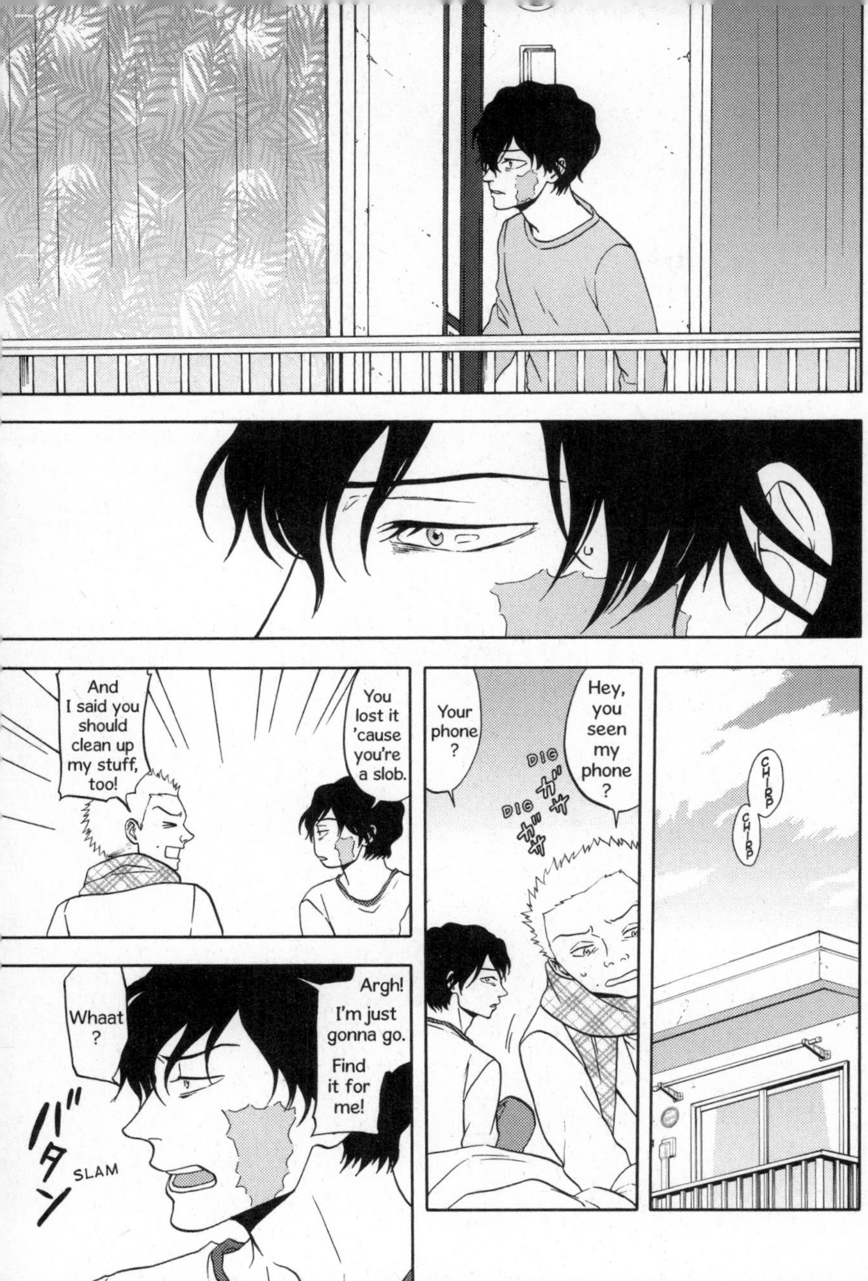
CHIRP
CHIRP
Hey, you seen my phone?
DIG
ガサ
DIG
ガサ
Your phone?
You lost it 'cause you're a slob.
And I said you should clean up my stuff, too!
Argh! I'm just gonna go.
Find it for me!
Whaat?
バタン
SLAM

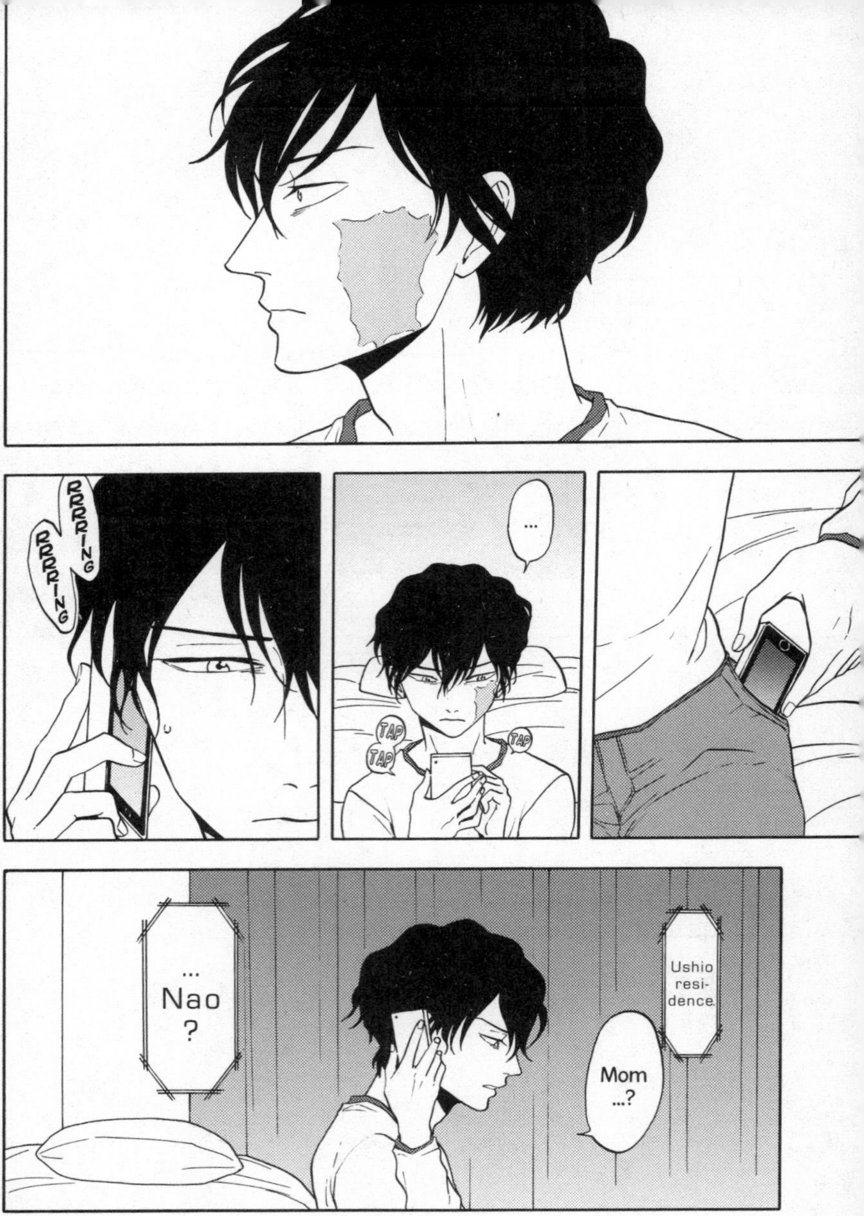
…
TAP
TAP
TAP
RRRRING
RRRRING
Ushio residence.
Mom …?
… Nao ?

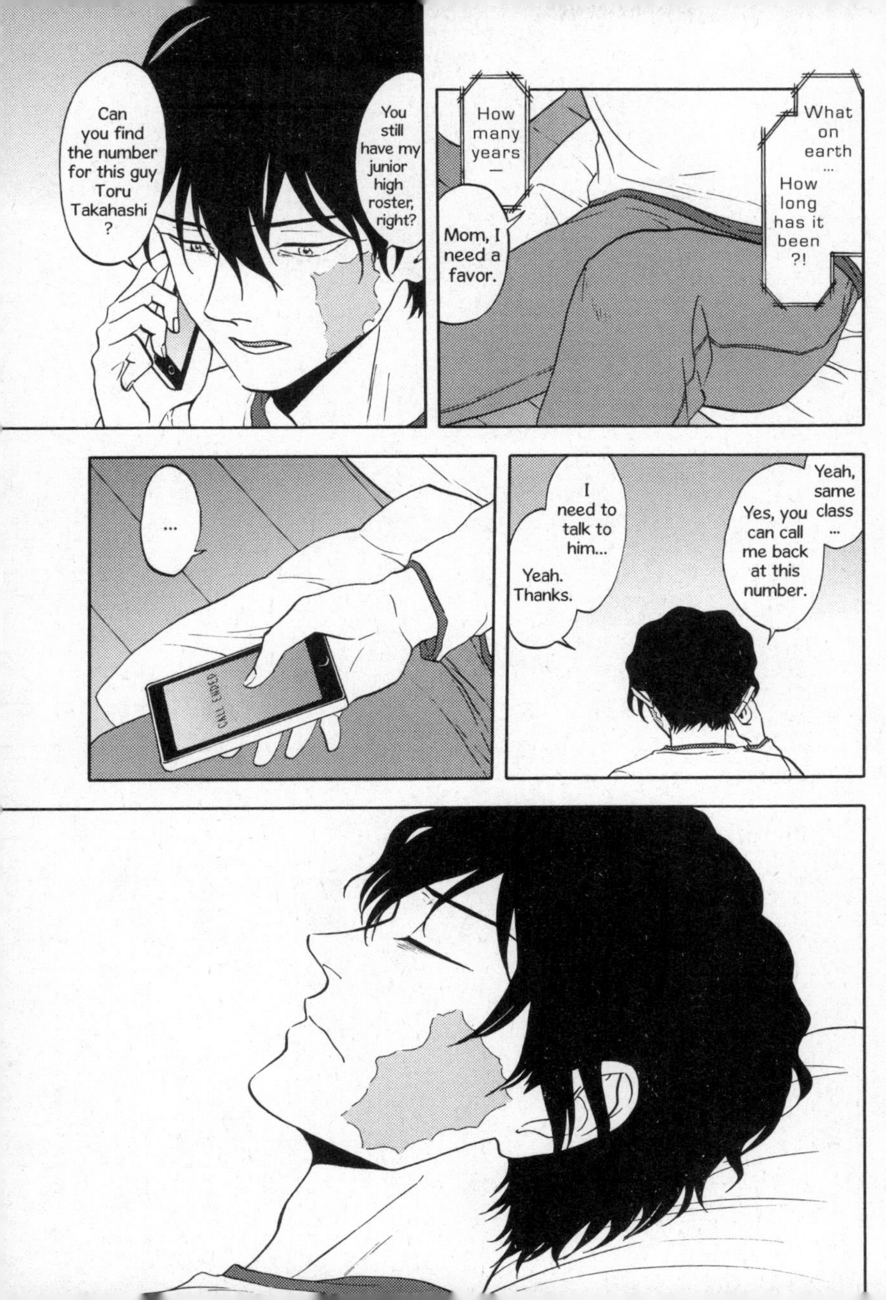
What on earth... How long has it been?!
How many years —
Mom, I need a favor.
You still have my junior high roster, right?
Can you find the number for this guy Toru Takahashi?
Yeah, same class...
Yes, you can call me back at this number.
I need to talk to him...
Yeah. Thanks.
...
CALL ENDED

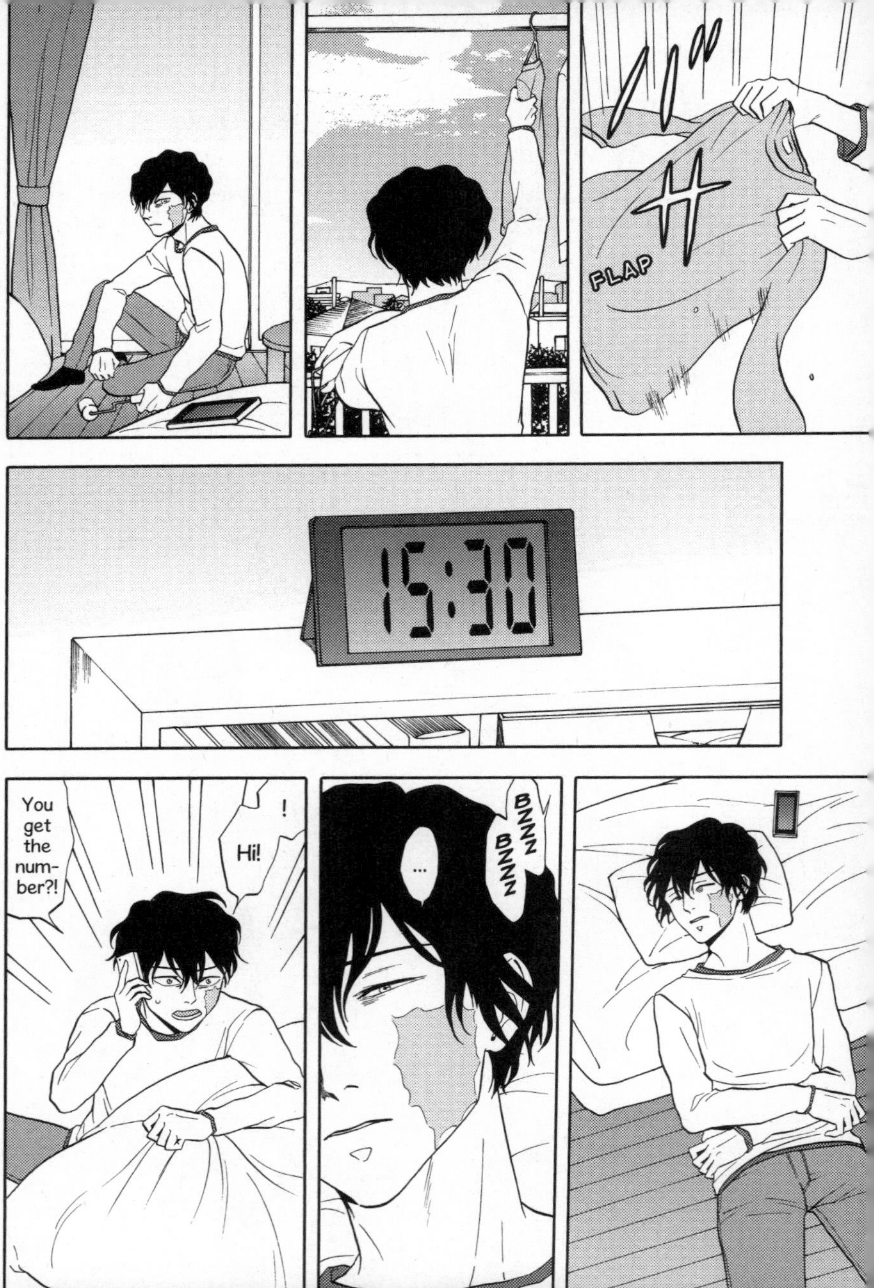
FLAP
15:30
...
BZZZ BZZZ
!
Hi!
You get the number?!

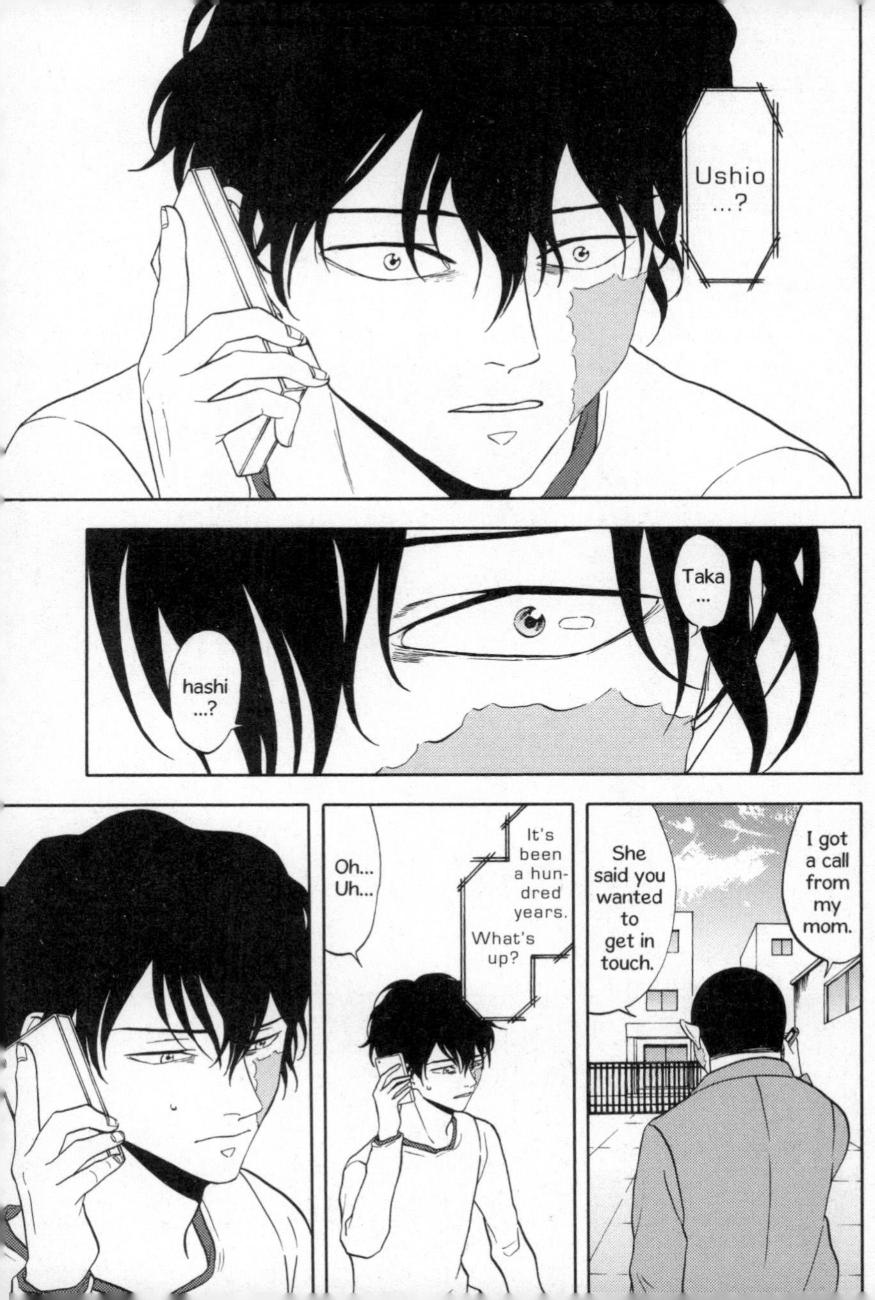
Ushio ...?
Taka ...
hashi ...?
I got a call from my mom.
She said you wanted to get in touch.
It's been a hun-dred years.
What's up?
Oh... Uh...

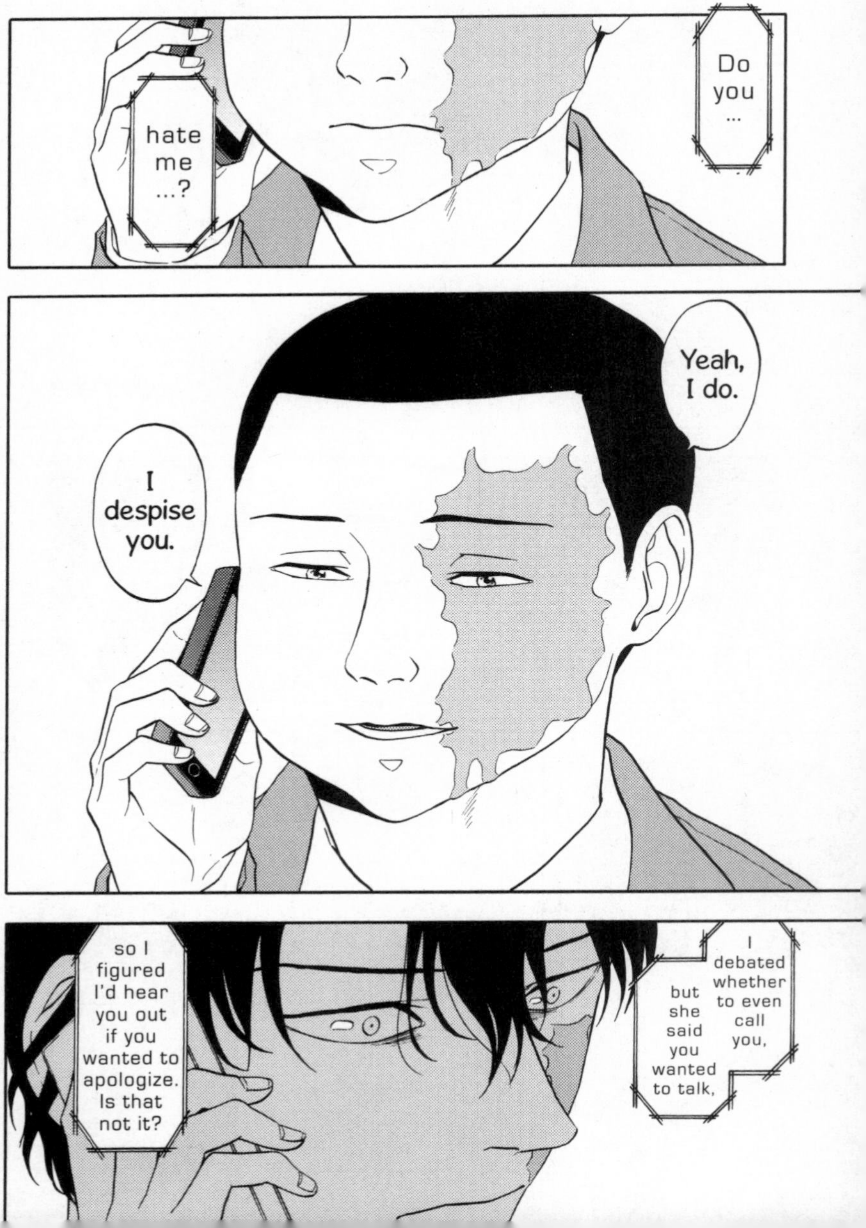
Do you ...
hate me ...?
Yeah, I do.
I despise you.
I debated whether to even call you,
but she said you wanted to talk,
so I figured I'd hear you out if you wanted to apologize. Is that not it?

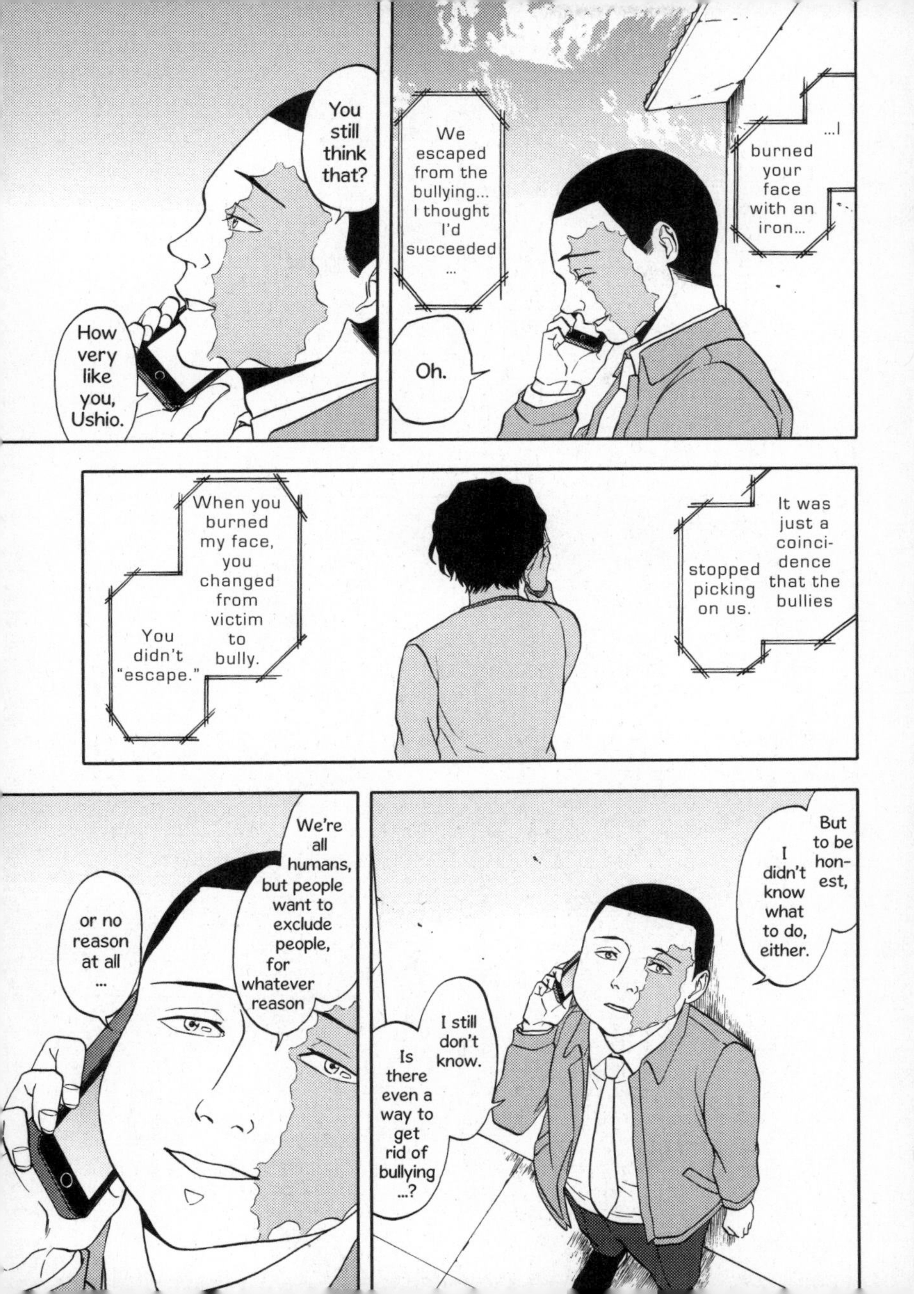
...I burned your face with an iron...
We escaped from the bullying... I thought I'd succeeded...
Oh.
You still think that?
How very like you, Ushio.
It was just a coincidence that the bullies stopped picking on us.
When you burned my face, you changed from victim to bully. You didn't "escape."
But to be honest, I didn't know what to do, either.
I still don't know. Is there even a way to get rid of bullying...?
We're all humans, but people want to exclude people, for whatever reason
or no reason at all...

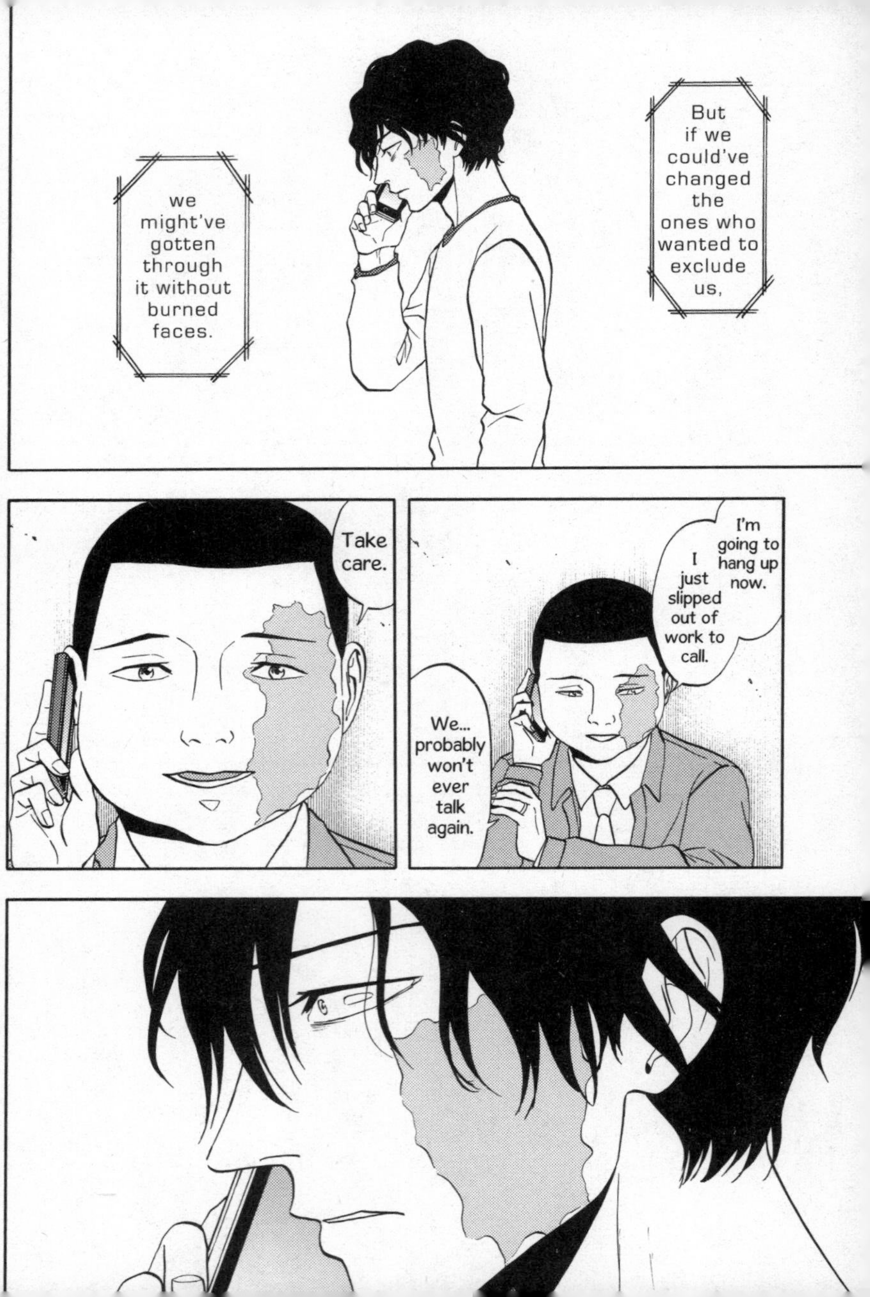
But if we could've changed the ones who wanted to exclude us,
we might've gotten through it without burned faces.
I'm going to hang up now.
I just slipped out of work to call.
We... probably won't ever talk again.
Take care.

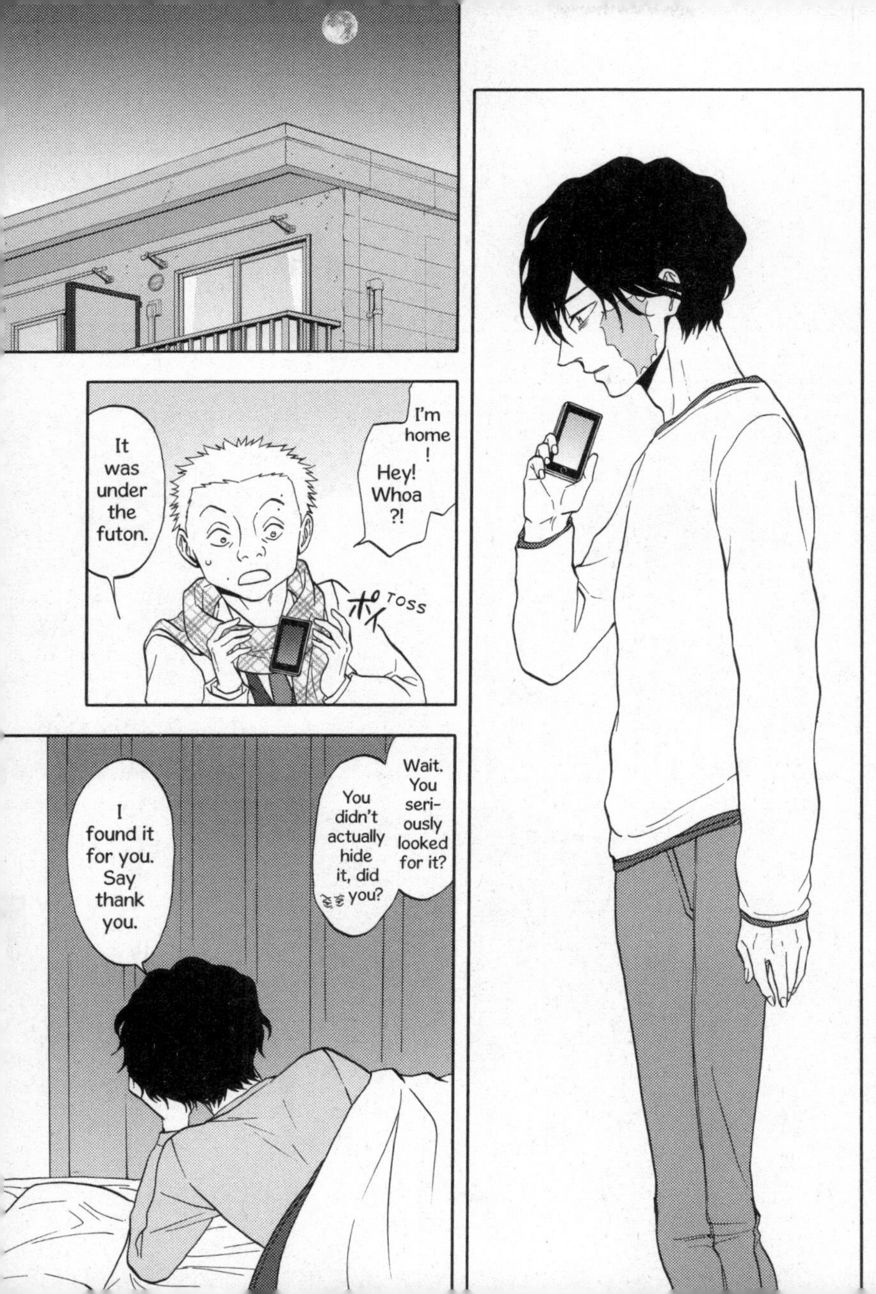
I'm home!
Hey! Whoa?!
It was under the futon.
TOSS
Wait. You seriously looked for it?
You didn't actually hide it, did you?
I found it for you. Say thank you.

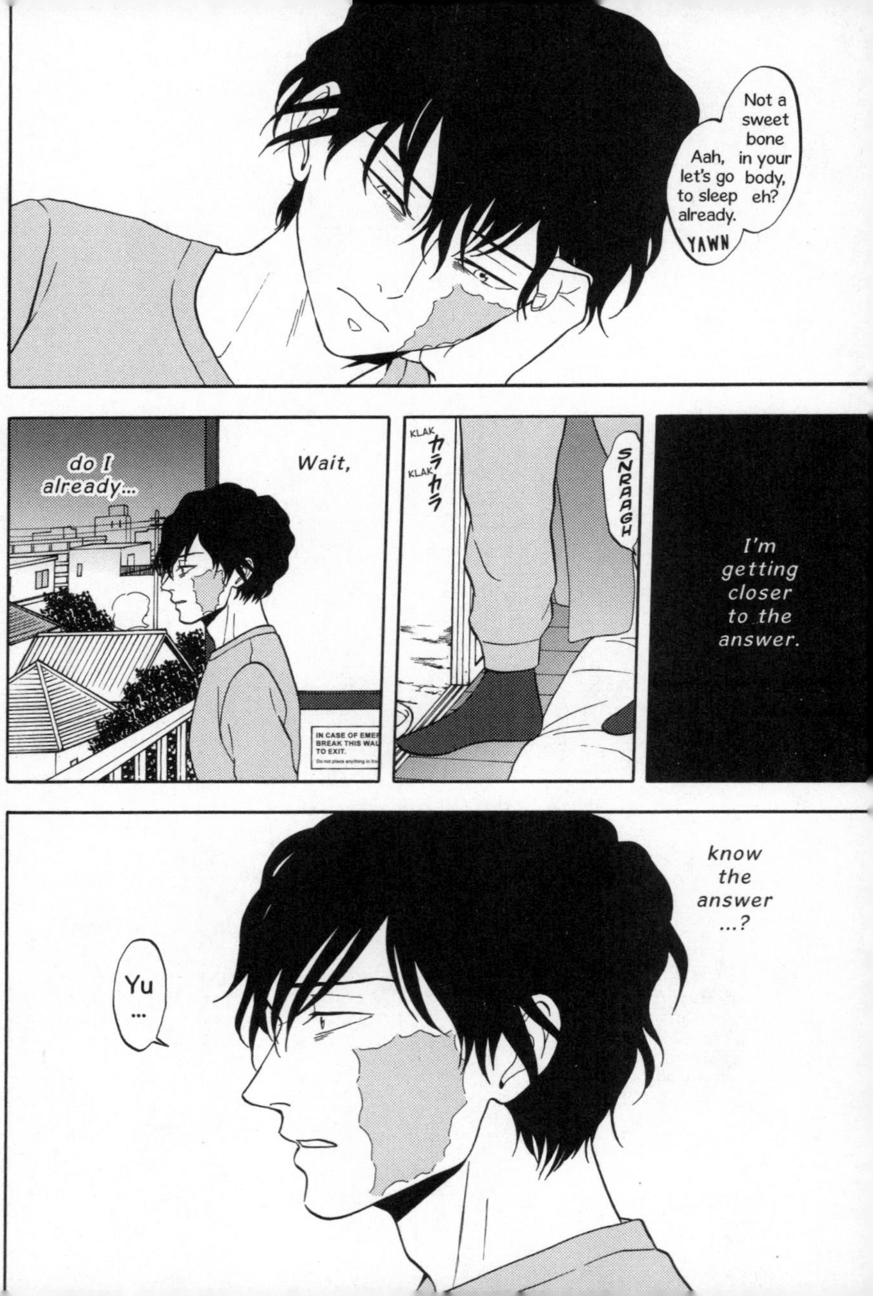
Not a sweet bone in your body, eh?
Aah, let's go to sleep already.
YAWN
I'm getting closer to the answer.
SNRAAGH
KLAK カラ
KLAK カラ
Wait,
do I already...
IN CASE OF EMER
BREAK THIS WAL
TO EXIT.
know the answer ...?
Yu ...

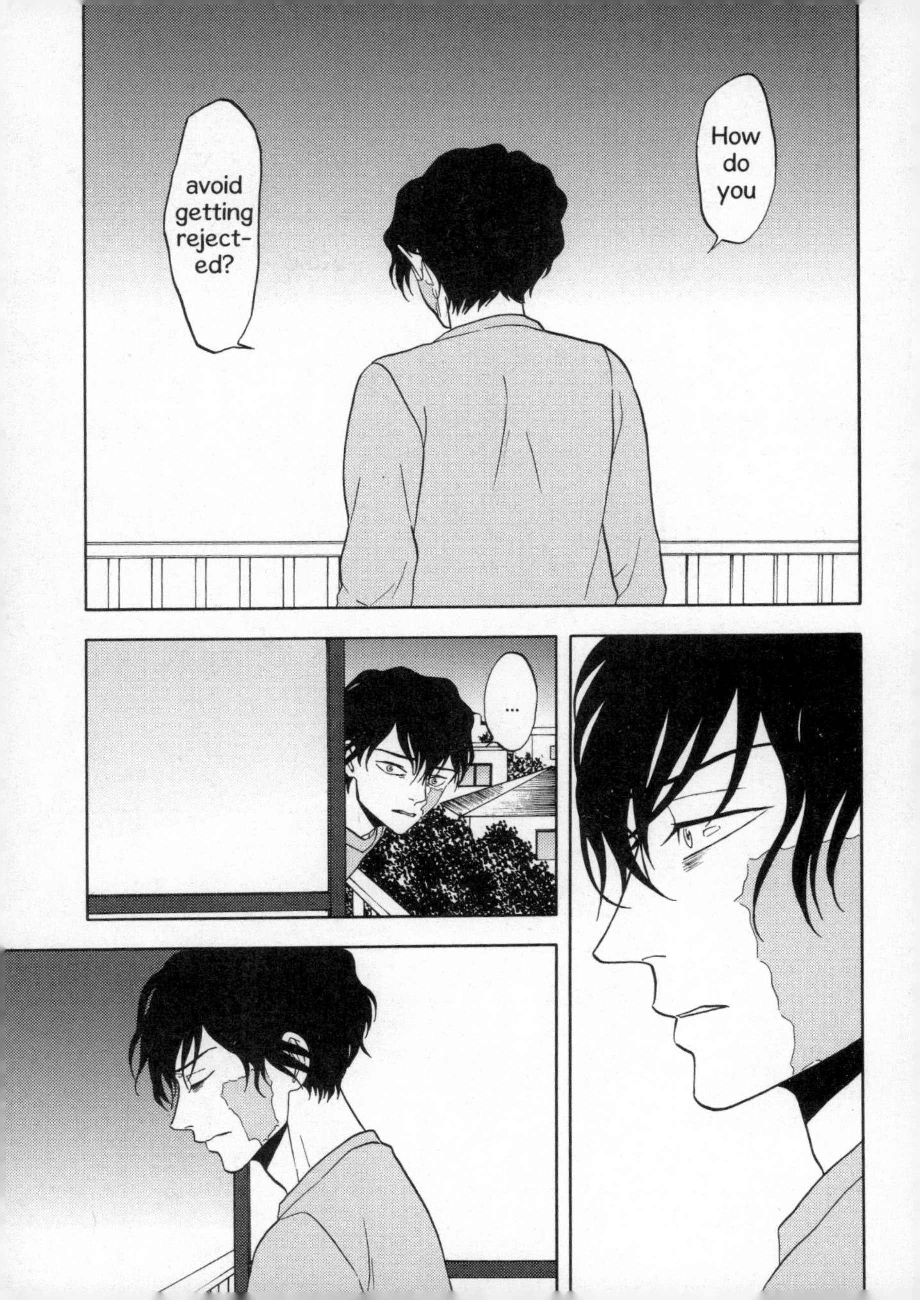
How do you
avoid getting reject-ed?
...

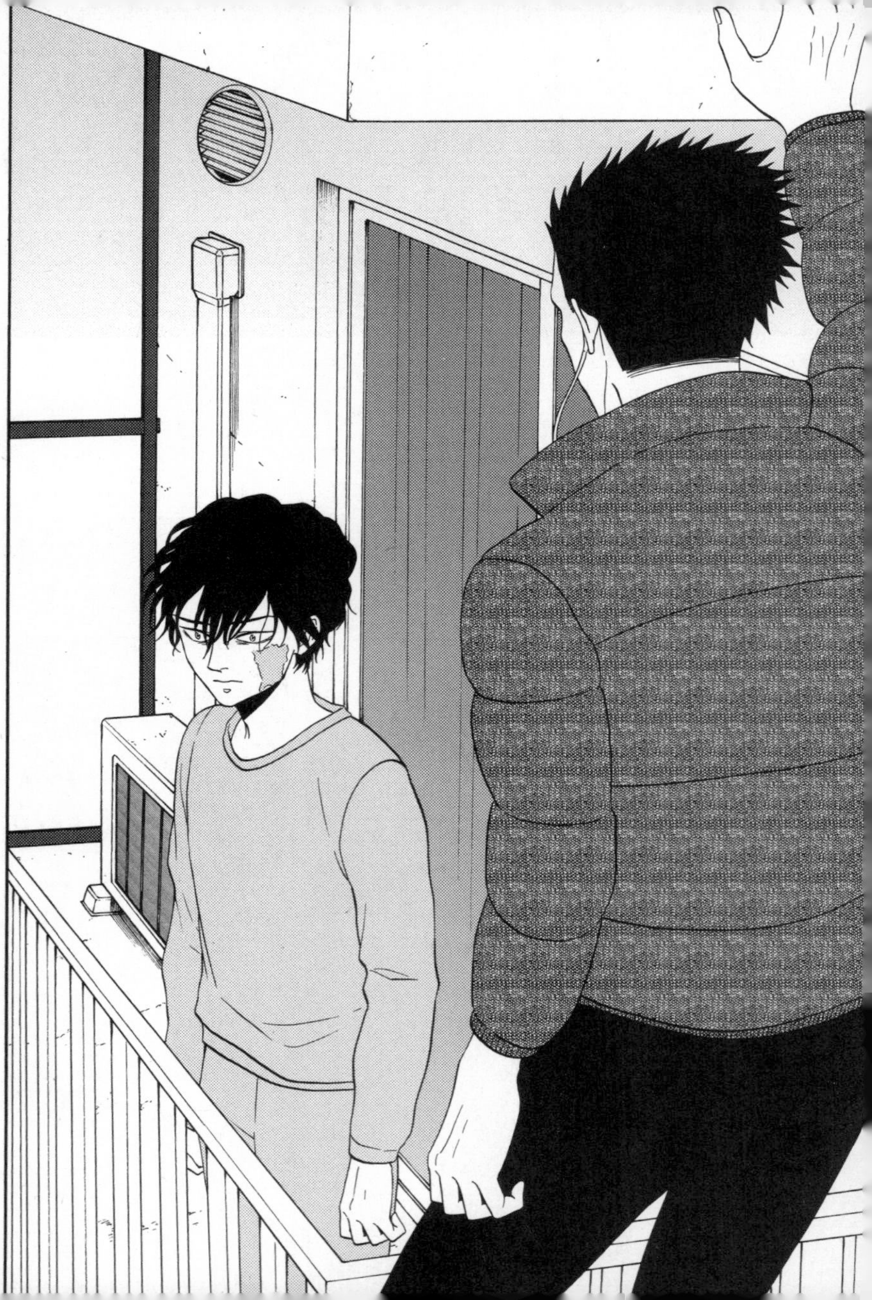

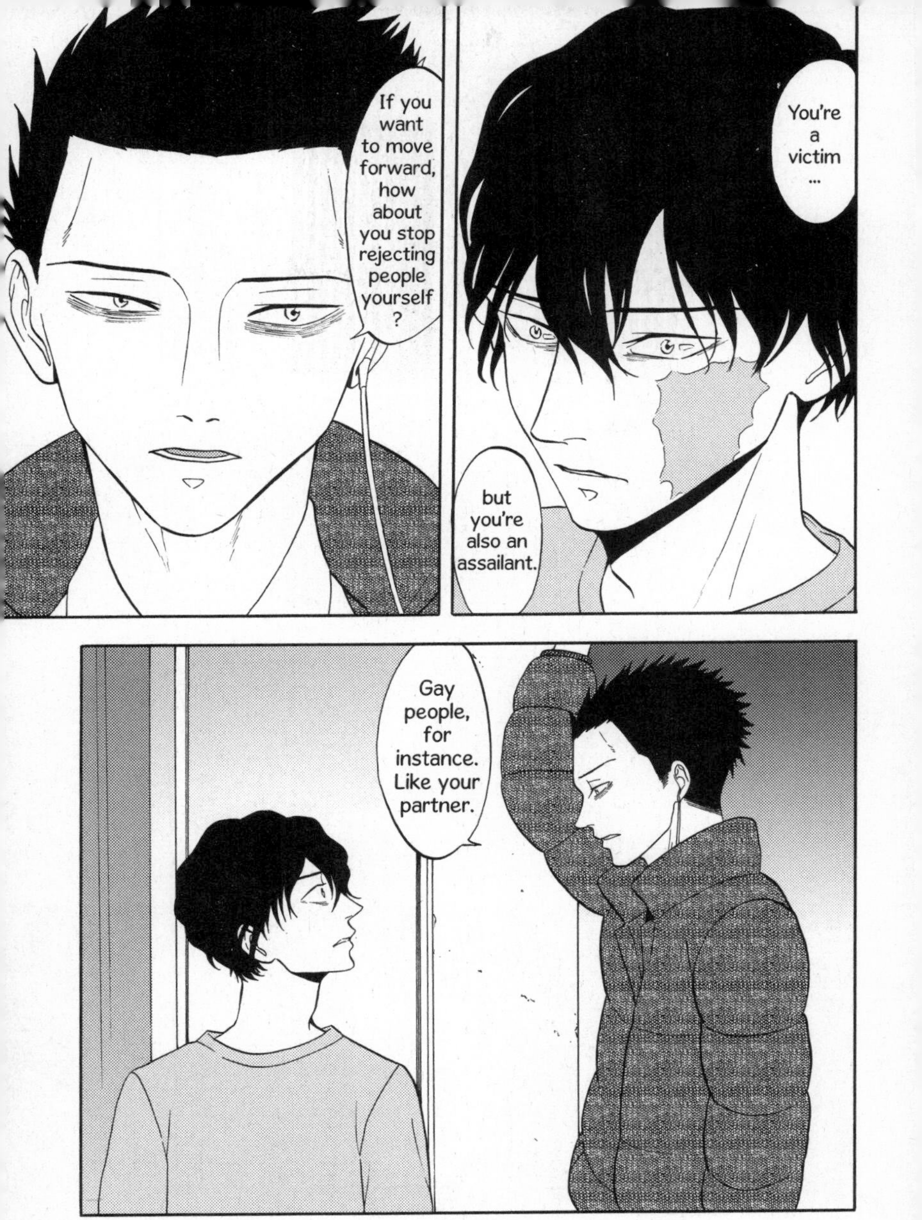
You're a victim ...
but you're also an assailant.
If you want to move forward, how about you stop rejecting people yourself?
Gay people, for instance. Like your partner.

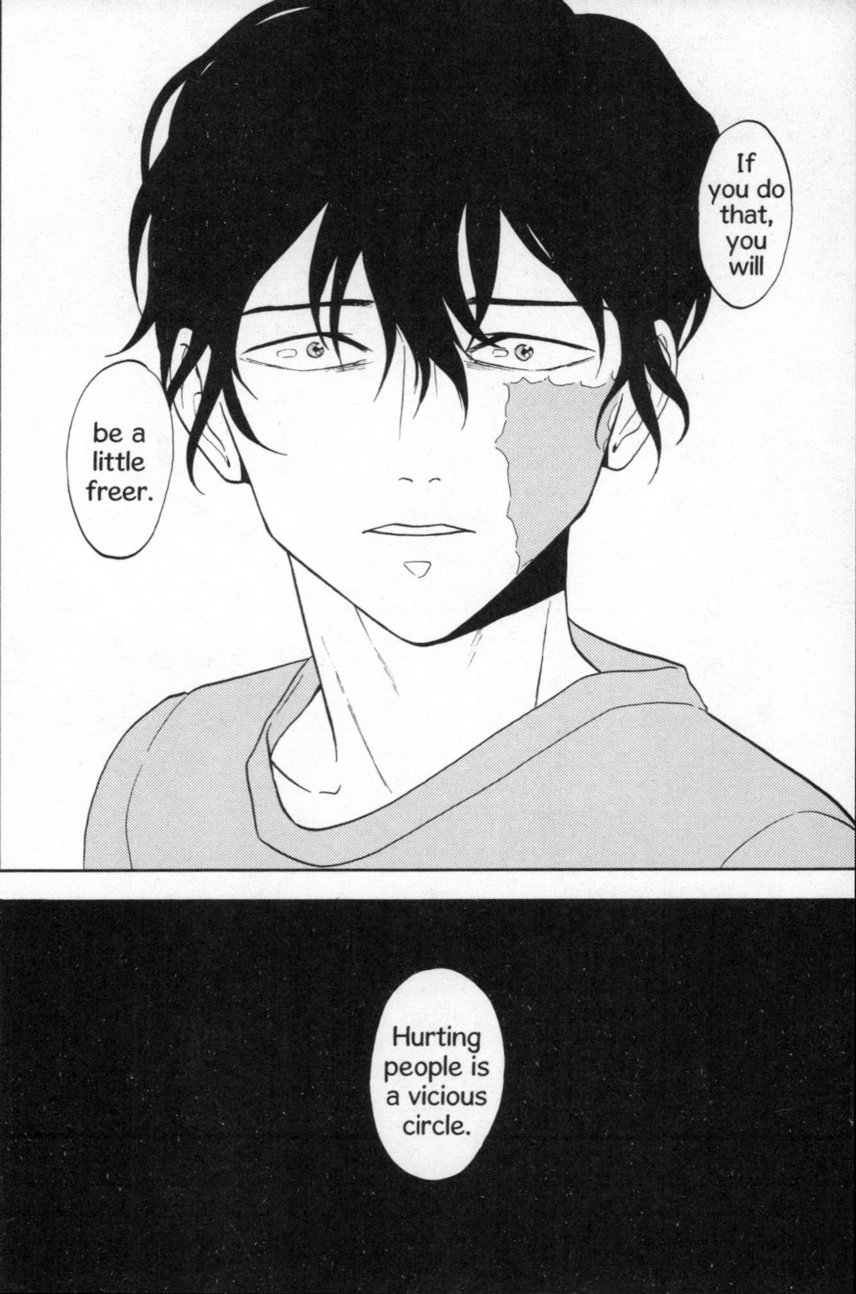
If you do that, you will
be a little freer.
Hurting people is a vicious circle.

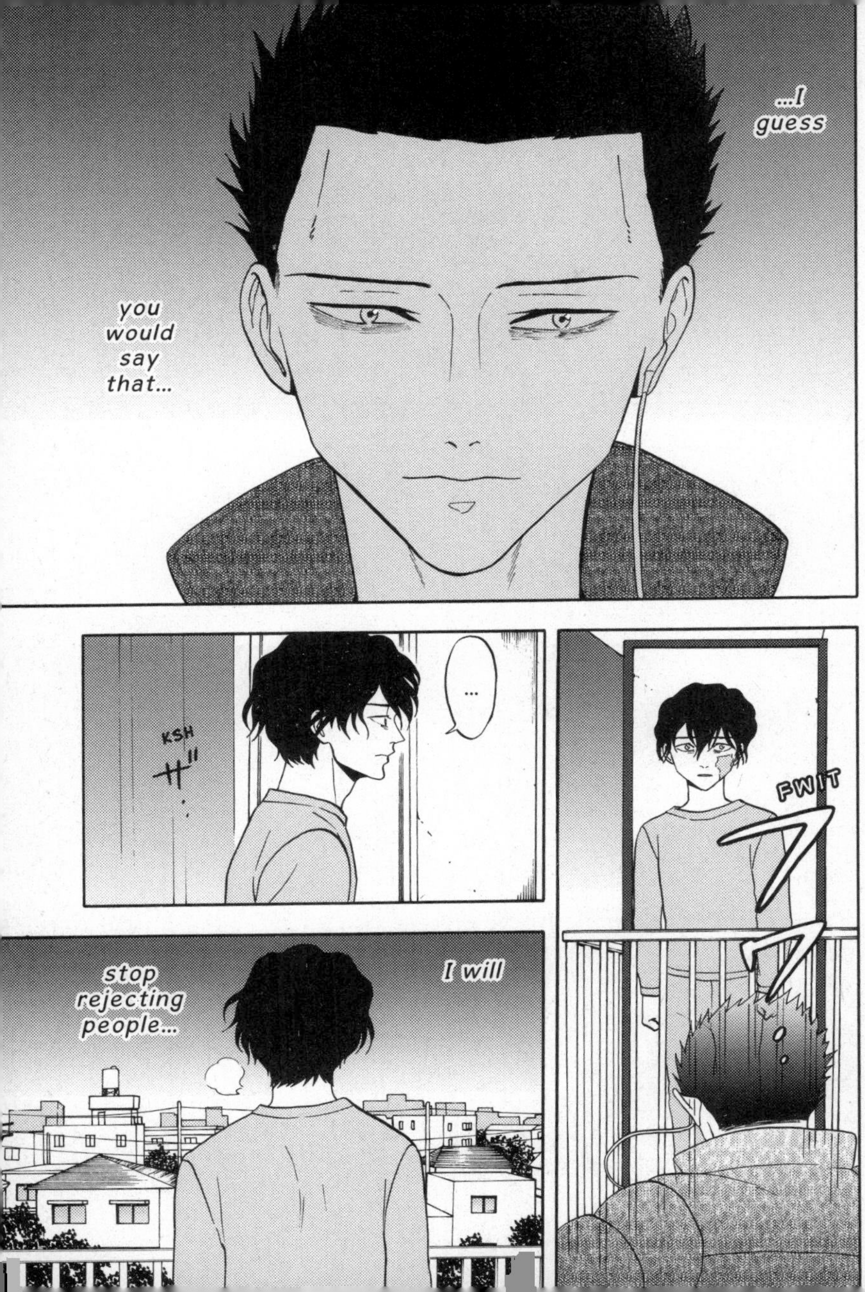
...I guess
you would say that...
FWIT
...
KSH
I will
stop rejecting people...

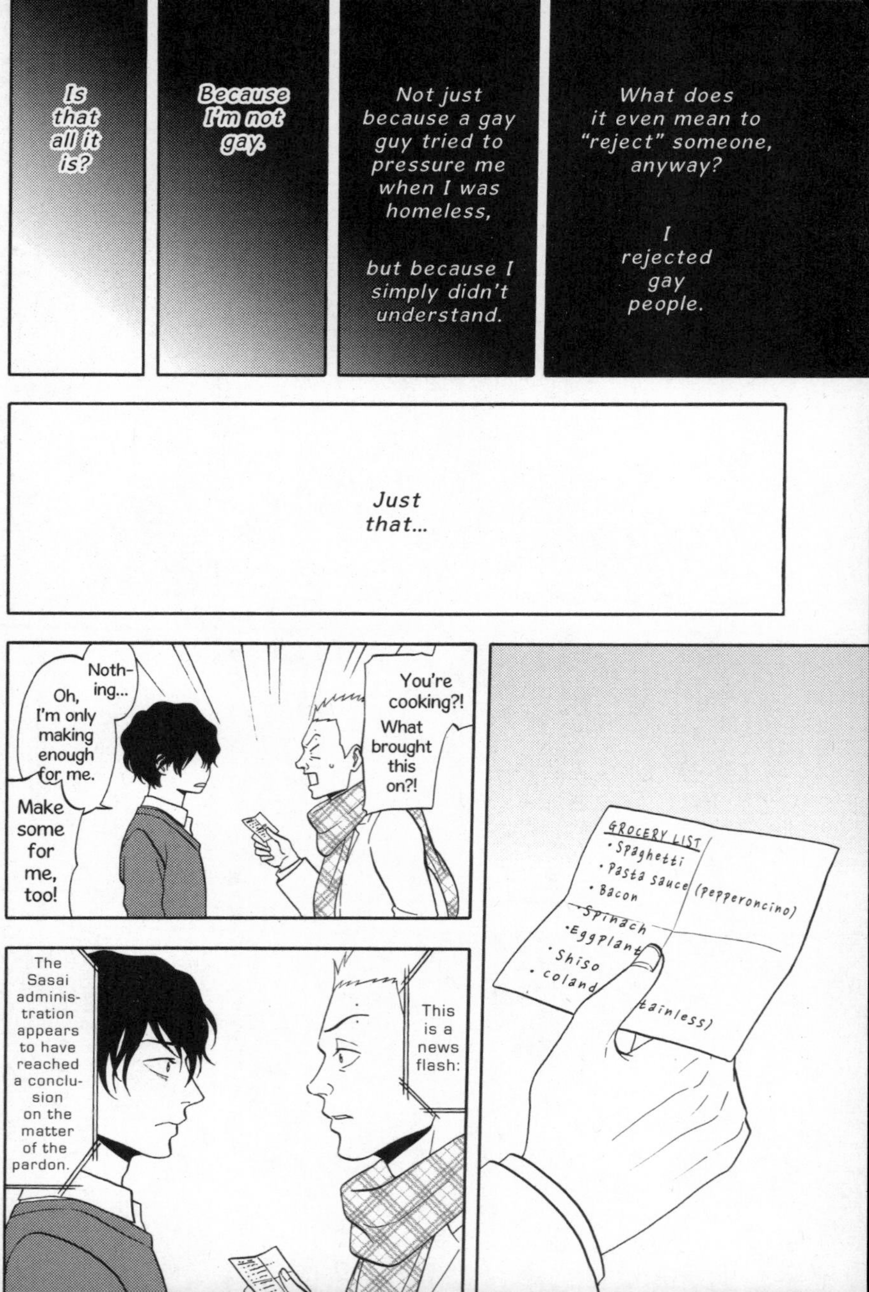
What does it even mean to "reject" someone, anyway?
I rejected gay people.
Not just because a gay guy tried to pressure me when I was homeless,
but because I simply didn't understand.
Because I'm not gay.
Is that all it is?
Just that...
GROCERY LIST
• Spaghetti
• Pasta sauce (pepperoncino)
• Bacon
• Spinach
• Eggplant
• Shiso
You're cooking?!
What brought this on?!
Nothing...
Oh, I'm only making enough for me.
Make some for me, too!
This is a news flash:
The Sasai administration appears to have reached a conclusion on the matter of the pardon.

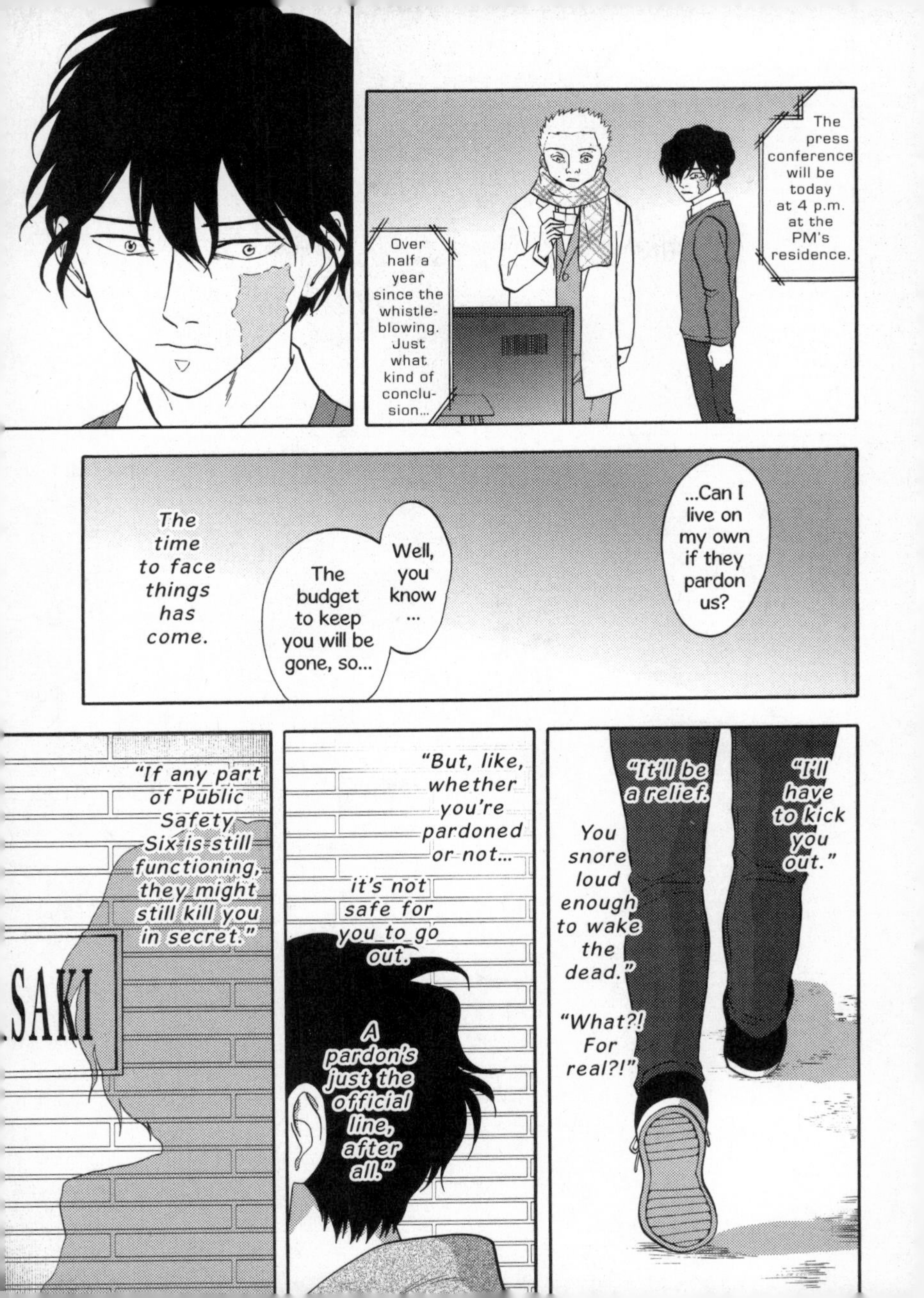
The press conference will be today at 4 p.m. at the PM's residence.
Over half a year since the whistle-blowing. Just what kind of conclu-sion...
...Can I live on my own if they pardon us?
Well, you know ...
The budget to keep you will be gone, so...
The time to face things has come.
"I'll have to kick you out."
"It'll be a relief.
You snore loud enough to wake the dead."
"What?! For real?!"
"But, like, whether you're pardoned or not...
it's not safe for you to go out.
A pardon's just the official line, after all."
"If any part of Public Safety Six is still functioning, they might still kill you in secret."
SAKI

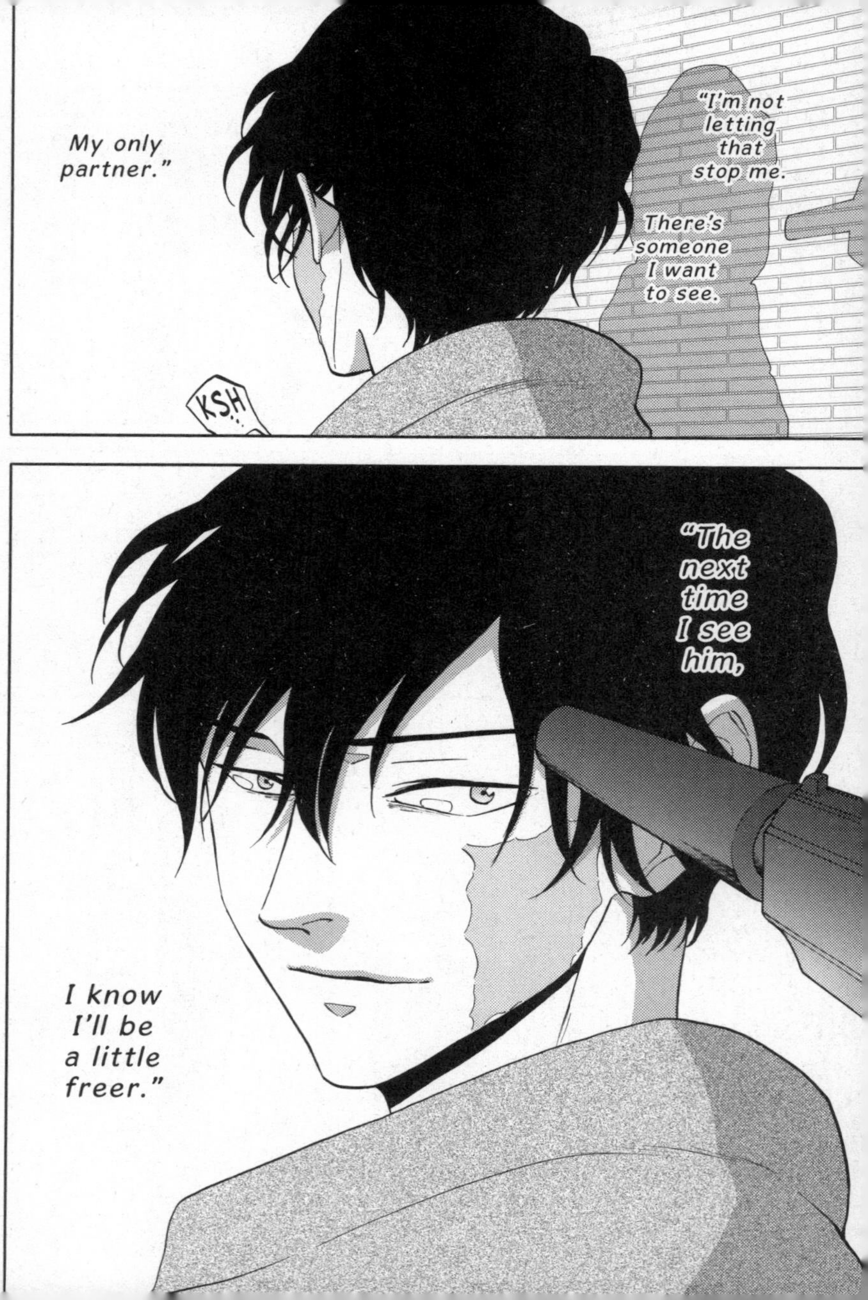
My only partner.”
“I'm not letting that stop me.
There's someone I want to see.
KSH
“The next time I see him,
I know I'll be a little freer.”

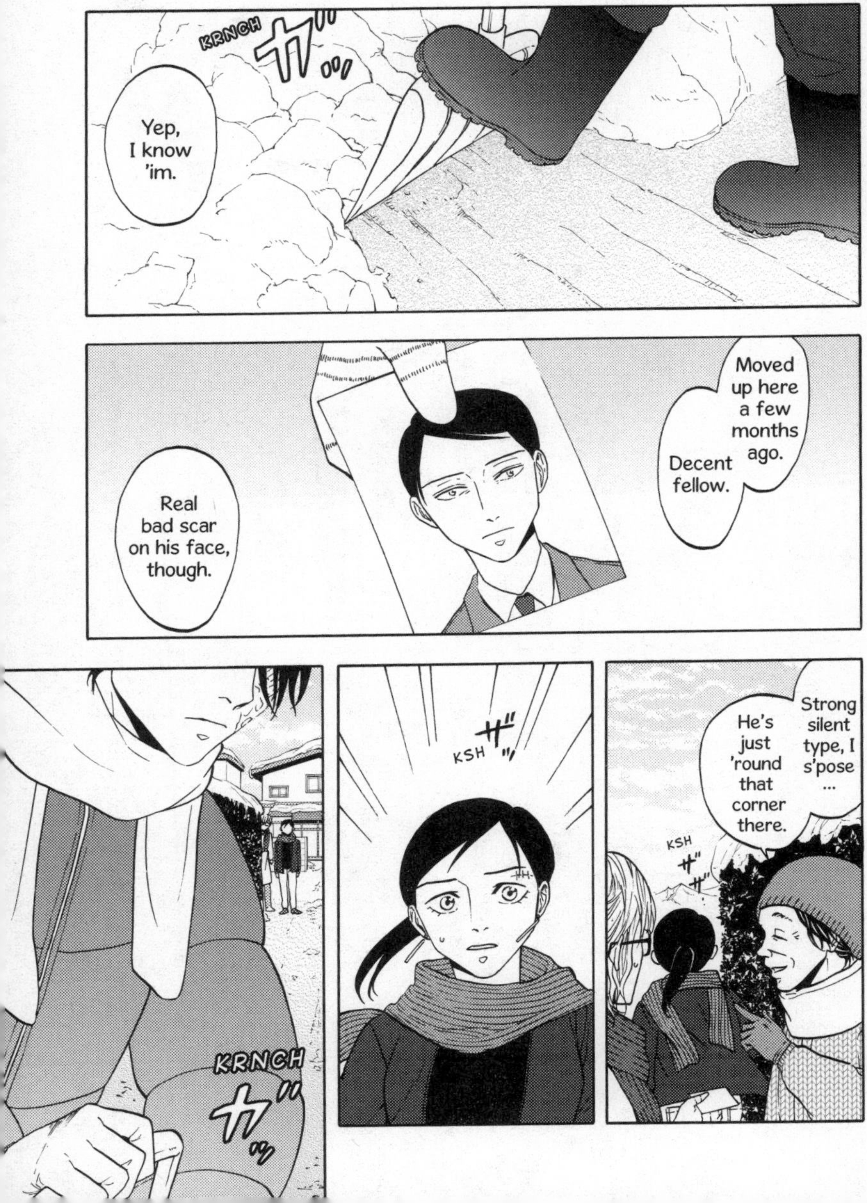
KRNCH
Yep, I know 'im.
Moved up here a few months ago.
Decent fellow.
Real bad scar on his face, though.
Strong silent type, I s'pose ...
He's just 'round that corner there.
KSH
KSH
KRNCH

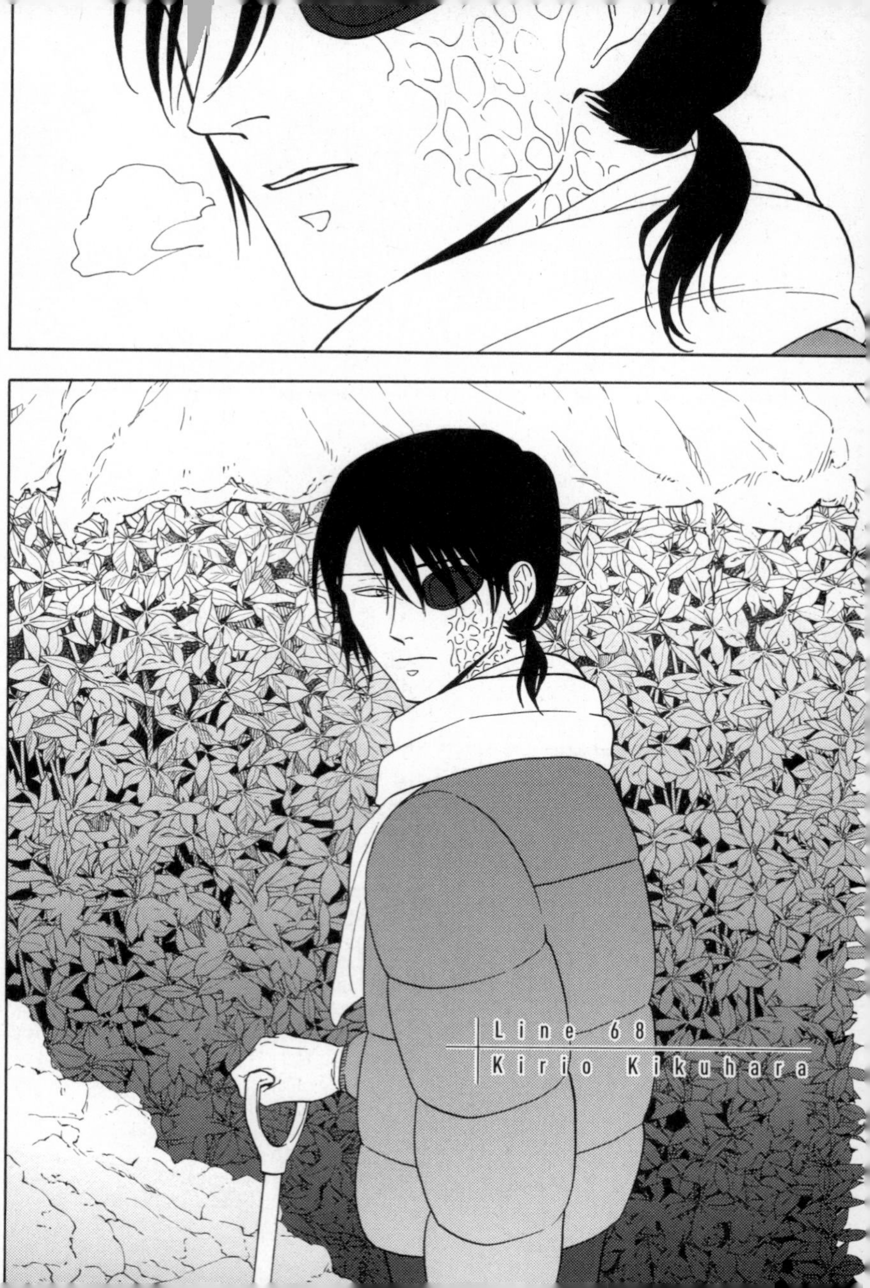
Line 68
Kirio Kikuhara

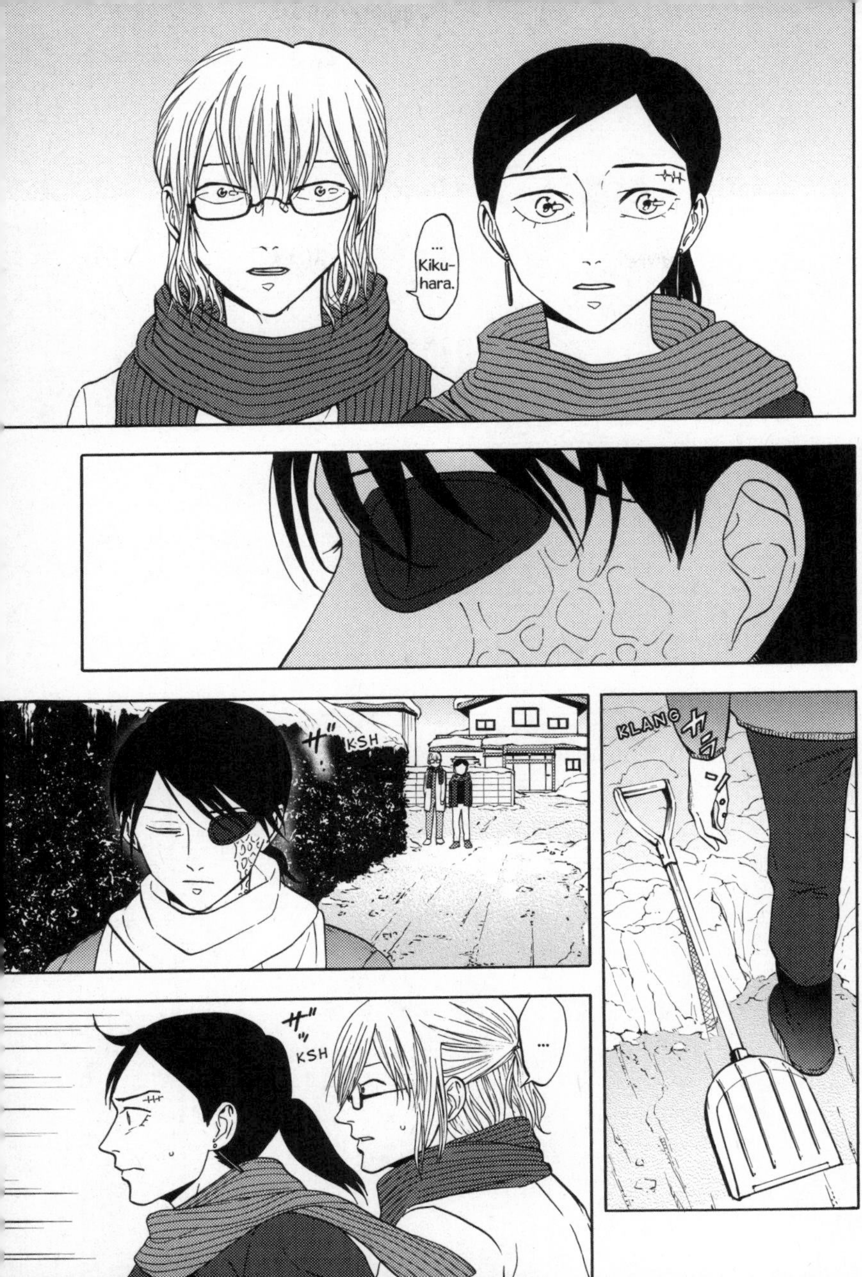

... Kiku-hara.
KLANG
KSH
...
KSH

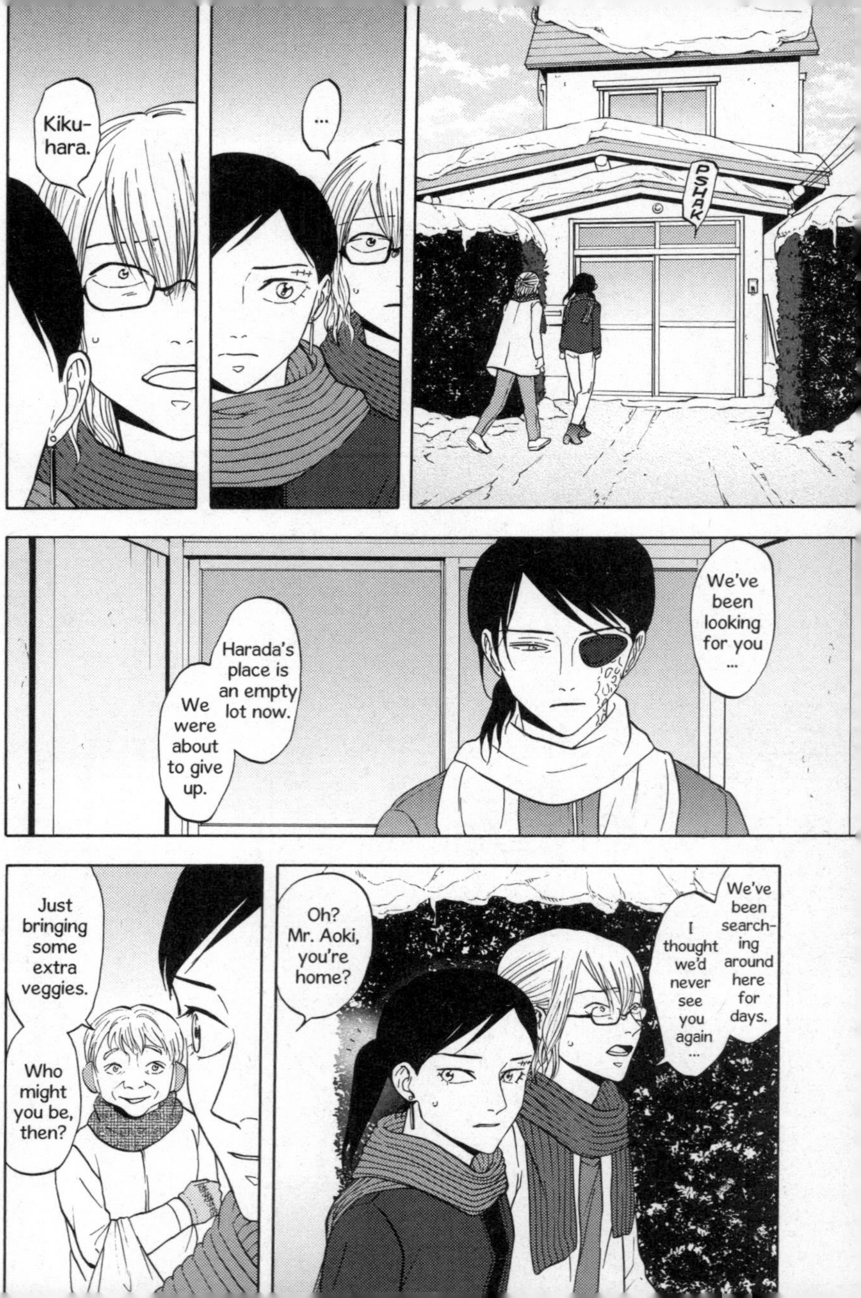
PSHAK
...
Kiku-hara.
We've been looking for you ...
Harada's place is an empty lot now.
We were about to give up.
We've been searching around here for days.
I thought we'd never see you again ...
Oh? Mr. Aoki, you're home?
Just bringing some extra veggies.
Who might you be, then?

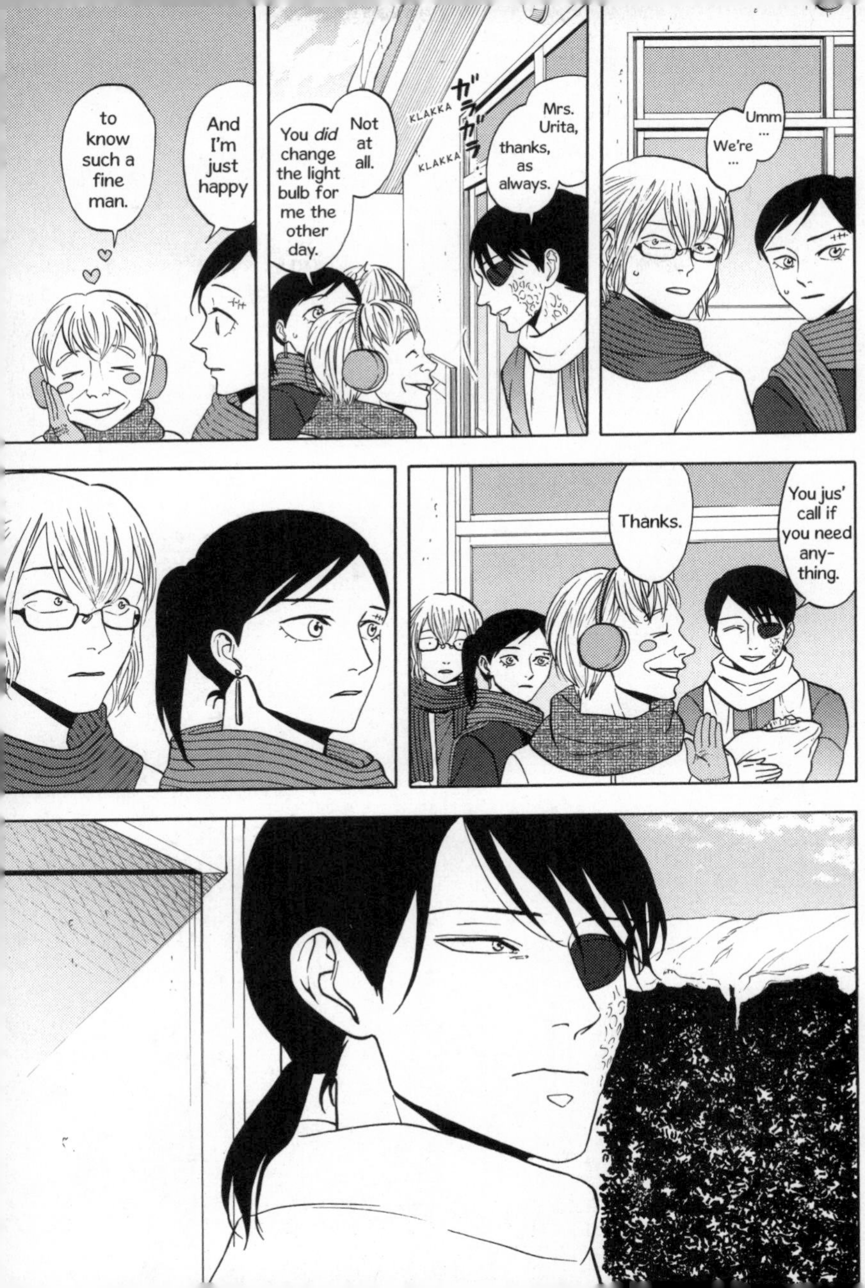
Umm...
We're...
Mrs. Urita, thanks, as always.
KLAKKA
ガラガラ
KLAKKA
Not at all.
You *did* change the light bulb for me the other day.
And I'm just happy
to know such a fine man.
You jus' call if you need any-thing.
Thanks.

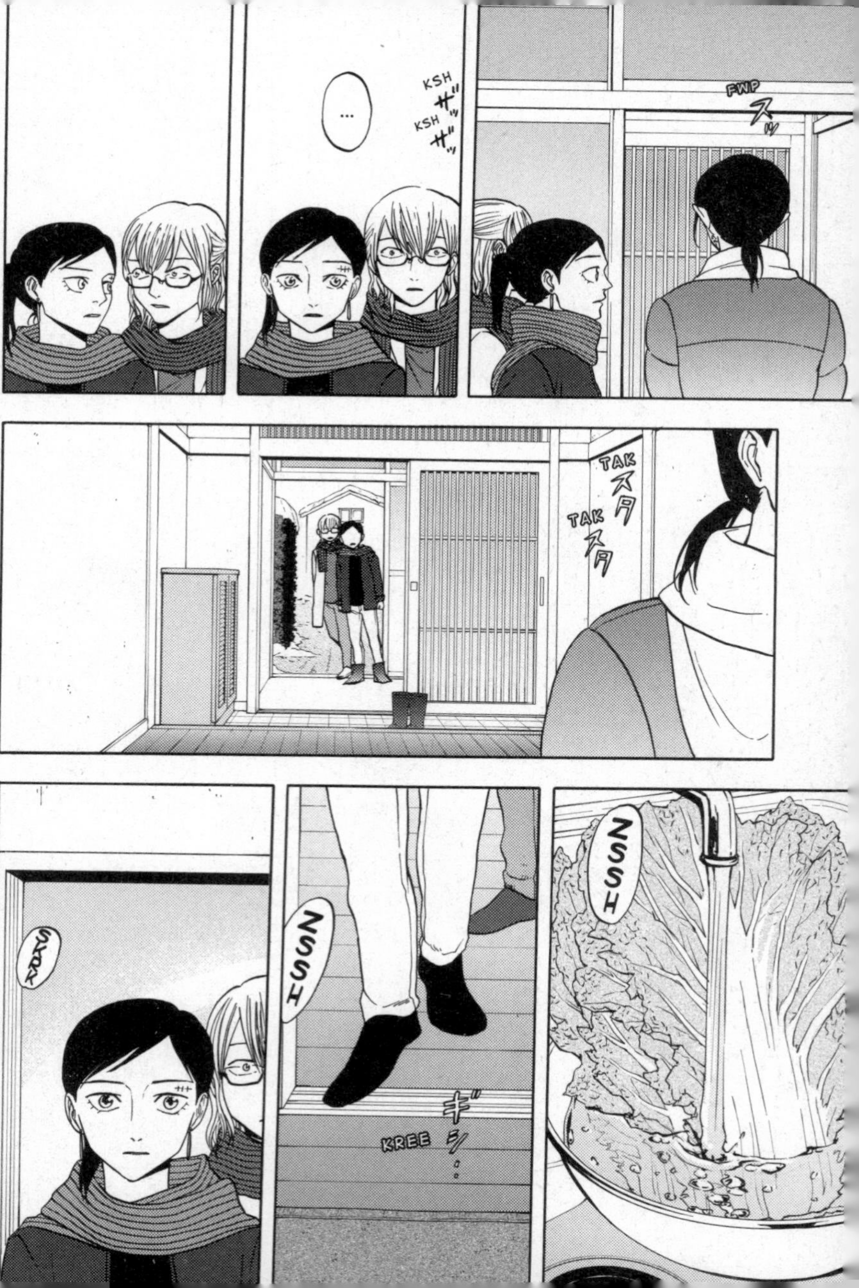
FWP
スッ
KSH
ザッ
KSH
ザッ
...
TAK
スタ
TAK
スタ
ZSSH
ZSSH
KREE
ギシ
SKRK

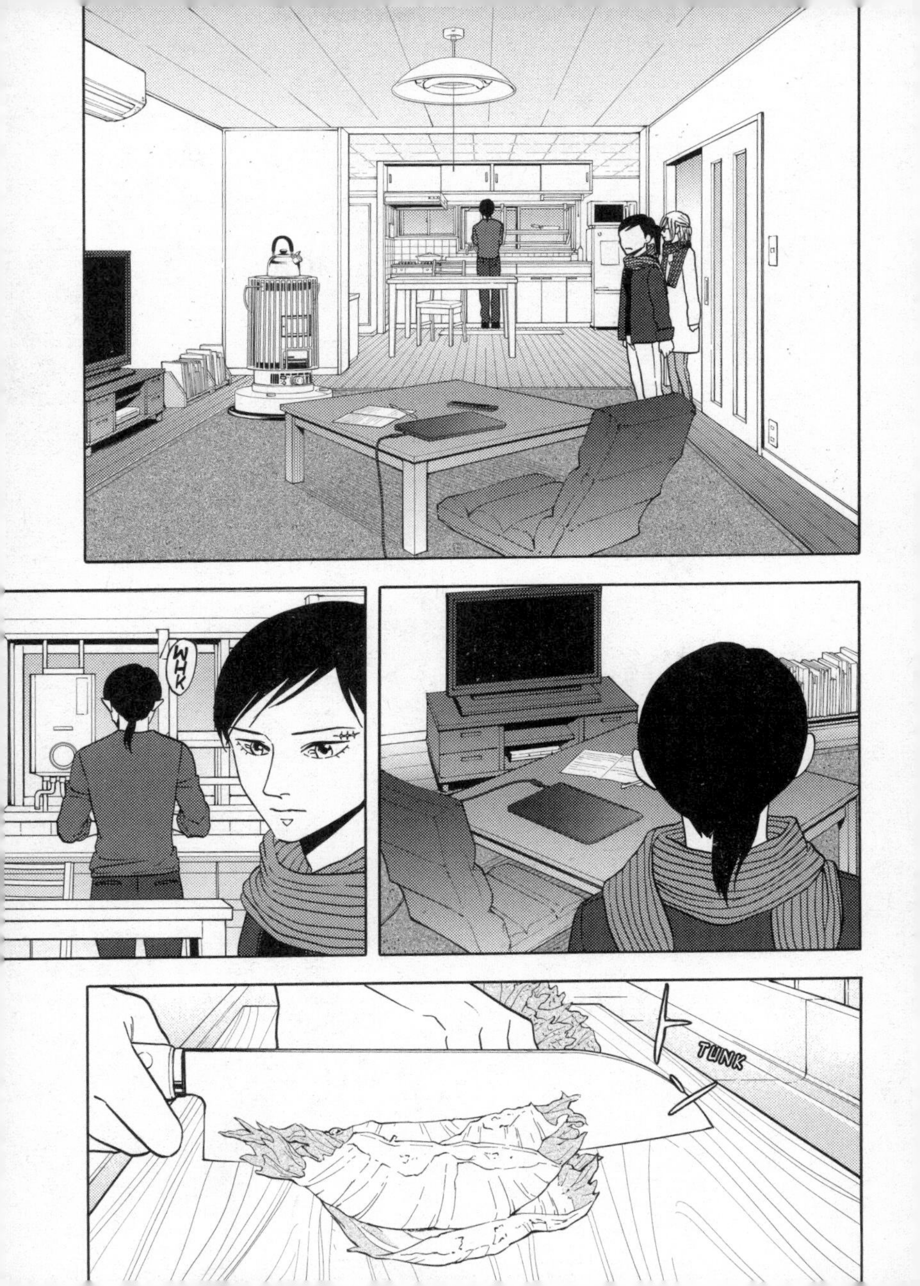
WHK
TUNK

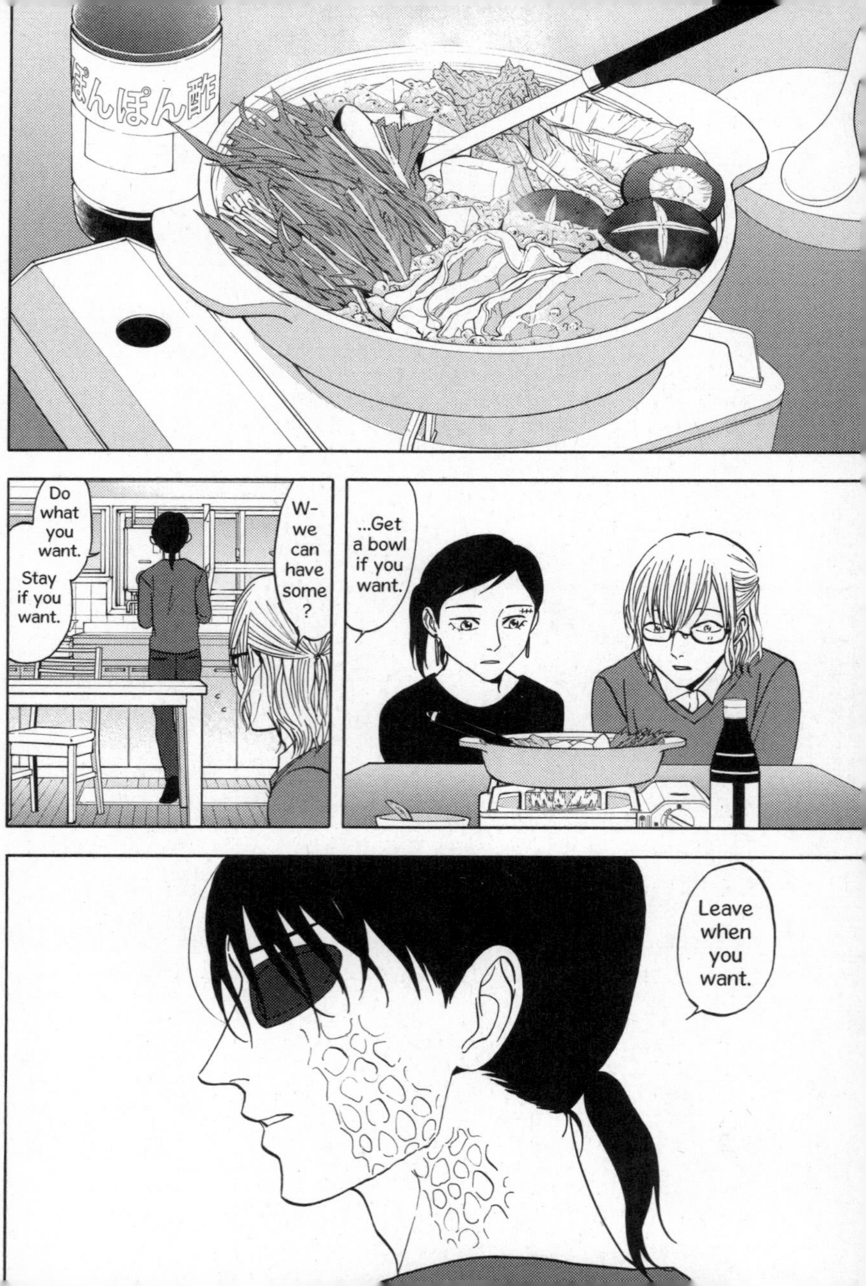
ぽんぽん酢
...Get a bowl if you want.
W-we can have some?
Do what you want.
Stay if you want.
Leave when you want.

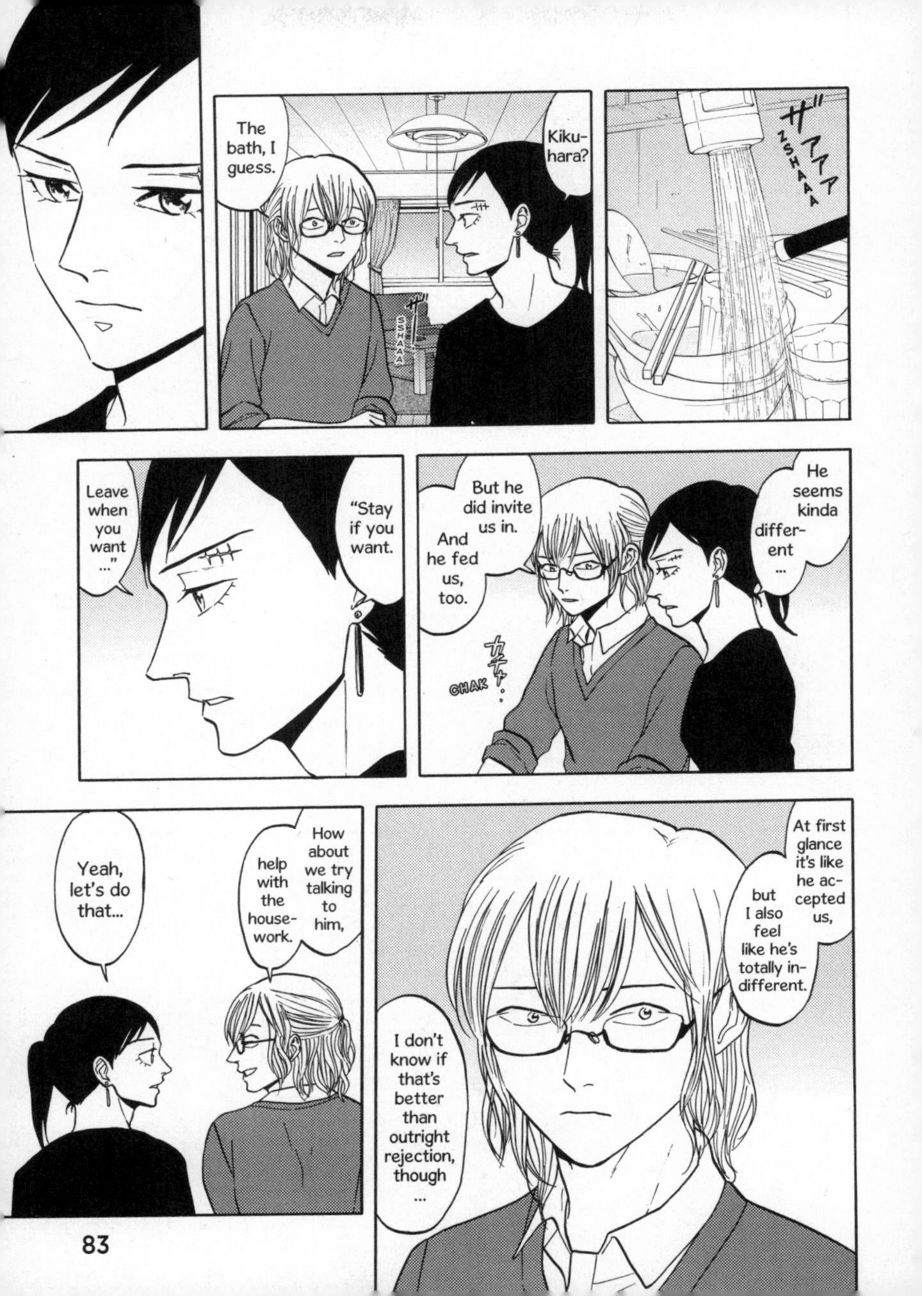
ザァァァ
ZSHAAA
Kiku-hara?
The bath, I guess.
SSHAAA
He seems kinda different...
But he did invite us in.
And he fed us, too.
カチャ
CHAK
"Stay if you want.
Leave when you want..."
At first glance it's like he accepted us,
but I also feel like he's totally indifferent.
I don't know if that's better than outright rejection, though...
How about we try talking to him,
help with the housework.
Yeah, let's do that...

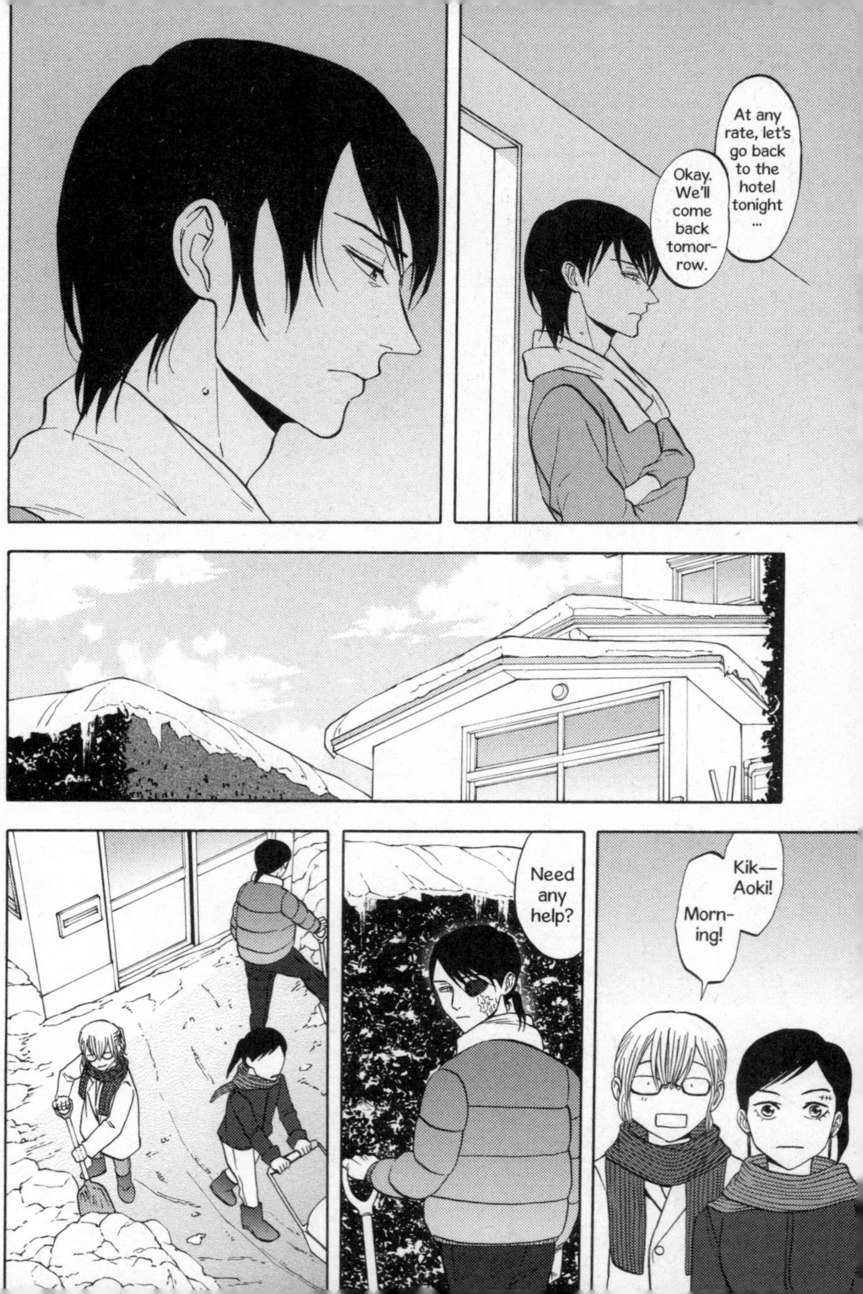
At any rate, let's go back to the hotel tonight ...
Okay. We'll come back tomor-row.
Kik— Aoki!
Morn-ing!
Need any help?

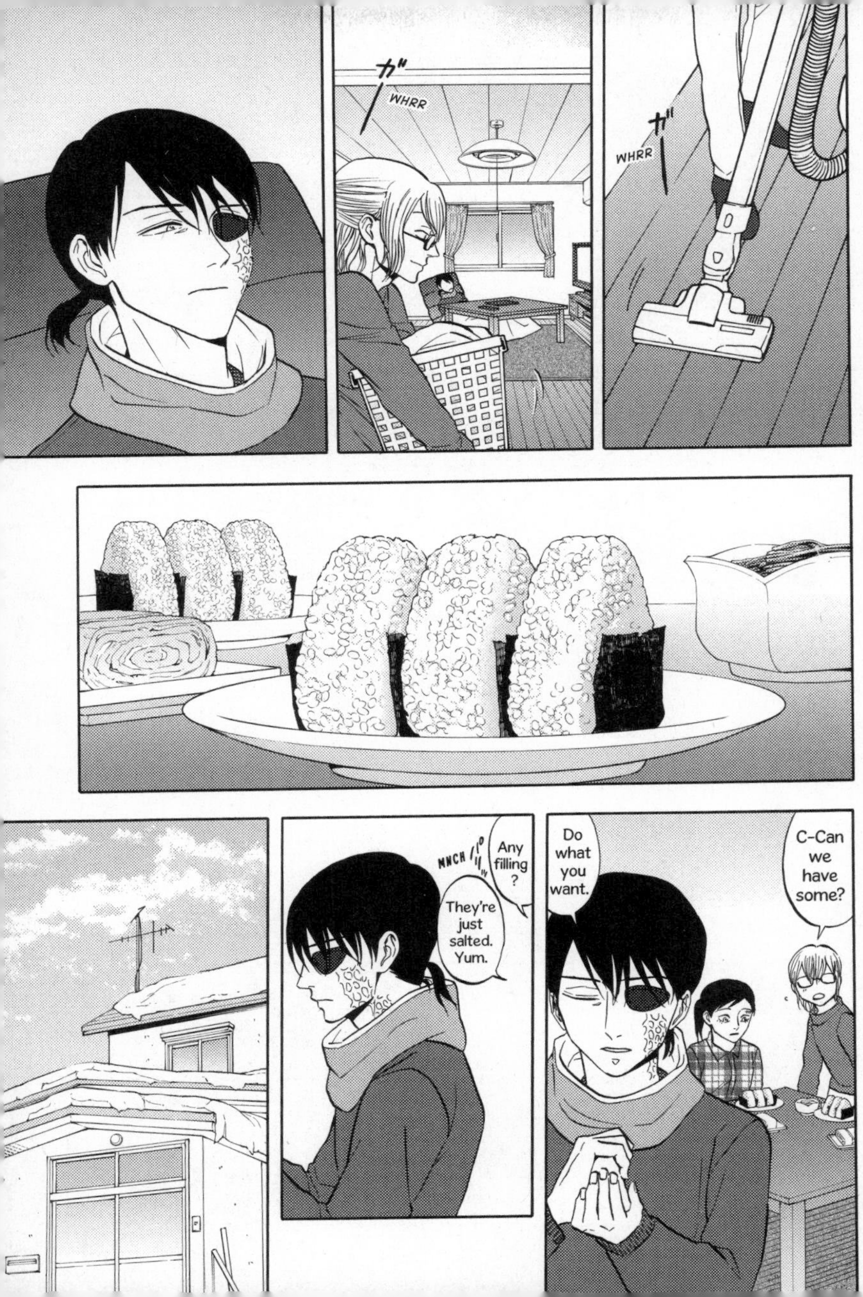
ガ
WHRR
ガ
WHRR
C-Can we have some?
Do what you want.
Any filling?
MNCH
They're just salted. Yum.

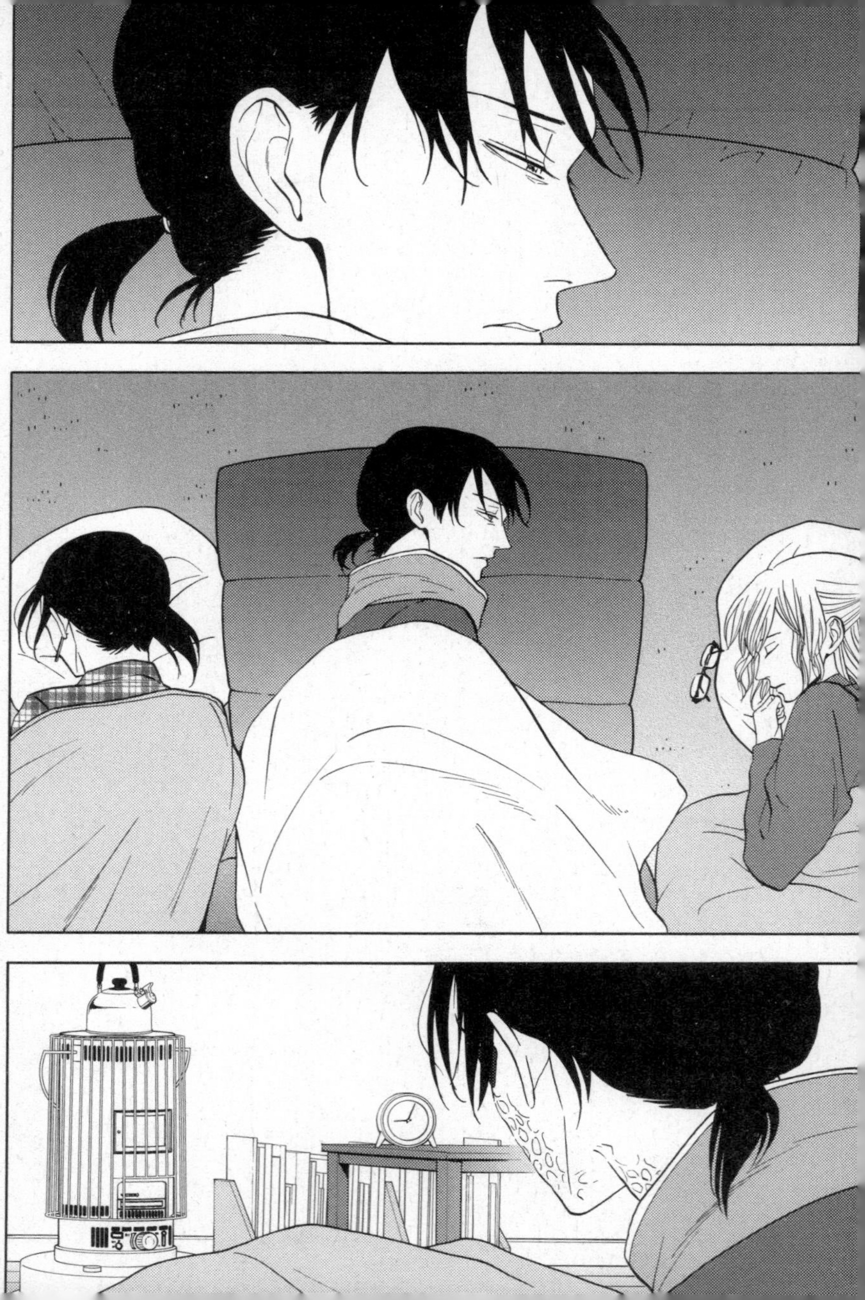

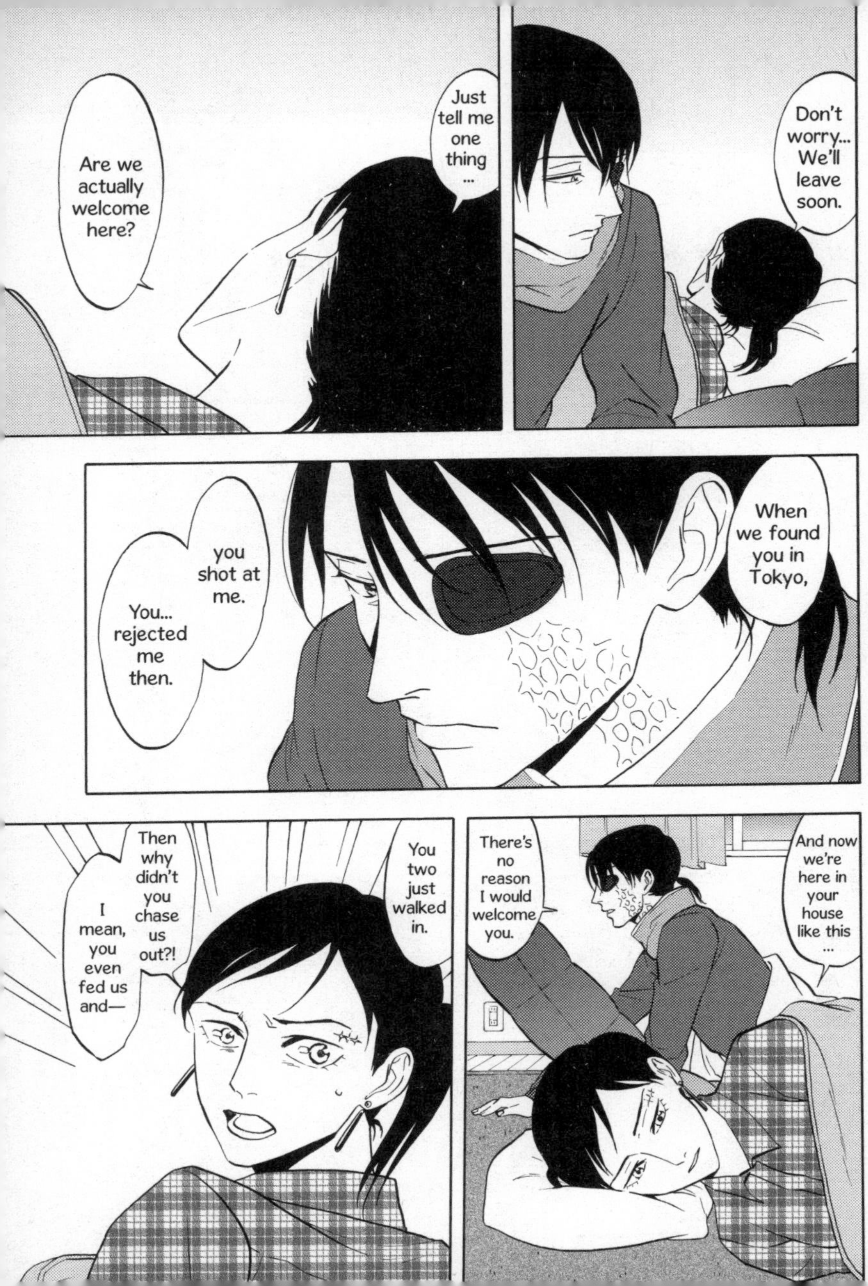
Don't worry... We'll leave soon.
Just tell me one thing ...
Are we actually welcome here?
When we found you in Tokyo,
you shot at me.
You... rejected me then.
And now we're here in your house like this ...
There's no reason I would welcome you.
You two just walked in.
Then why didn't you chase us out?!
I mean, you even fed us and—

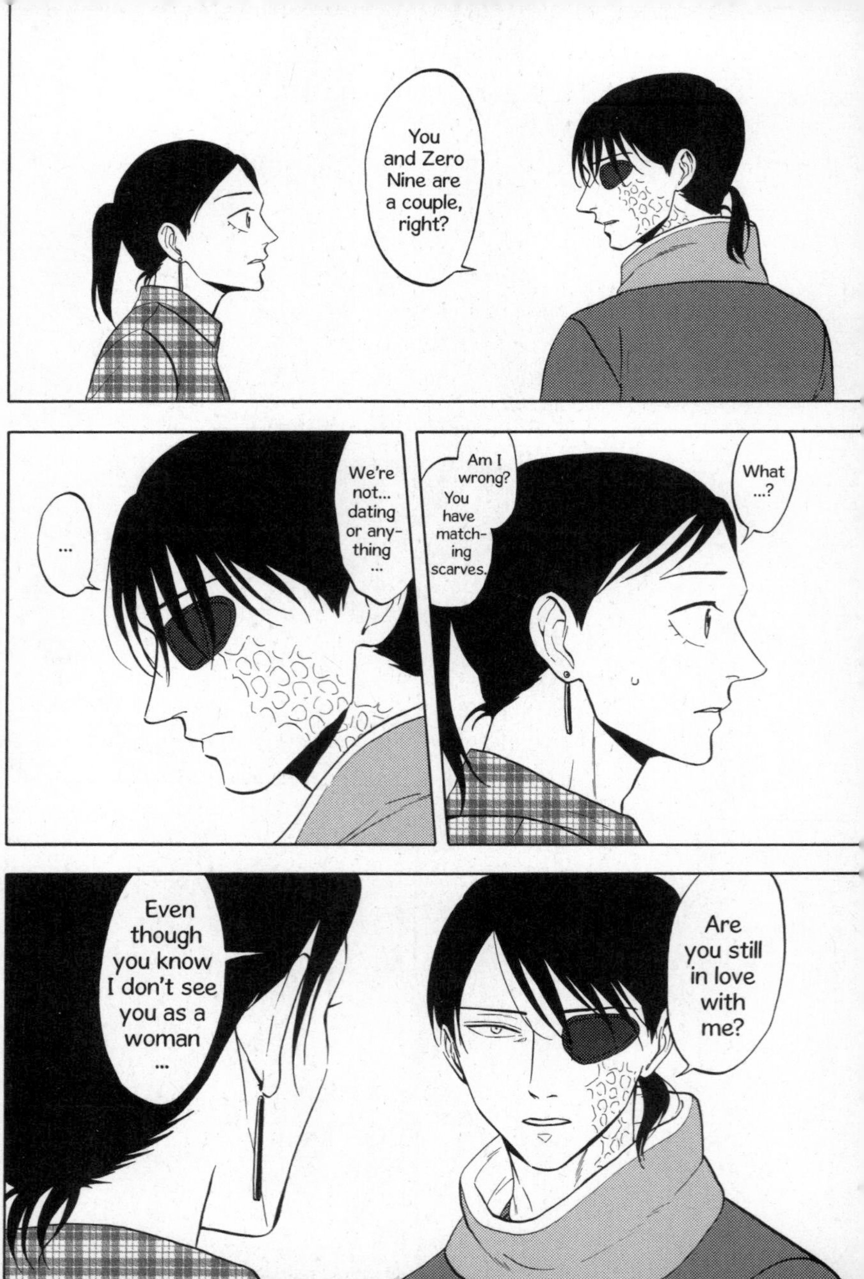
You and Zero Nine are a couple, right?
What ...?
Am I wrong? You have matching scarves.
We're not... dating or anything ...
...
Are you still in love with me?
Even though you know I don't see you as a woman ...

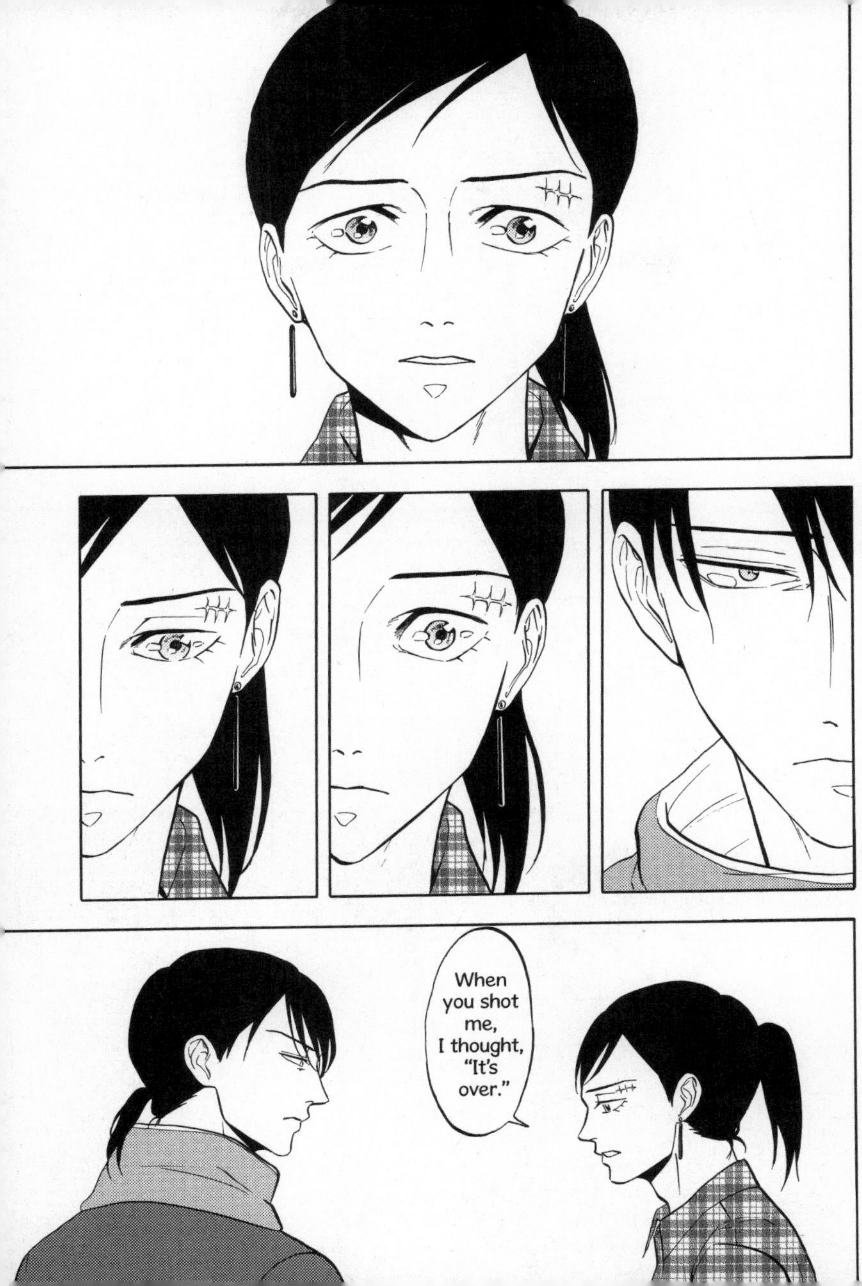
When you shot me, I thought, "It's over."

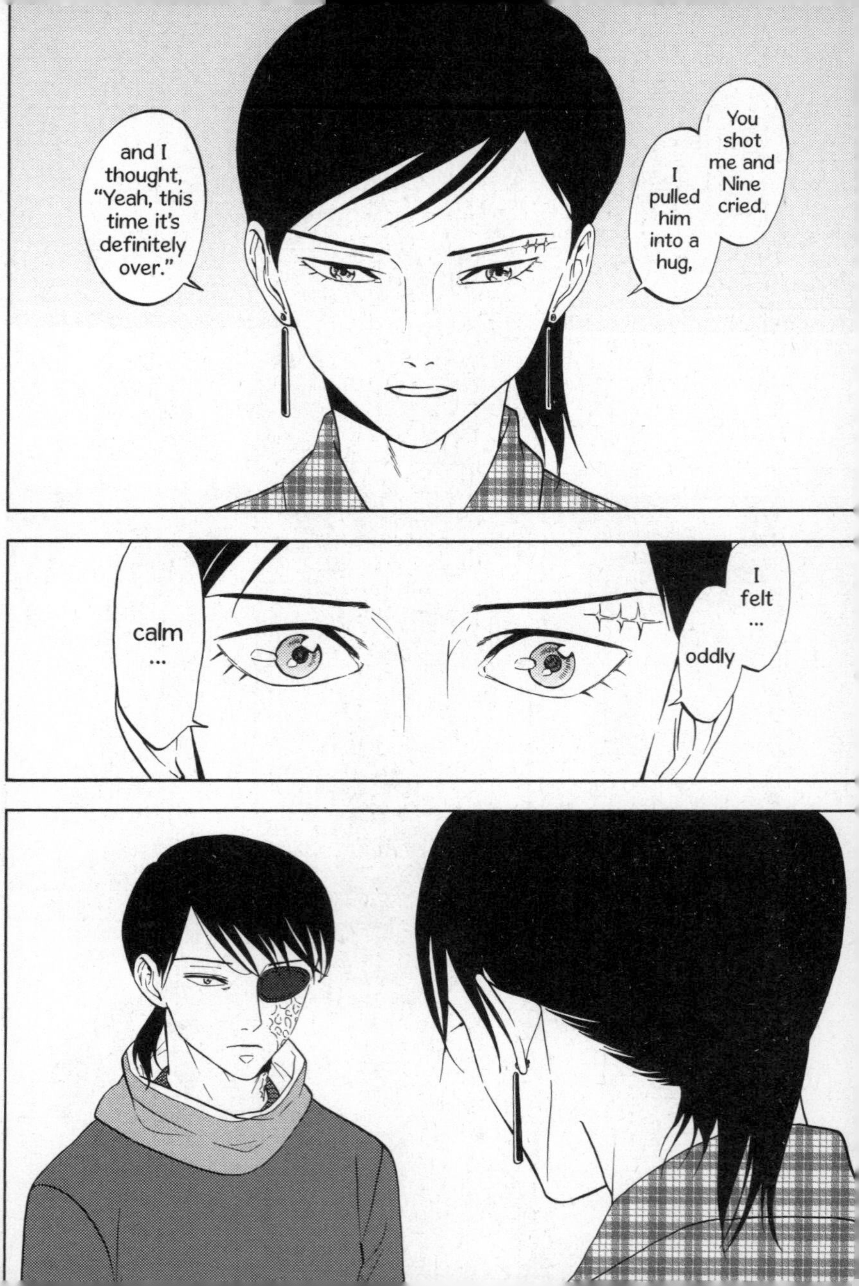
You shot me and Nine cried.
I pulled him into a hug,
and I thought, "Yeah, this time it's definitely over."
I felt ... oddly
calm ...

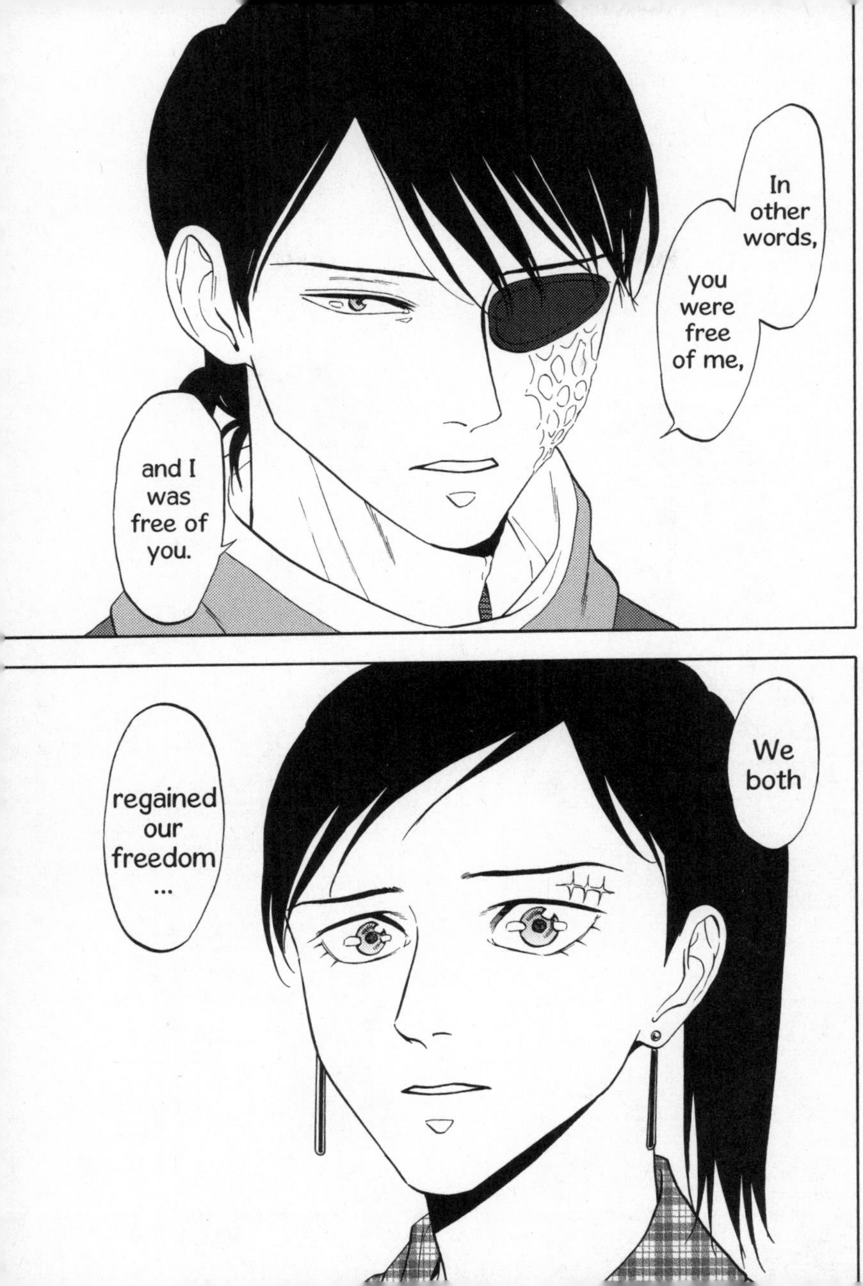
In other words,
you were free of me,
and I was free of you.
We both
regained our freedom ...

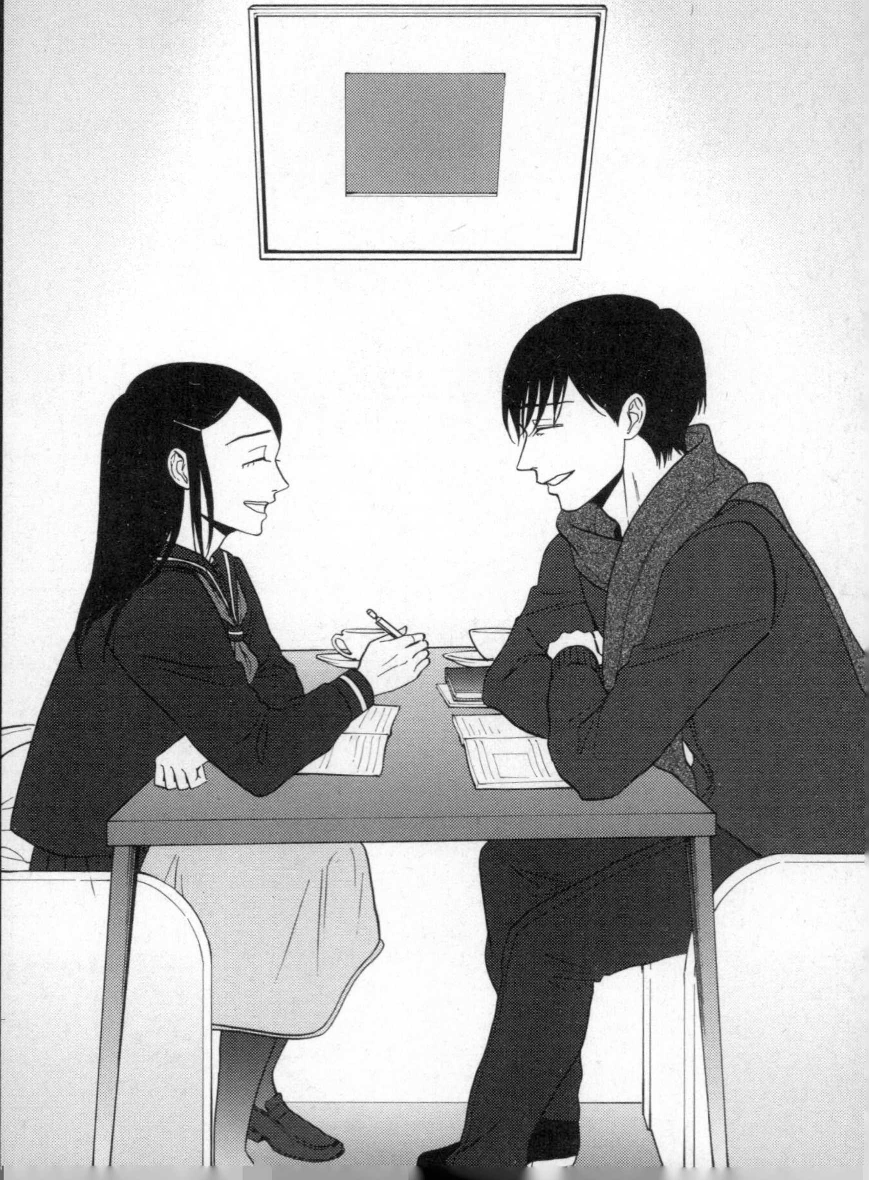

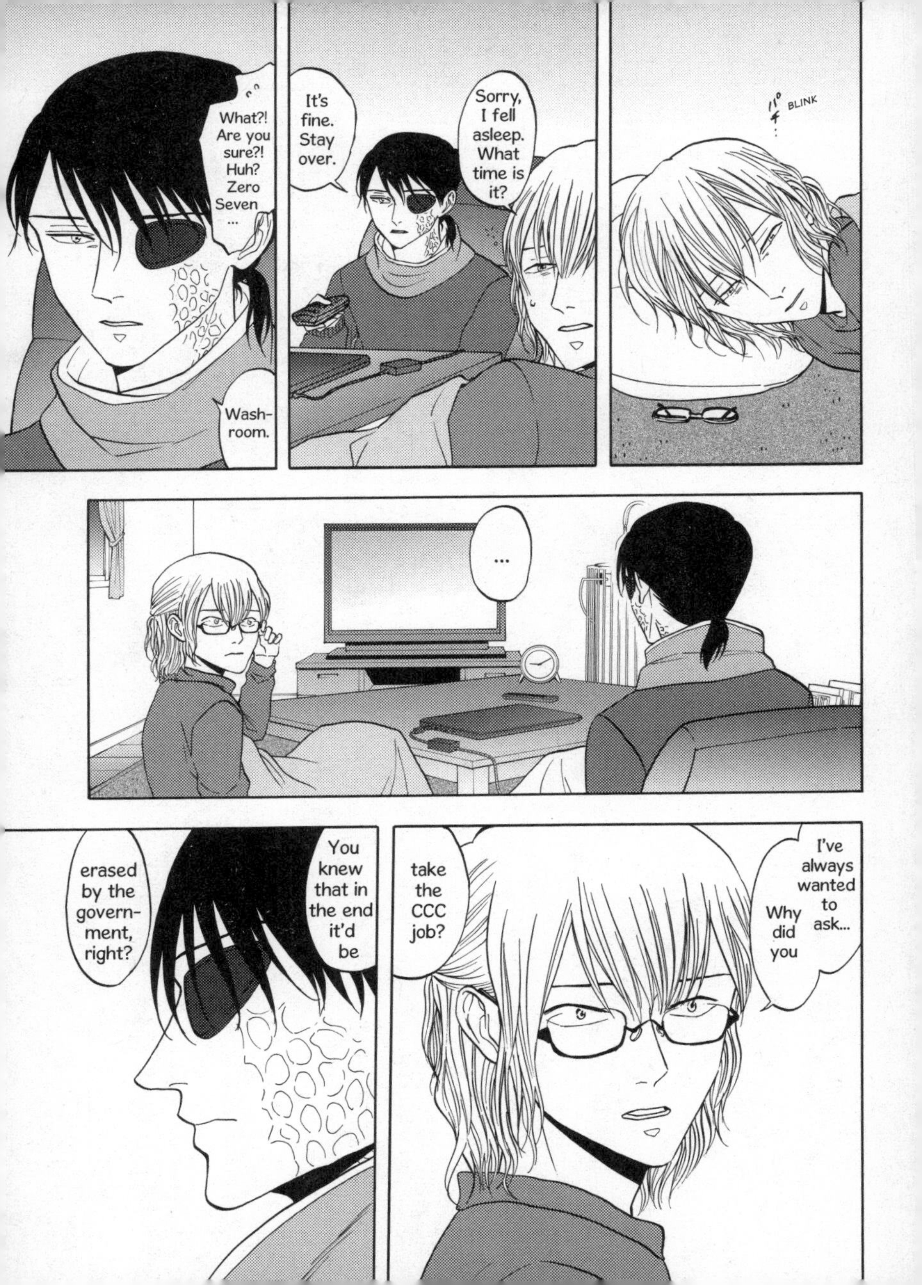
BLINK
Sorry, I fell asleep. What time is it?
It's fine. Stay over.
What?! Are you sure?! Huh? Zero Seven ...
Wash-room.
...
I've always wanted to ask...
Why did you take the CCC job?
You knew that in the end it'd be erased by the government, right?

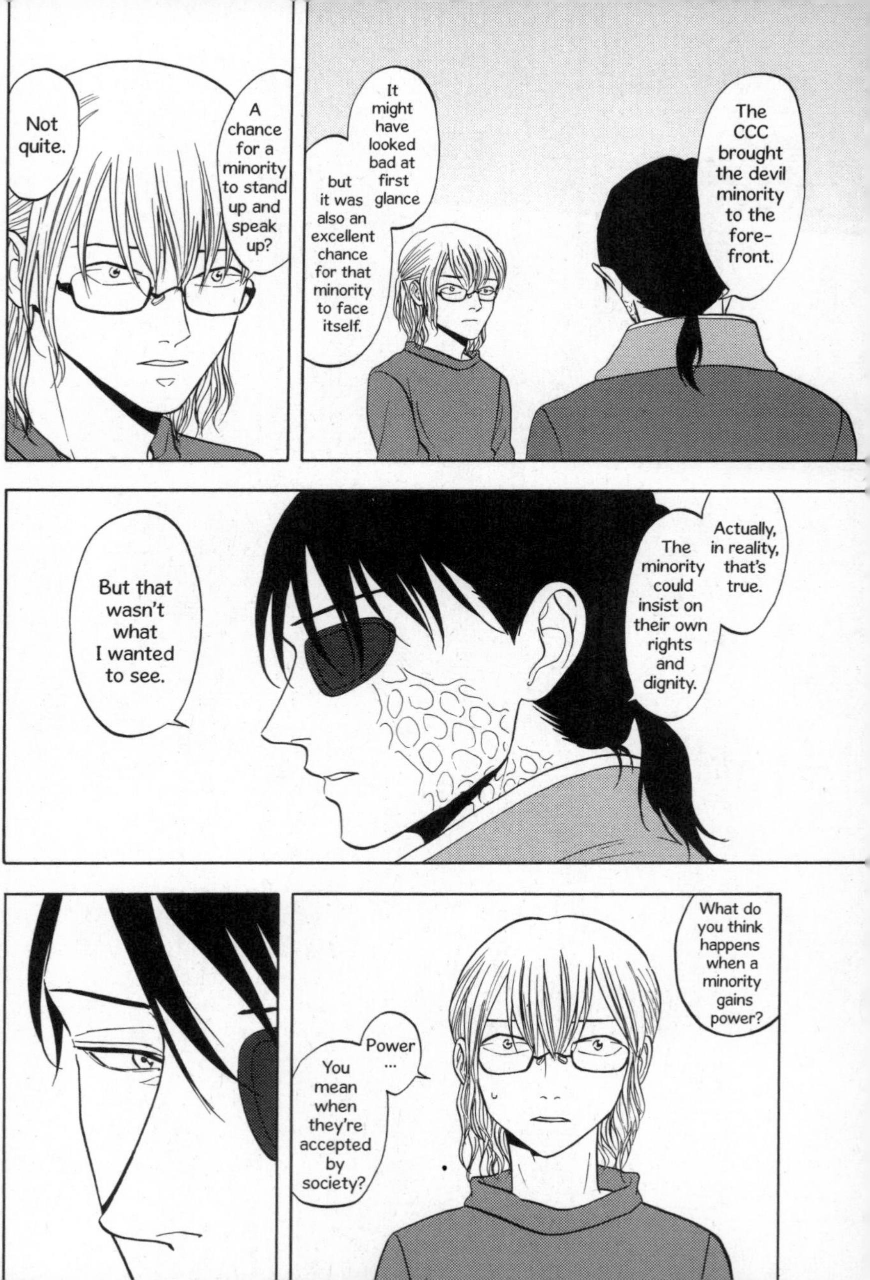
The CCC brought the devil minority to the fore-front.
It might have looked bad at first glance
but it was also an excellent chance for that minority to face itself.
A chance for a minority to stand up and speak up?
Not quite.
Actually, in reality, that's true.
The minority could insist on their own rights and dignity.
But that wasn't what I wanted to see.
What do you think happens when a minority gains power?
Power ...
You mean when they're accepted by society?

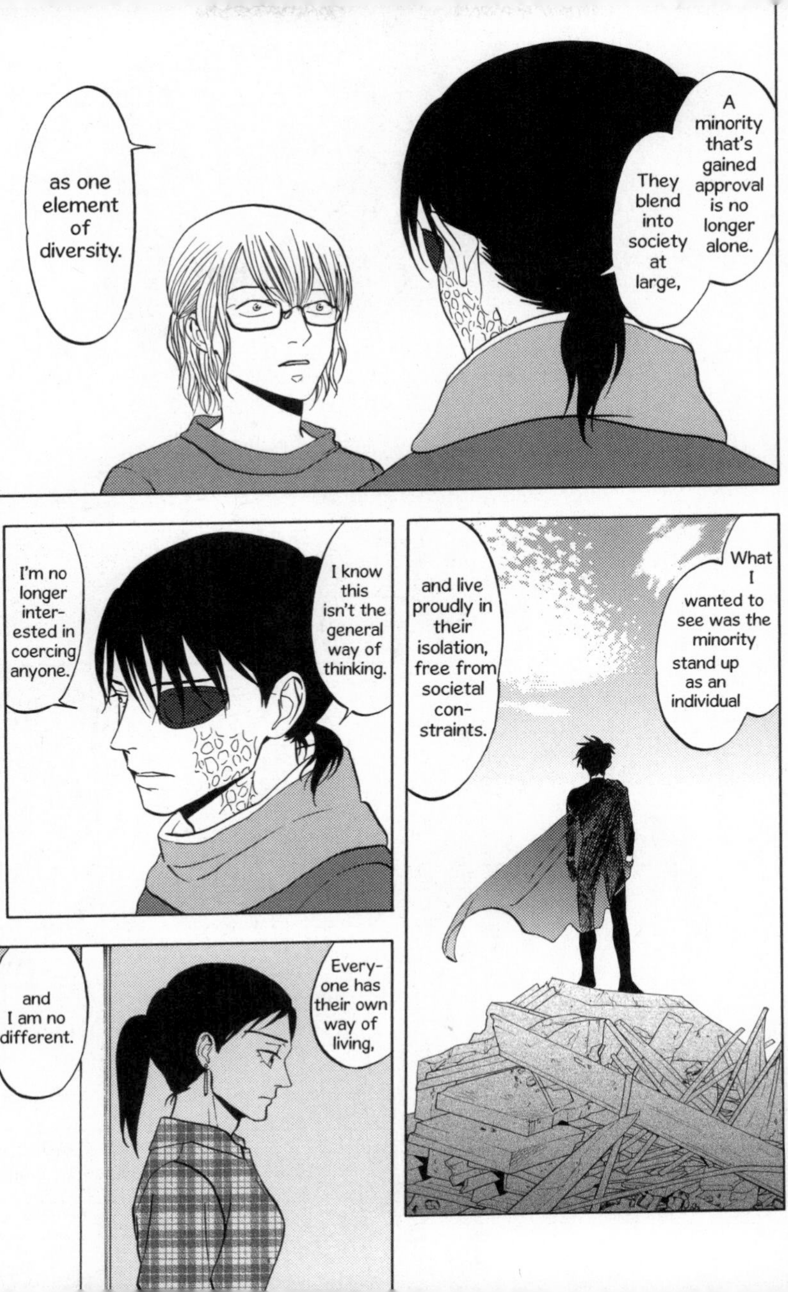
A minority that's gained approval is no longer alone.
They blend into society at large,
as one element of diversity.
What I wanted to see was the minority stand up as an individual
and live proudly in their isolation, free from societal constraints.
I know this isn't the general way of thinking.
I'm no longer interested in coercing anyone.
Every-one has their own way of living,
and I am no different.

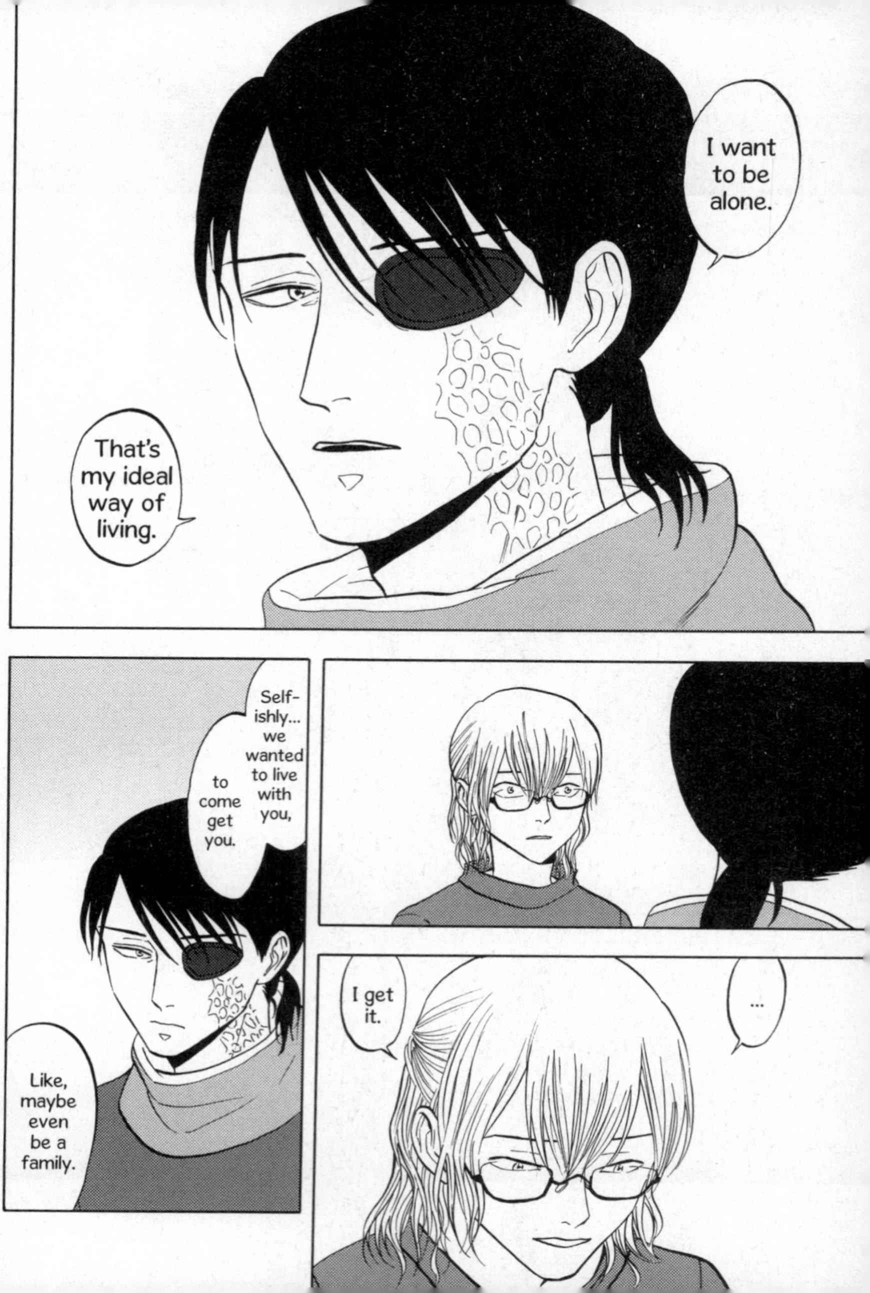

I want to be alone.
That's my ideal way of living.
...
I get it.
Self-ishly... we wanted to live with you, to come get you.
Like, maybe even be a family.

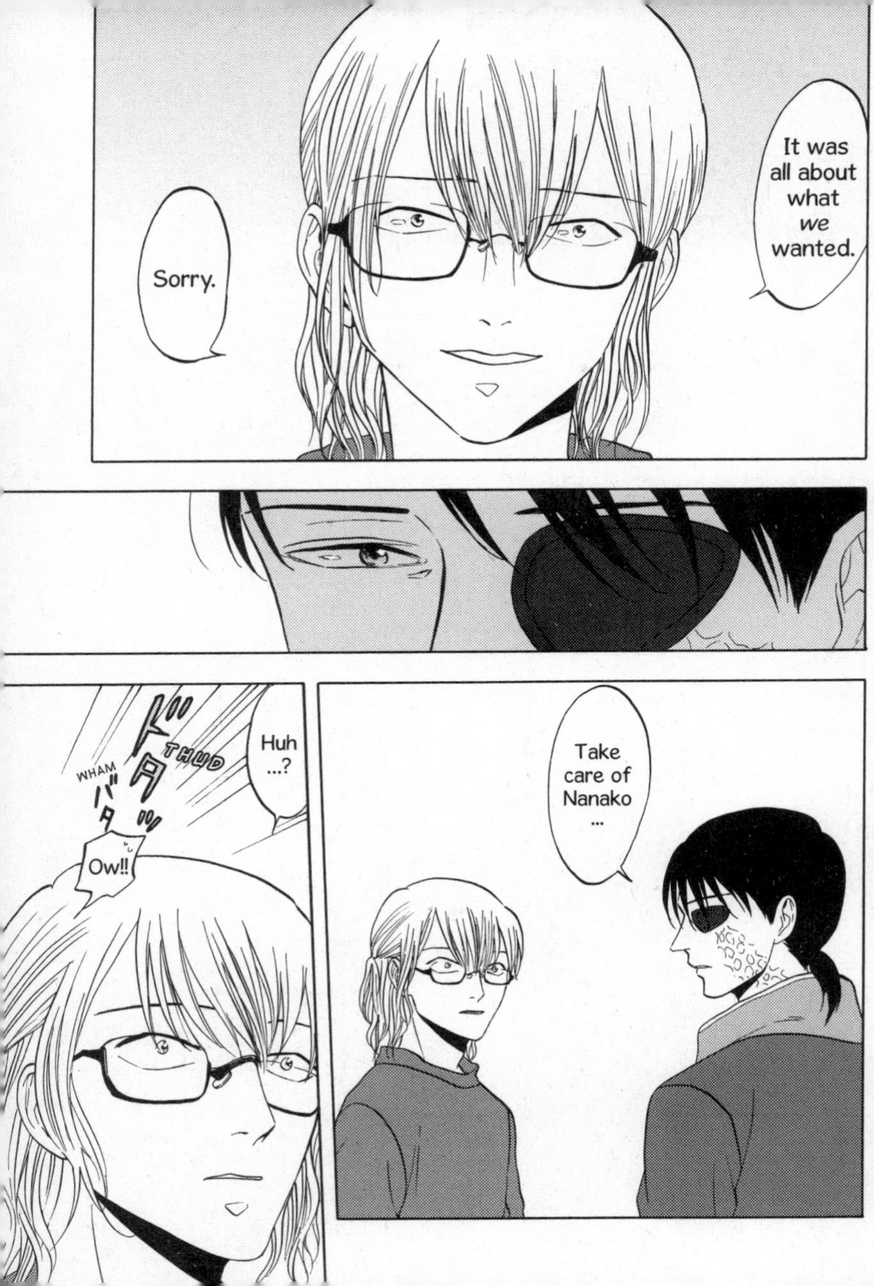
It was all about what *we* wanted.
Sorry.
Take care of Nanako ...
Huh ...?
THUD
WHAM
Ow!!

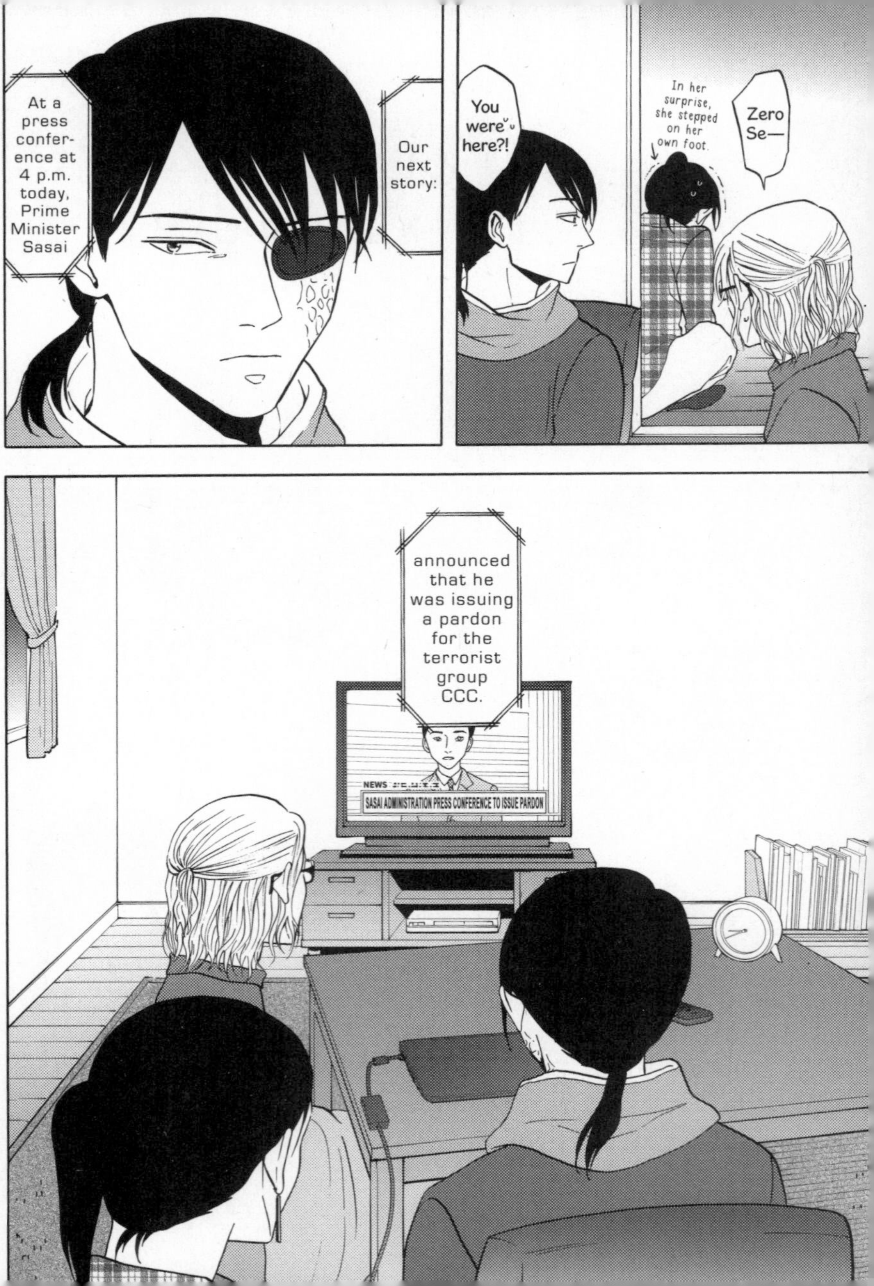
Zero Se—
In her surprise, she stepped on her own foot.
You were here?!
Our next story:
At a press conference at 4 p.m. today, Prime Minister Sasai
announced that he was issuing a pardon for the terrorist group CCC.
NEWS
SASAI ADMINISTRATION PRESS CONFERENCE TO ISSUE PARDON

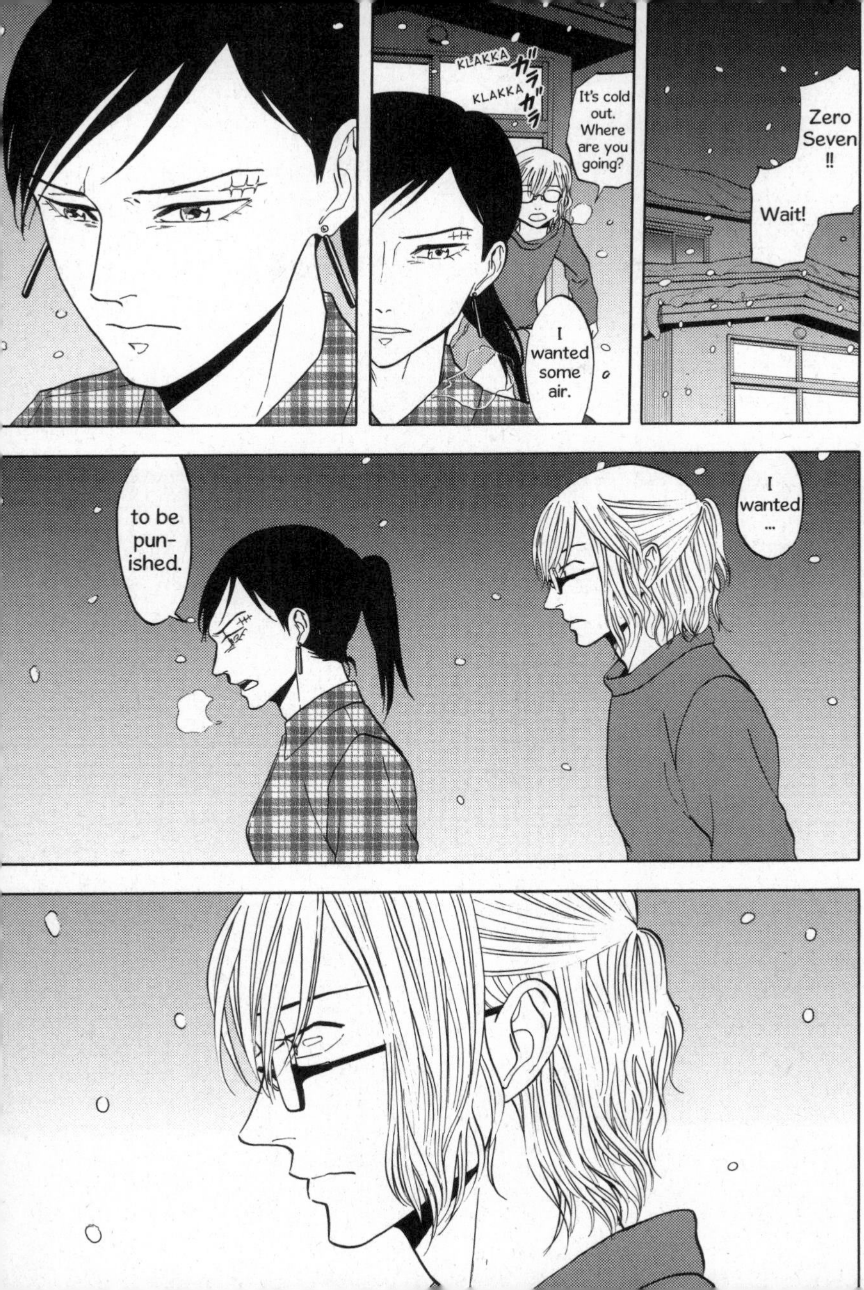
Zero Seven !!
Wait!
KLAKKA ガラ
KLAKKA ガラ
It's cold out. Where are you going?
I wanted some air.
I wanted ...
to be pun-ished.

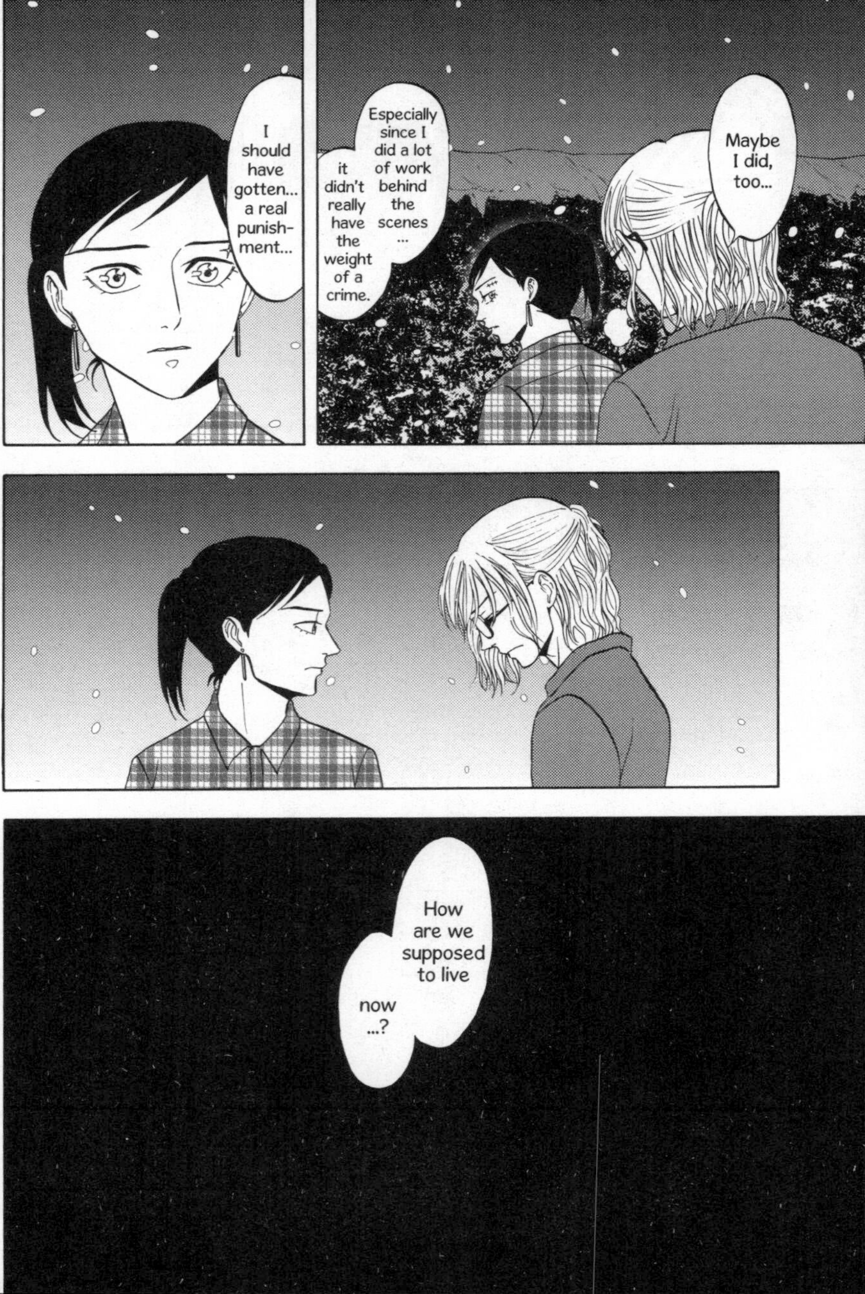
Maybe I did, too...
Especially since I did a lot of work behind the scenes...
it didn't really have the weight of a crime.
I should have gotten... a real punishment...
How are we supposed to live
now ...?

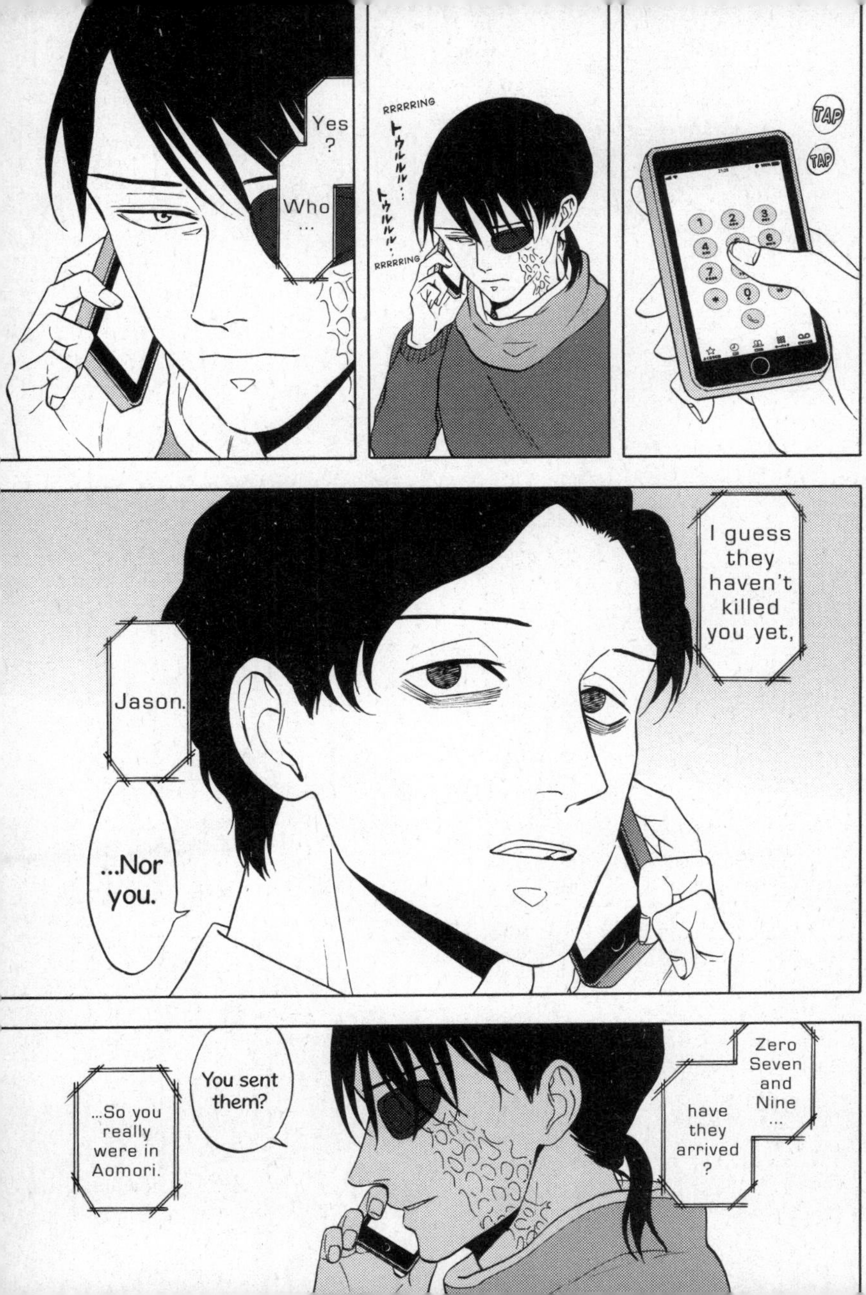
TAP
TAP
RRRRRING
トゥルルル…
トゥルルル…
RRRRRING
Yes?
Who…
I guess they haven't killed you yet,
Jason.
...Nor you.
Zero Seven and Nine…
have they arrived?
You sent them?
...So you really were in Aomori.

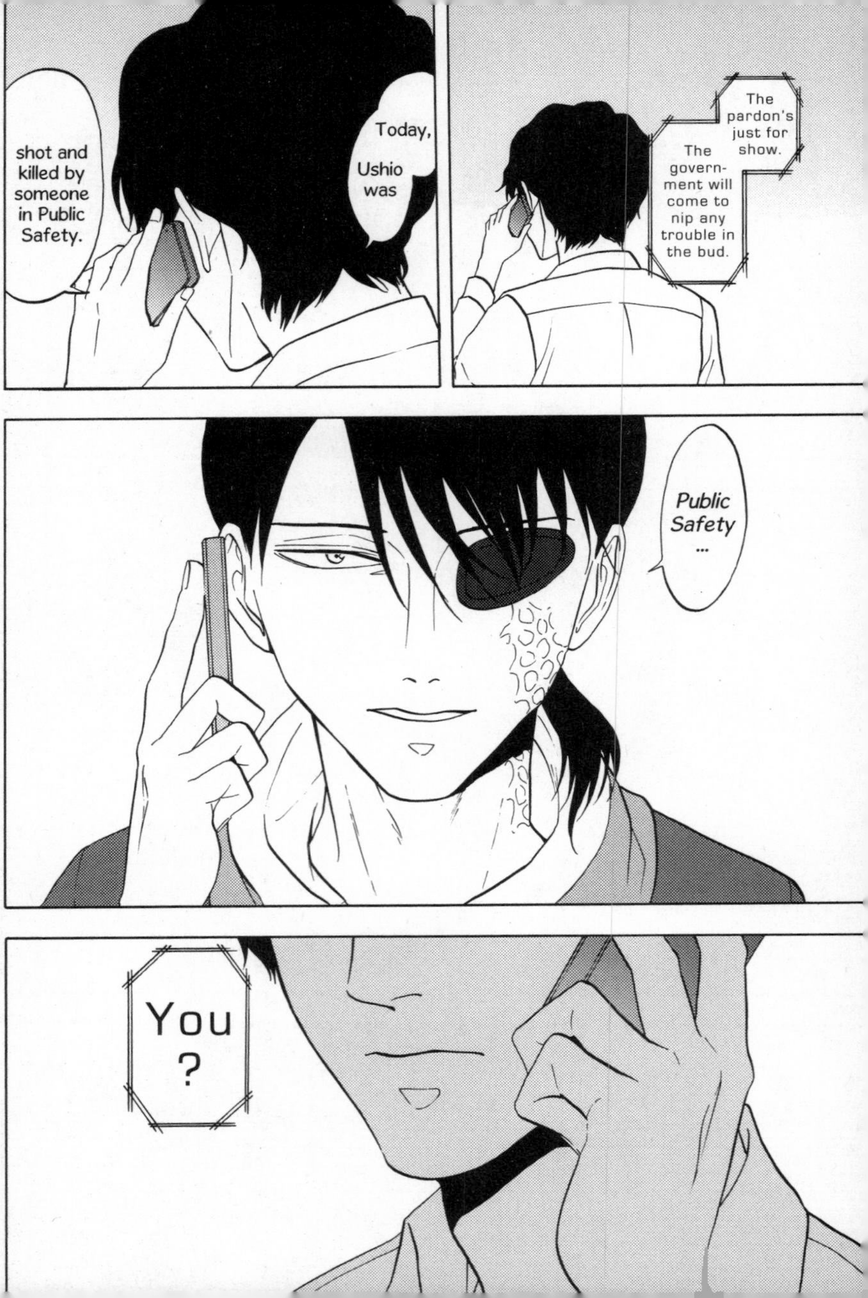
The pardon's just for show.
The government will come to nip any trouble in the bud.
Today, Ushio was
shot and killed by someone in Public Safety.
Public Safety ...
You ?

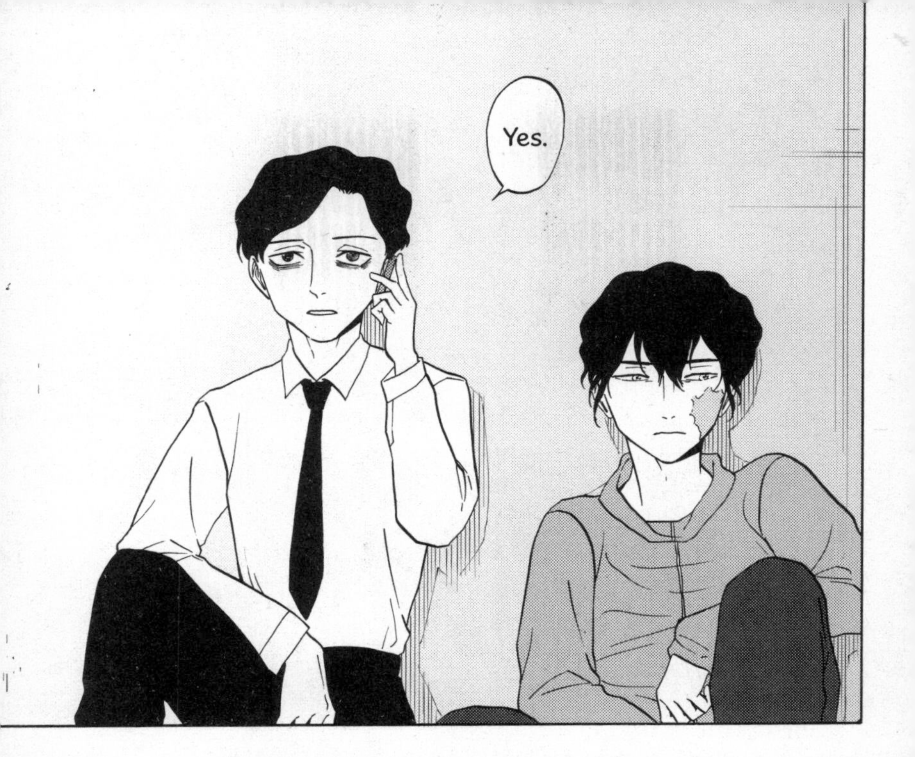
Yes.
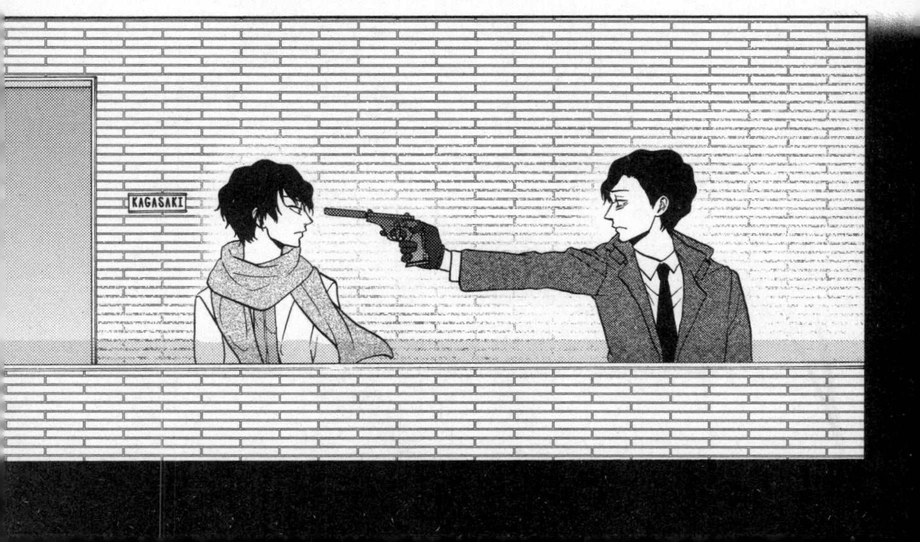
KAGASAKI

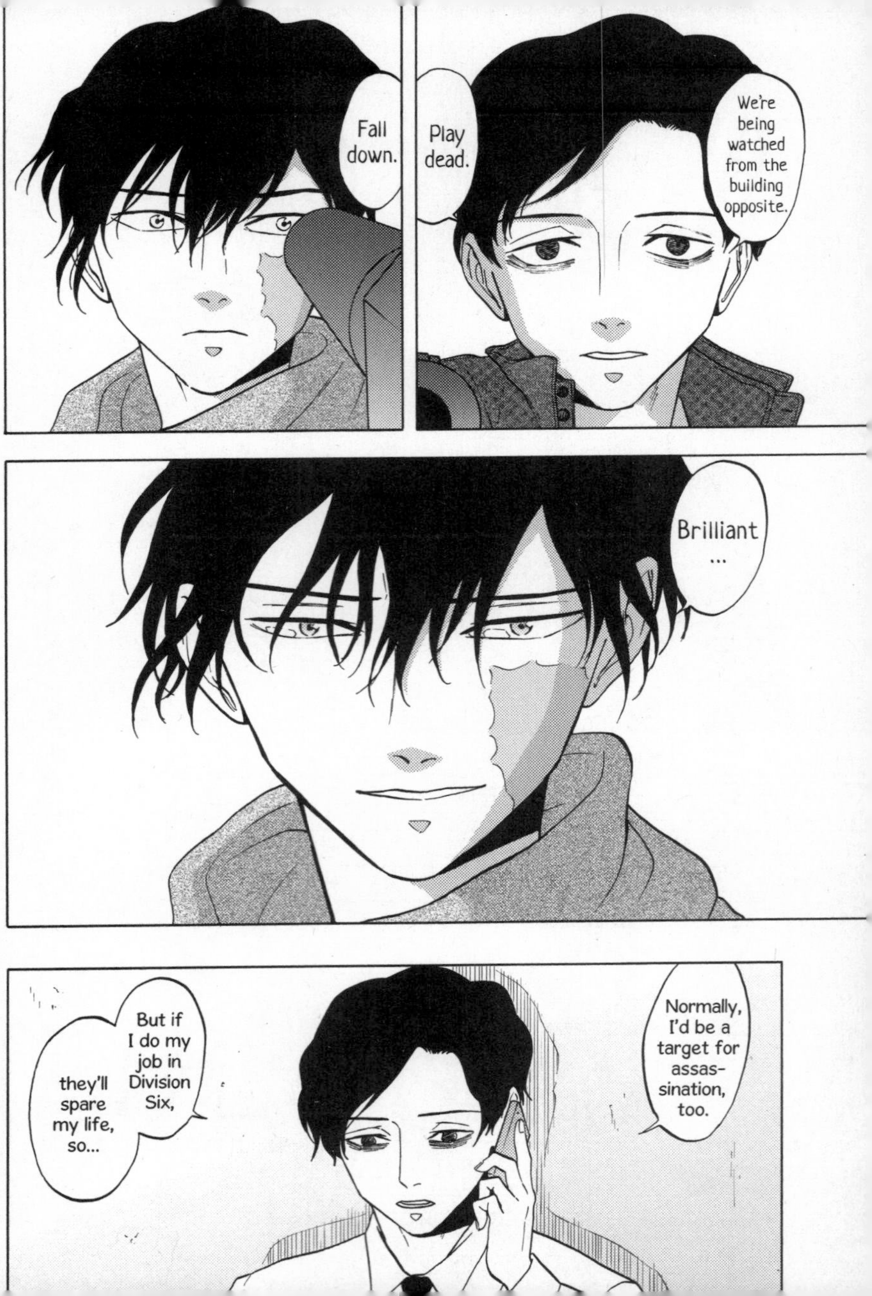
We're being watched from the building opposite.
Play dead.
Fall down.
Brilliant ...
Normally, I'd be a target for assas-sination, too.
But if I do my job in Division Six,
they'll spare my life, so...

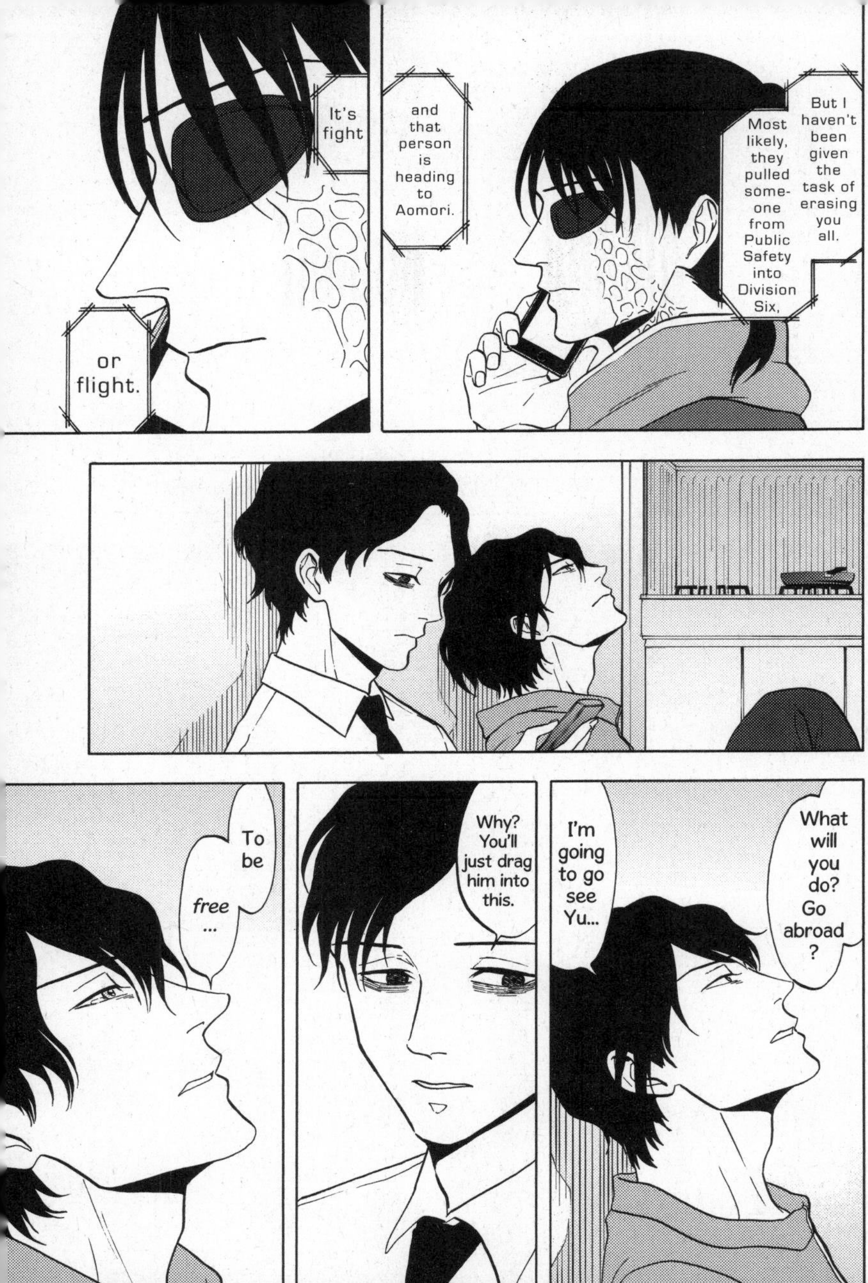
But I haven't been given the task of erasing you all.
Most likely, they pulled some-one from Public Safety into Division Six,
and that person is heading to Aomori.
It's fight
or flight.
What will you do? Go abroad?
I'm going to go see Yu...
Why? You'll just drag him into this.
To be *free*...

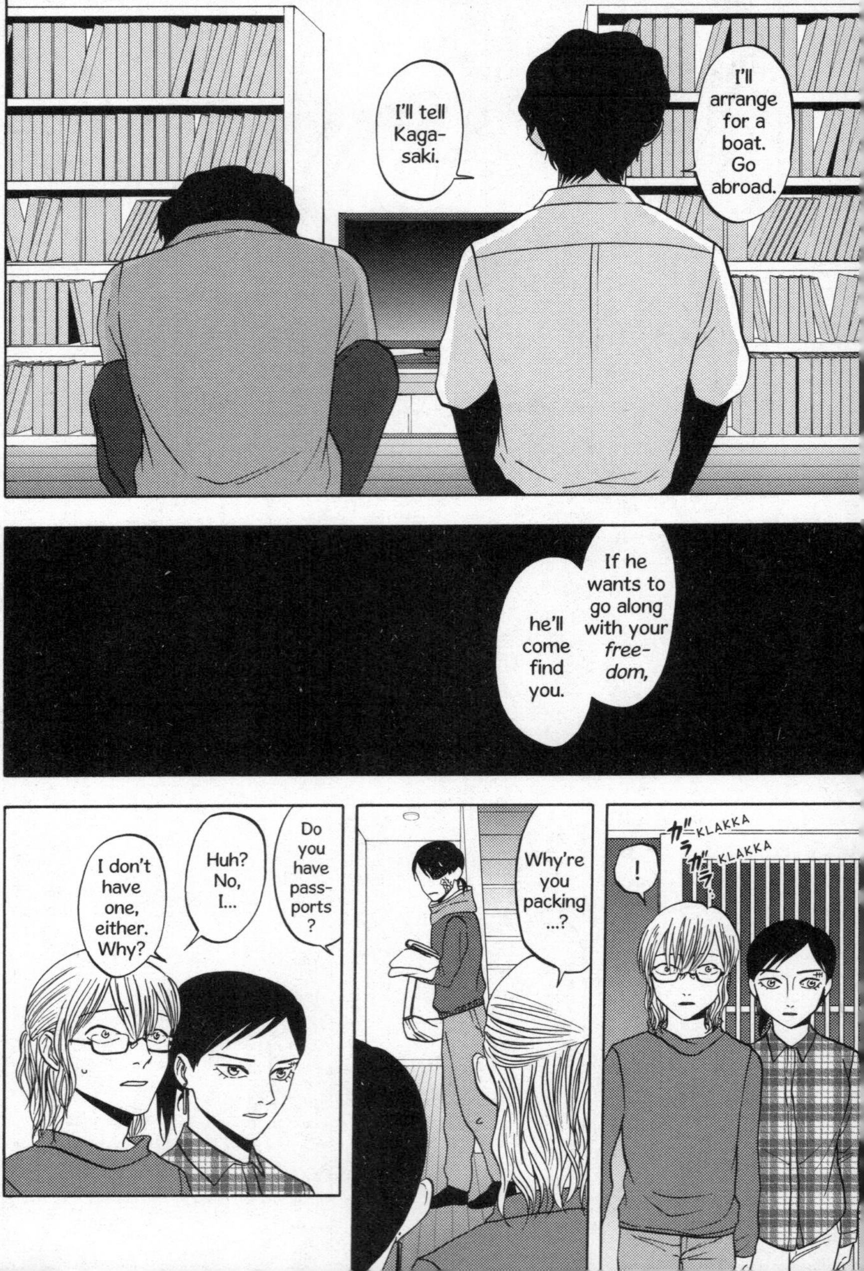
I'll arrange for a boat. Go abroad.
I'll tell Kaga-saki.
If he wants to go along with your *free-dom,*
he'll come find you.
ガラ KLAKKA
ガラ KLAKKA
!
Why're you packing ...?
Do you have pass-ports ?
Huh? No, I...
I don't have one, either. Why?

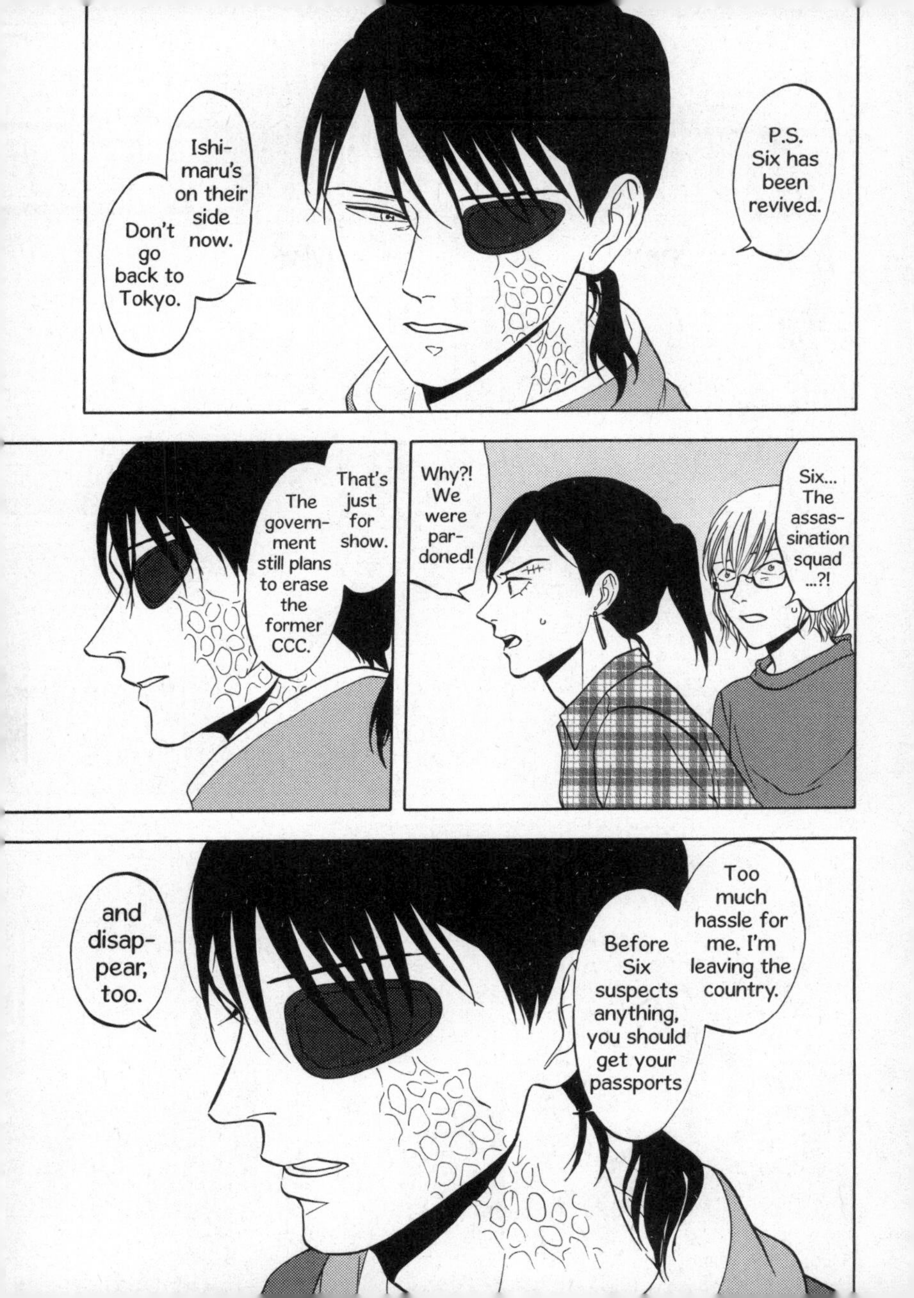

P.S. Six has been revived.
Ishi-maru's on their side now.
Don't go back to Tokyo.
Six... The assas-sination squad ...?!
Why?! We were par-doned!
That's just for show.
The govern-ment still plans to erase the former CCC.
Too much hassle for me. I'm leaving the country.
Before Six suspects anything, you should get your passports
and disap-pear, too.

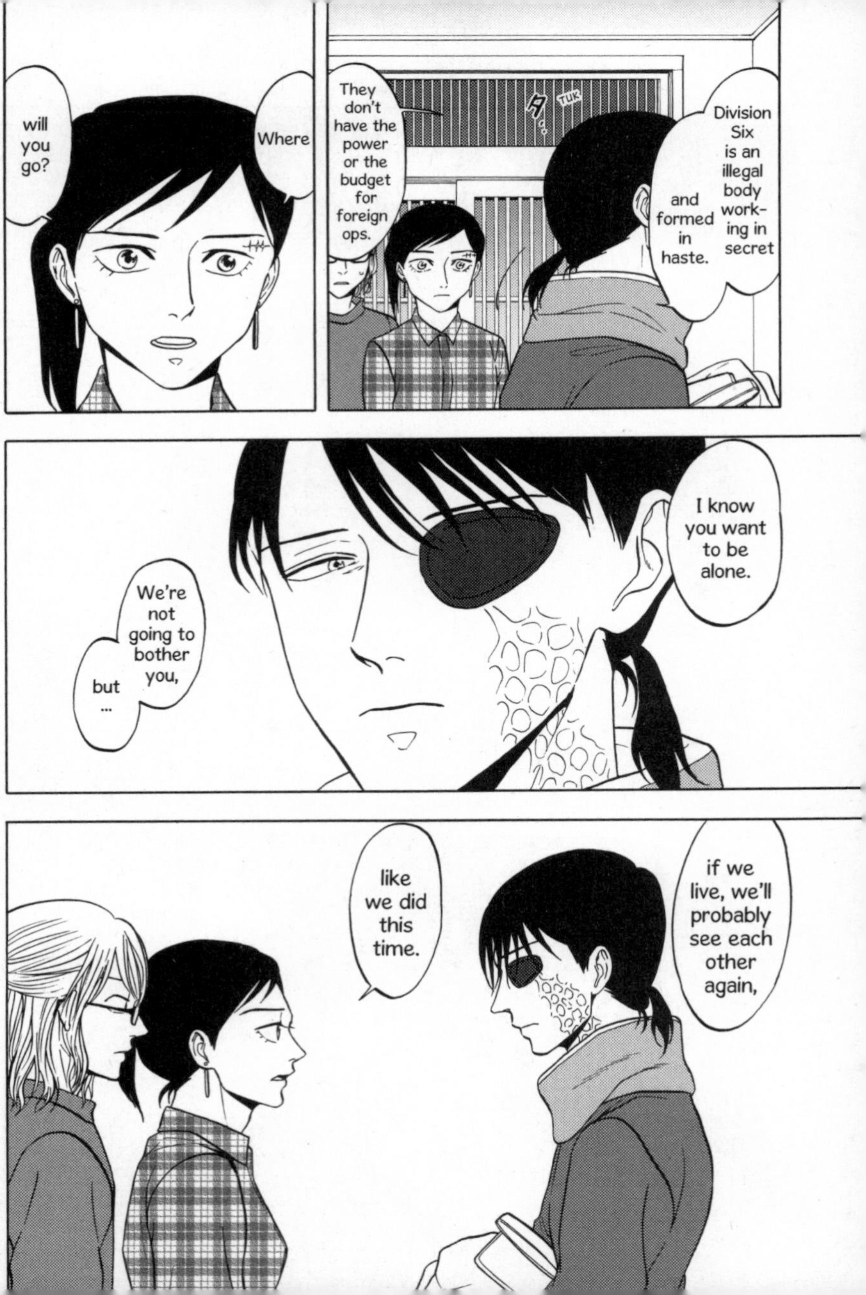
Division Six is an illegal body working in secret
and formed in haste.
TUK
They don't have the power or the budget for foreign ops.
Where
will you go?
I know you want to be alone.
We're not going to bother you,
but ...
if we live, we'll probably see each other again,
like we did this time.

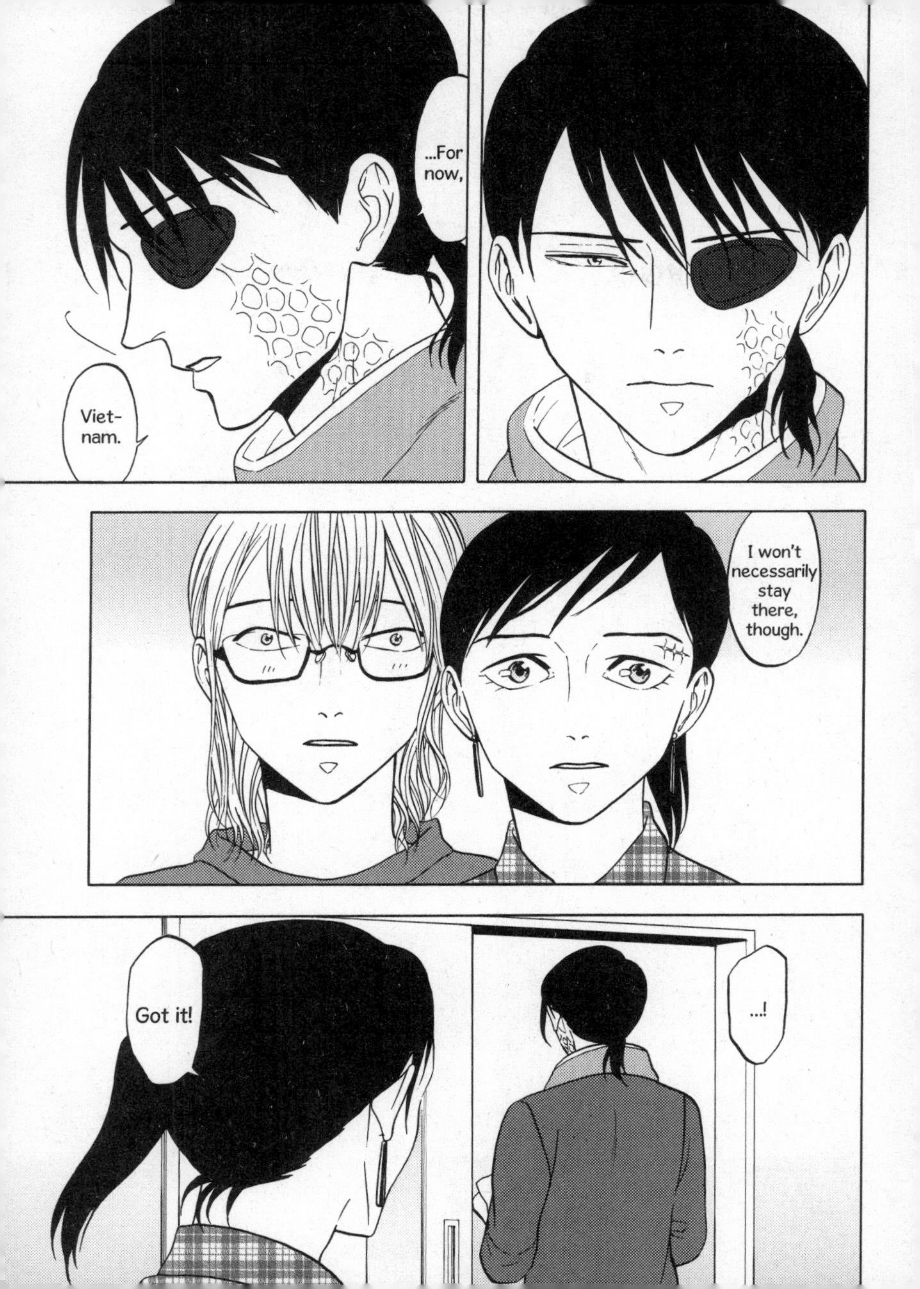
...For now,
Viet-nam.
I won't necessarily stay there, though.
...!
Got it!

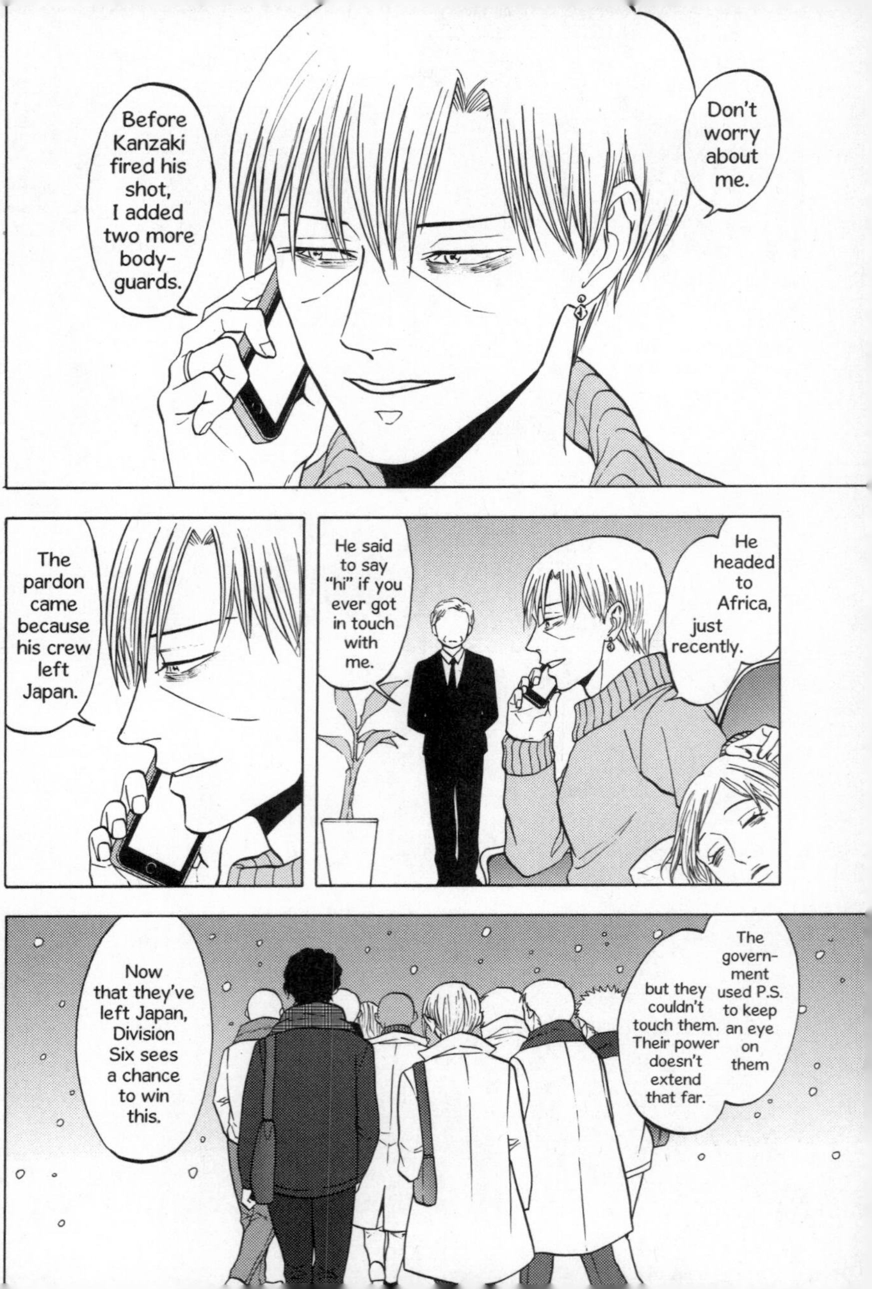
Don't worry about me.
Before Kanzaki fired his shot, I added two more body-guards.
He headed to Africa, just recently.
He said to say "hi" if you ever got in touch with me.
The pardon came because his crew left Japan.
The government used P.S. to keep an eye on them
but they couldn't touch them. Their power doesn't extend that far.
Now that they've left Japan, Division Six sees a chance to win this.

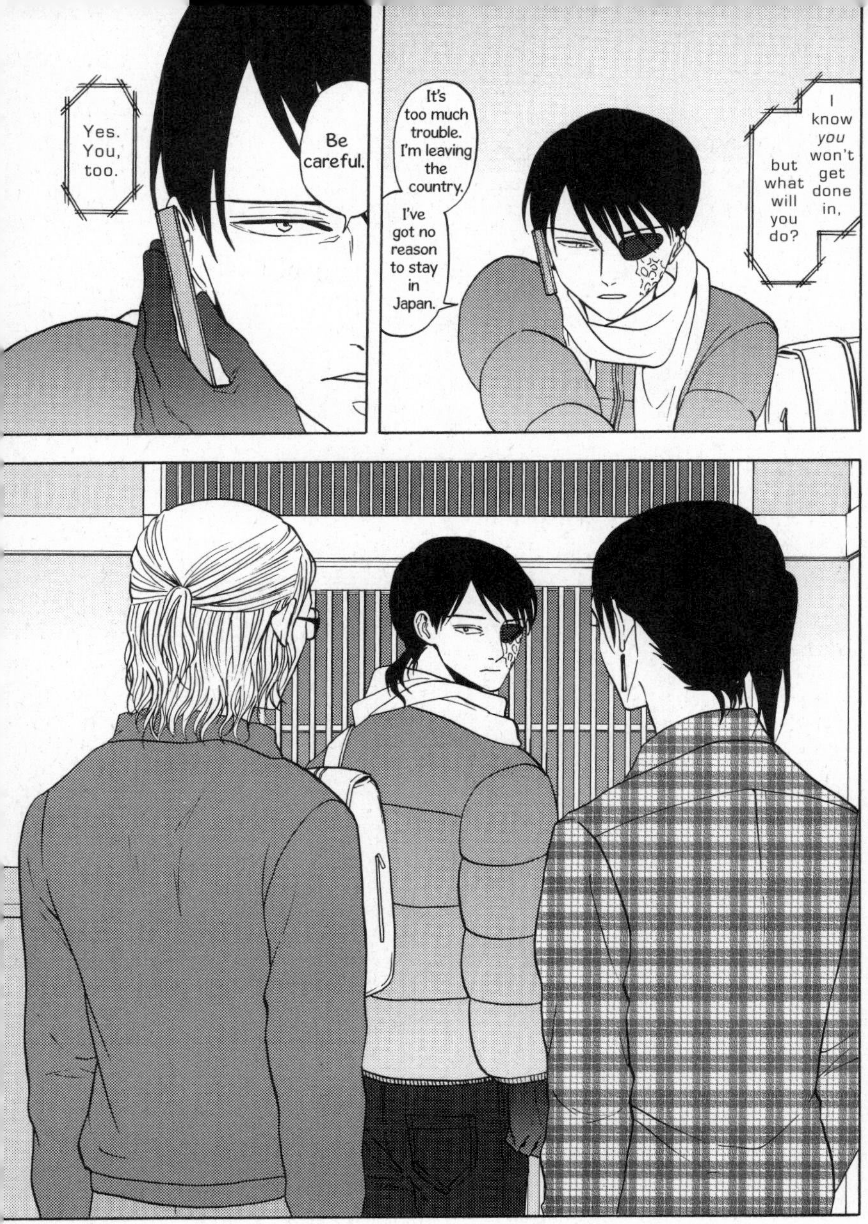
I know *you* won't get done in,
but what will you do?
It's too much trouble. I'm leaving the country.
I've got no reason to stay in Japan.
Be careful.
Yes. You, too.

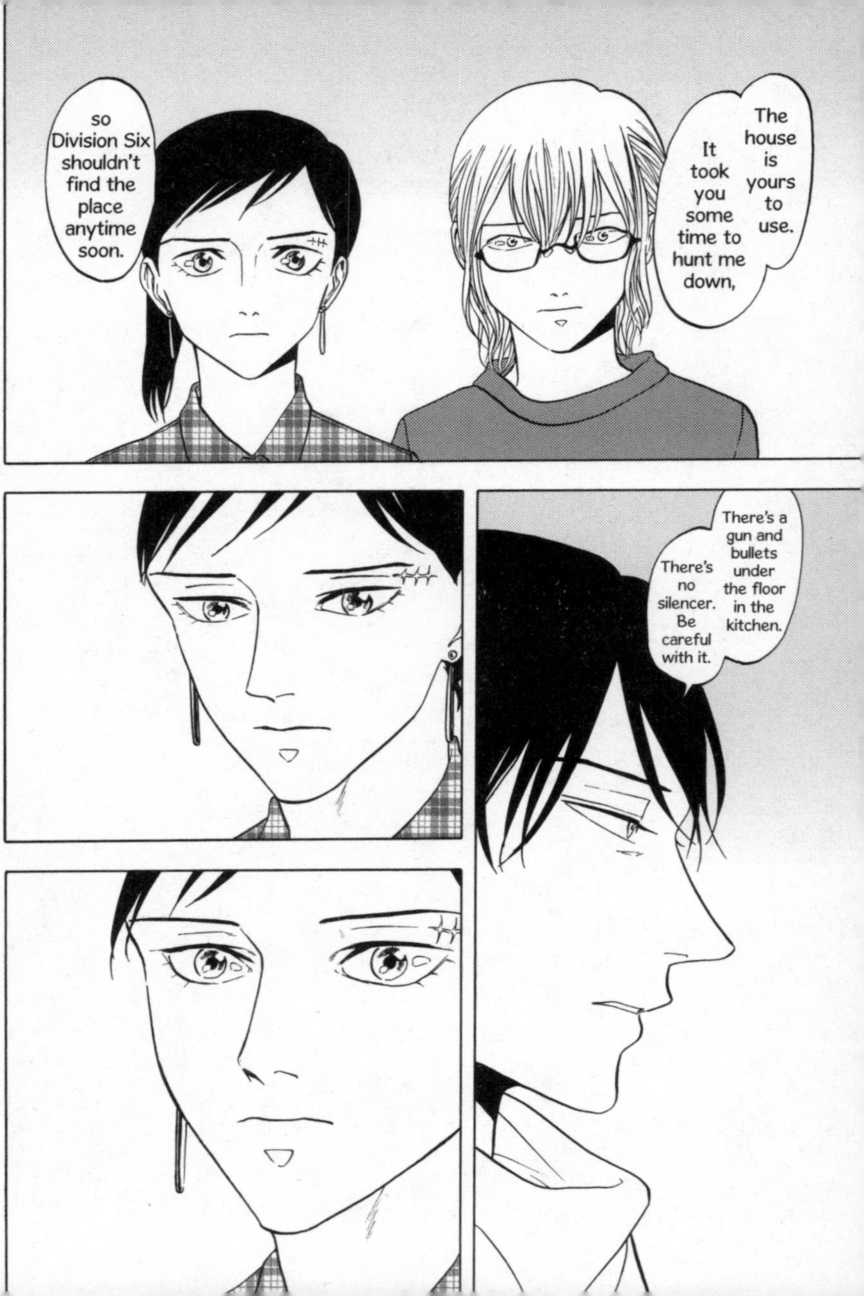
The house is yours to use.
It took you some time to hunt me down,
so Division Six shouldn't find the place anytime soon.
There's a gun and bullets under the floor in the kitchen.
There's no silencer. Be careful with it.

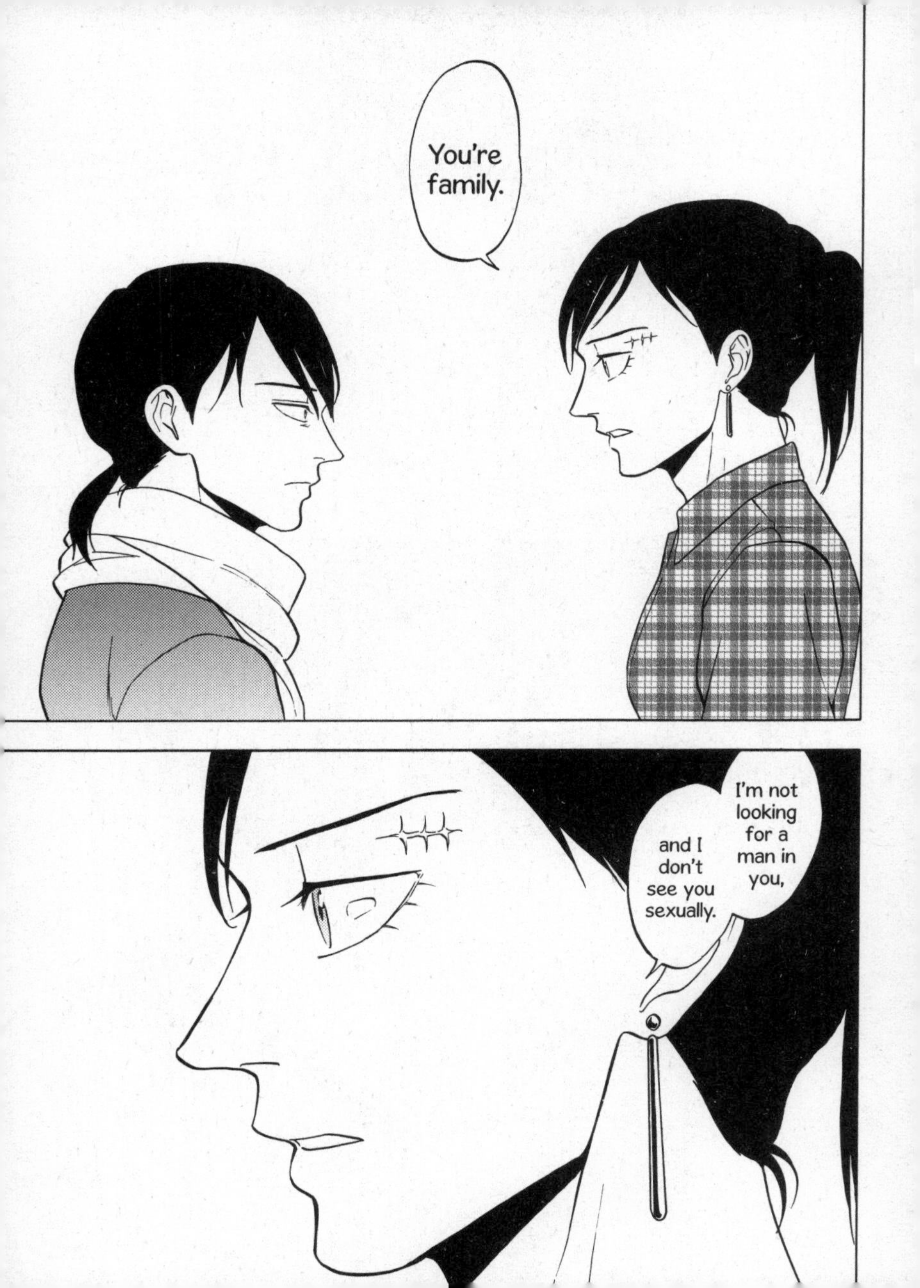
You're family.
I'm not looking for a man in you,
and I don't see you sexually.

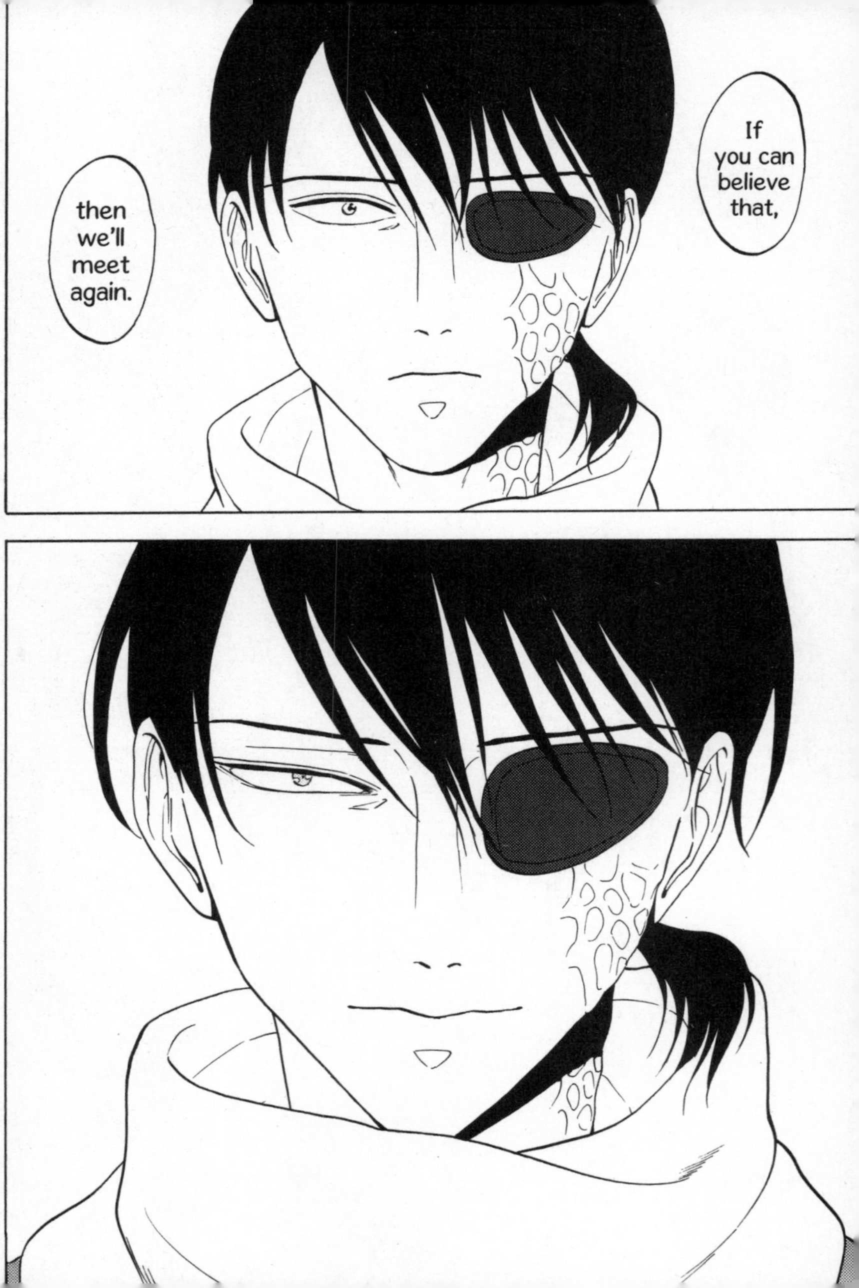
If you can believe that,
then we'll meet again.

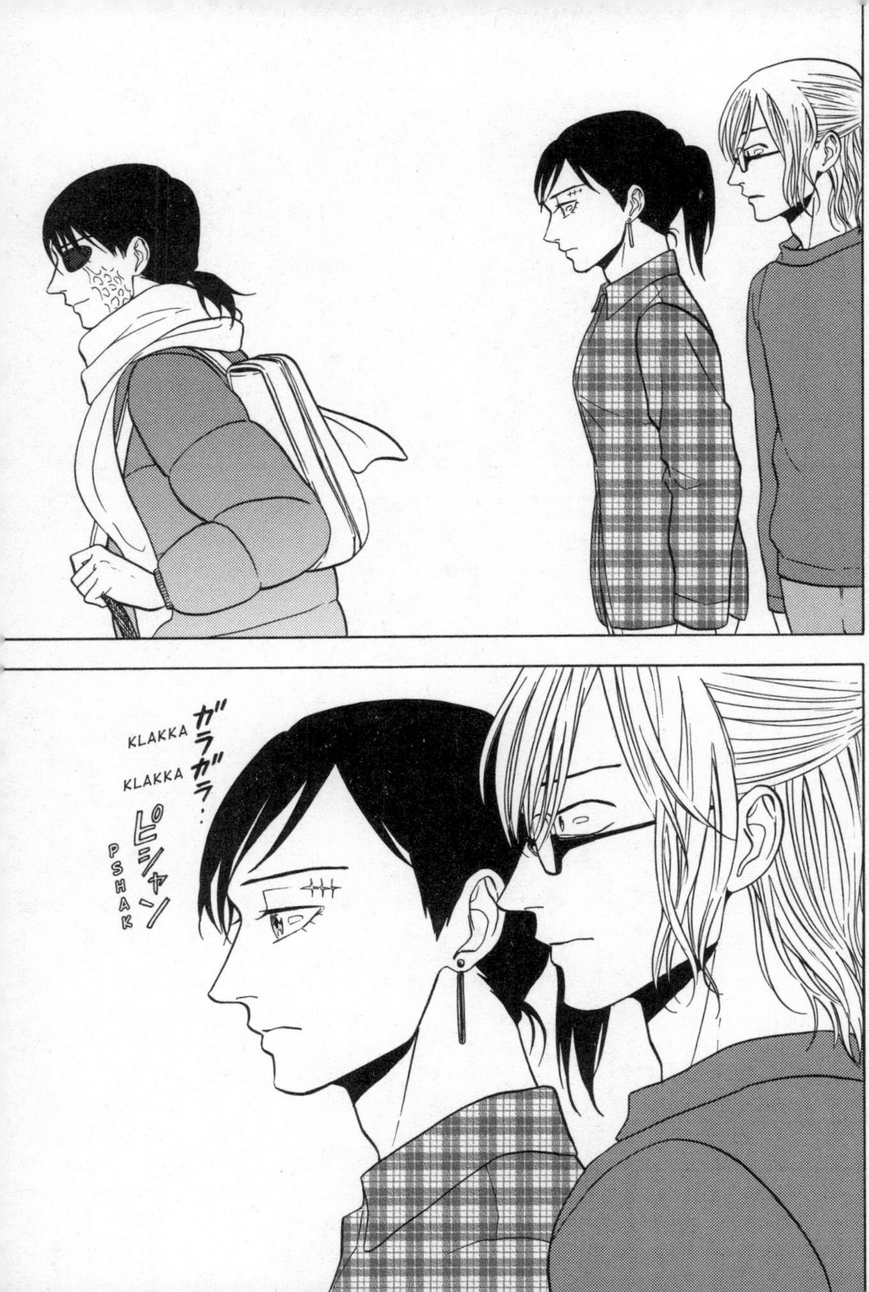
ガラガラ…
KLAKKA KLAKKA
ピシャーン
PSHAK

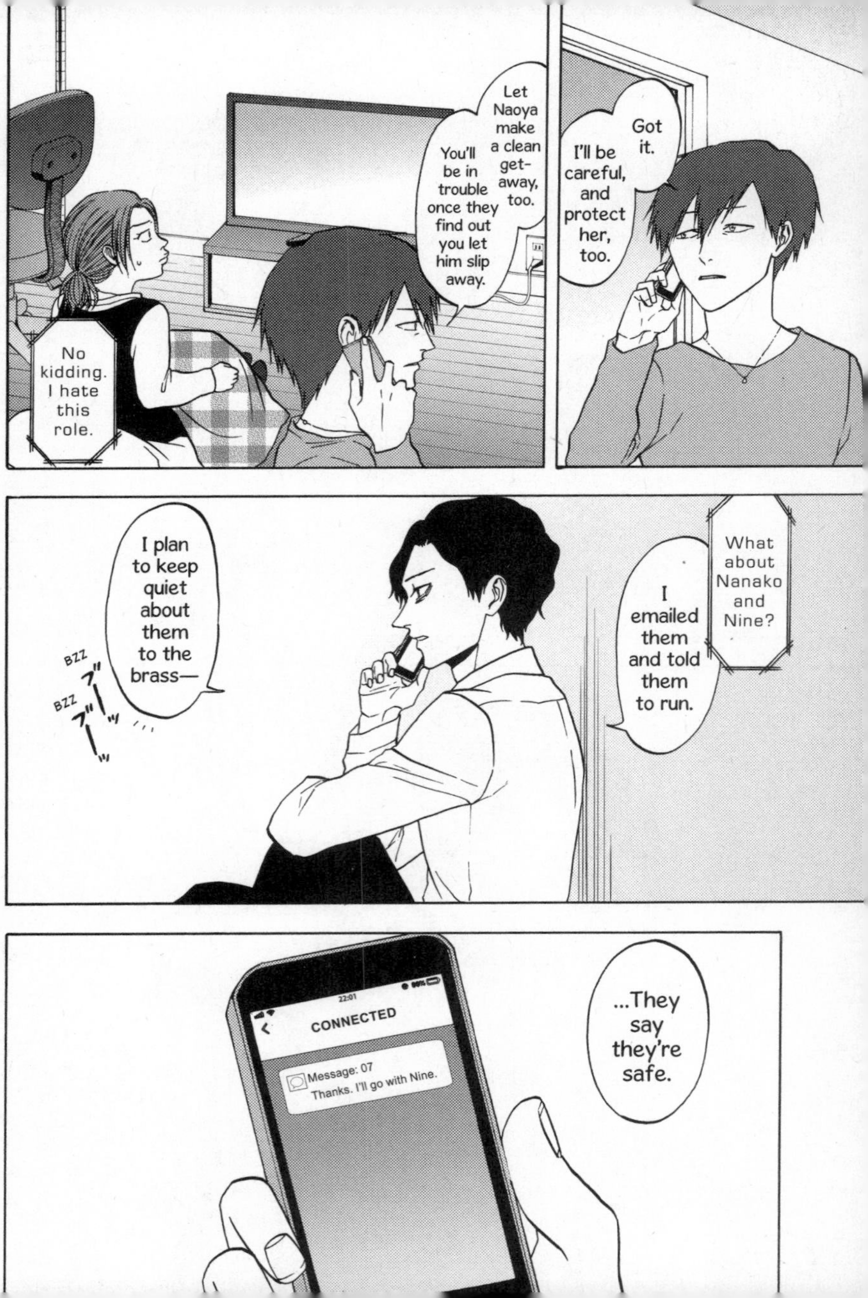
Got it.
I'll be careful, and protect her, too.
Let Naoya make a clean get-away, too.
You'll be in trouble once they find out you let him slip away.
No kidding. I hate this role.
What about Nanako and Nine?
I emailed them and told them to run.
I plan to keep quiet about them to the brass—
BZZ ブー
BZZ ブー
22:01
CONNECTED
Message: 07
Thanks. I'll go with Nine.
...They say they're safe.

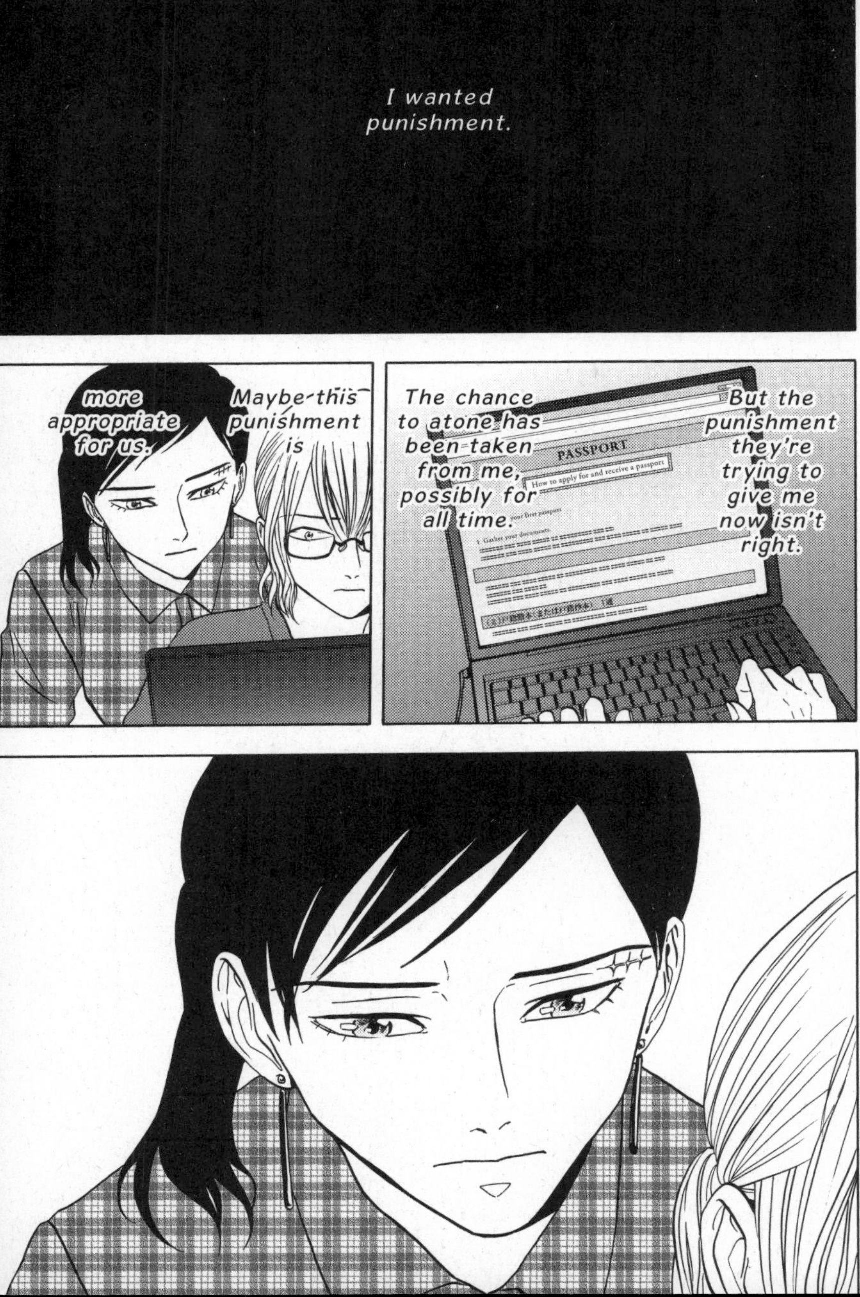
I wanted punishment.
But the punishment they're trying to give me now isn't right.
The chance to atone has been taken from me, possibly for all time.
PASSPORT
How to apply for and receive a passport
Maybe this punishment is
more appropriate for us.

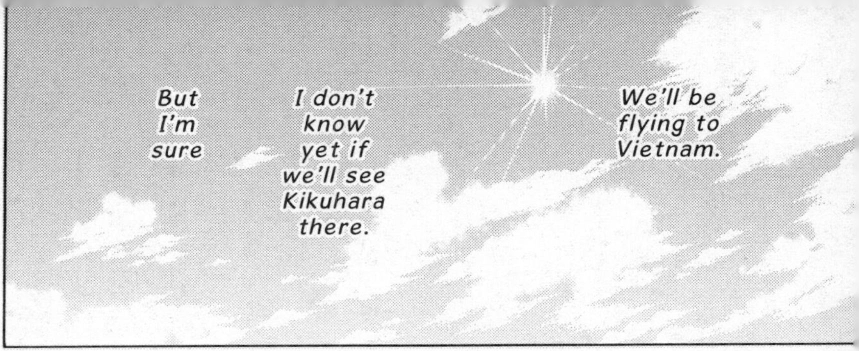
We'll be flying to Vietnam.
I don't know yet if we'll see Kikuhara there.
But I'm sure

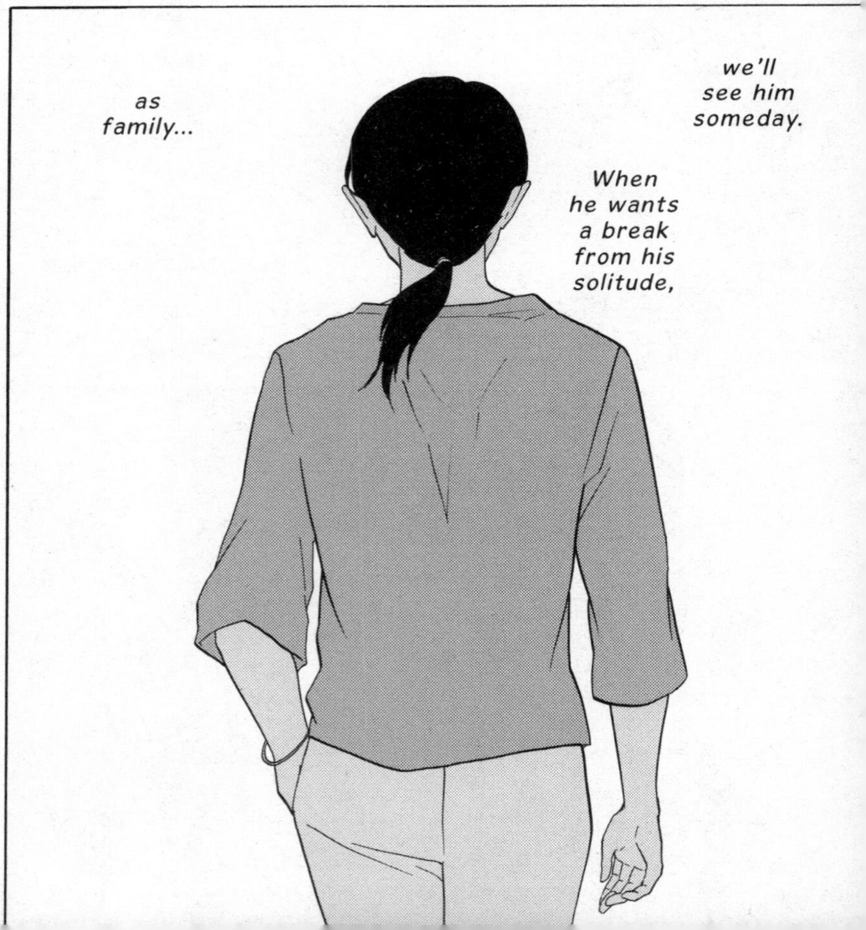
we'll see him someday.
When he wants a break from his solitude,
as family...

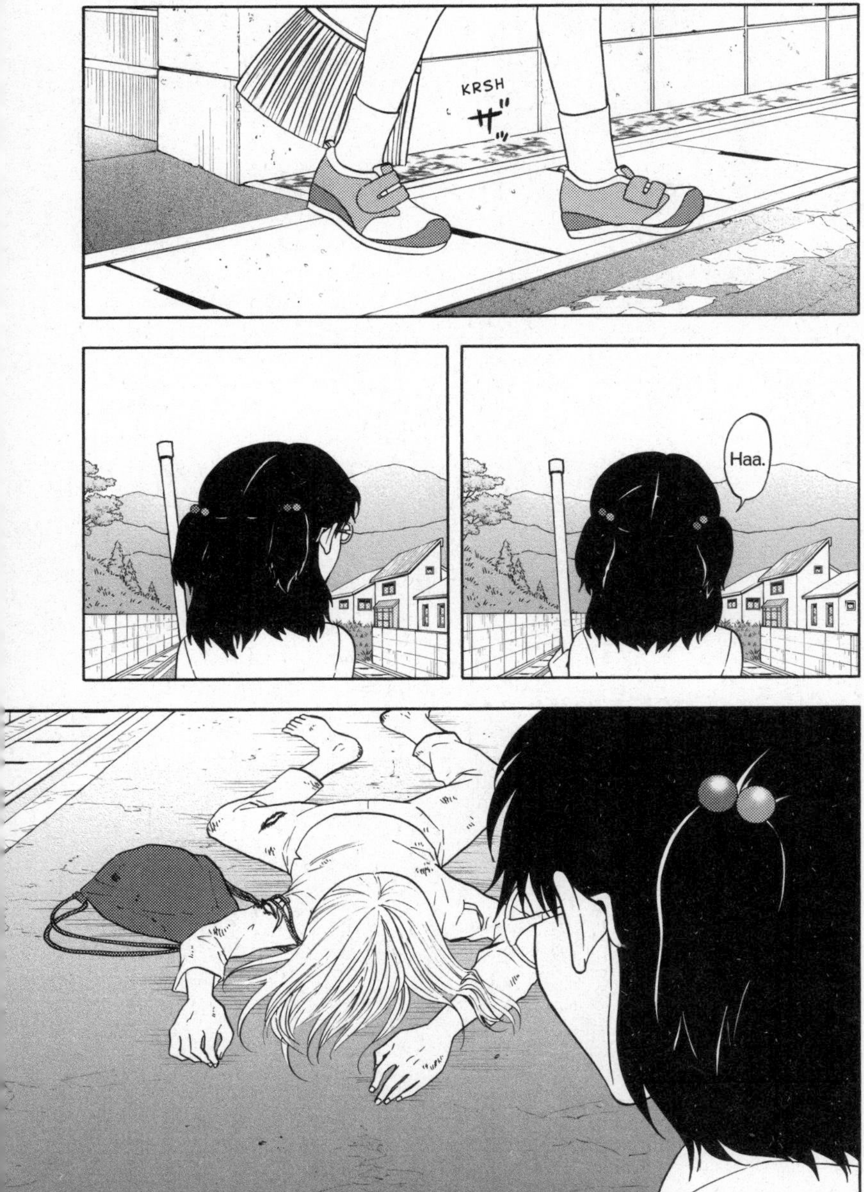
KRSH
ザッ
Haa.

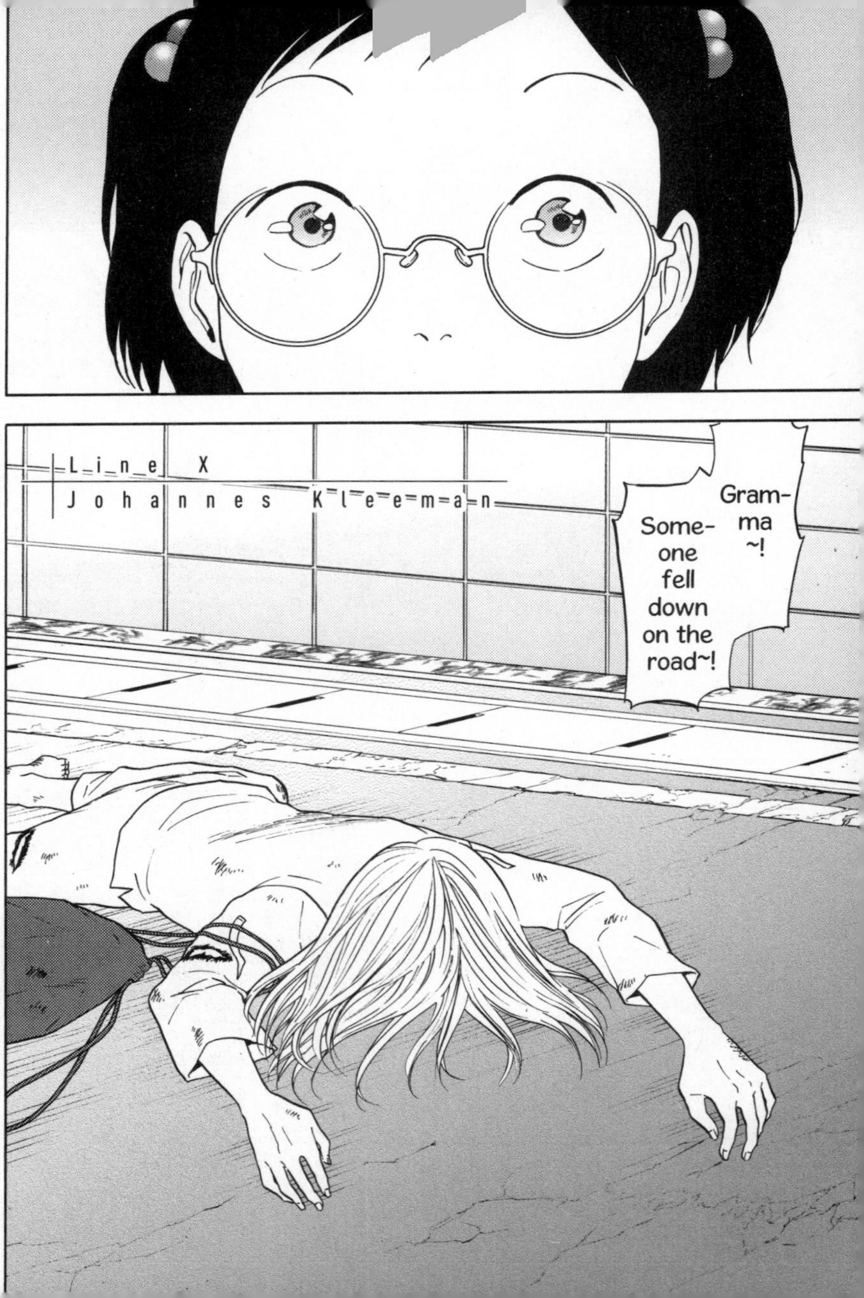
Gramma~!
Someone fell down on the road~!
Line X
Johannes Kleeman

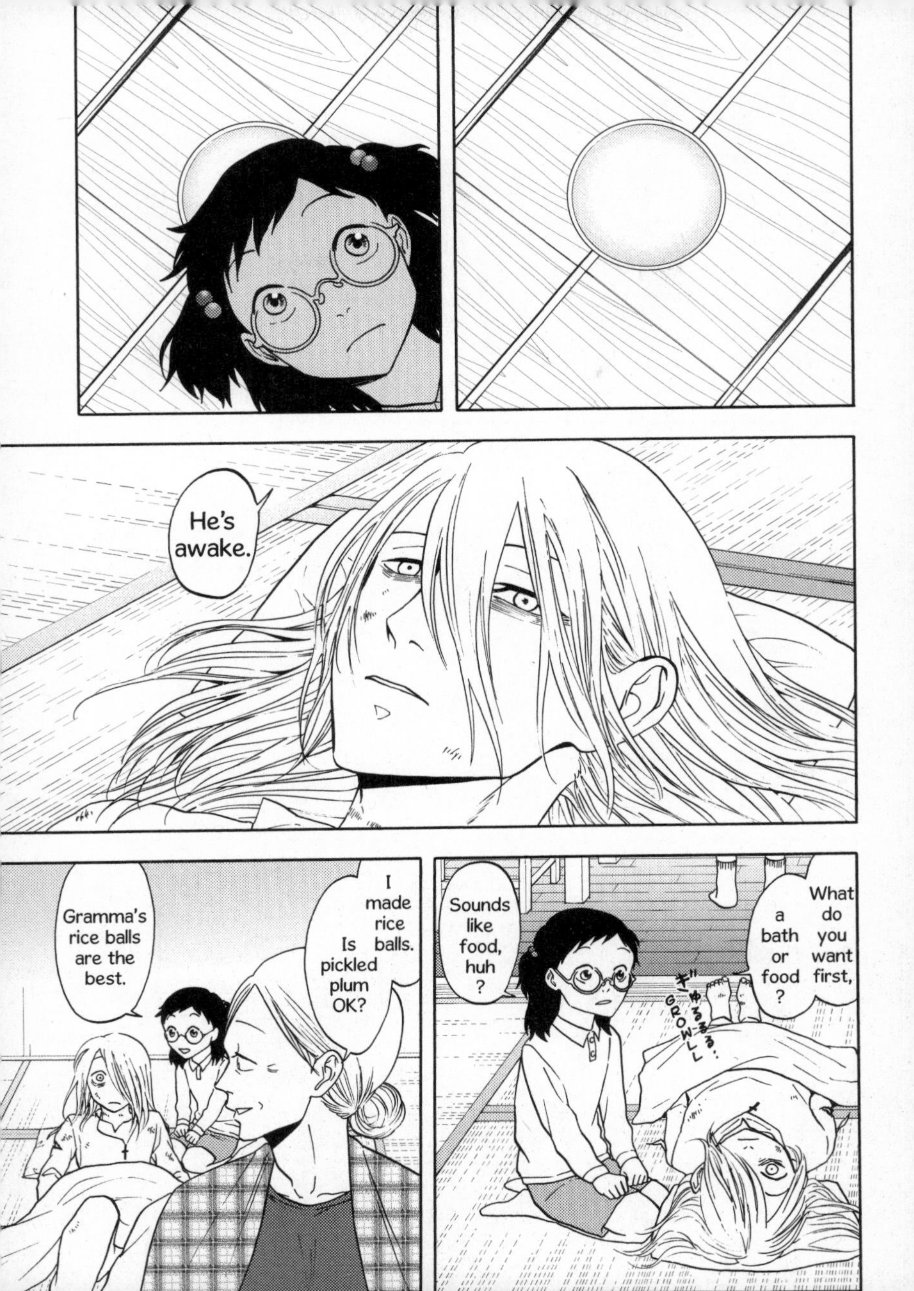
He's awake.
What do you want first, a bath or food?
GROWLL
Sounds like food, huh?
I made rice balls. Is pickled plum OK?
Gramma's rice balls are the best.

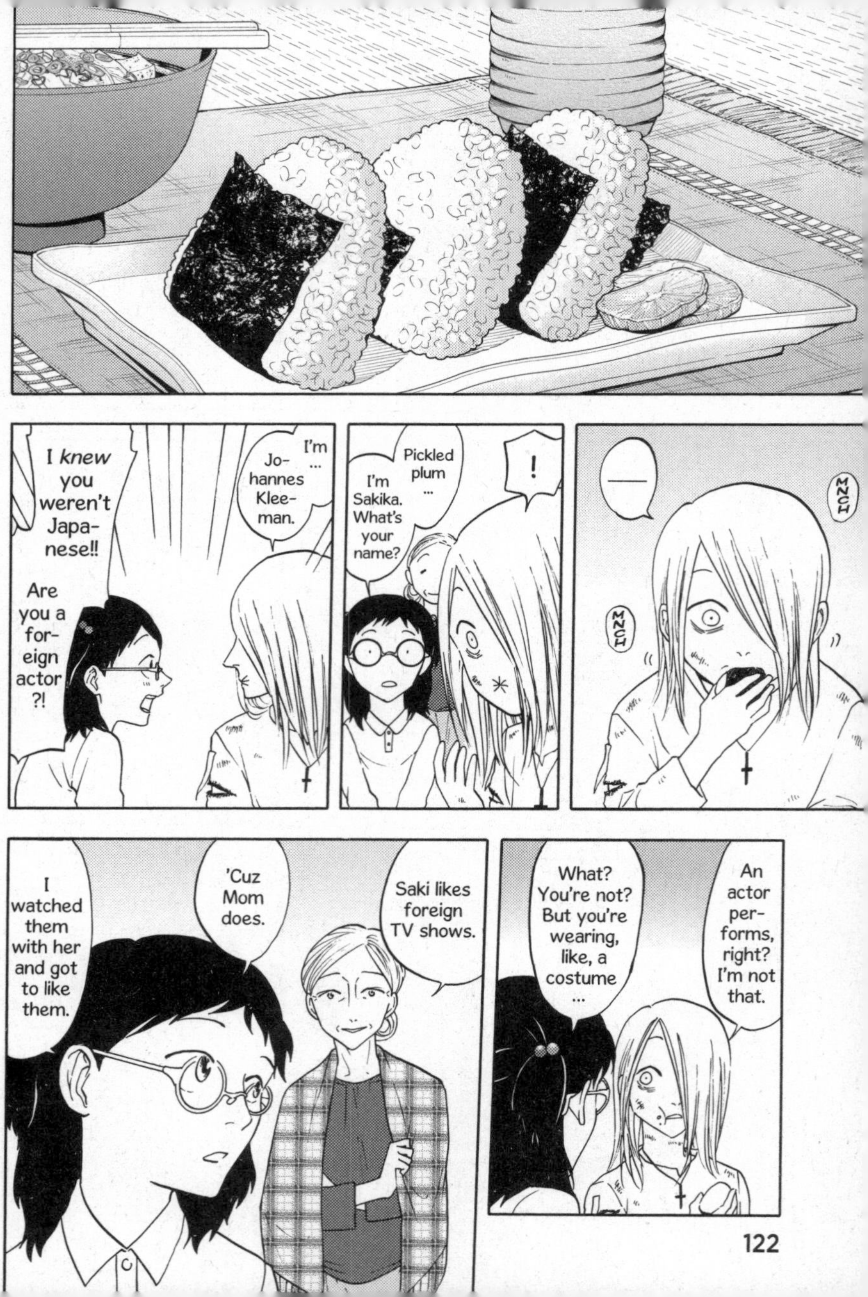
——
MNCH
MNCH
!
Pickled plum ...
I'm Sakika. What's your name?
I'm ...
Johannes Kleeman.
I *knew* you weren't Japanese!!
Are you a foreign actor ?!
An actor performs, right? I'm not that.
What? You're not? But you're wearing, like, a costume ...
Saki likes foreign TV shows.
'Cuz Mom does.
I watched them with her and got to like them.

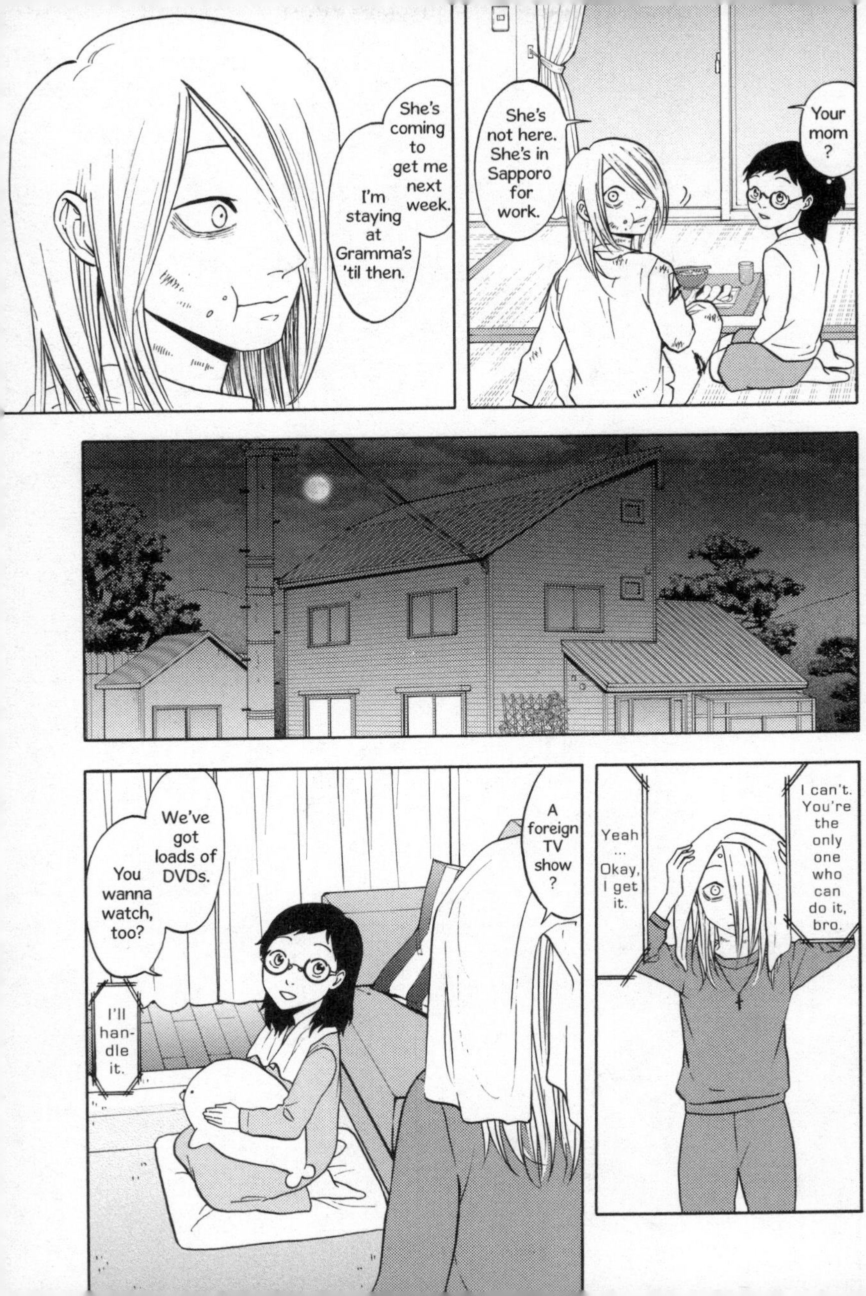
Your mom?
She's not here. She's in Sapporo for work.
She's coming to get me next week.
I'm staying at Gramma's 'til then.
I can't. You're the only one who can do it, bro.
Yeah... Okay, I get it.
A foreign TV show?
We've got loads of DVDs.
You wanna watch, too?
I'll handle it.

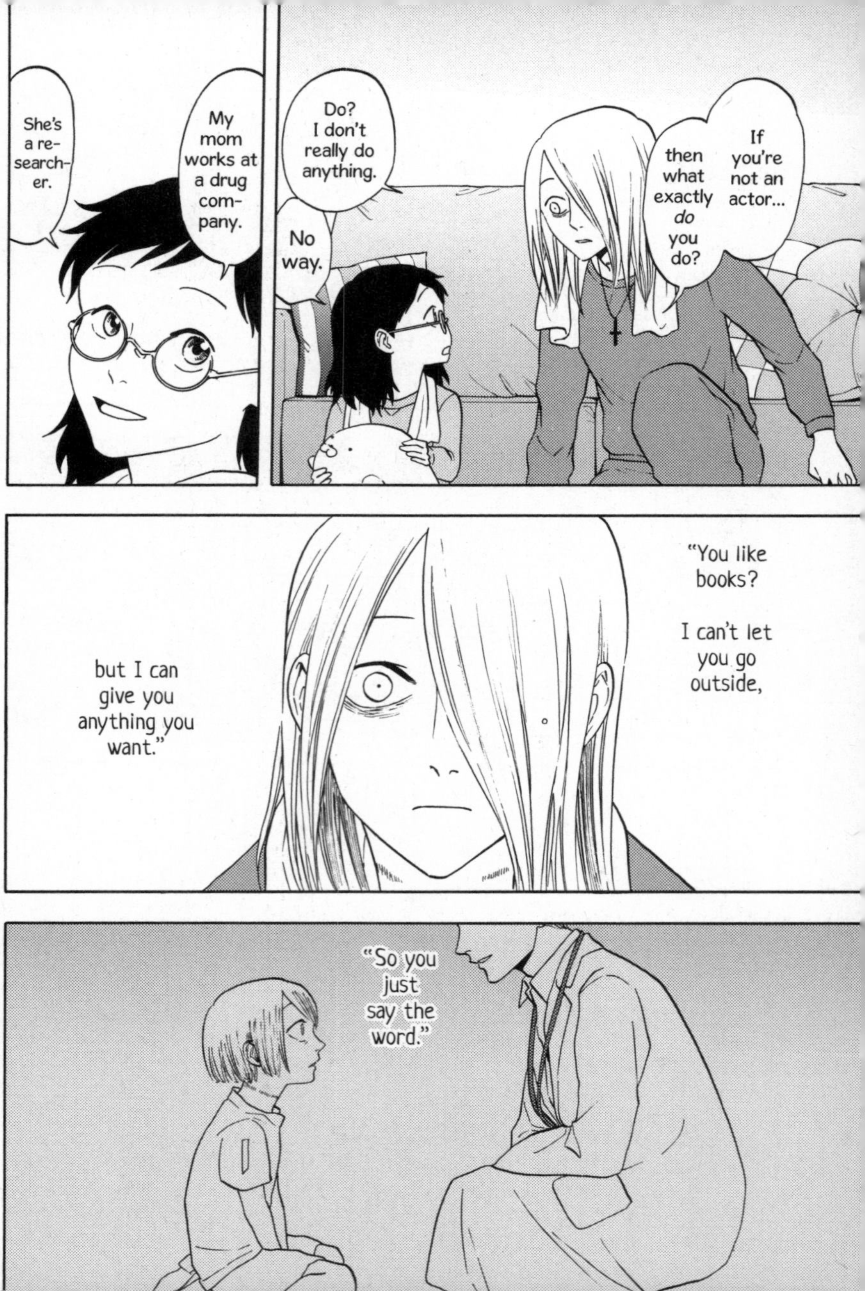
If you're not an actor...
then what exactly *do* you do?
Do? I don't really do anything.
No way.
My mom works at a drug com-pany.
She's a re-search-er.
"You like books? I can't let you go outside,
but I can give you anything you want."
"So you just say the word."

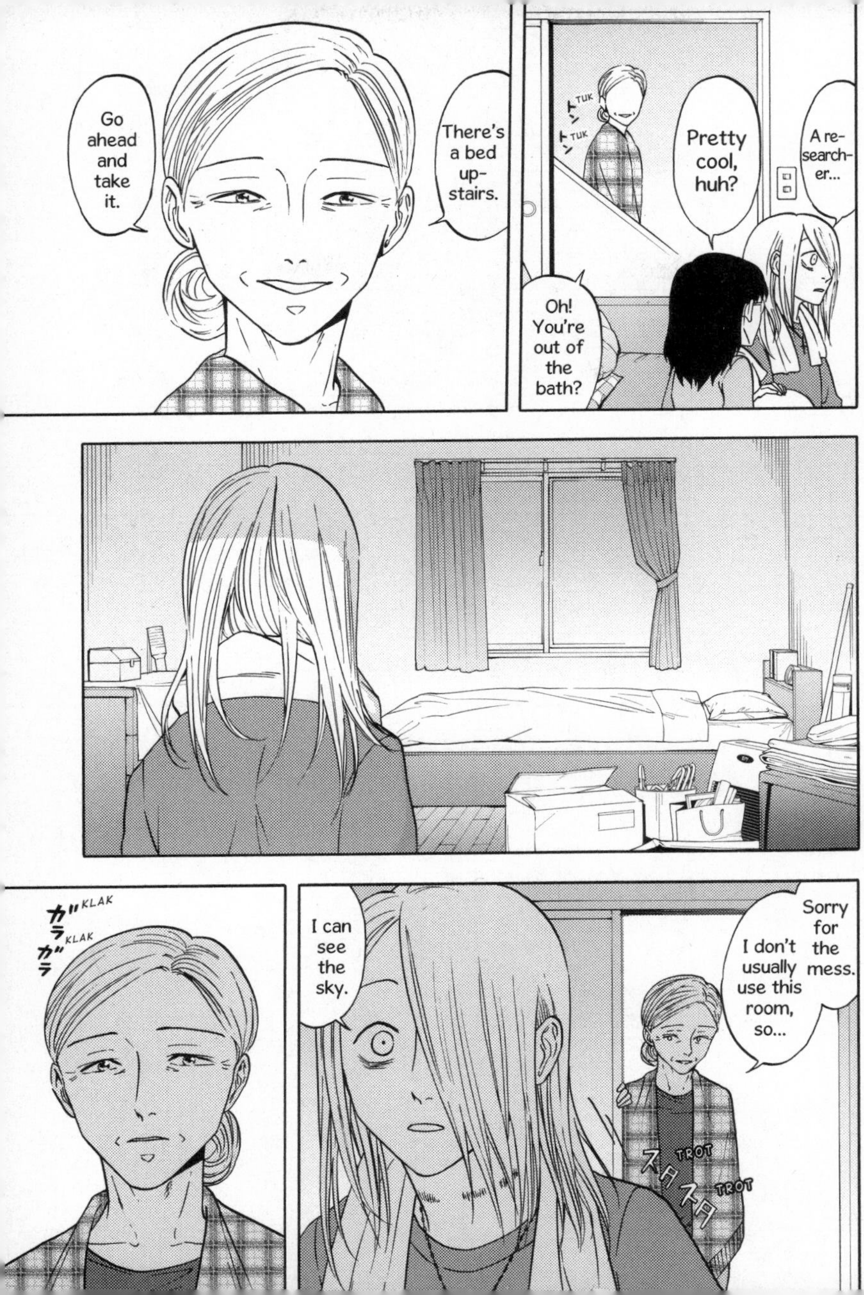
A re-searcher...
Pretty cool, huh?
トン TUK
トン TUK
Oh! You're out of the bath?
There's a bed up-stairs.
Go ahead and take it.
Sorry for the mess.
I don't usually use this room, so...
I can see the sky.
スタ TROT
スタ TROT
ガラ KLAK
ガラ KLAK

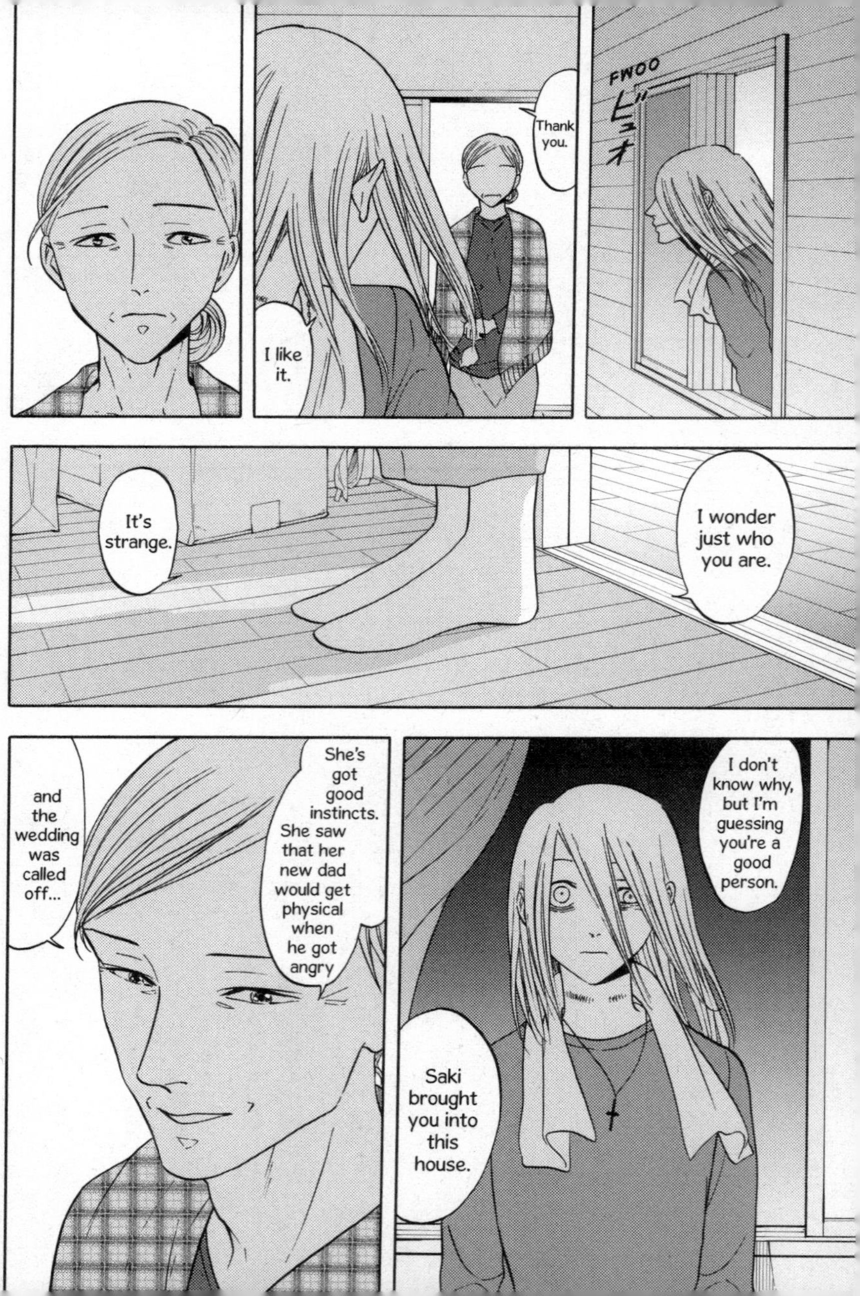
FWOO
ビュオ
Thank you.
I like it.
I wonder just who you are.
It's strange.
I don't know why, but I'm guessing you're a good person.
Saki brought you into this house.
She's got good instincts. She saw that her new dad would get physical when he got angry
and the wedding was called off...

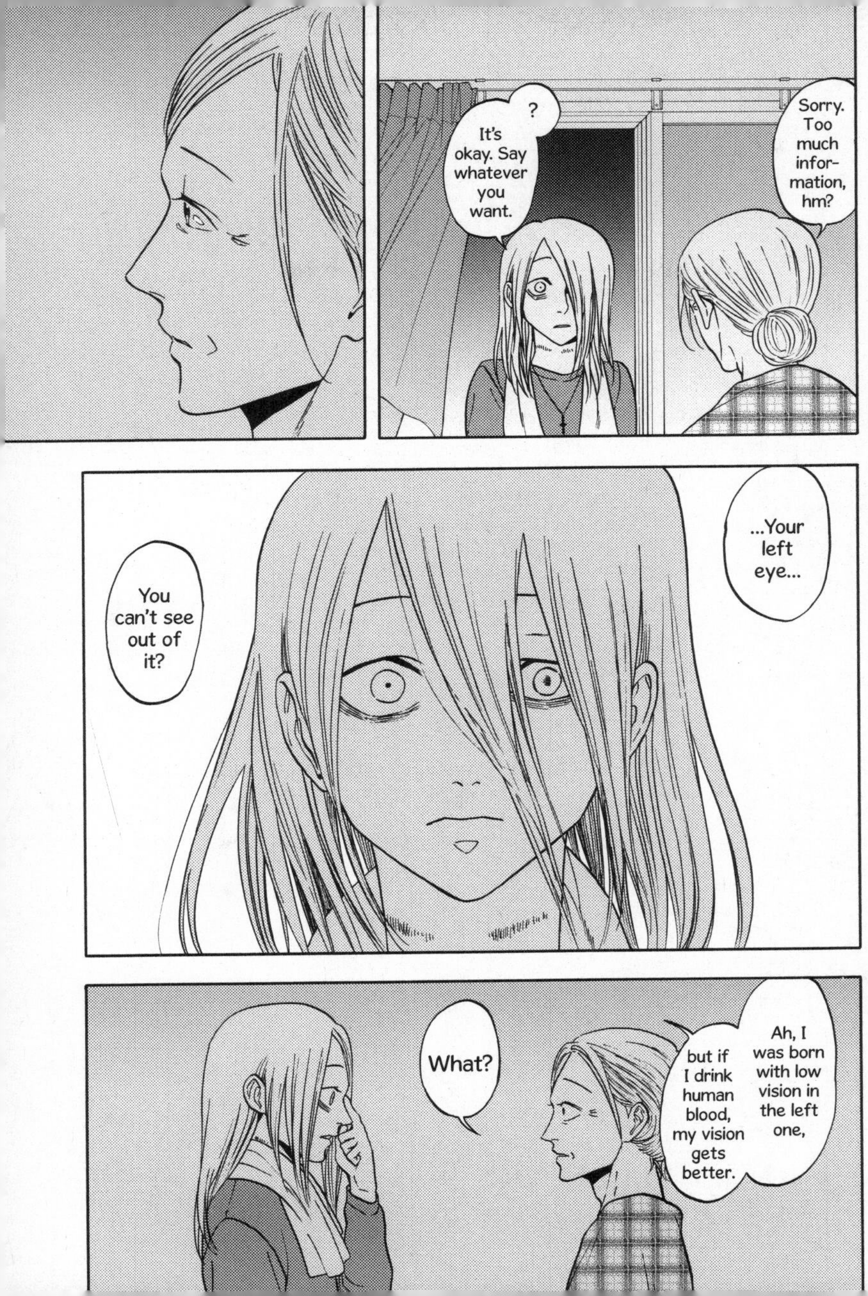
Sorry. Too much information, hm?
?
It's okay. Say whatever you want.
...Your left eye...
You can't see out of it?
Ah, I was born with low vision in the left one,
but if I drink human blood, my vision gets better.
What?

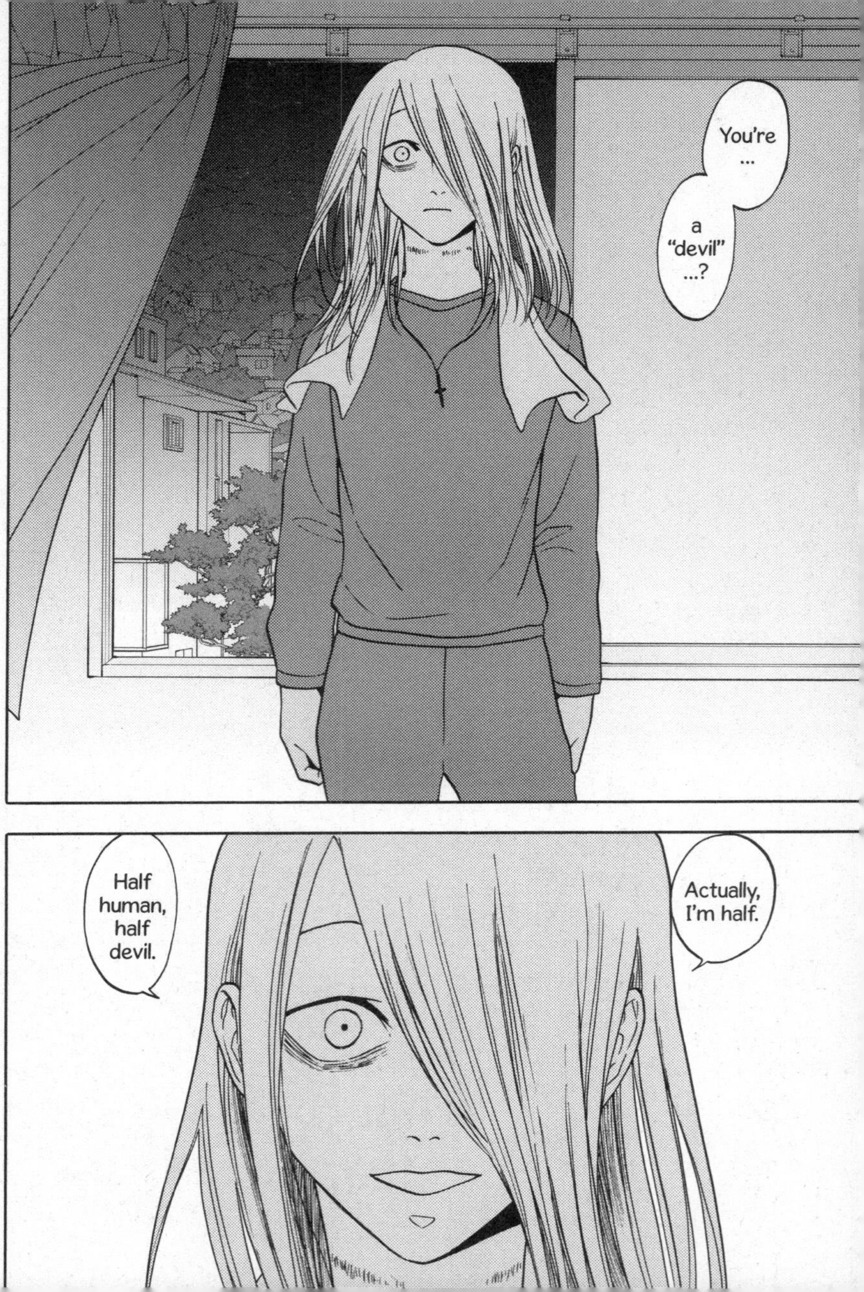
You're ...
a "devil" ...?
Actually, I'm half.
Half human, half devil.

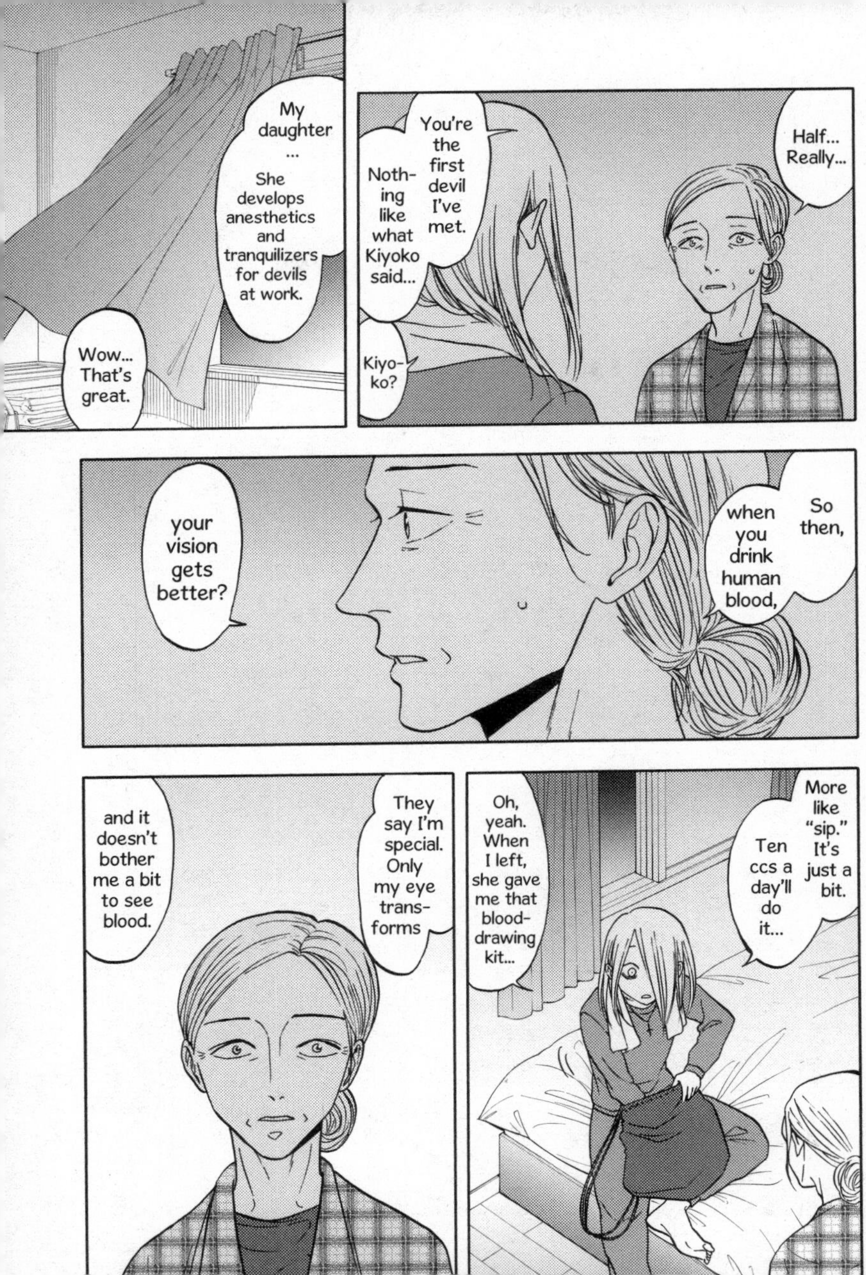
Half... Really...
You're the first devil I've met.
Nothing like what Kiyoko said...
Kiyoko?
My daughter ... She develops anesthetics and tranquilizers for devils at work.
Wow... That's great.
So then, when you drink human blood,
your vision gets better?
More like "sip." It's just a bit.
Ten ccs a day'll do it...
Oh, yeah. When I left, she gave me that blood-drawing kit...
They say I'm special. Only my eye transforms
and it doesn't bother me a bit to see blood.

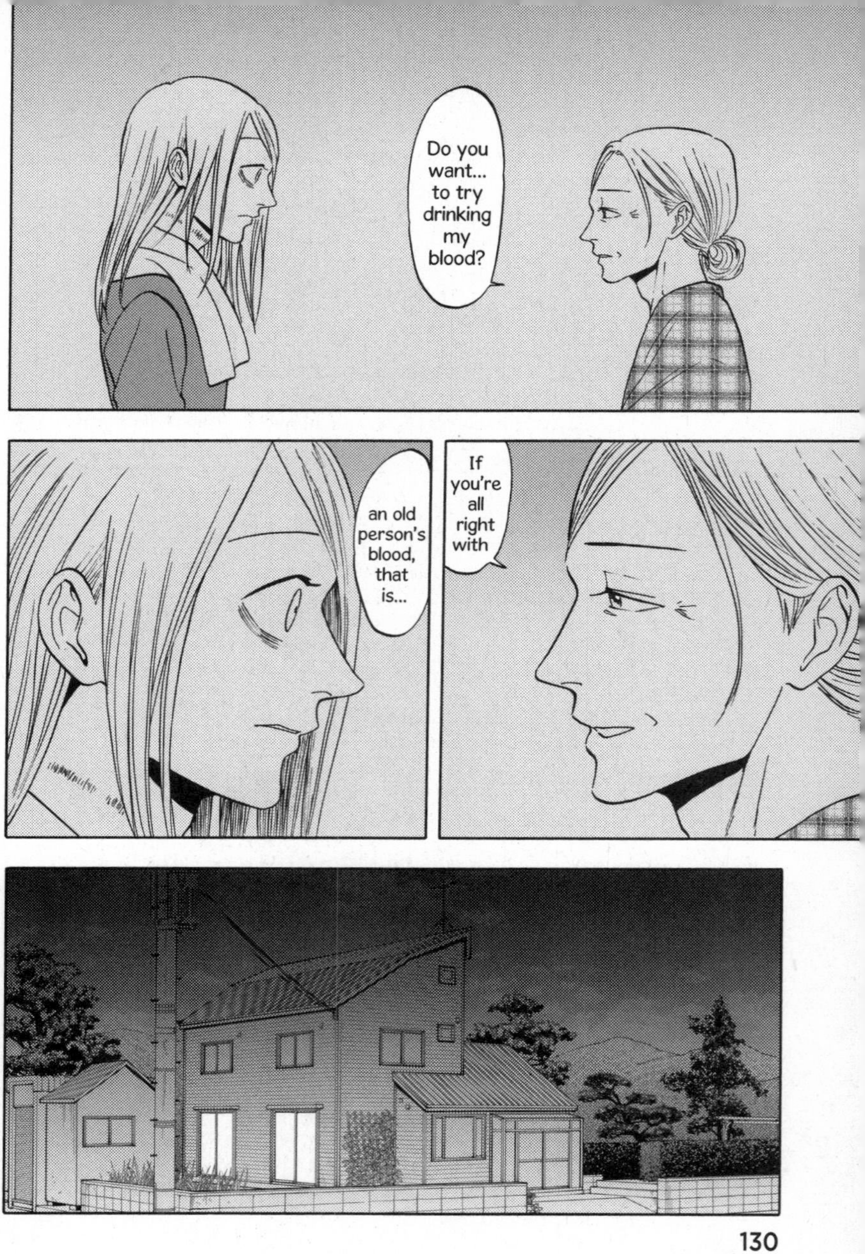
Do you want... to try drinking my blood?
If you're all right with
an old person's blood, that is...

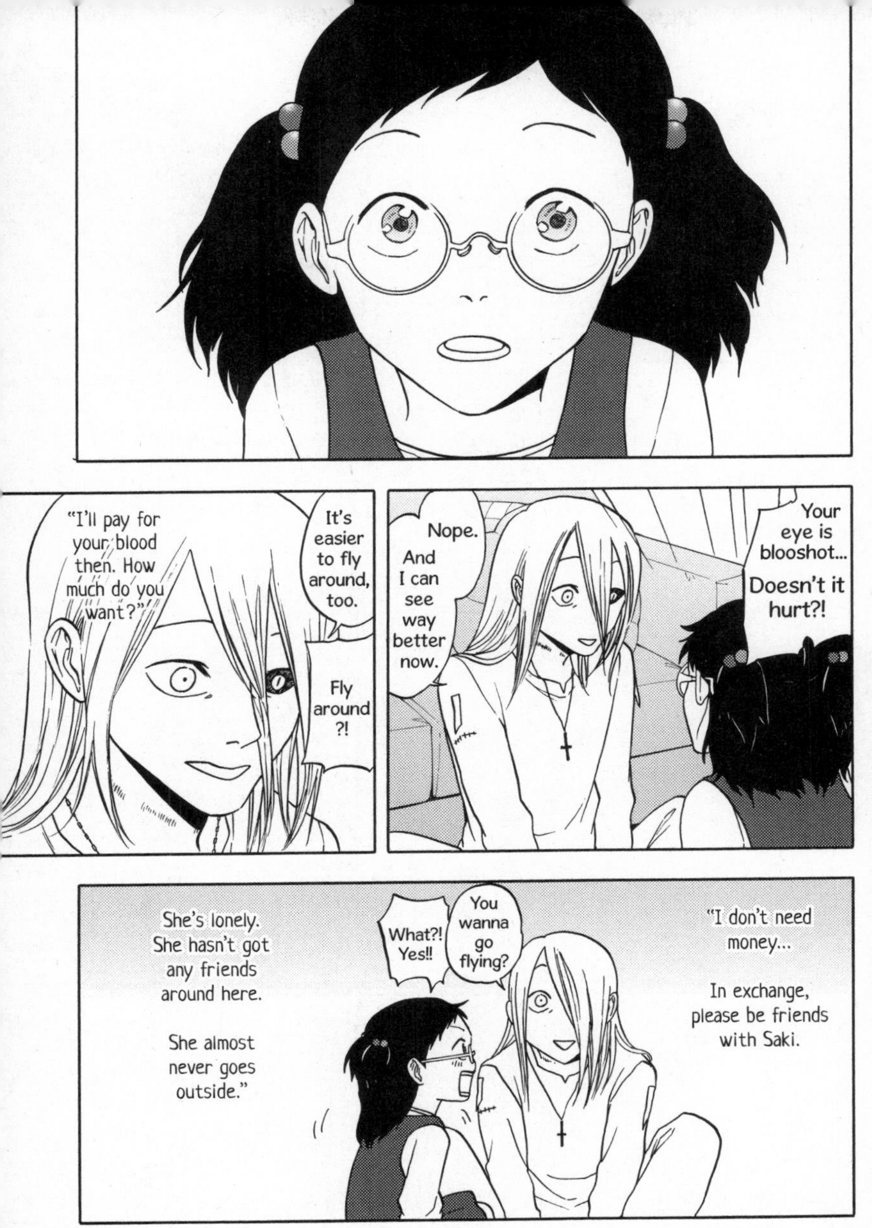
Your eye is blooshot...
Doesn't it hurt?!
Nope.
And I can see way better now.
It's easier to fly around, too.
Fly around ?!
"I'll pay for your blood then. How much do you want?"
"I don't need money...
In exchange, please be friends with Saki.
You wanna go flying?
What?! Yes!!
She's lonely. She hasn't got any friends around here.
She almost never goes outside."

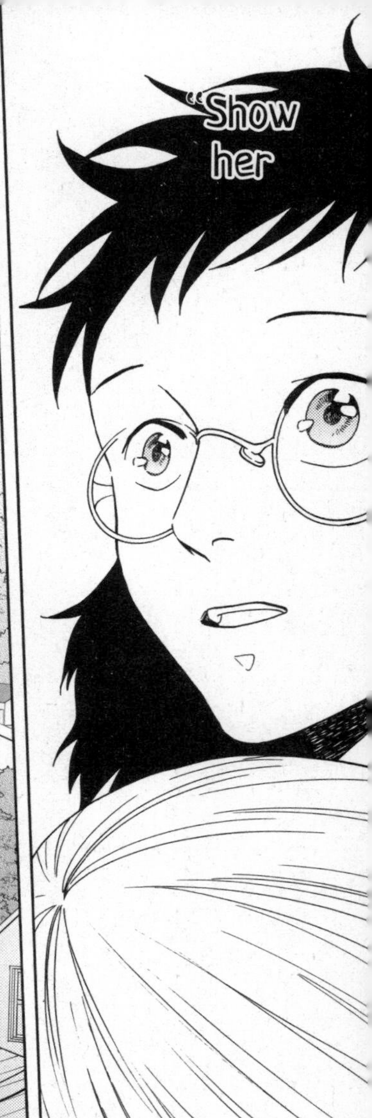
"Show her
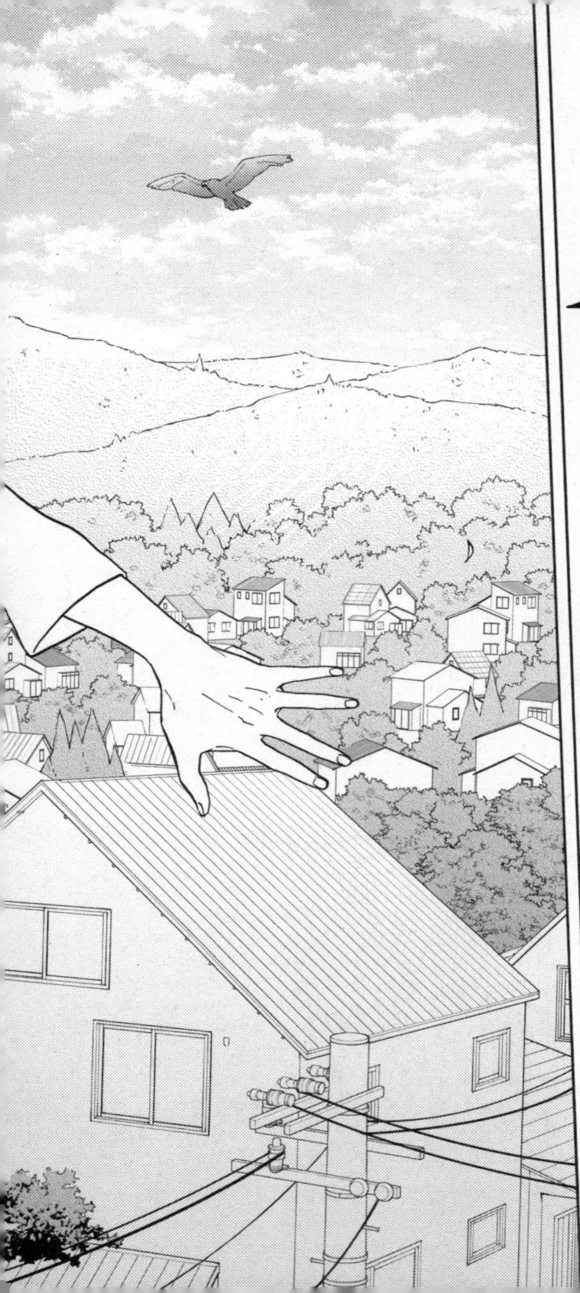

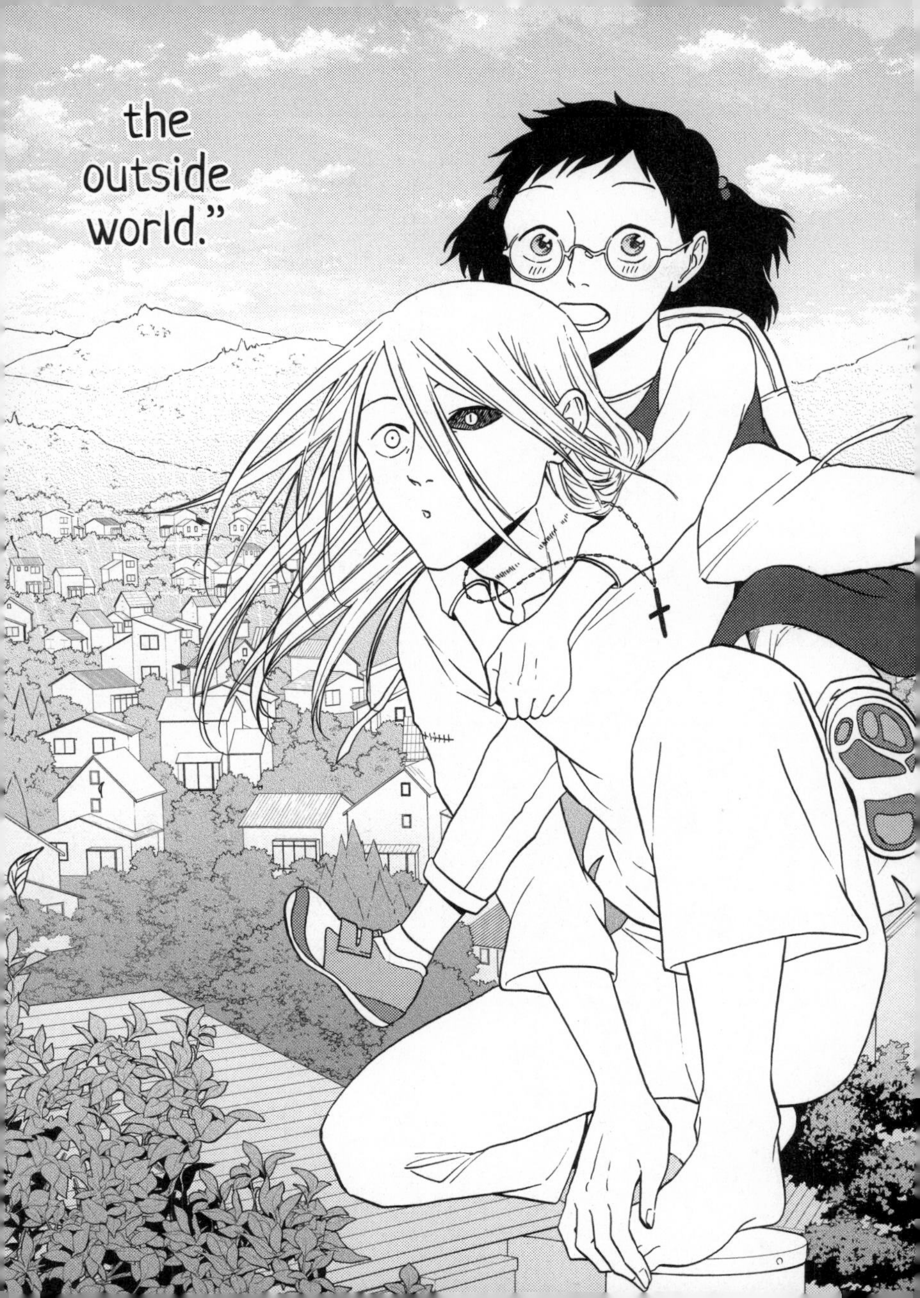
the outside world."

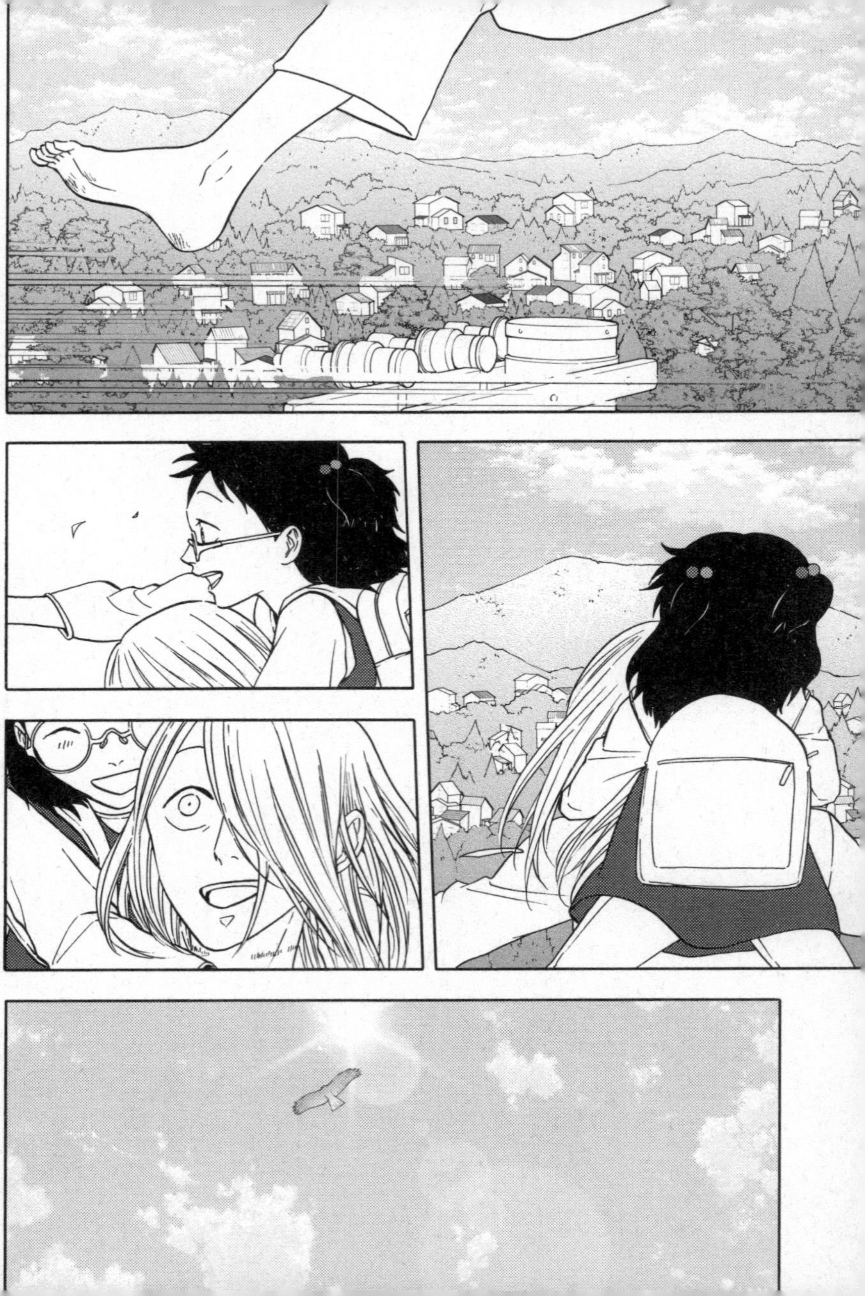

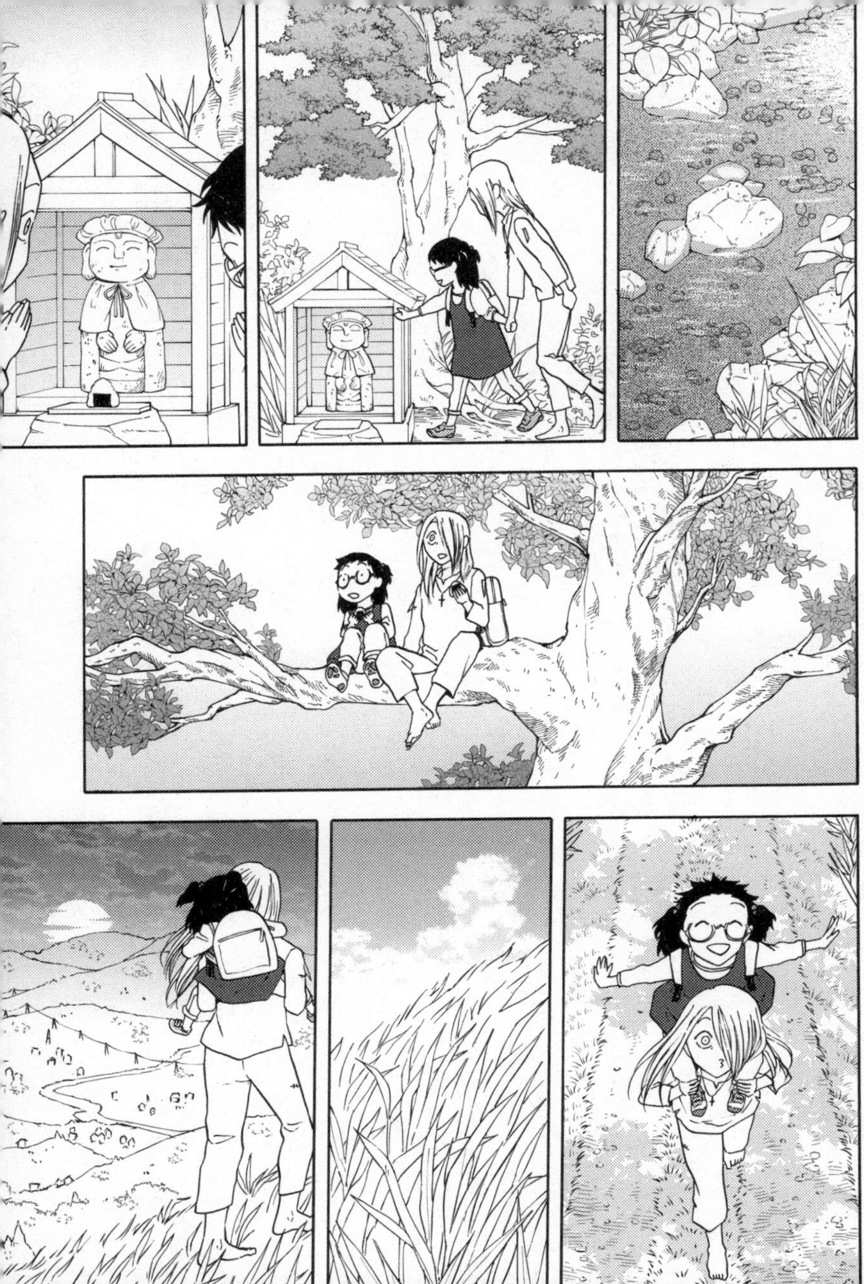

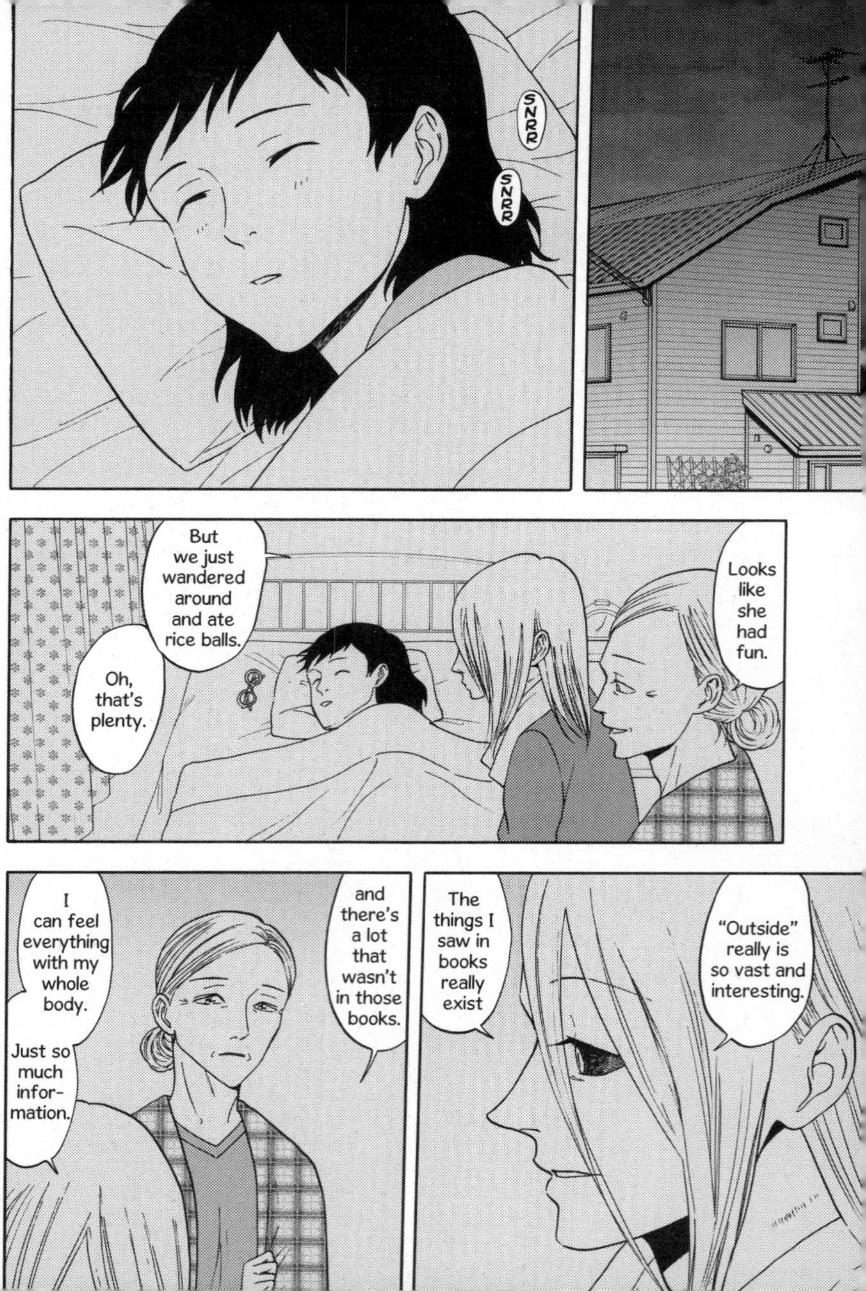
SNRR
SNRR
Looks like she had fun.
But we just wandered around and ate rice balls.
Oh, that's plenty.
“Outside” really is so vast and interesting.
The things I saw in books really exist
and there's a lot that wasn't in those books.
I can feel everything with my whole body.
Just so much information.

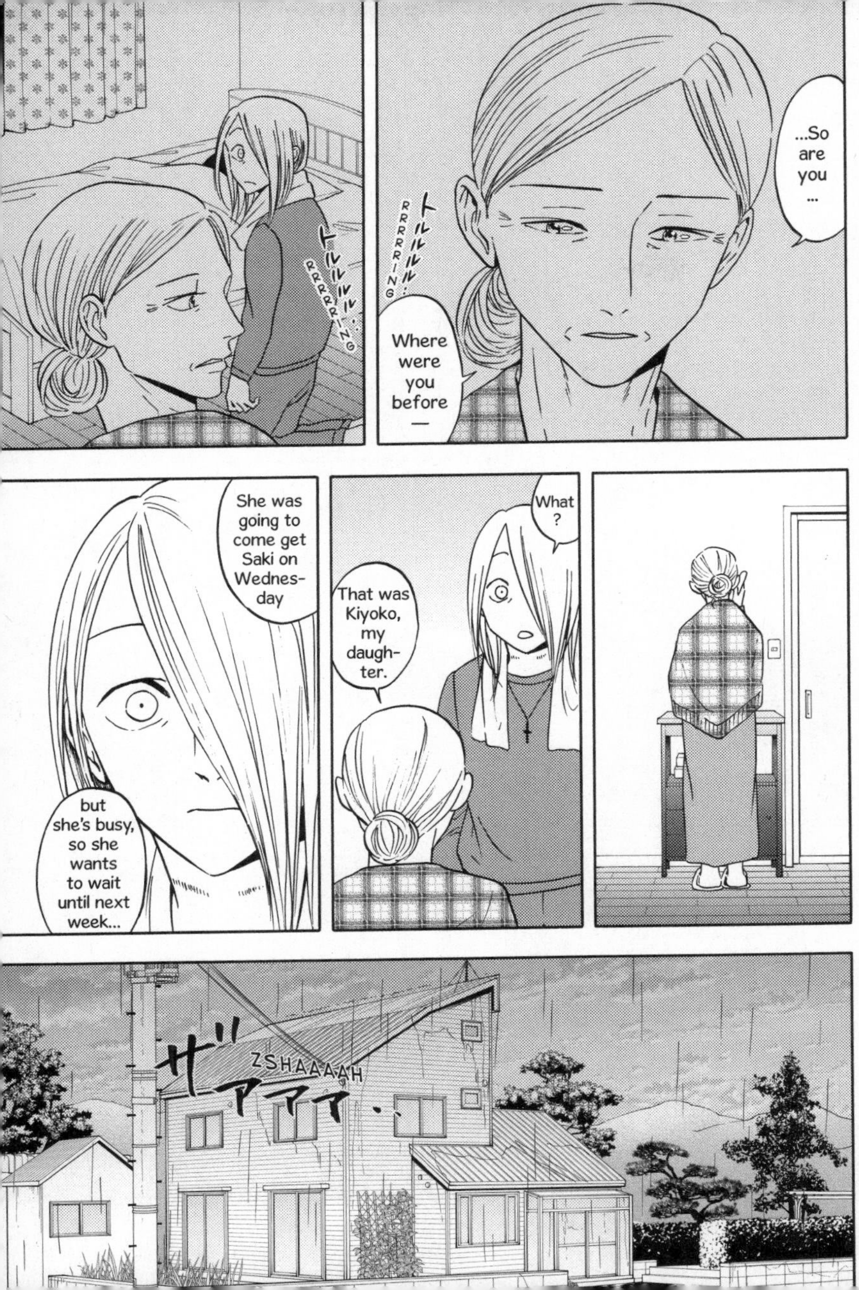
...So are you ...
トゥルルル
RRRRRING
Where were you before —
トゥルルル・・・
RRRRRING
What?
That was Kiyoko, my daughter.
She was going to come get Saki on Wednesday
but she's busy, so she wants to wait until next week...
ザアアア
ZSHAAAAH

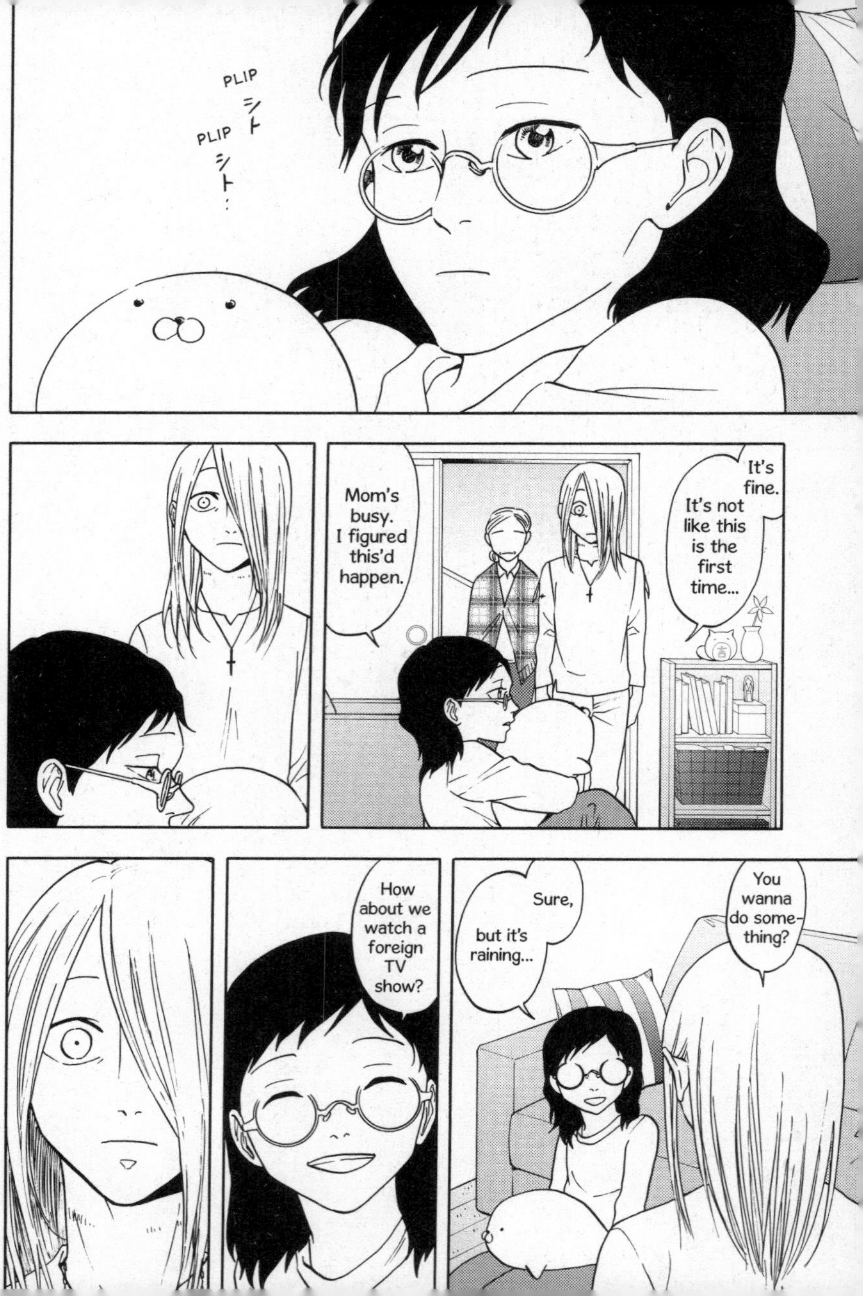
PLIP
シト
PLIP
シト
It's fine. It's not like this is the first time...
Mom's busy. I figured this'd happen.
You wanna do something?
Sure,
but it's raining...
How about we watch a foreign TV show?

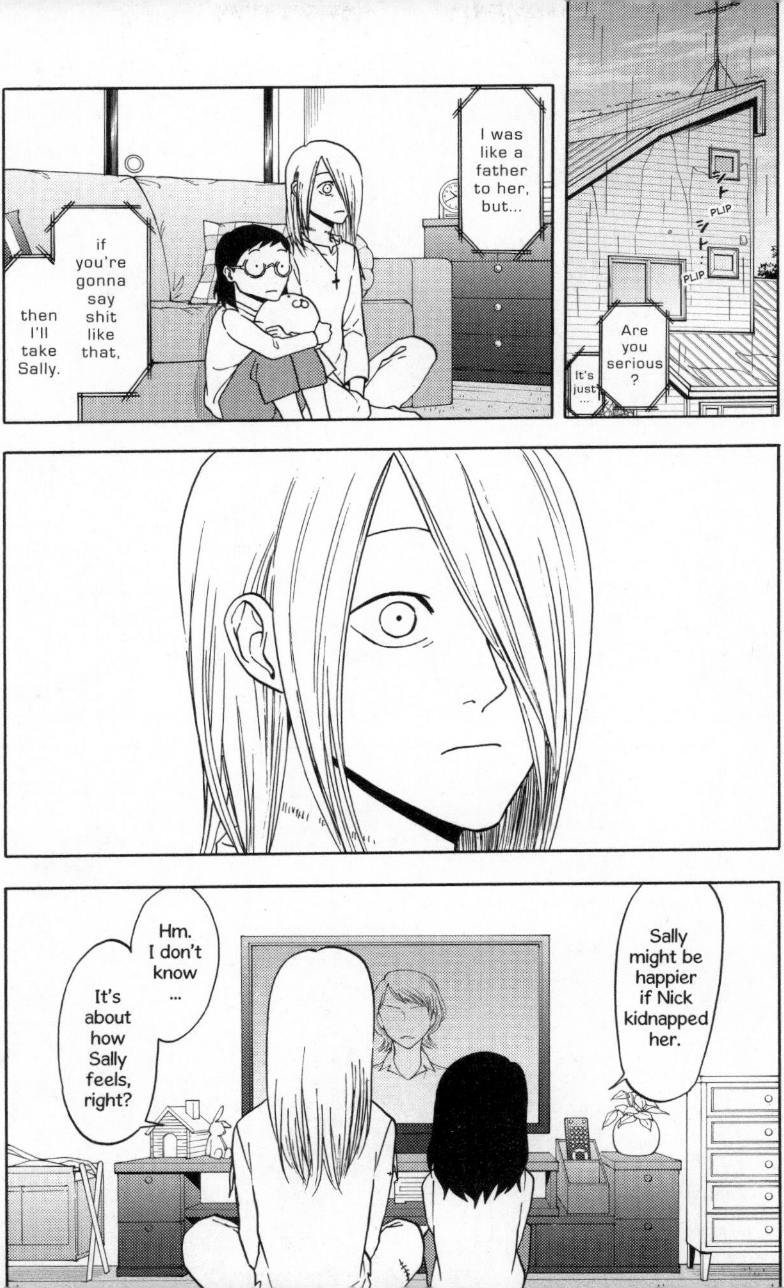
PLIP
PLIP
Are you serious?
It's just...
I was like a father to her, but...
if you're gonna say shit like that,
then I'll take Sally.
Sally might be happier if Nick kidnapped her.
Hm. I don't know...
It's about how Sally feels, right?

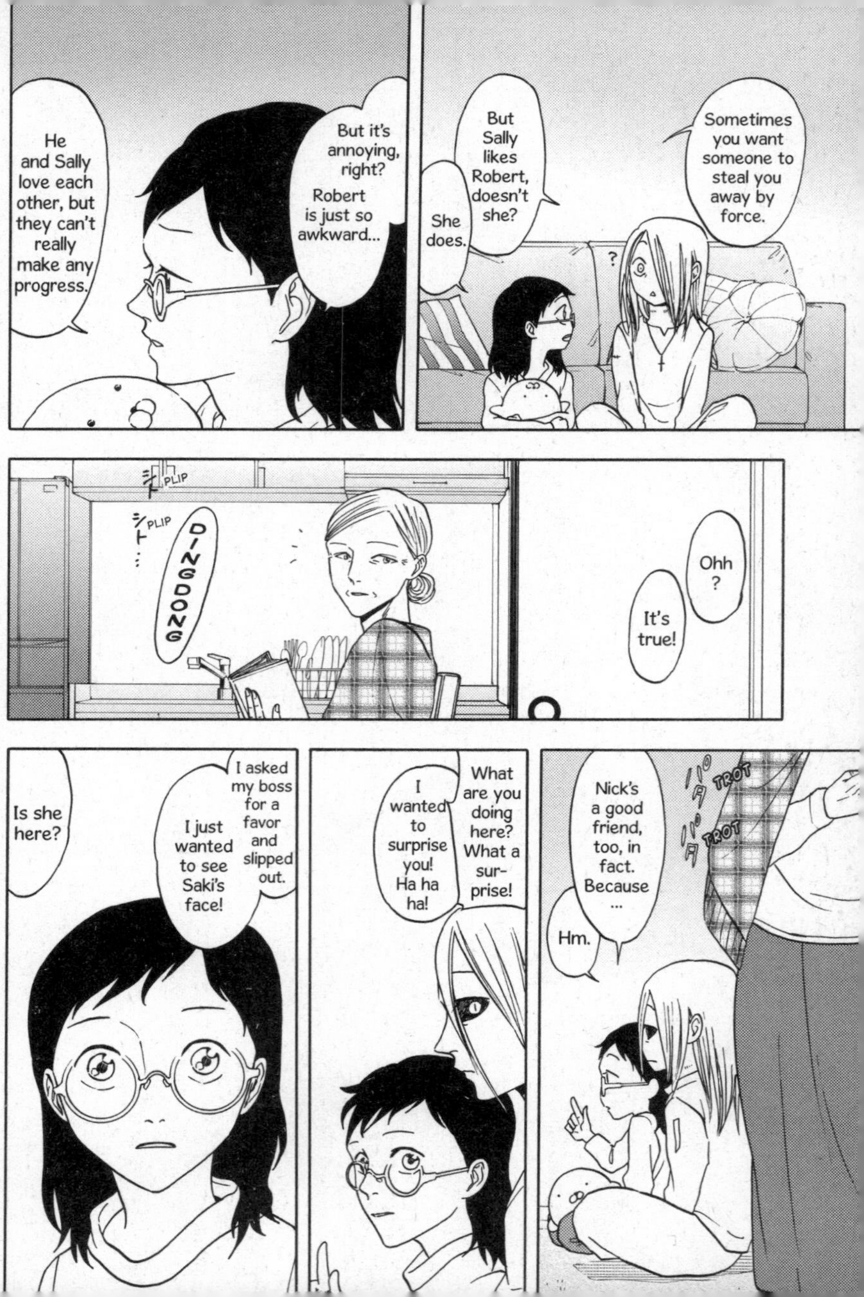
Sometimes you want someone to steal you away by force.
?
But Sally likes Robert, doesn't she?
She does.
But it's annoying, right?
Robert is just so awkward...
He and Sally love each other, but they can't really make any progress.
Ohh?
It's true!
DINGDONG
PLIP
PLIP
TROT
TROT
Nick's a good friend, too, in fact. Because ...
Hm.
What are you doing here? What a surprise!
I wanted to surprise you! Ha ha ha!
I asked my boss for a favor and slipped out.
I just wanted to see Saki's face!
Is she here?

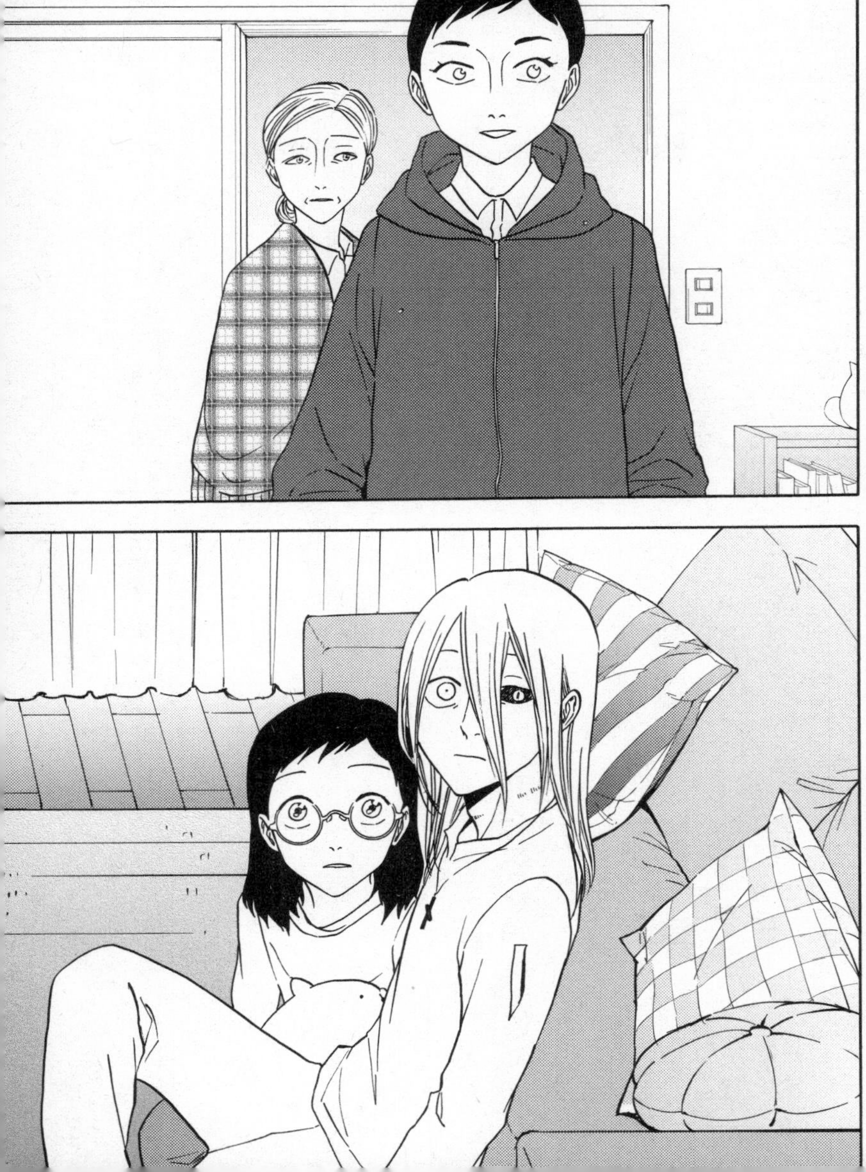

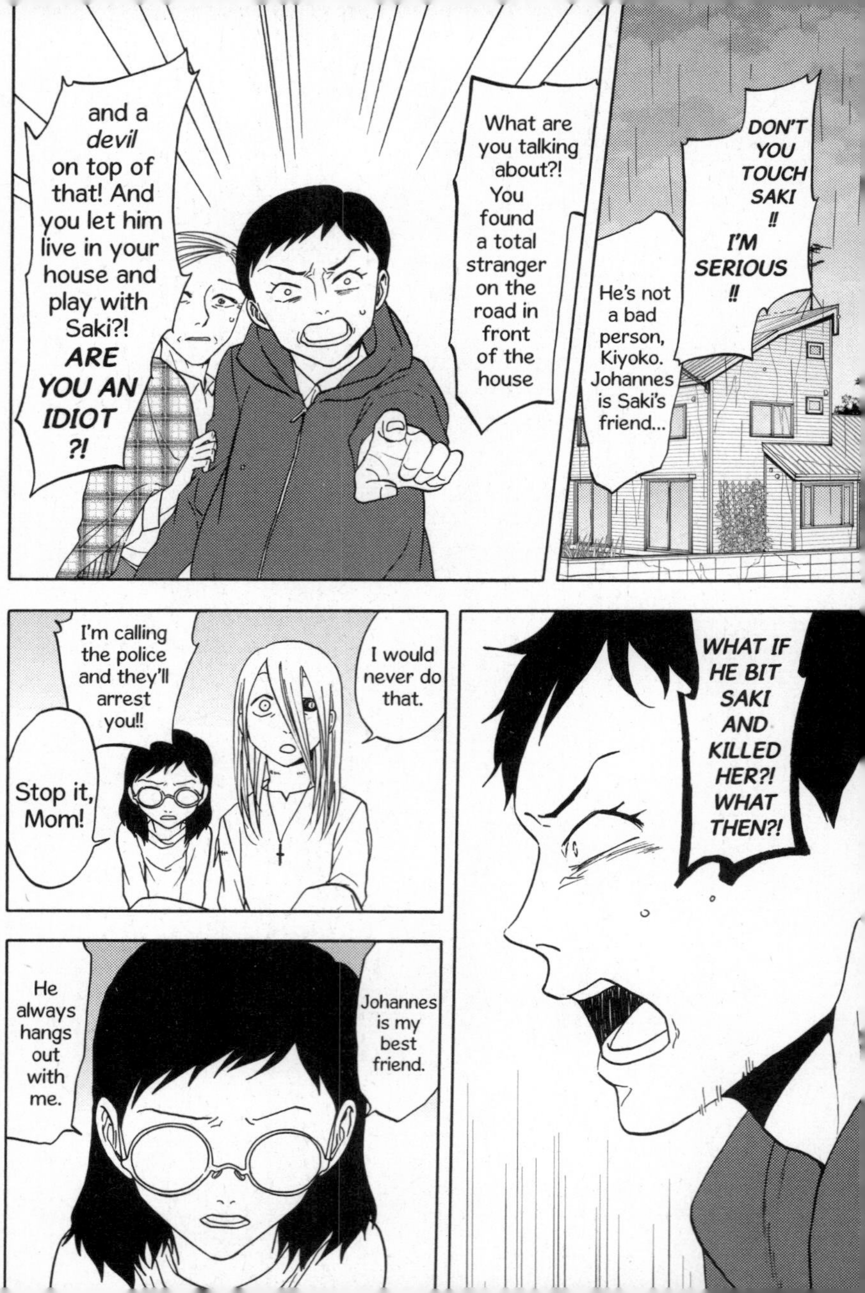
DON'T YOU TOUCH SAKI!! I'M SERIOUS!!
He's not a bad person, Kiyoko. Johannes is Saki's friend...
What are you talking about?! You found a total stranger on the road in front of the house
and a *devil* on top of that! And you let him live in your house and play with Saki?! ARE YOU AN IDIOT?!
WHAT IF HE BIT SAKI AND KILLED HER?! WHAT THEN?!
I would never do that.
I'm calling the police and they'll arrest you!!
Stop it, Mom!
Johannes is my best friend.
He always hangs out with me.

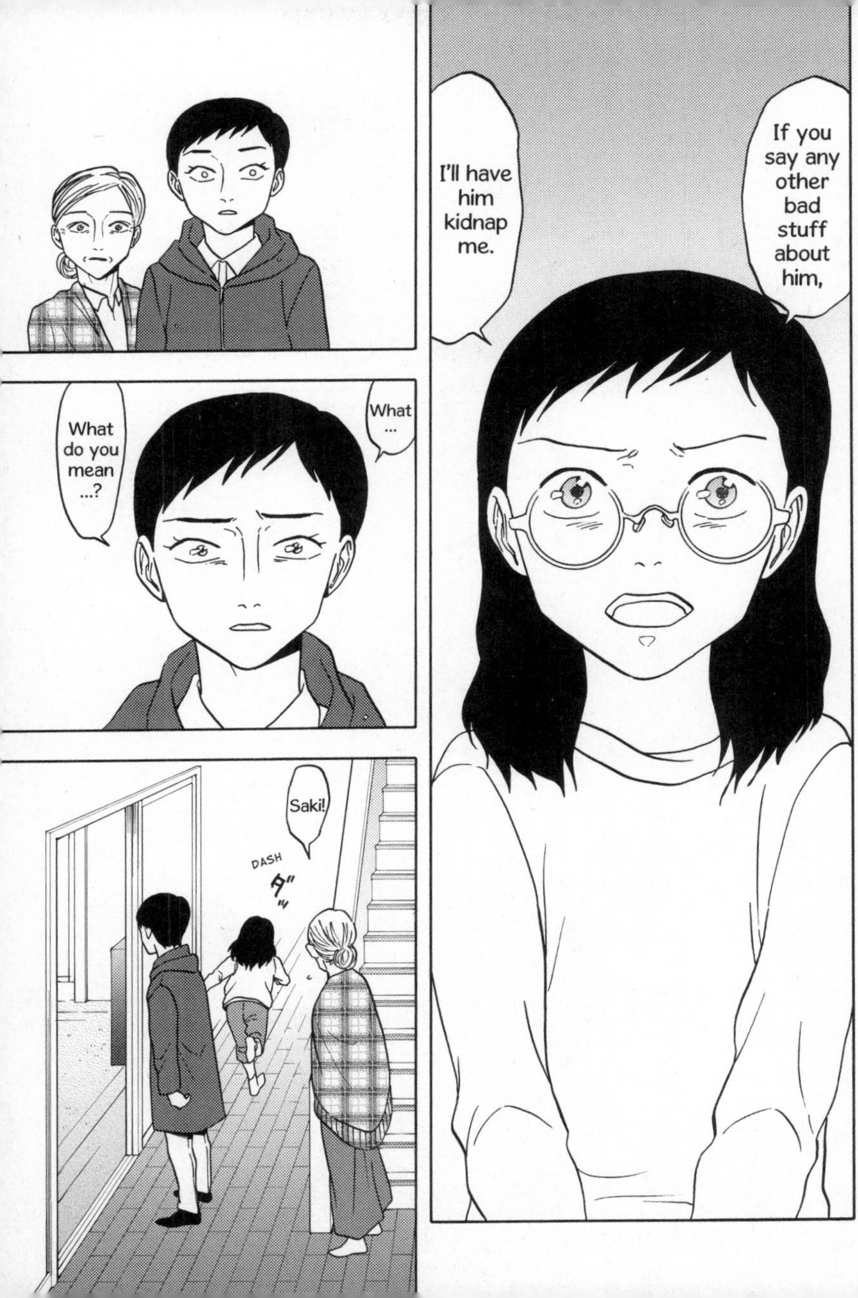

If you say any other bad stuff about him,
I'll have him kidnap me.
What ...
What do you mean ...?
Saki!
DASH
ダッ

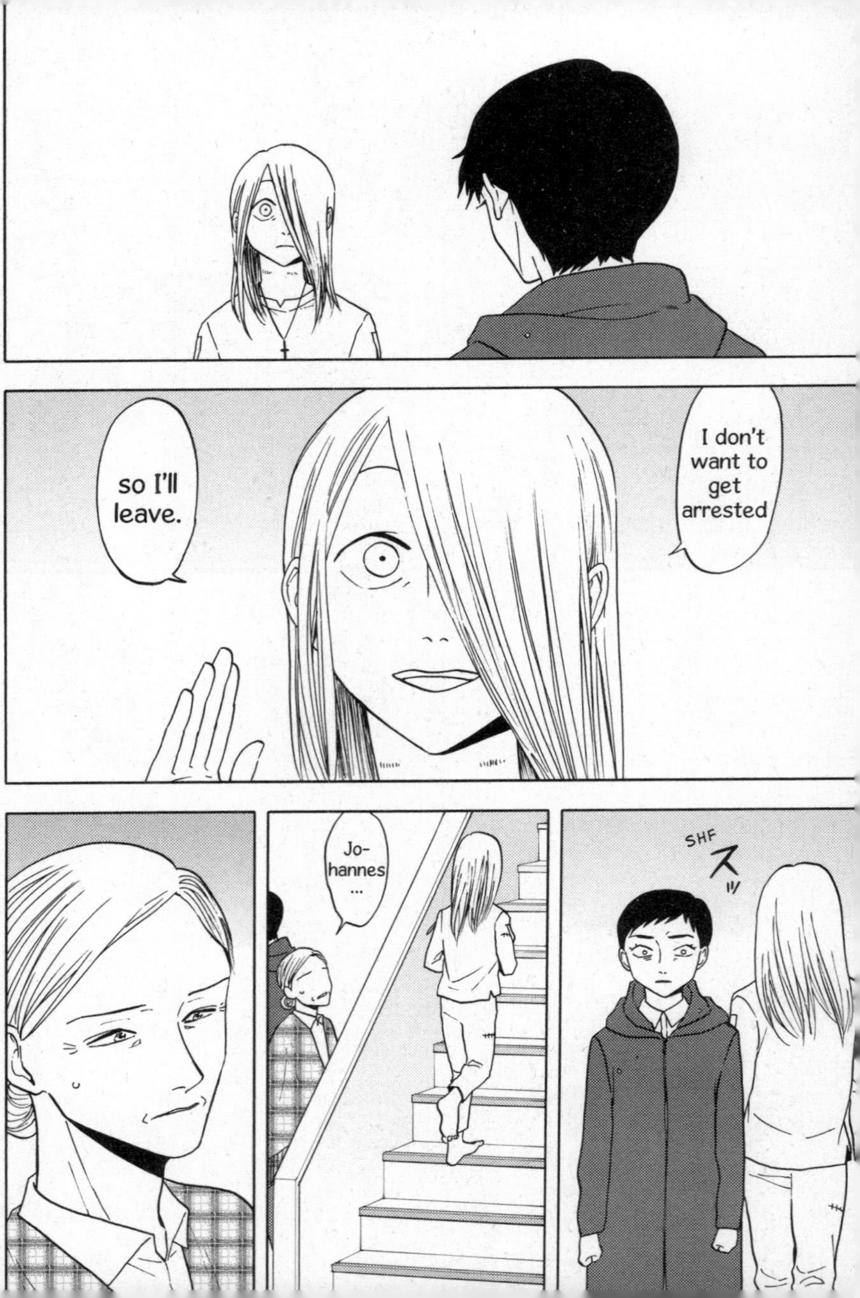
I don't want to get arrested
so I'll leave.
SHF
スッ
Jo-hannes ...

Jo-
hannes,
wait.

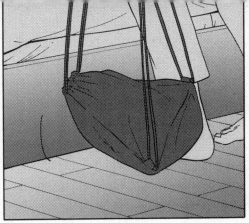

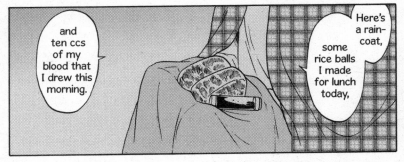

and
ten ccs
of my
blood that
I drew this
morning.

Here's
a rain-
coat,
some
rice balls
I made
for lunch
today,

Tell
Saki

I'll
take
off
from
up
here,
okay?

It's
fine.

I'm
sorry.
My
daugh-
ter's
...

Are
you
sure
?

This is
super
helpful!

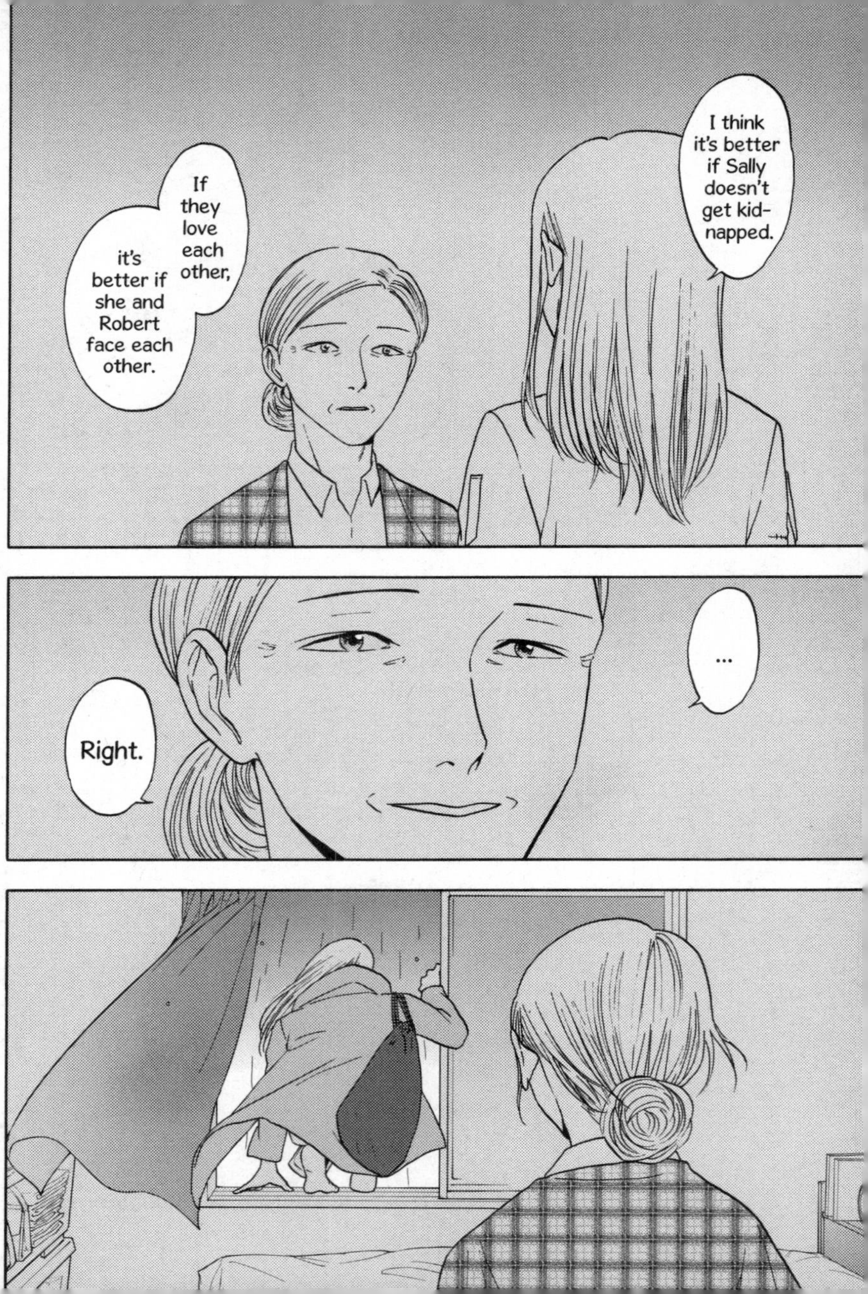
I think it's better if Sally doesn't get kid-napped.
If they love each other,
it's better if she and Robert face each other.
...
Right.

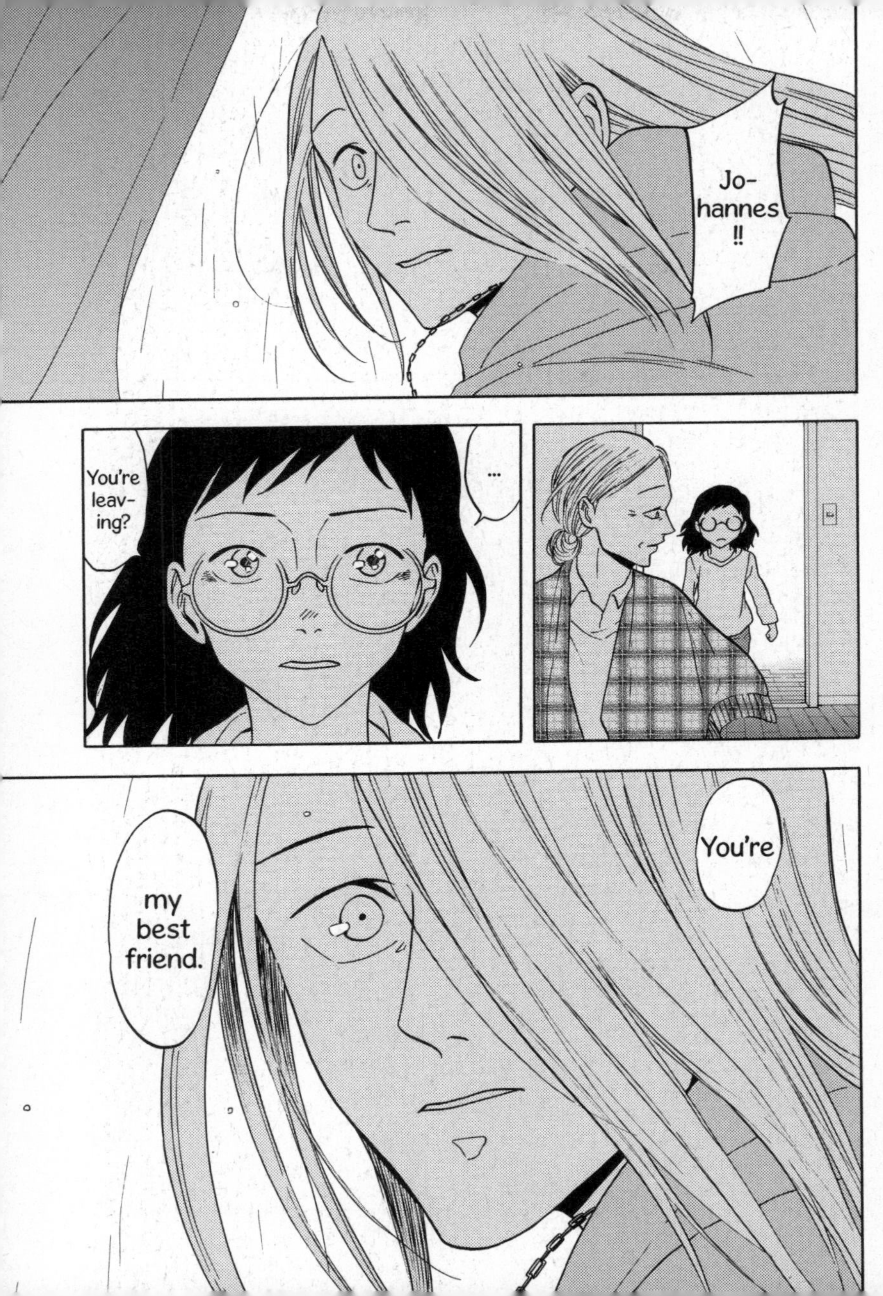
Jo-hannes!!
...
You're leav-ing?
You're
my best friend.

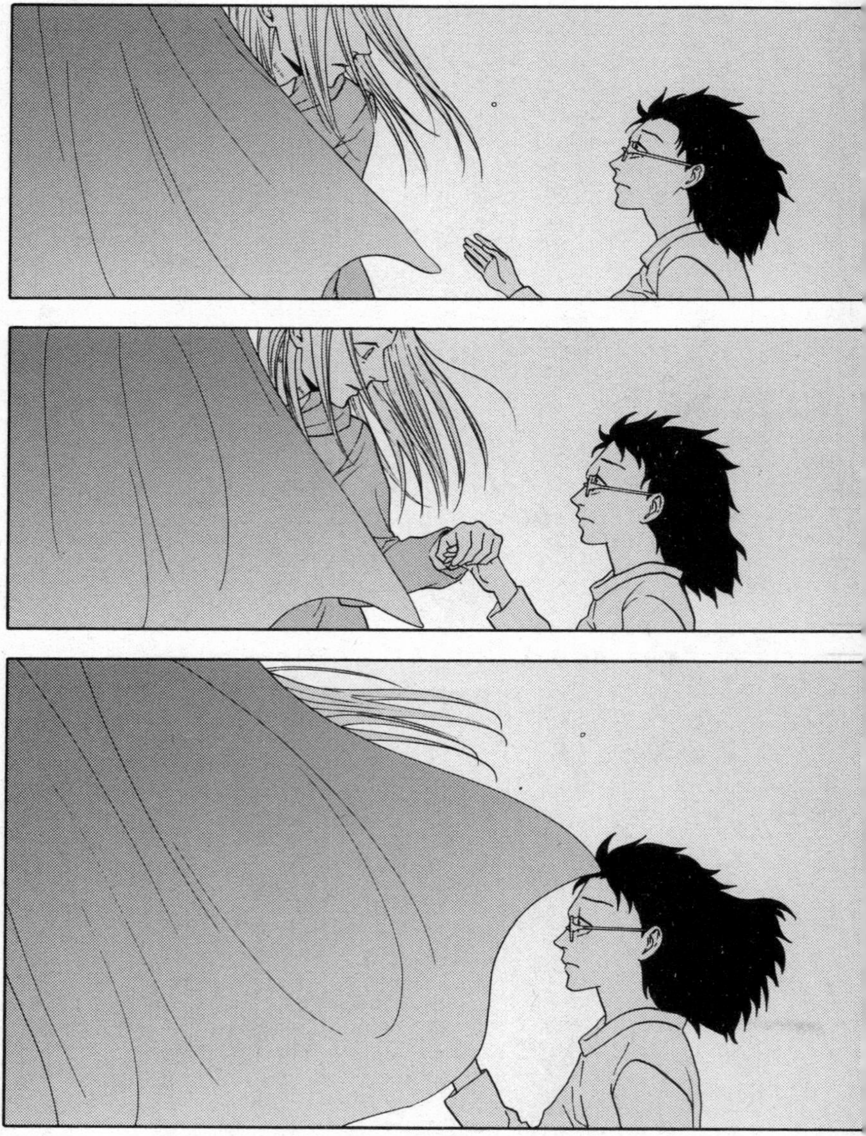

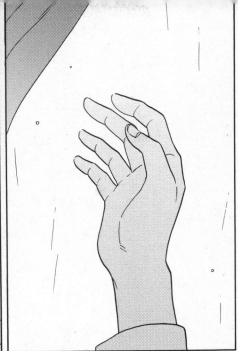

Thanks for being here for me.

Now go, Johannes.

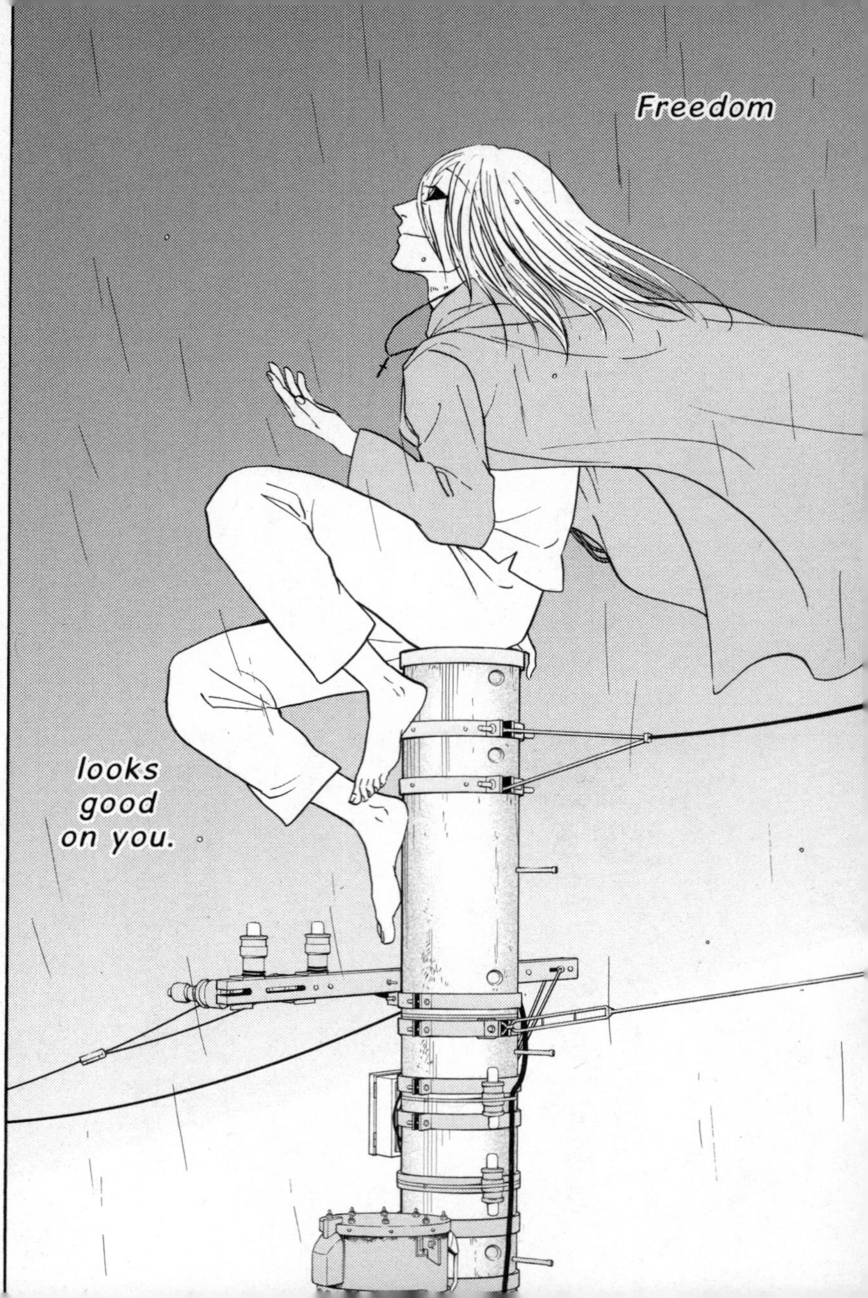
Freedom
looks good on you.

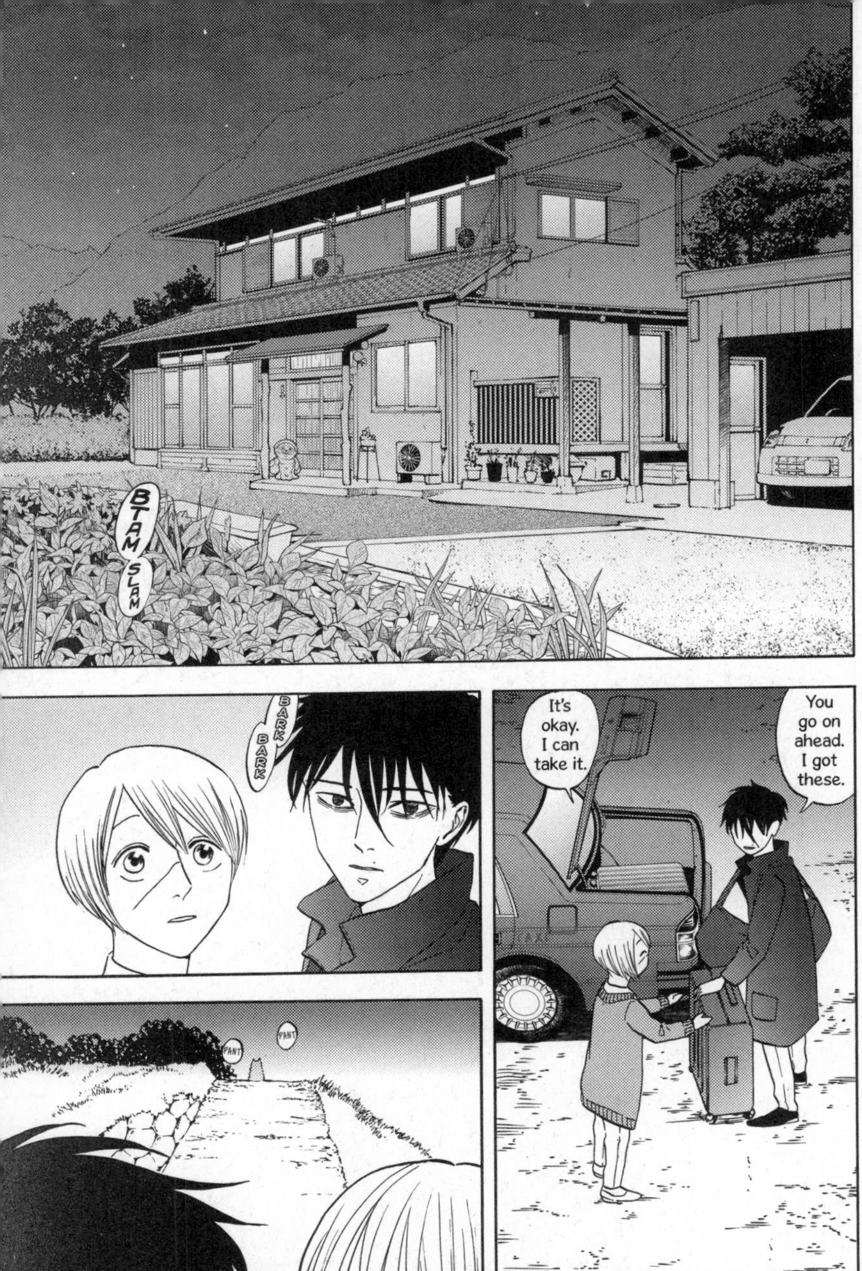
BTAM
SLAM
You go on ahead. I got these.
It's okay. I can take it.
BARK BARK
PANT
PANT

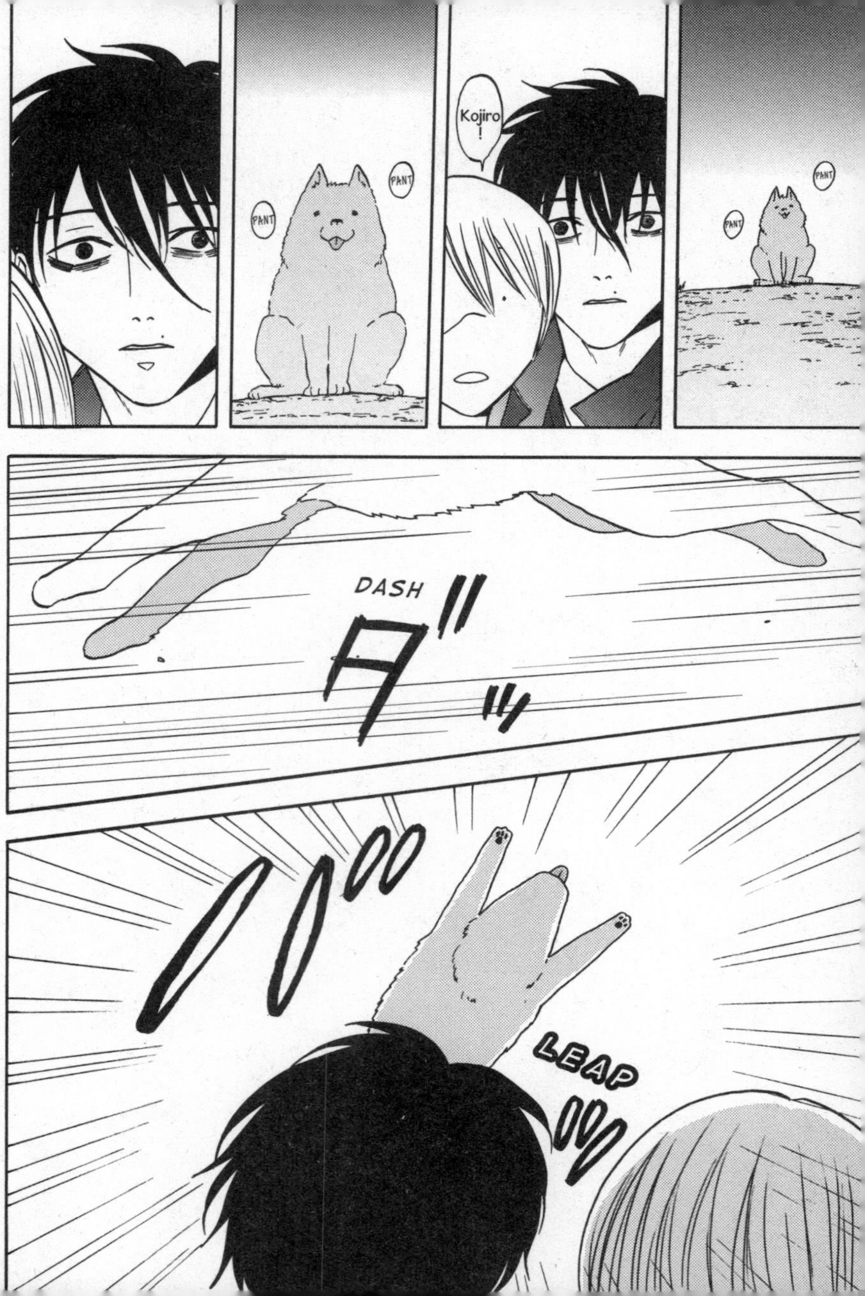
PANT
PANT
Kojiro!
PANT
PANT
DASH
ダッ
LEAP

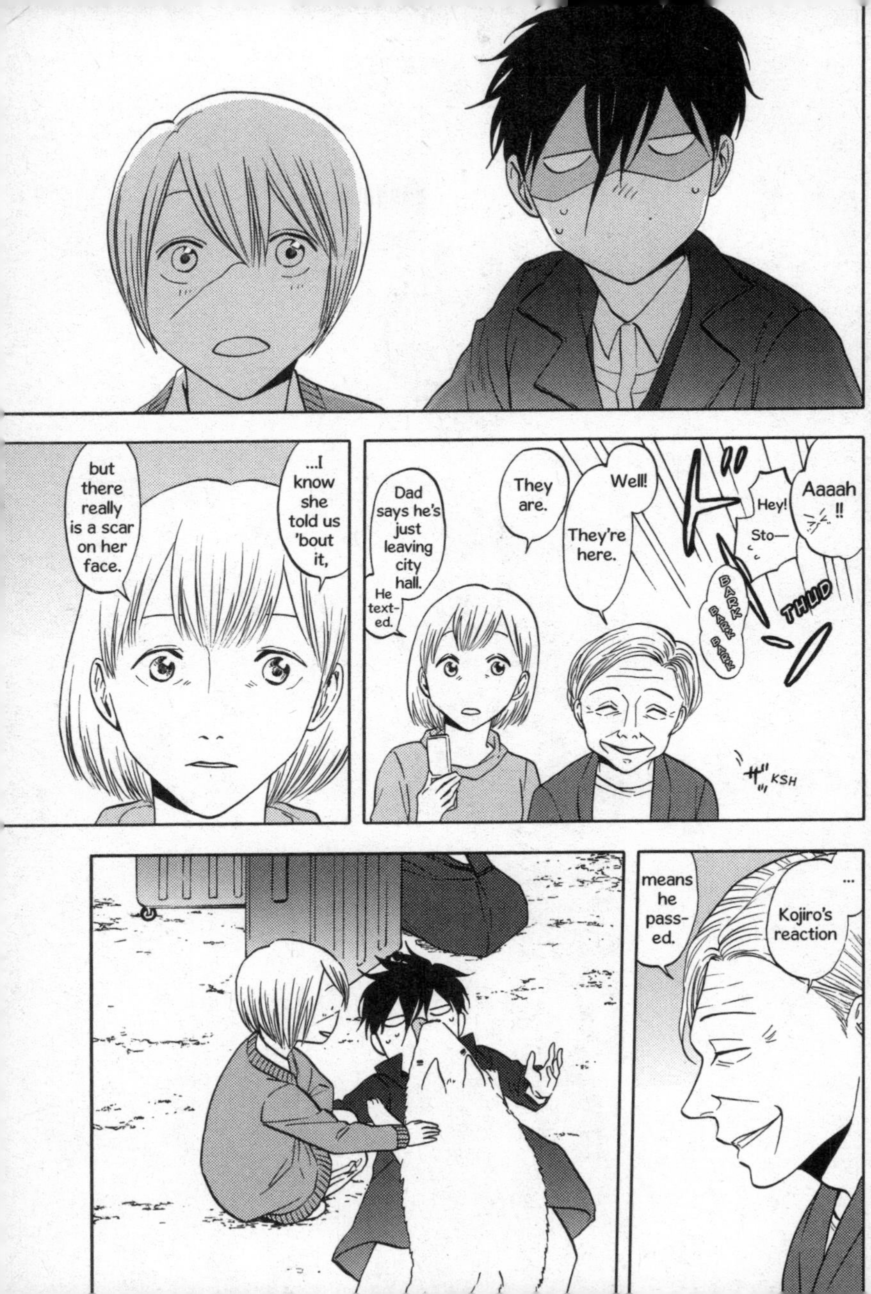
Aaaah!!
Hey! Sto—
THUD
BARK BARK BARK
Well! They're here.
They are.
Dad says he's just leaving city hall. He texted.
KSH
...I know she told us 'bout it,
but there really is a scar on her face.
... Kojiro's reaction
means he passed.

Line 69

Yuuki Anzai and Tsukasa Taira

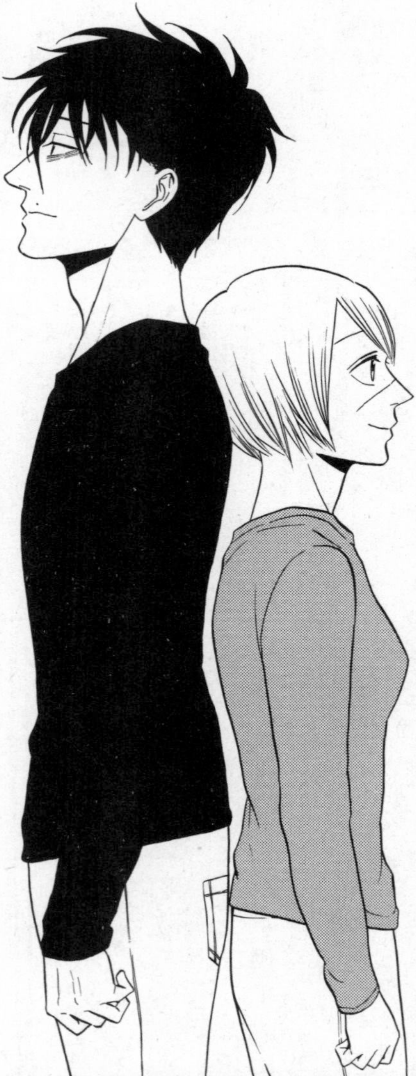

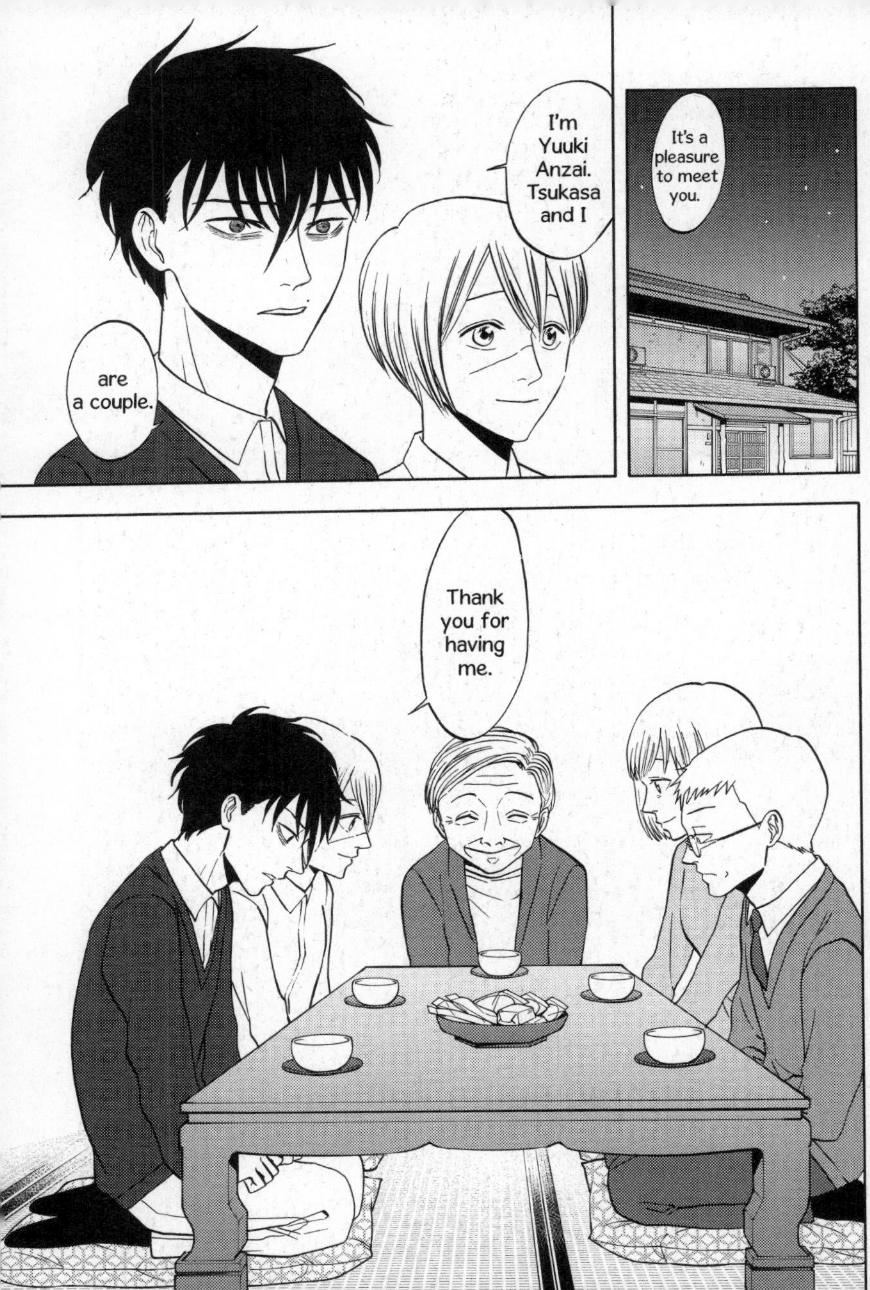
It's a pleasure to meet you.
I'm Yuuki Anzai. Tsukasa and I
are a couple.
Thank you for having me.

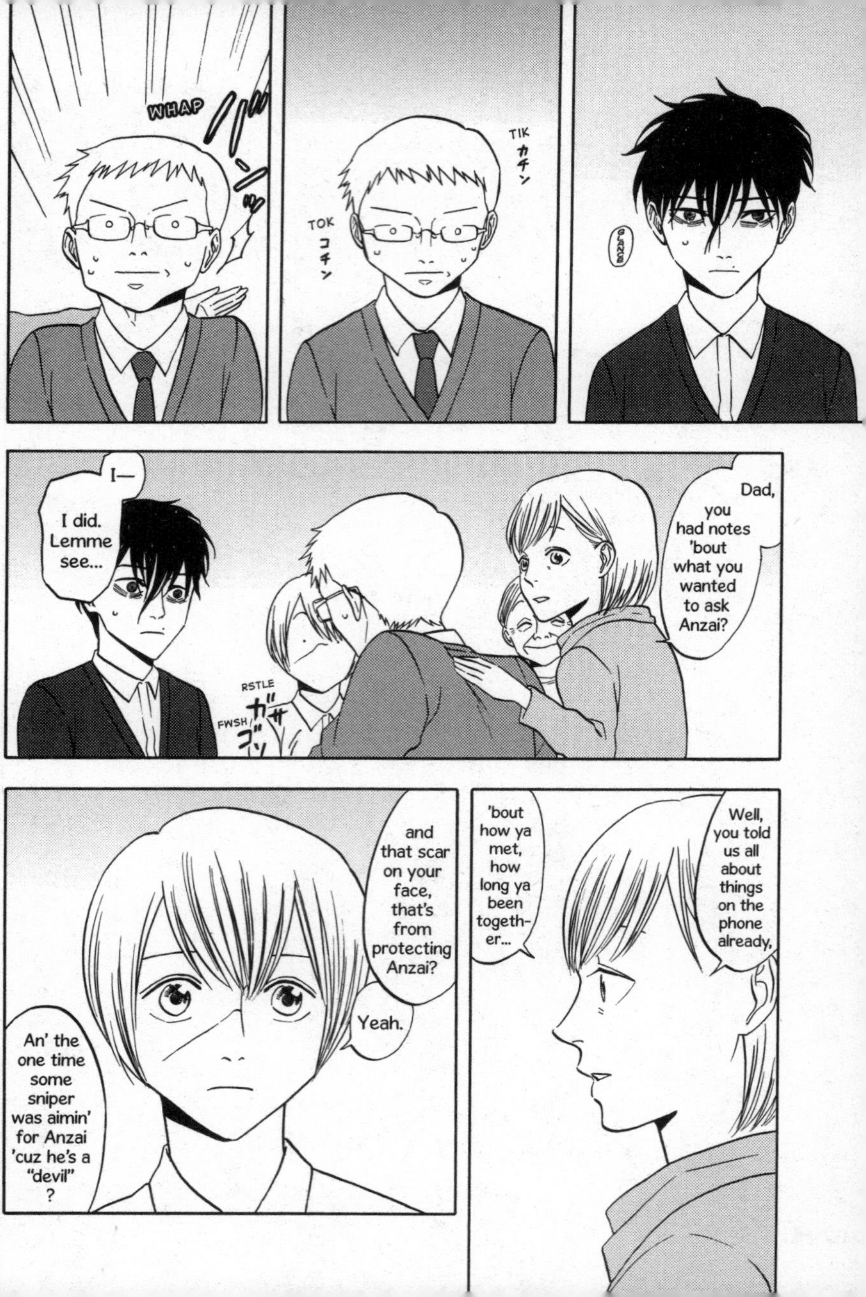
GLANCE
TIK カチン
TOK コチン
WHAP
Dad, you had notes 'bout what you wanted to ask Anzai?
RSTLE ガサ
FWSH ゴソ
I—
I did. Lemme see...
Well, you told us all about things on the phone already,
'bout how ya met, how long ya been togeth-er...
and that scar on your face, that's from protecting Anzai?
Yeah.
An' the one time some sniper was aimin' for Anzai 'cuz he's a "devil"?

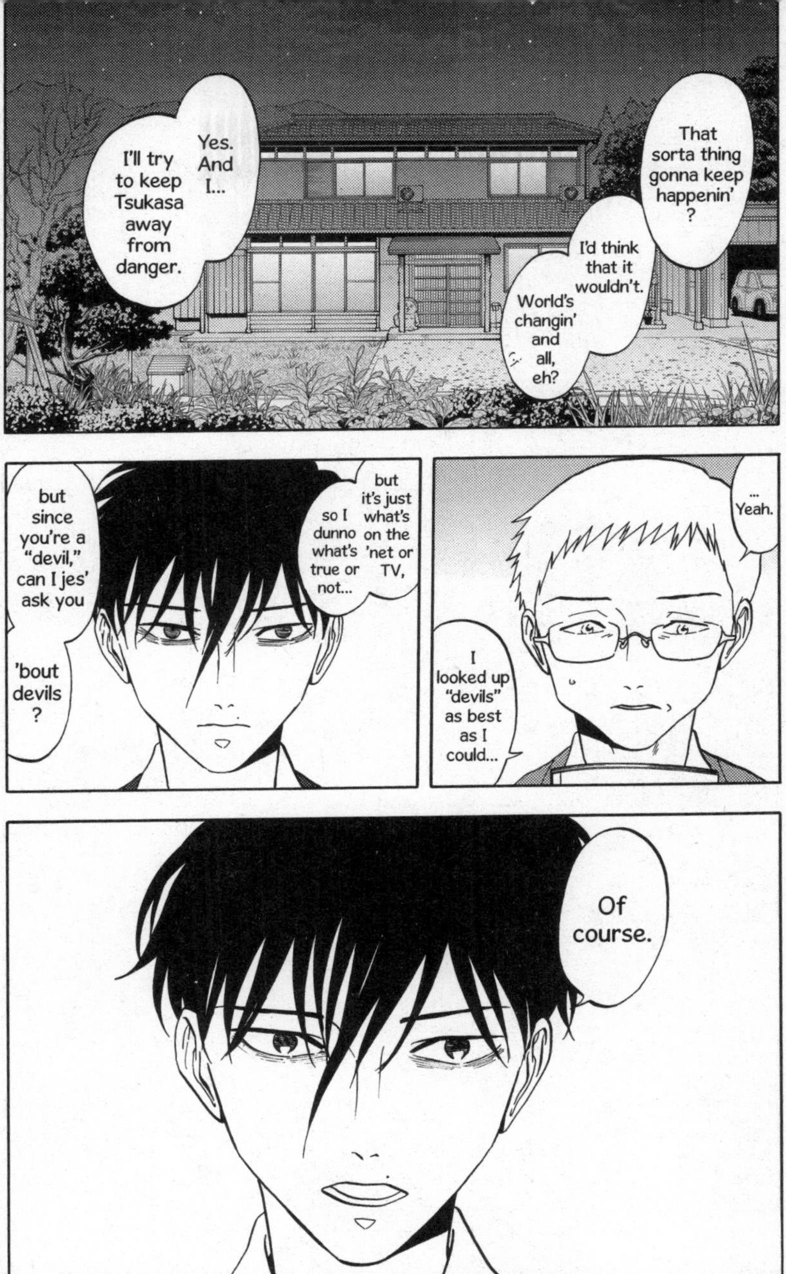
That sorta thing gonna keep happenin'?
I'd think that it wouldn't.
World's changin' and all, eh?
Yes. And I...
I'll try to keep Tsukasa away from danger.
... Yeah.
I looked up "devils" as best as I could...
but it's just what's on the 'net or TV,
so I dunno what's true or not...
but since you're a "devil," can I jes' ask you
'bout devils?
Of course.

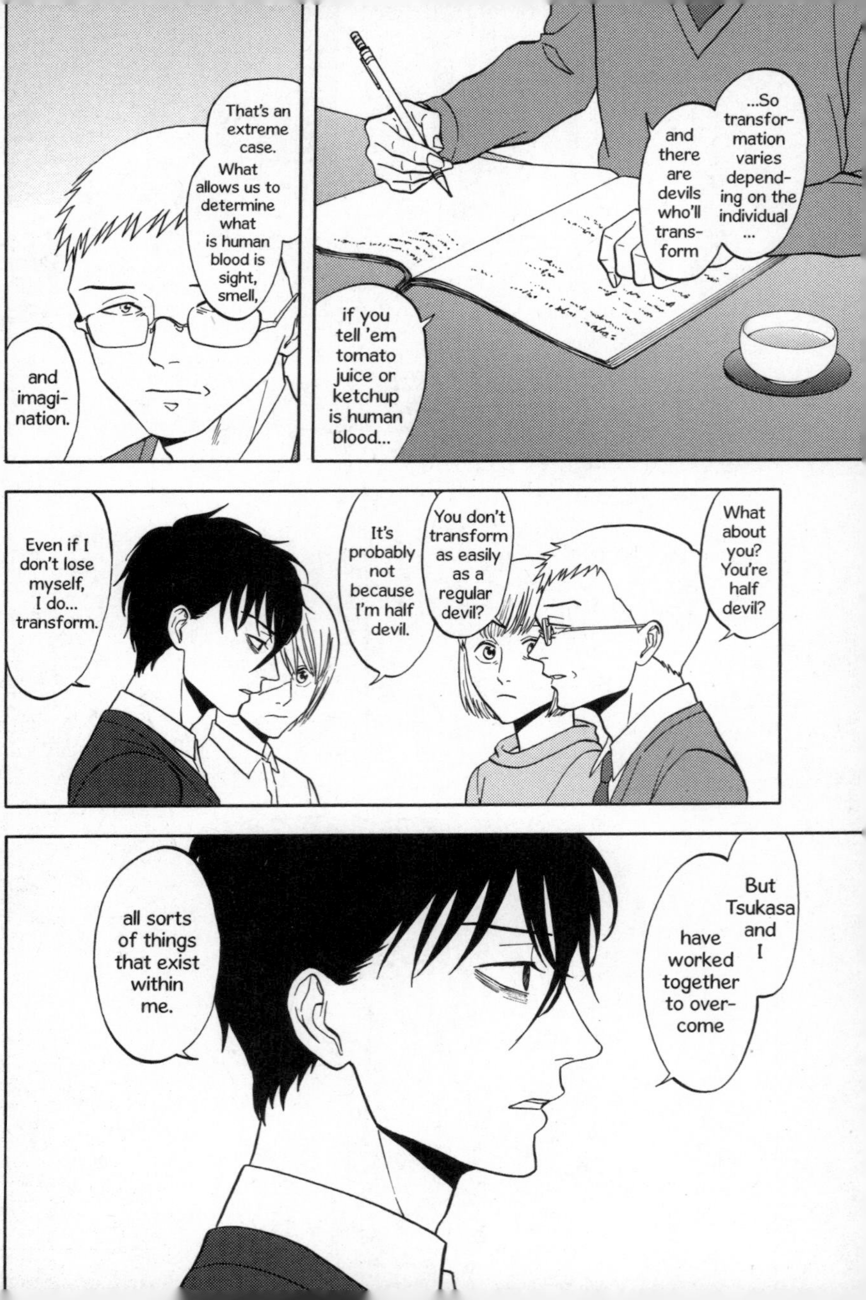
...So transformation varies depending on the individual...
and there are devils who'll transform
if you tell 'em tomato juice or ketchup is human blood...
That's an extreme case.
What allows us to determine what is human blood is sight, smell,
and imagination.
What about you? You're half devil?
You don't transform as easily as a regular devil?
It's probably not because I'm half devil.
Even if I don't lose myself, I do... transform.
But Tsukasa and I have worked together to overcome
all sorts of things that exist within me.

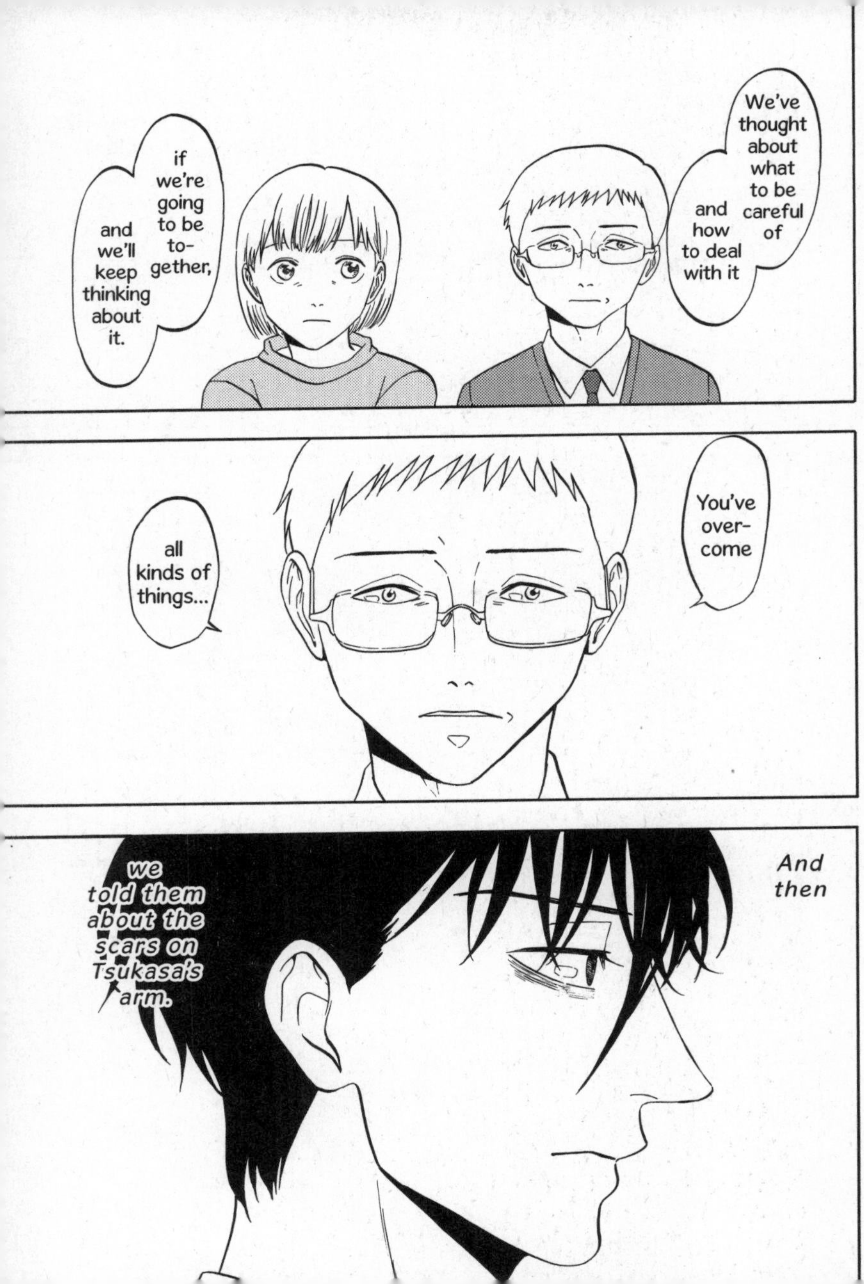
We've thought about what to be careful of
and how to deal with it
if we're going to be to- gether,
and we'll keep thinking about it.
You've over- come
all kinds of things...
And then
we told them about the scars on Tsukasa's arm.

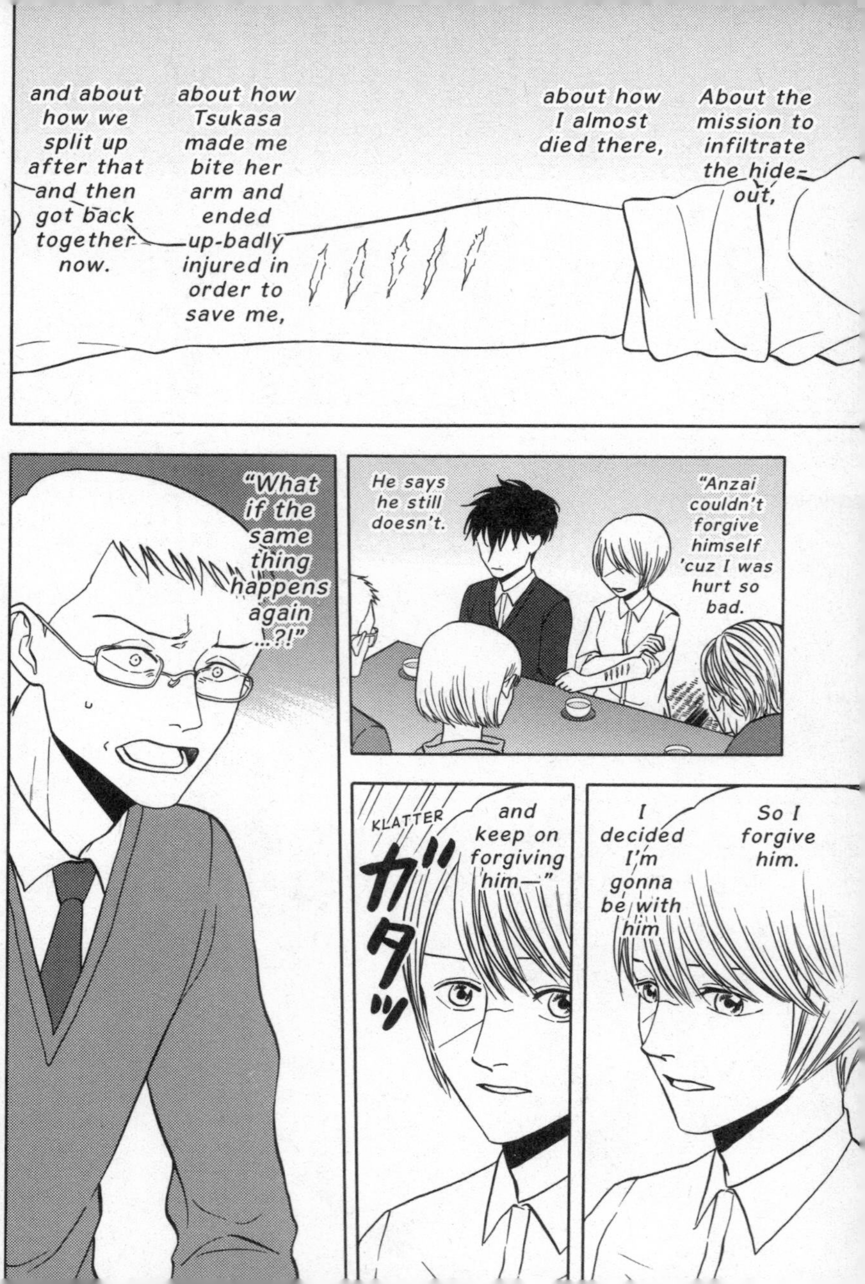
About the mission to infiltrate the hide-out,
about how I almost died there,
about how Tsukasa made me bite her arm and ended up badly injured in order to save me,
and about how we split up after that and then got back together now.
"Anzai couldn't forgive himself 'cuz I was hurt so bad.
He says he still doesn't.
So I forgive him.
I decided I'm gonna be with him
and keep on forgiving him—"
KLATTER
ガタッ
"What if the same thing happens again...?!"

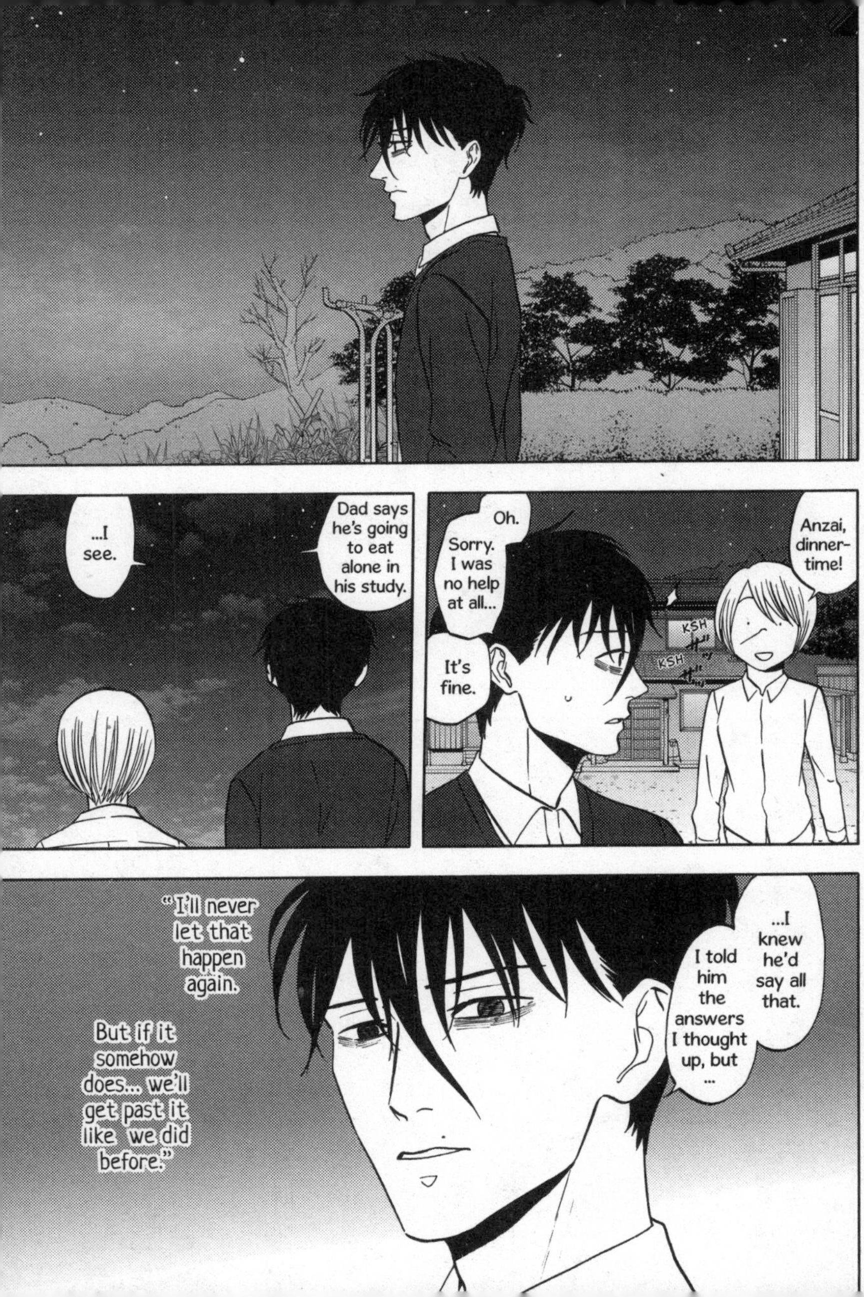
Anzai, dinner-time!
Oh. Sorry. I was no help at all...
KSH
KSH
It's fine.
Dad says he's going to eat alone in his study.
...I see.
...I knew he'd say all that.
I told him the answers I thought up, but ...
“I'll never let that happen again.
But if it somehow does... we'll get past it like we did before.”

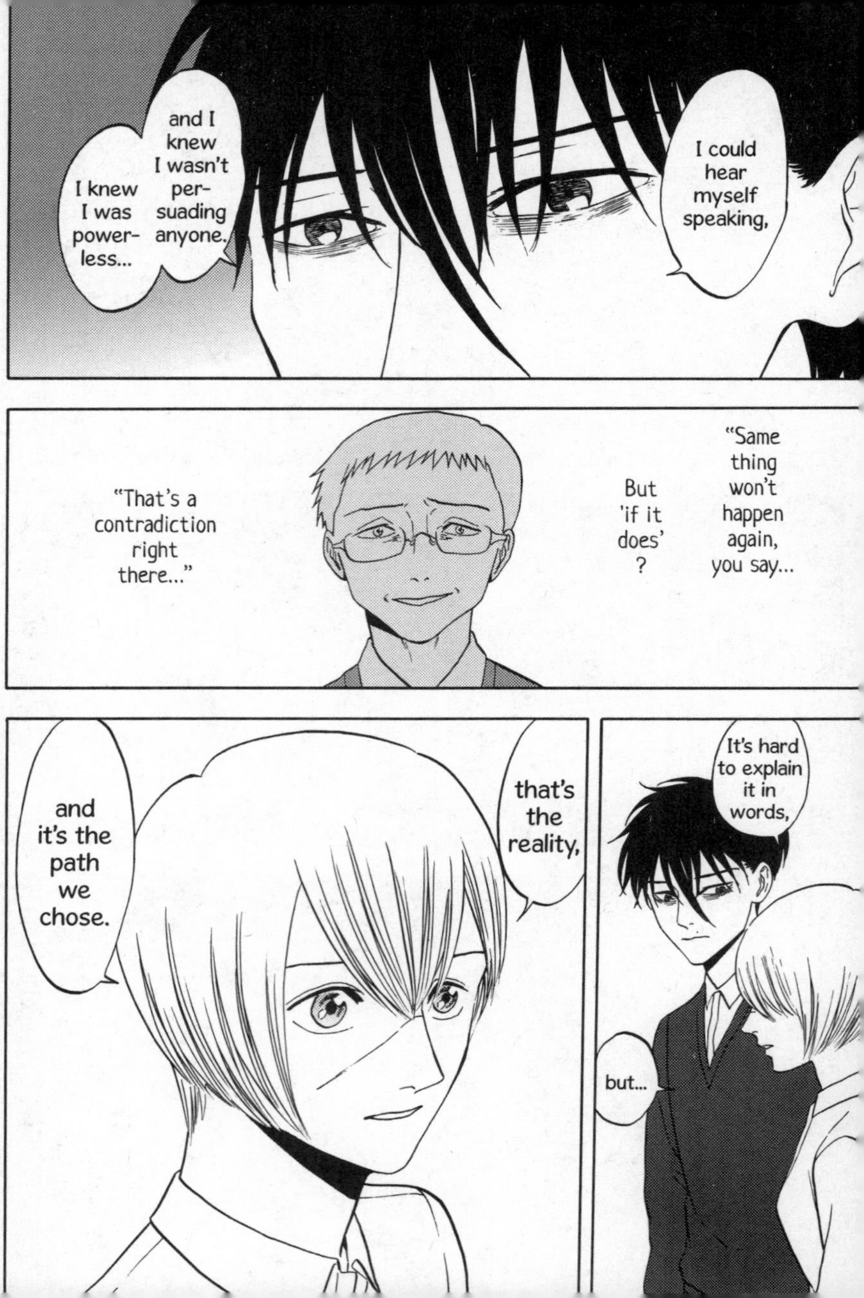
I could hear myself speaking,
and I knew I wasn't persuading anyone.
I knew I was powerless...
"Same thing won't happen again, you say...
But 'if it does' ?
"That's a contradiction right there..."
It's hard to explain it in words,
but...
that's the reality,
and it's the path we chose.

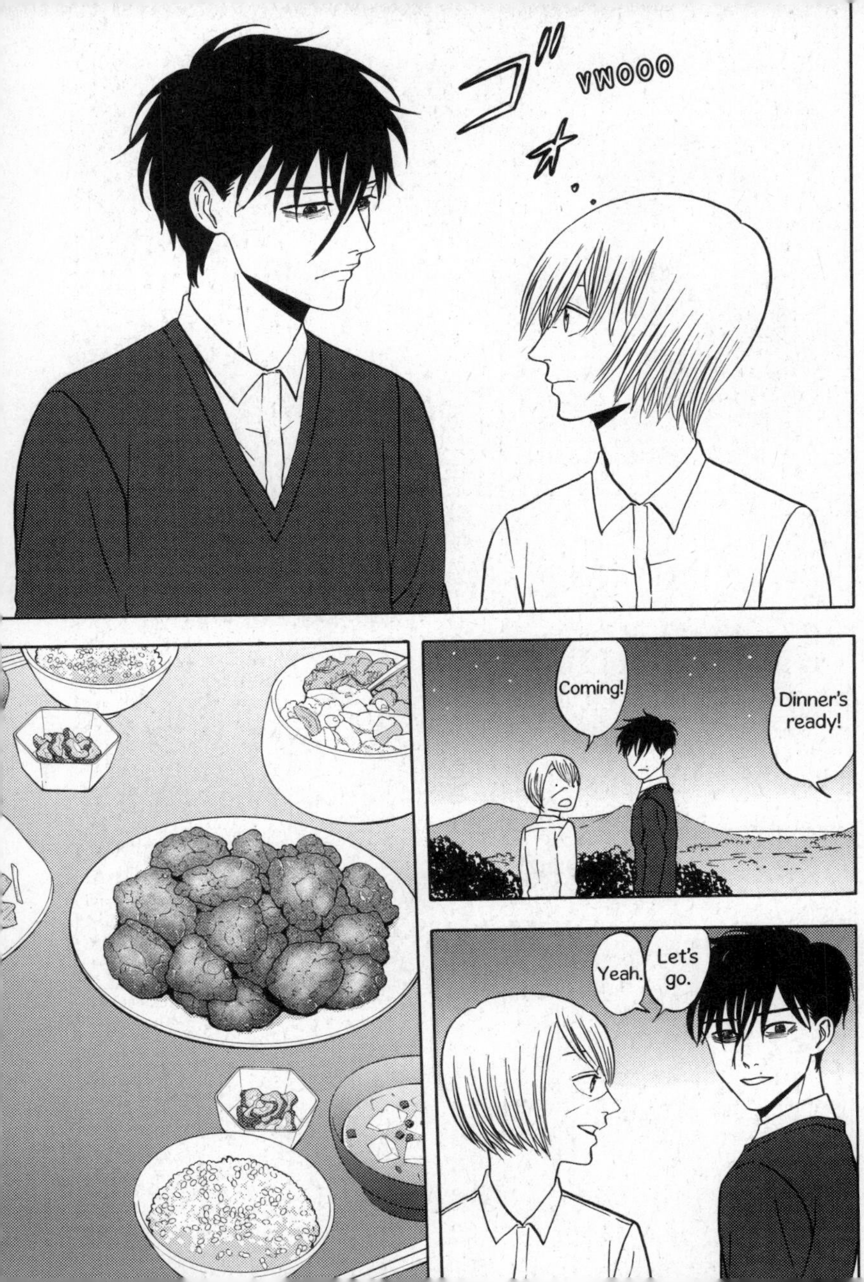
ゴォ
VWOOO
Dinner's ready!
Coming!
Let's go.
Yeah.

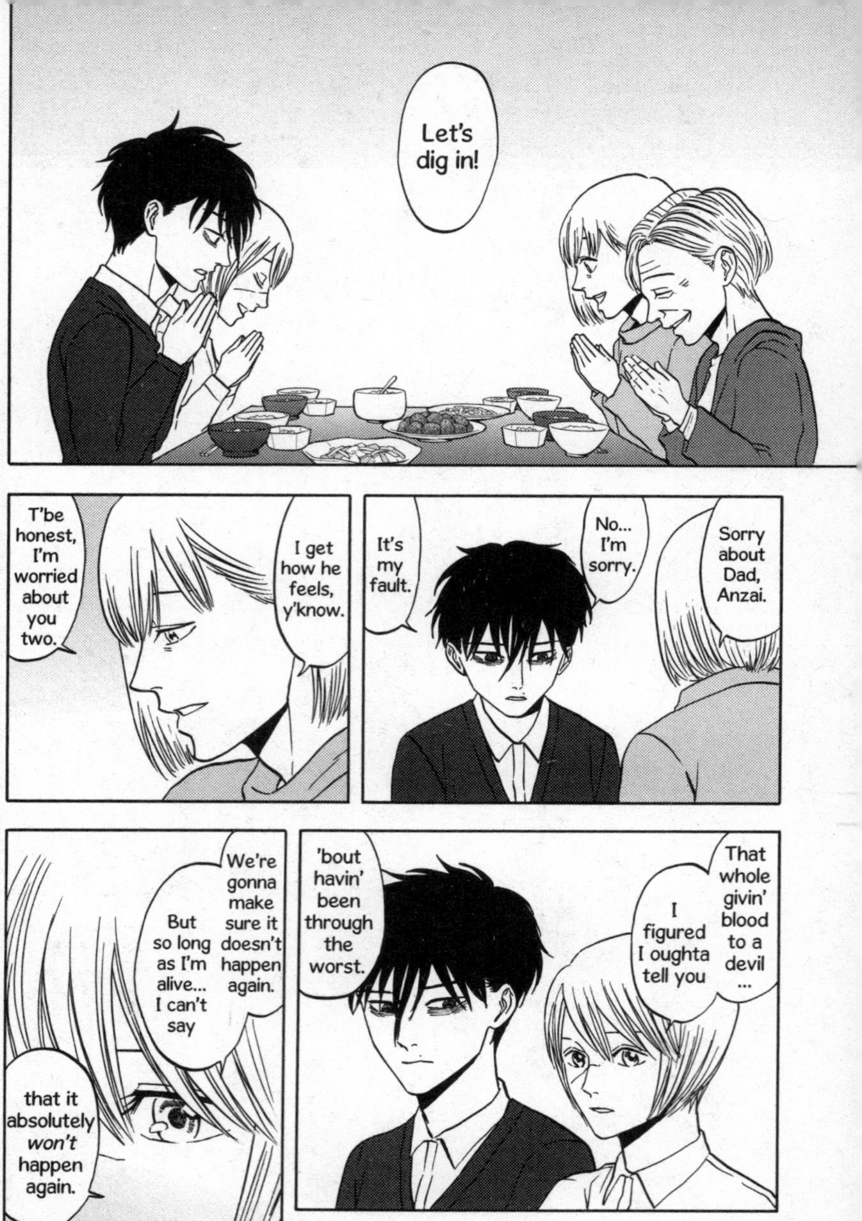
Let's dig in!
Sorry about Dad, Anzai.
No... I'm sorry.
It's my fault.
I get how he feels, y'know.
T'be honest, I'm worried about you two.
That whole givin' blood to a devil ...
I figured I oughta tell you
'bout havin' been through the worst.
We're gonna make sure it doesn't happen again.
But so long as I'm alive... I can't say
that it absolutely *won't* happen again.

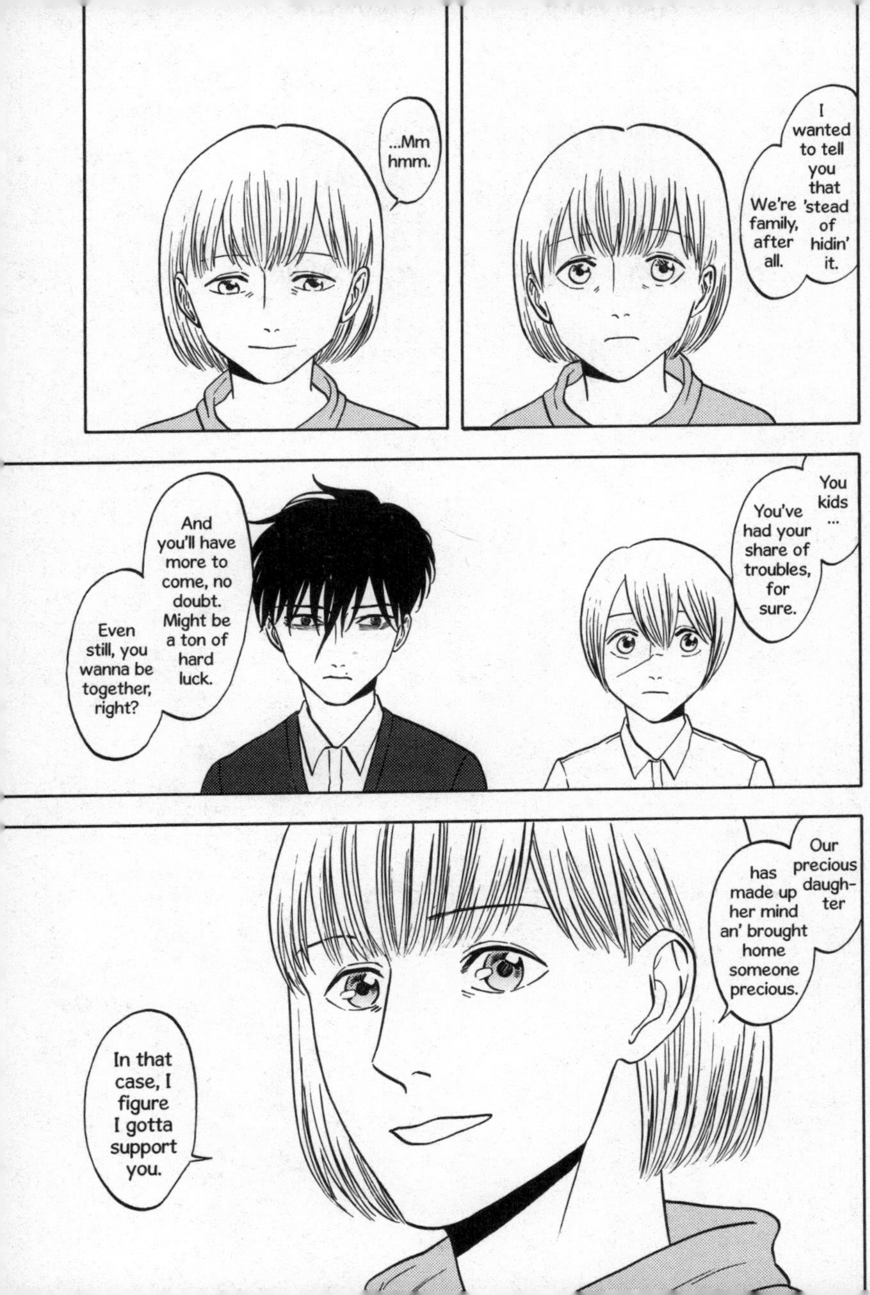
I wanted to tell you that 'stead of hidin' it.
We're family, after all.
...Mm hmm.
You kids ...
You've had your share of troubles, for sure.
And you'll have more to come, no doubt. Might be a ton of hard luck.
Even still, you wanna be together, right?
Our precious daugh-ter
has made up her mind an' brought home someone precious.
In that case, I figure I gotta support you.

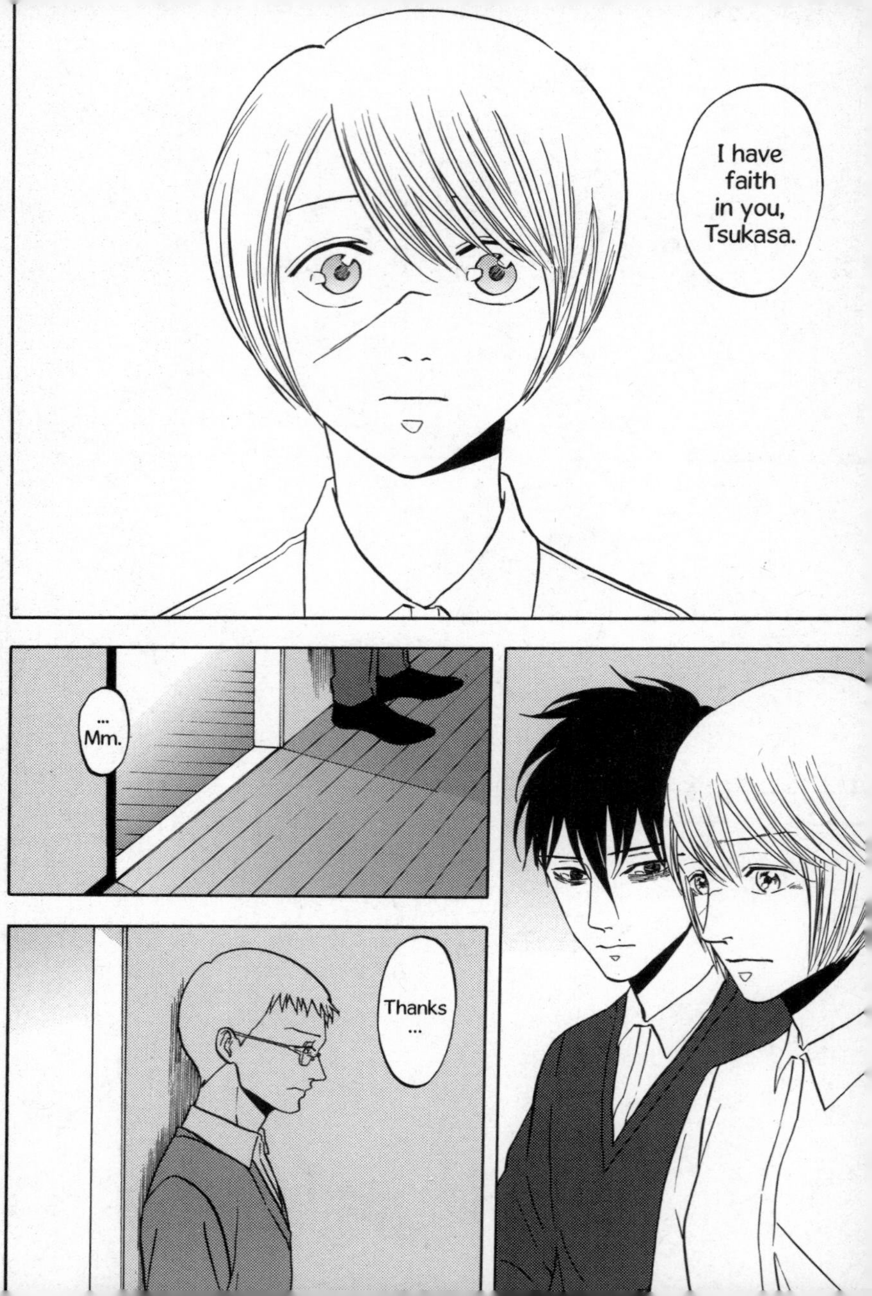
I have faith in you, Tsukasa.
... Mm.
Thanks ...

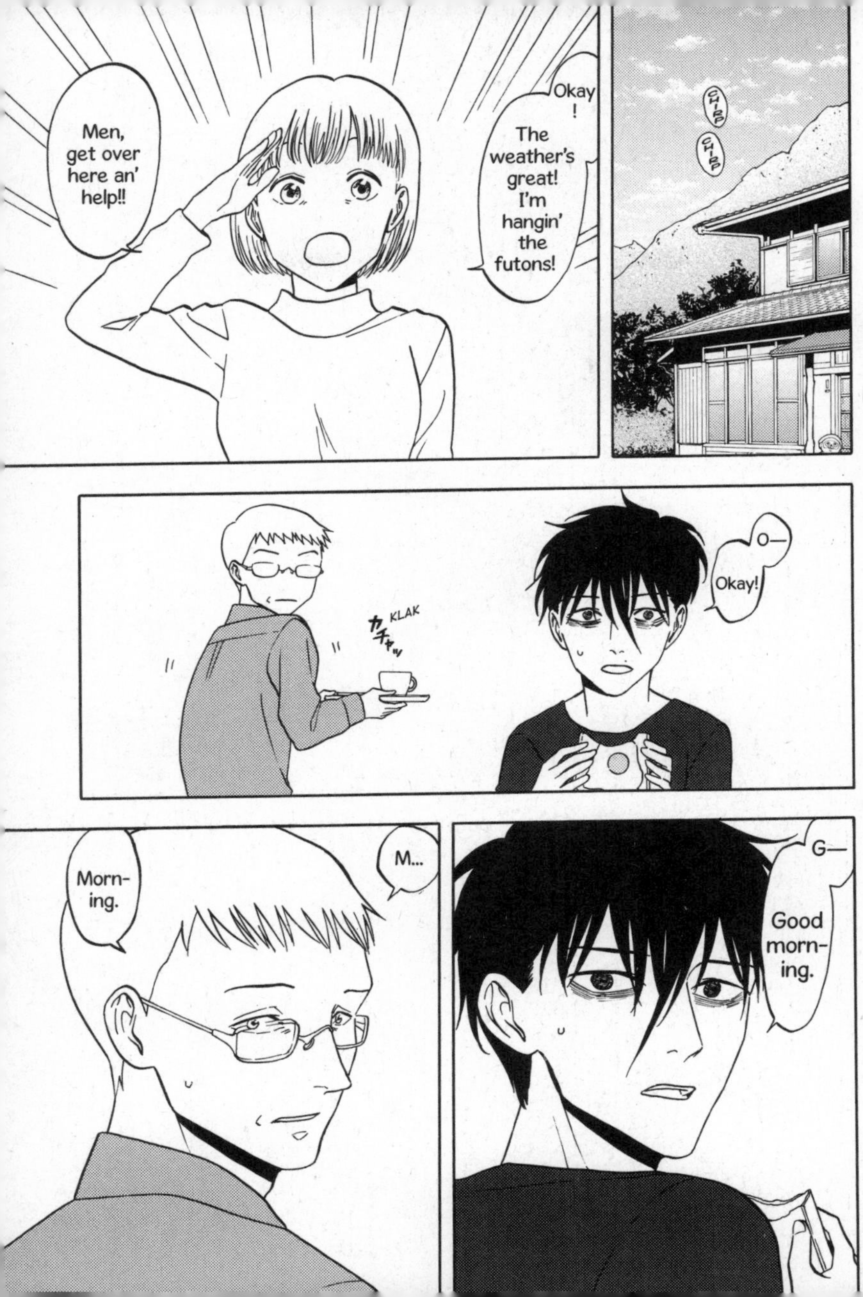
CHIRP
CHIRP
Okay!
The weather's great! I'm hangin' the futons!
Men, get over here an' help!!
O—
Okay!
KLAK
カチャッ
G—
Good morning.
M...
Morning.

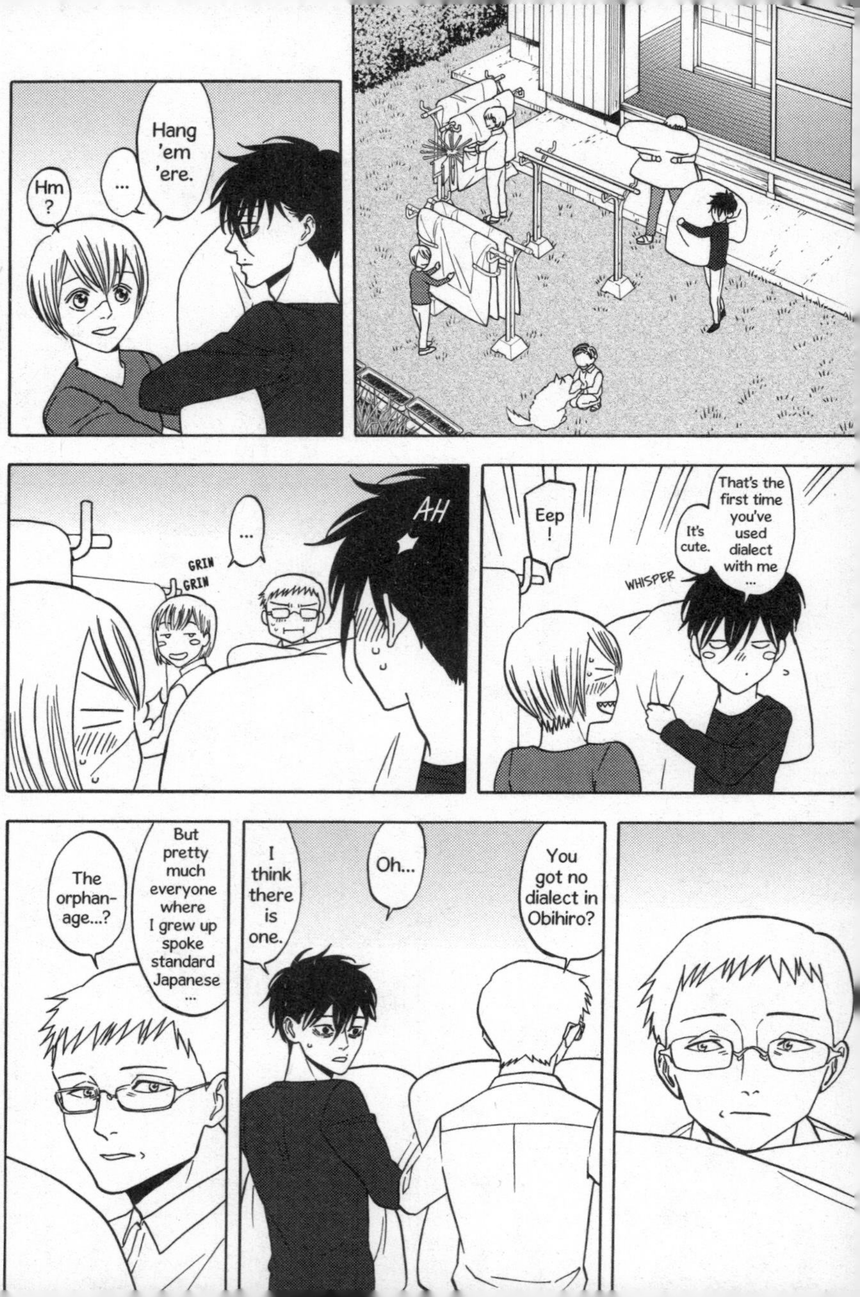
Hang 'em 'ere.
...
Hm?
That's the first time you've used dialect with me ...
It's cute.
WHISPER
Eep!
AH
...
GRIN GRIN
You got no dialect in Obihiro?
Oh...
I think there is one.
But pretty much everyone where I grew up spoke standard Japanese ...
The orphan-age...?

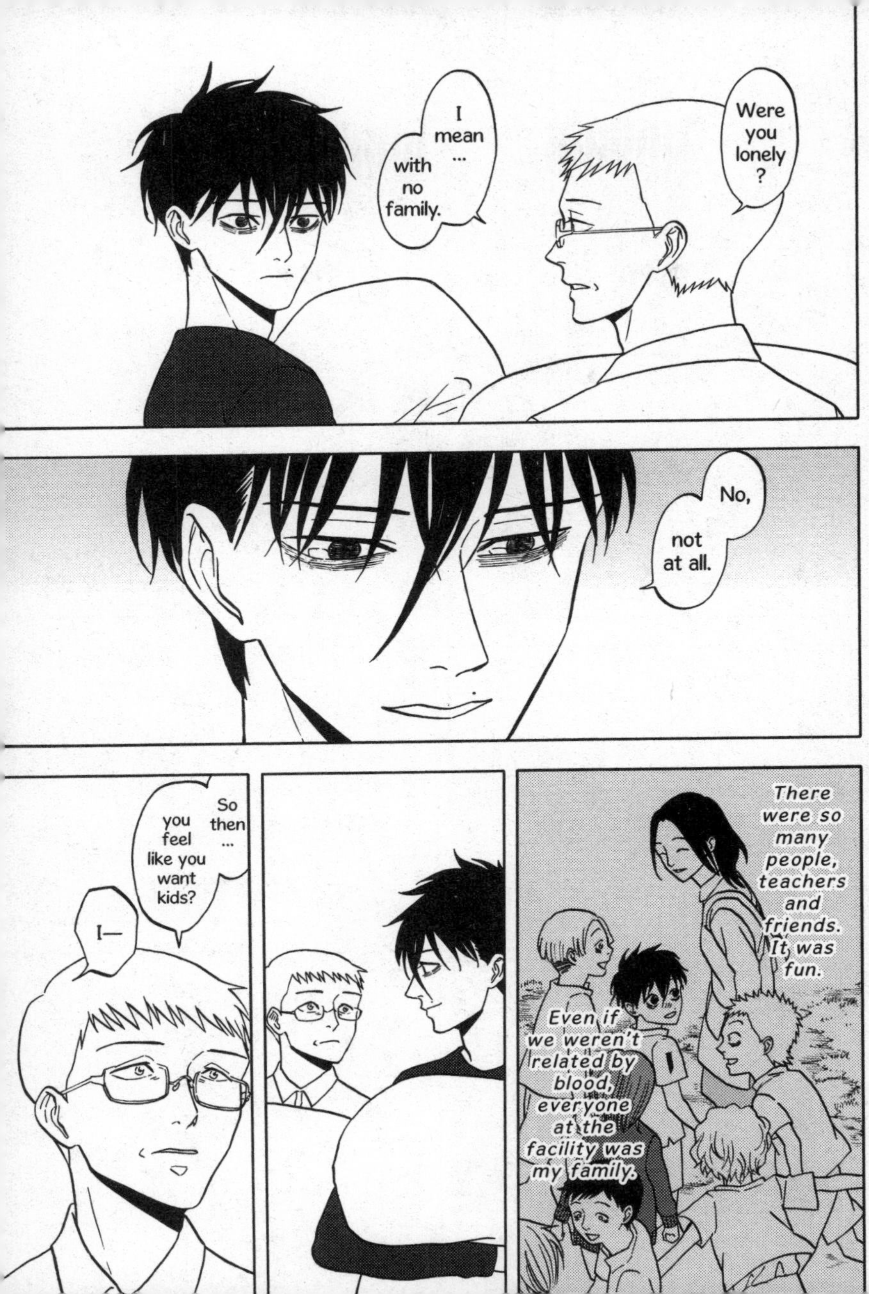
Were you lonely?
I mean... with no family.
No, not at all.
There were so many people, teachers and friends. It was fun.
Even if we weren't related by blood, everyone at the facility was my family.
So then... you feel like you want kids?
I—

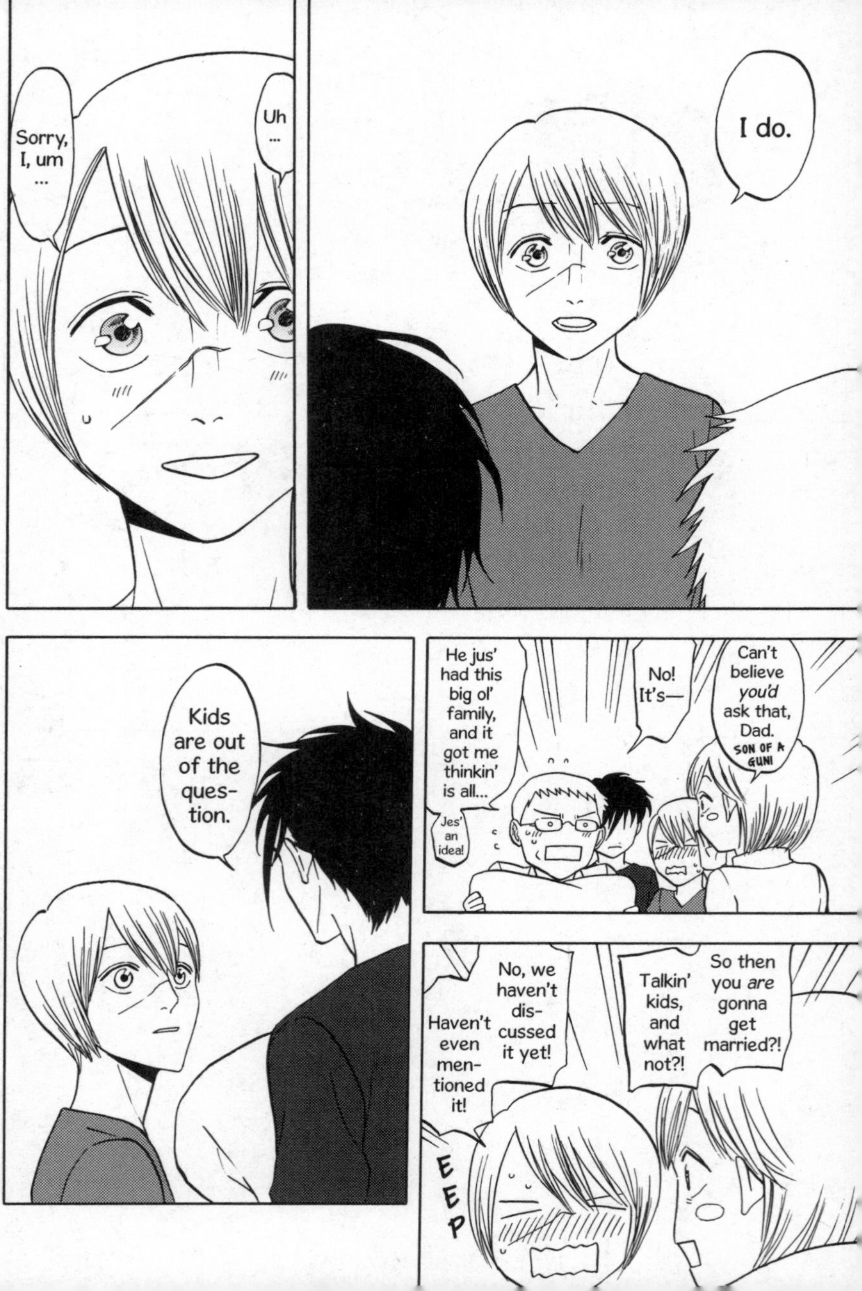
I do.
Uh ...
Sorry, I, um ...
Can't believe *you'd* ask that, Dad.
SON OF A GUN!
No! It's—
He jus' had this big ol' family, and it got me thinkin' is all...
Jes' an idea!
So then you *are* gonna get married?!
Talkin' kids, and what not?!
No, we haven't dis-cussed it yet!
Haven't even men-tioned it!
EEP
Kids are out of the ques-tion.

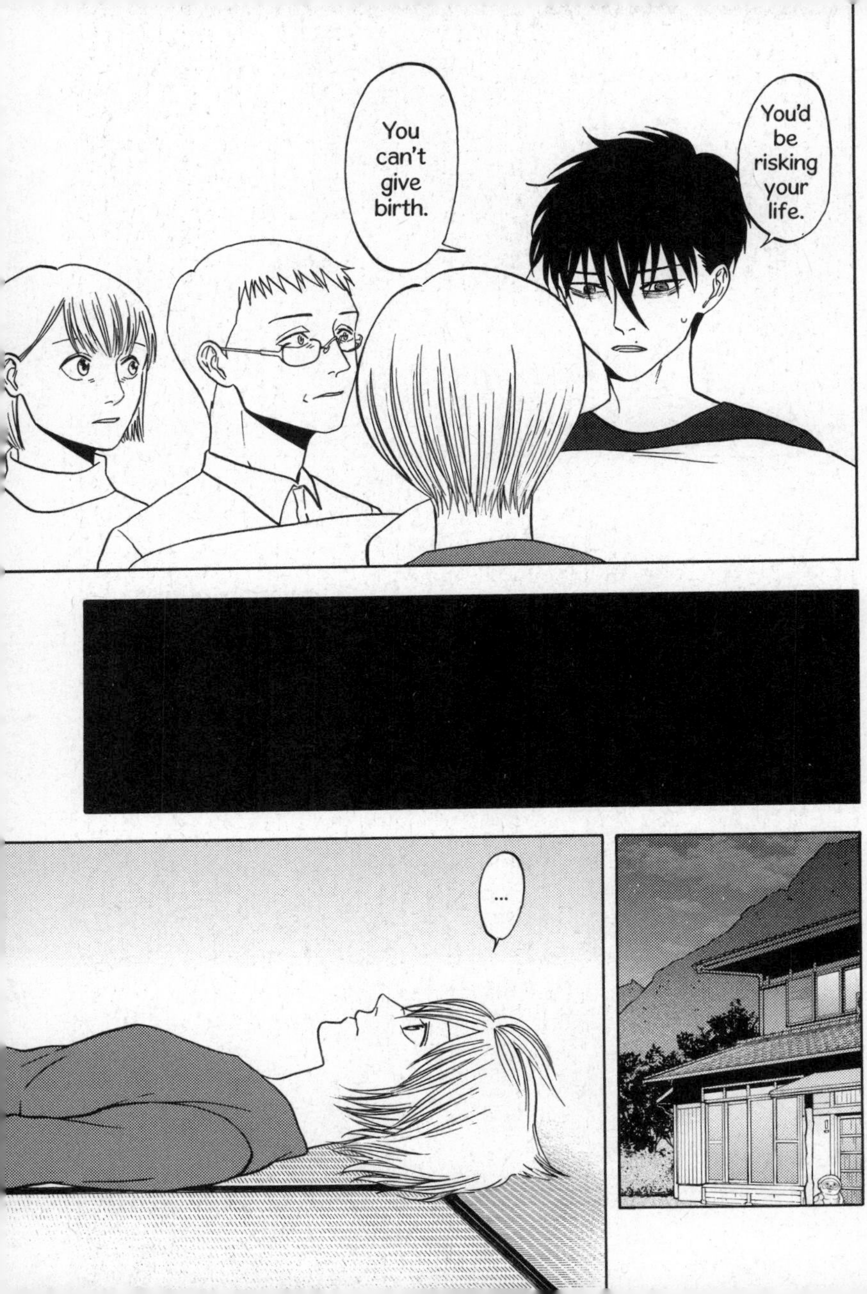
You'd be risking your life.
You can't give birth.
...

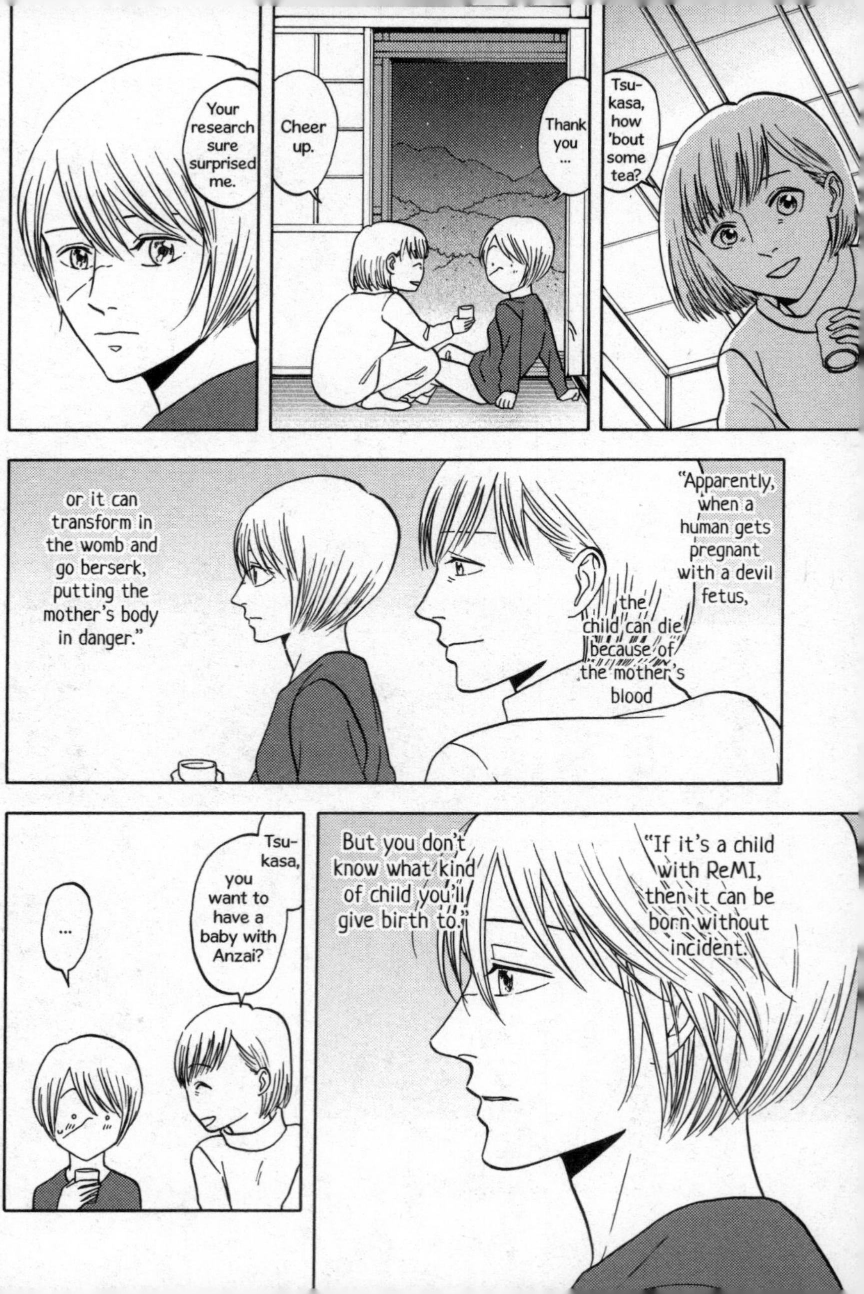
Tsu-kasa, how 'bout some tea?
Thank you ...
Cheer up.
Your research sure surprised me.
"Apparently, when a human gets pregnant with a devil fetus,
the child can die because of the mother's blood
or it can transform in the womb and go berserk, putting the mother's body in danger."
"If it's a child with ReMI, then it can be born without incident.
But you don't know what kind of child you'll give birth to."
Tsu-kasa, you want to have a baby with Anzai?
...

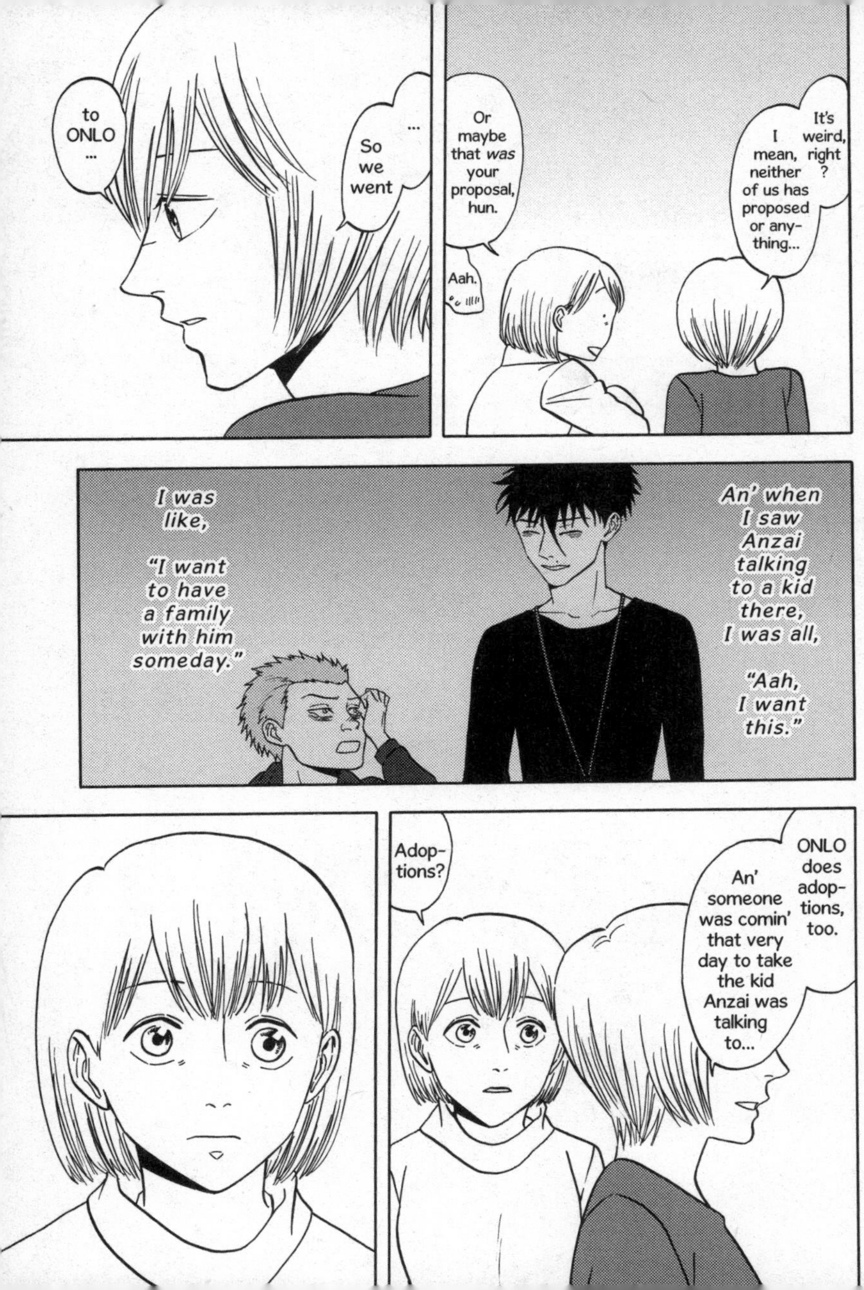
It's weird, right?
I mean, neither of us has proposed or anything...
Or maybe that *was* your proposal, hun.
Aah.
... So we went
to ONLO ...
An' when I saw Anzai talking to a kid there, I was all,
"Aah, I want this."
I was like,
"I want to have a family with him someday."
ONLO does adoptions, too.
An' someone was comin' that very day to take the kid Anzai was talking to...
Adoptions?

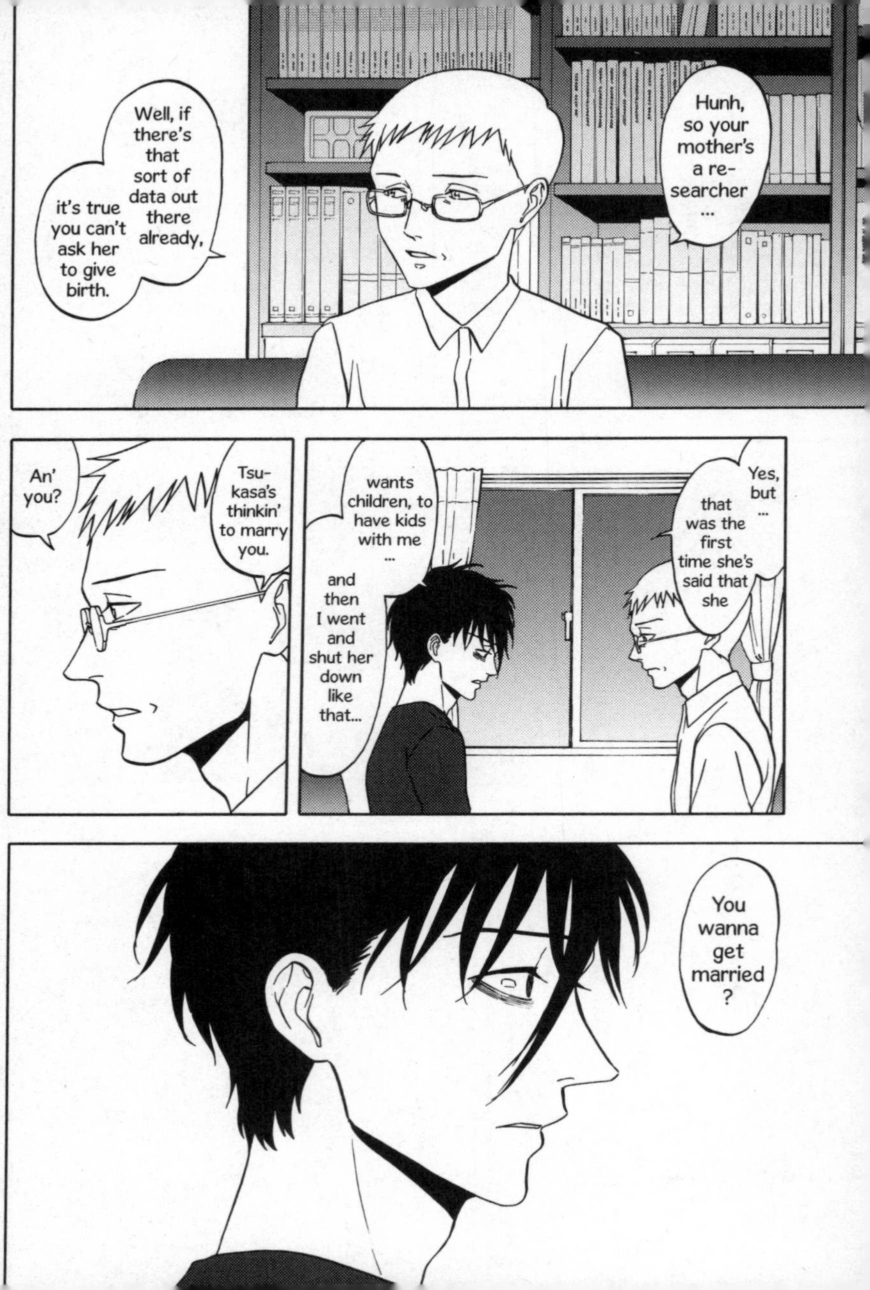
Hunh, so your mother's a re-searcher ...
Well, if there's that sort of data out there already,
it's true you can't ask her to give birth.
Yes, but ...
that was the first time she's said that she
wants children, to have kids with me ...
and then I went and shut her down like that...
Tsu-kasa's thinkin' to marry you.
An' you?
You wanna get married ?

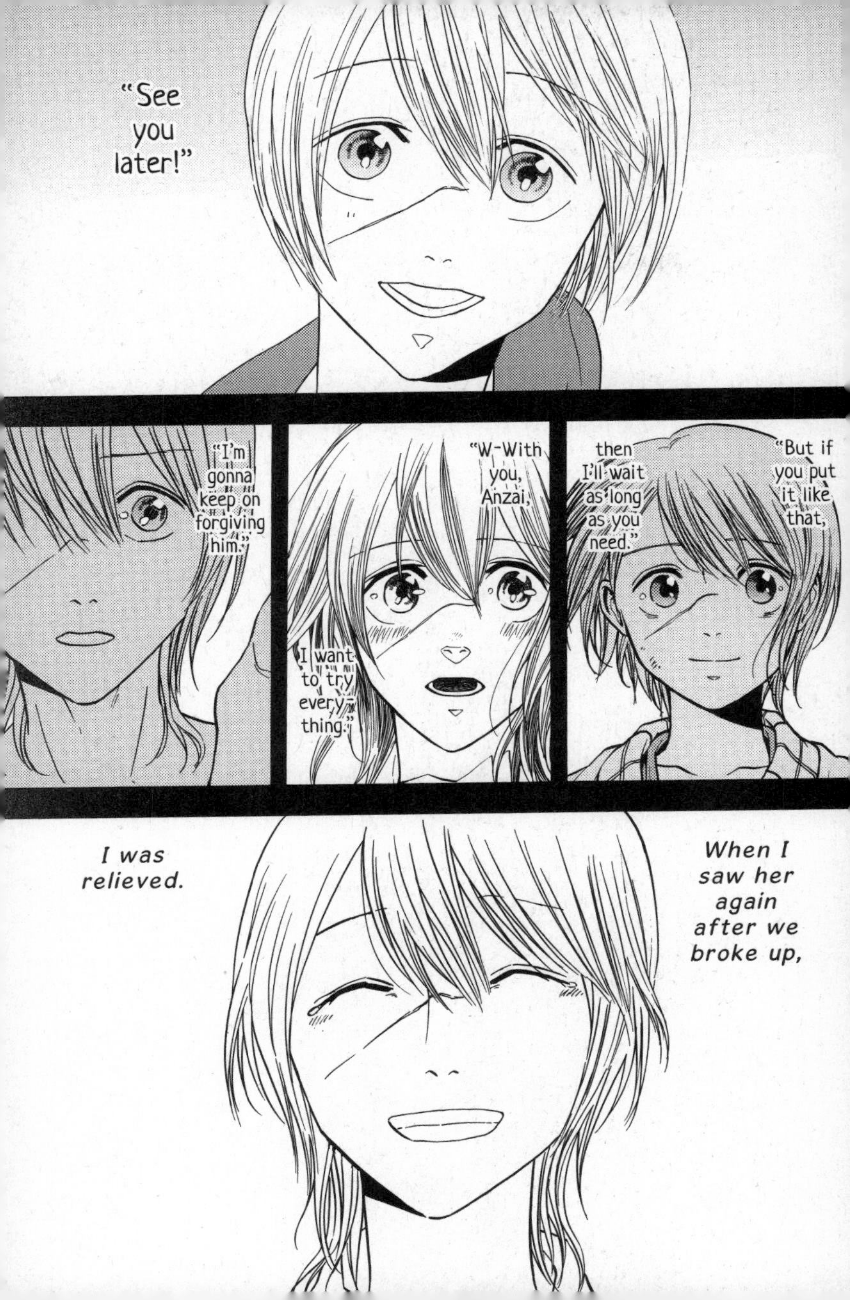
"See you later!"
"But if you put it like that,
then I'll wait as long as you need."
"W-With you, Anzai,
I want to try every-thing."
"I'm gonna keep on forgiving him."
When I saw her again after we broke up,
I was relieved.

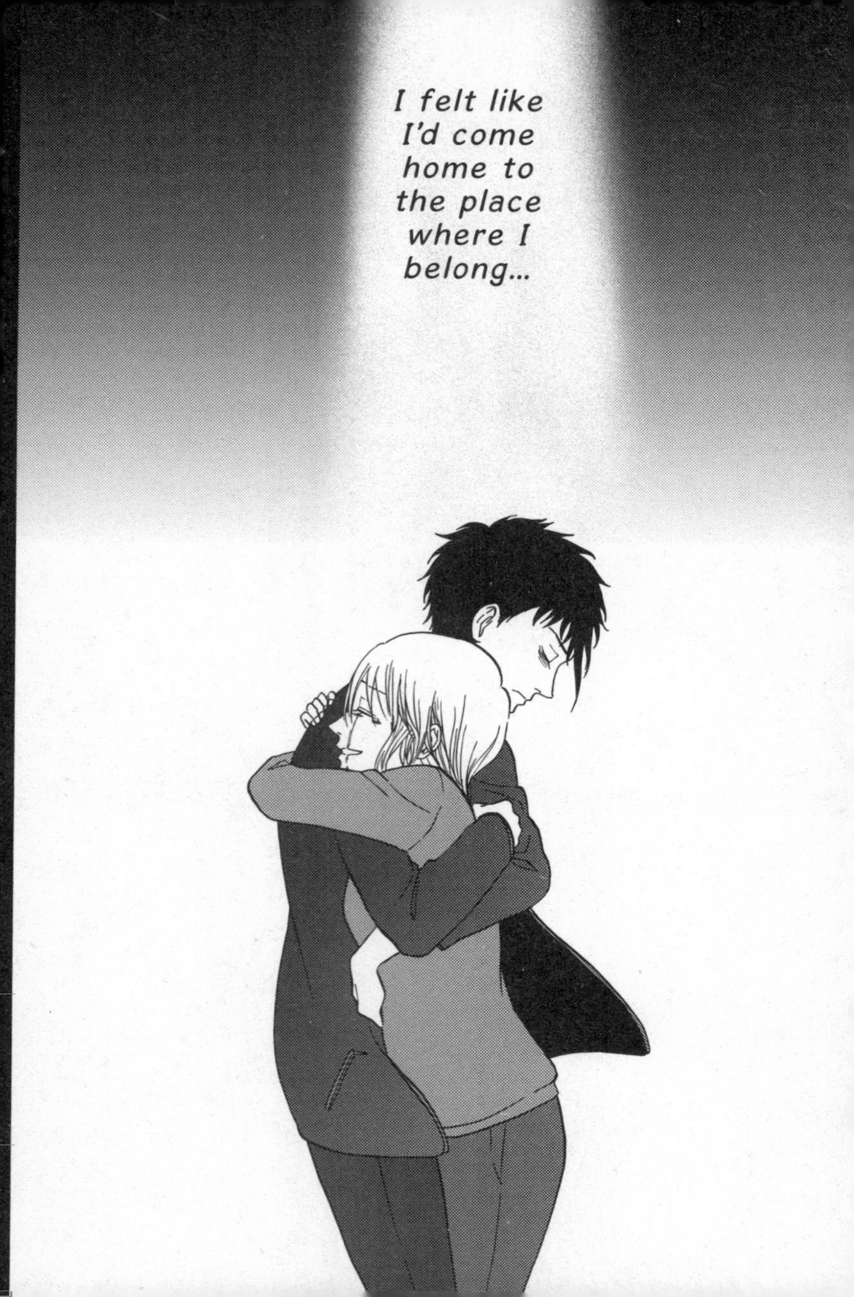
I felt like I'd come home to the place where I belong...

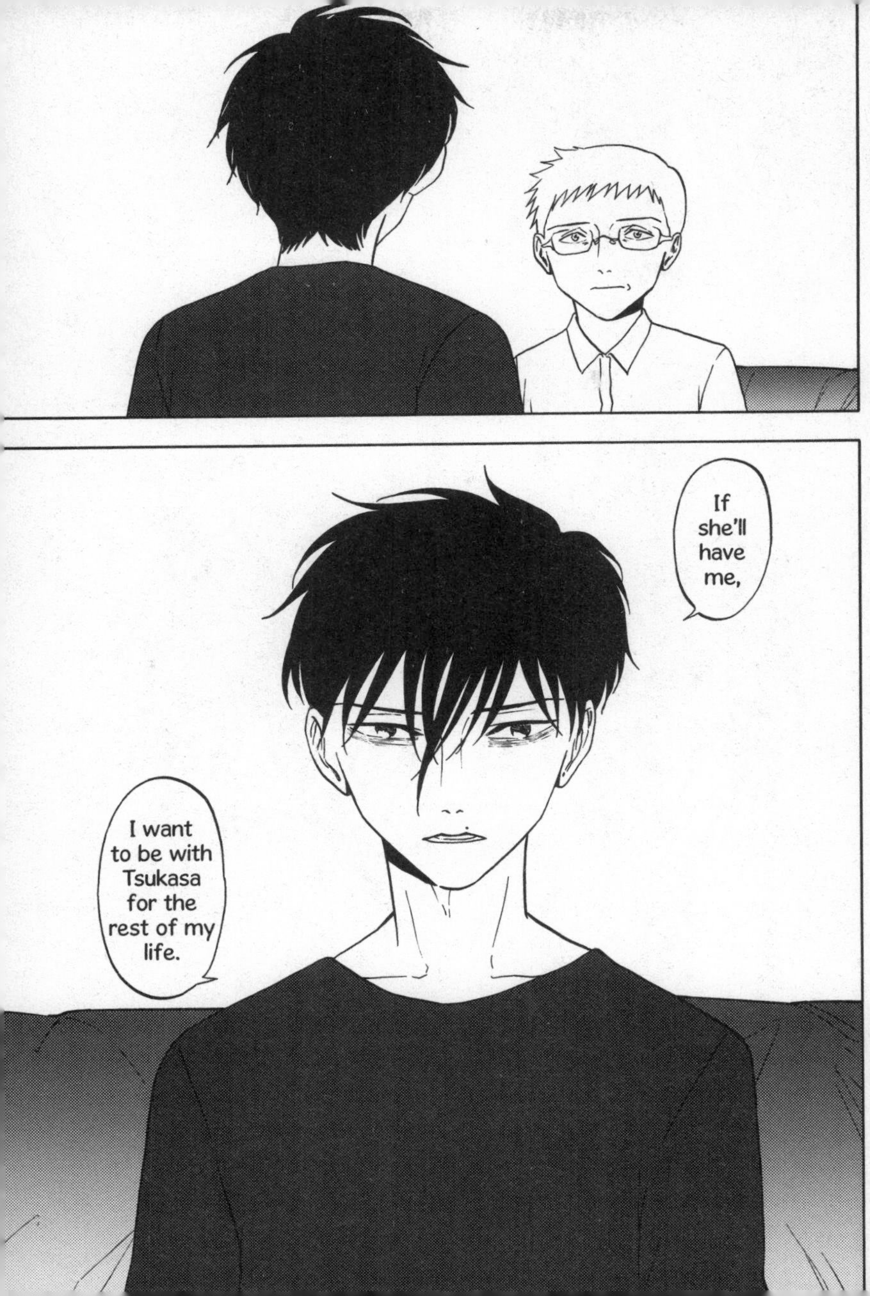
If she'll have me,
I want to be with Tsukasa for the rest of my life.

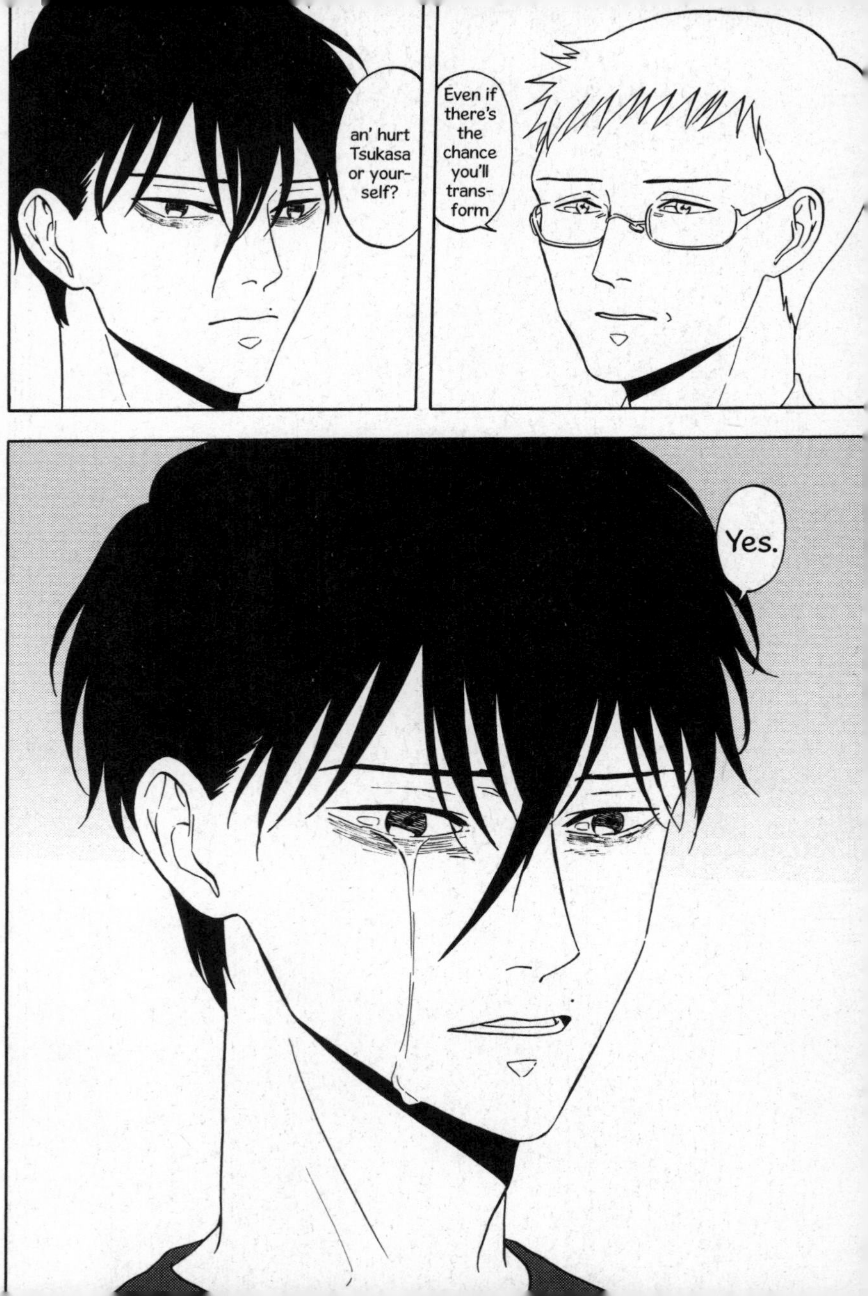
Even if there's the chance you'll trans-form
an' hurt Tsukasa or your-self?
Yes.

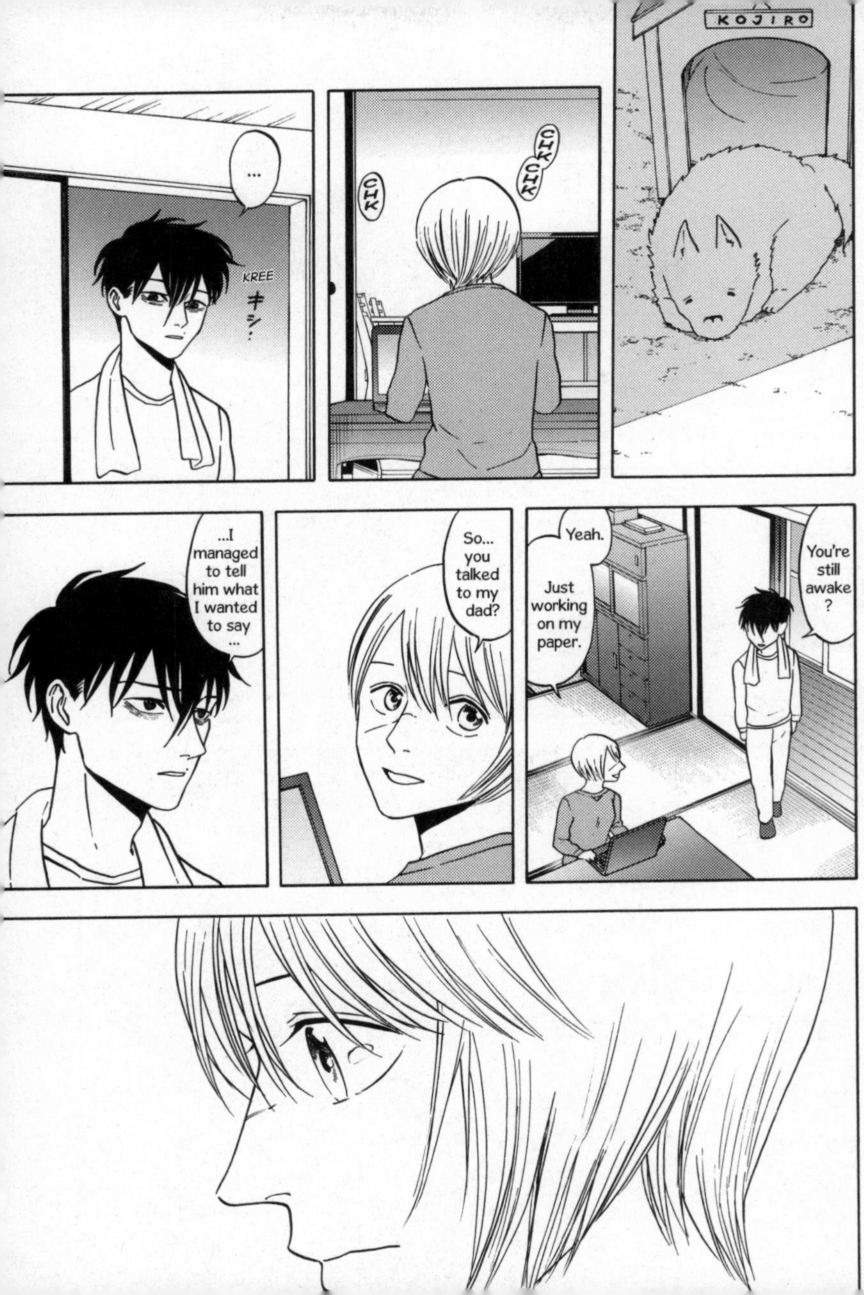
KOJIRO
CHK CHK
CHK
...
KREE
キシ…
You're still awake?
Yeah.
Just working on my paper.
So... you talked to my dad?
...I managed to tell him what I wanted to say ...

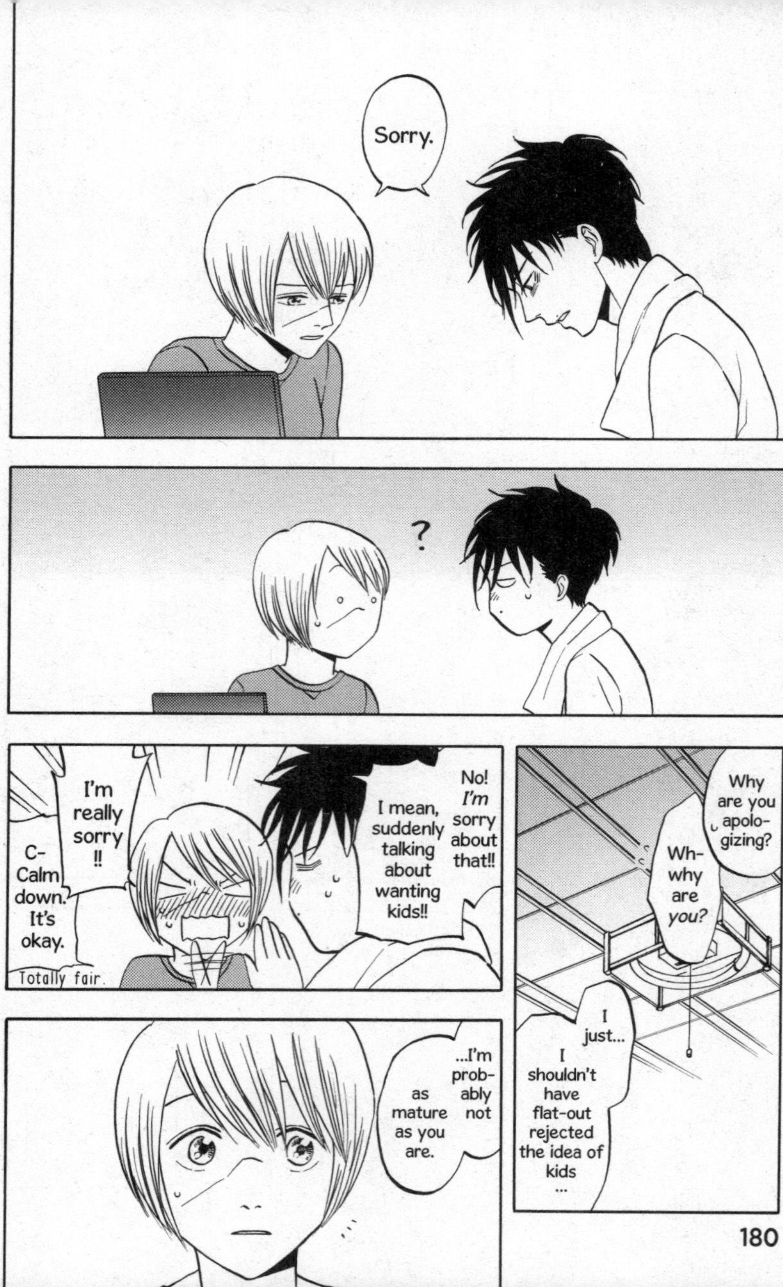
Sorry.
?
Why are you apolo-gizing?
Wh-why are you?
I just...
I shouldn't have flat-out rejected the idea of kids ...
No! I'm sorry about that!!
I mean, suddenly talking about wanting kids!!
I'm really sorry !!
C-Calm down. It's okay.
Totally fair.
...I'm prob-ably not as mature as you are.

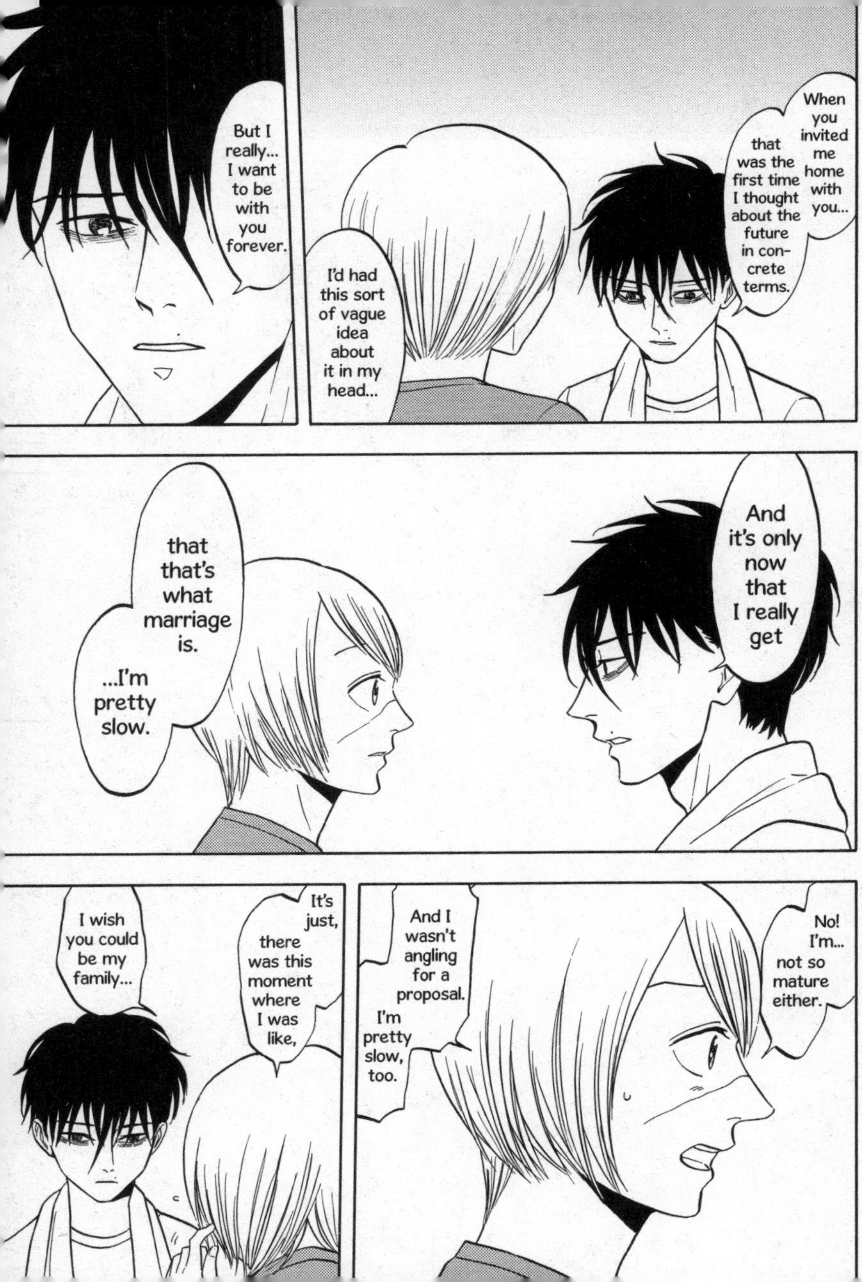
When you invited me home with you...
that was the first time I thought about the future in concrete terms.
I'd had this sort of vague idea about it in my head...
But I really... I want to be with you forever.
And it's only now that I really get
that that's what marriage is.
...I'm pretty slow.
No! I'm... not so mature either.
And I wasn't angling for a proposal.
I'm pretty slow, too.
It's just, there was this moment where I was like,
I wish you could be my family...

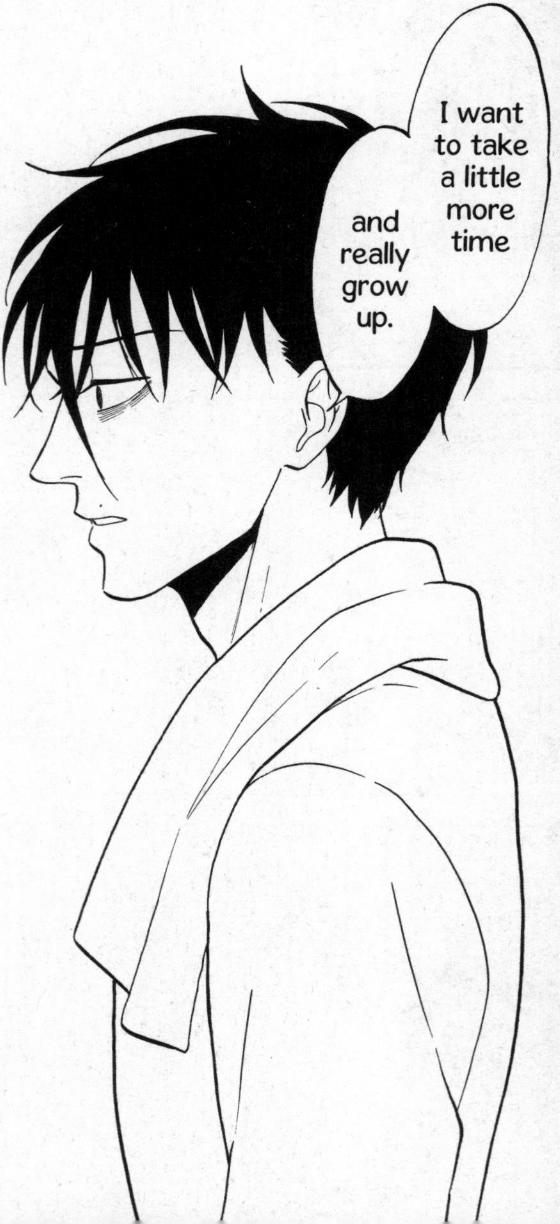
I want to take a little more time and really grow up.

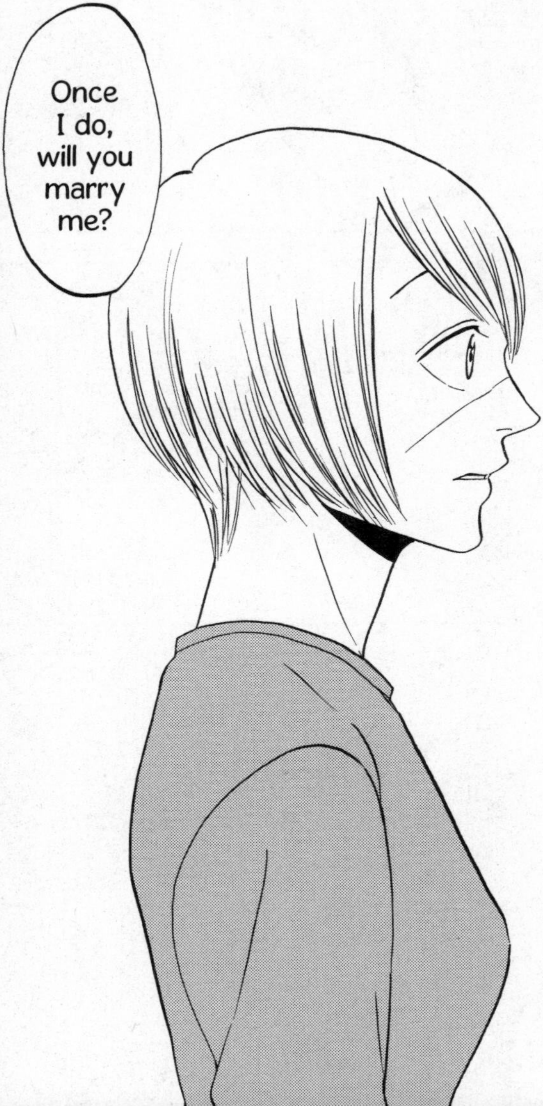
Once I do, will you marry me?

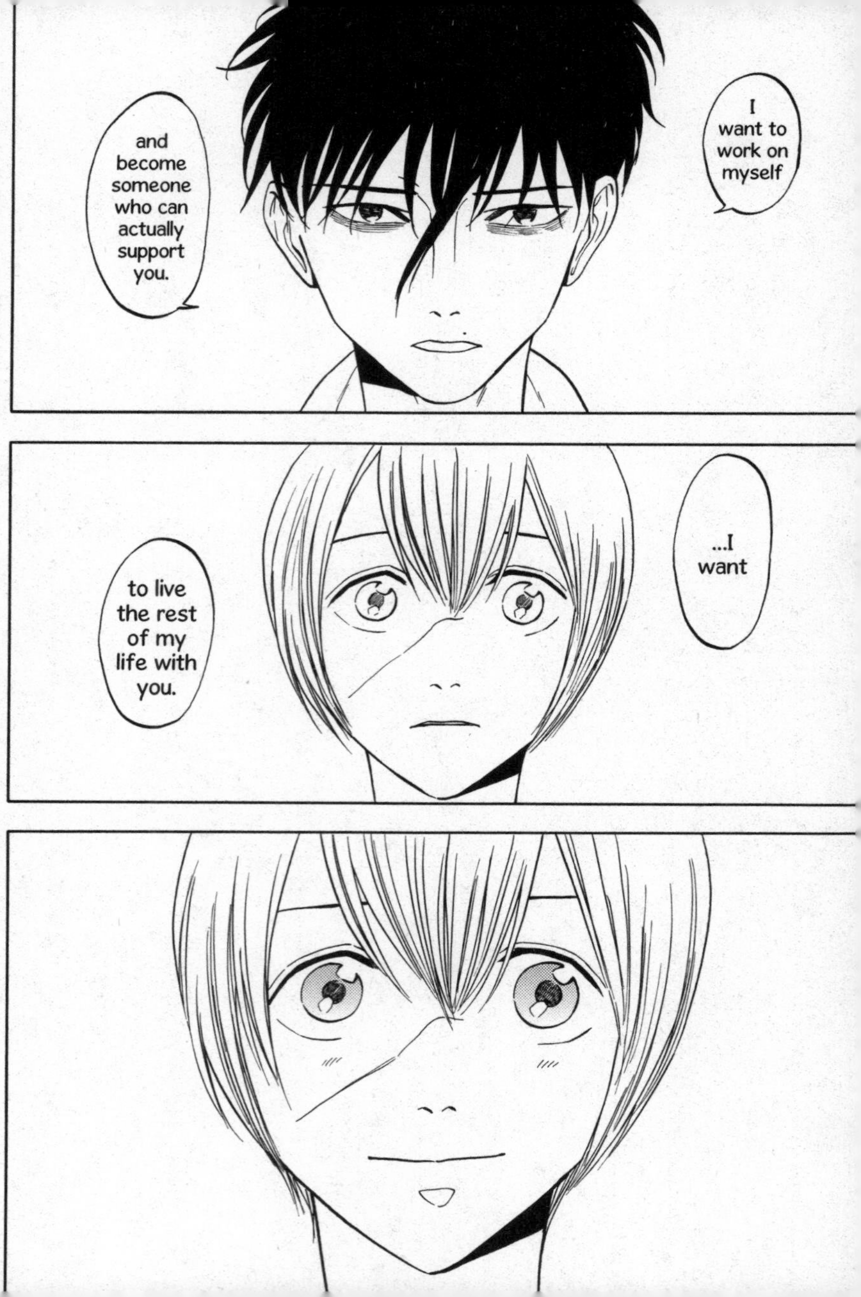
I want to work on myself
and become someone who can actually support you.
...I want
to live the rest of my life with you.

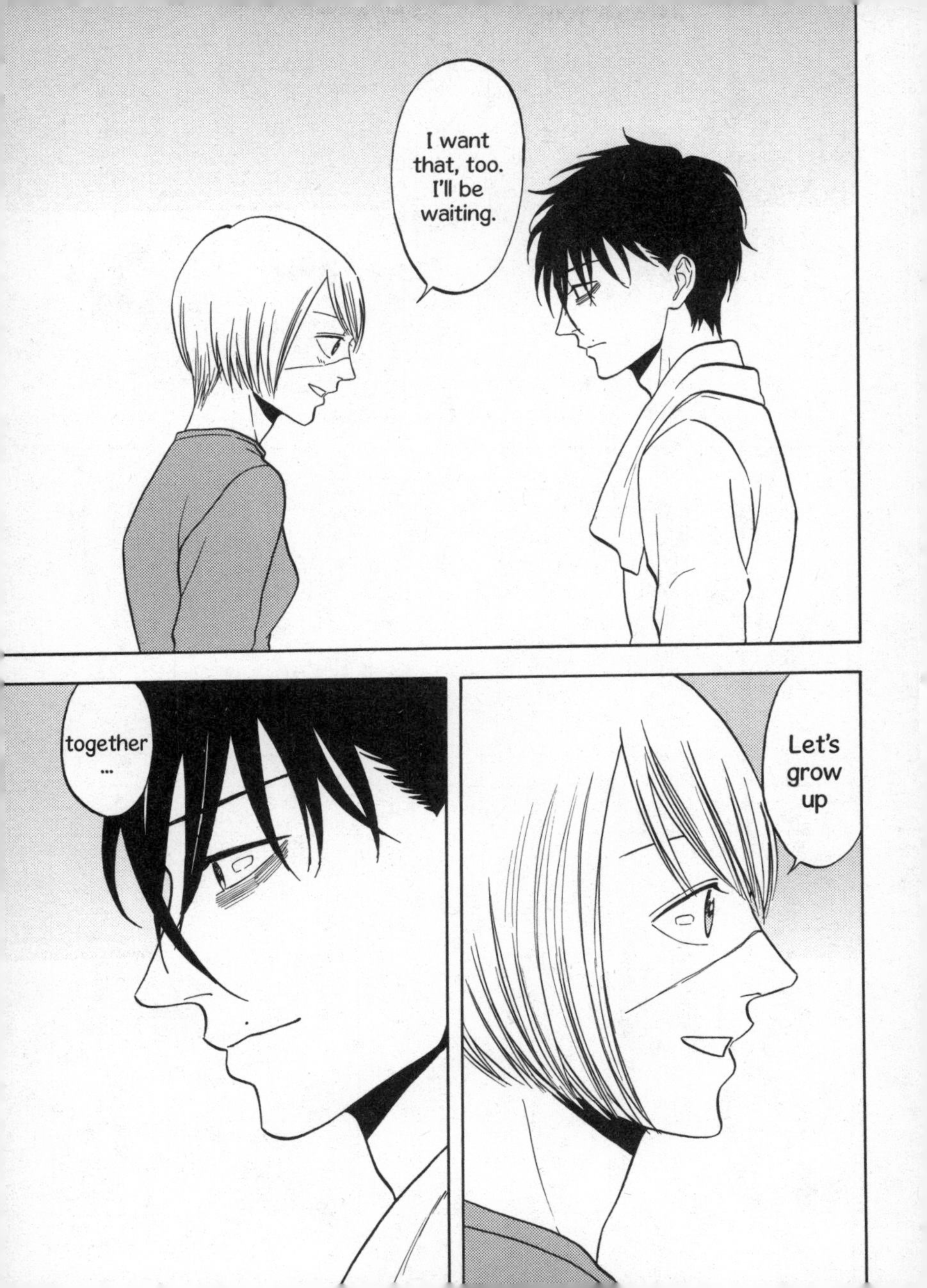
I want that, too. I'll be waiting.
Let's grow up
together …

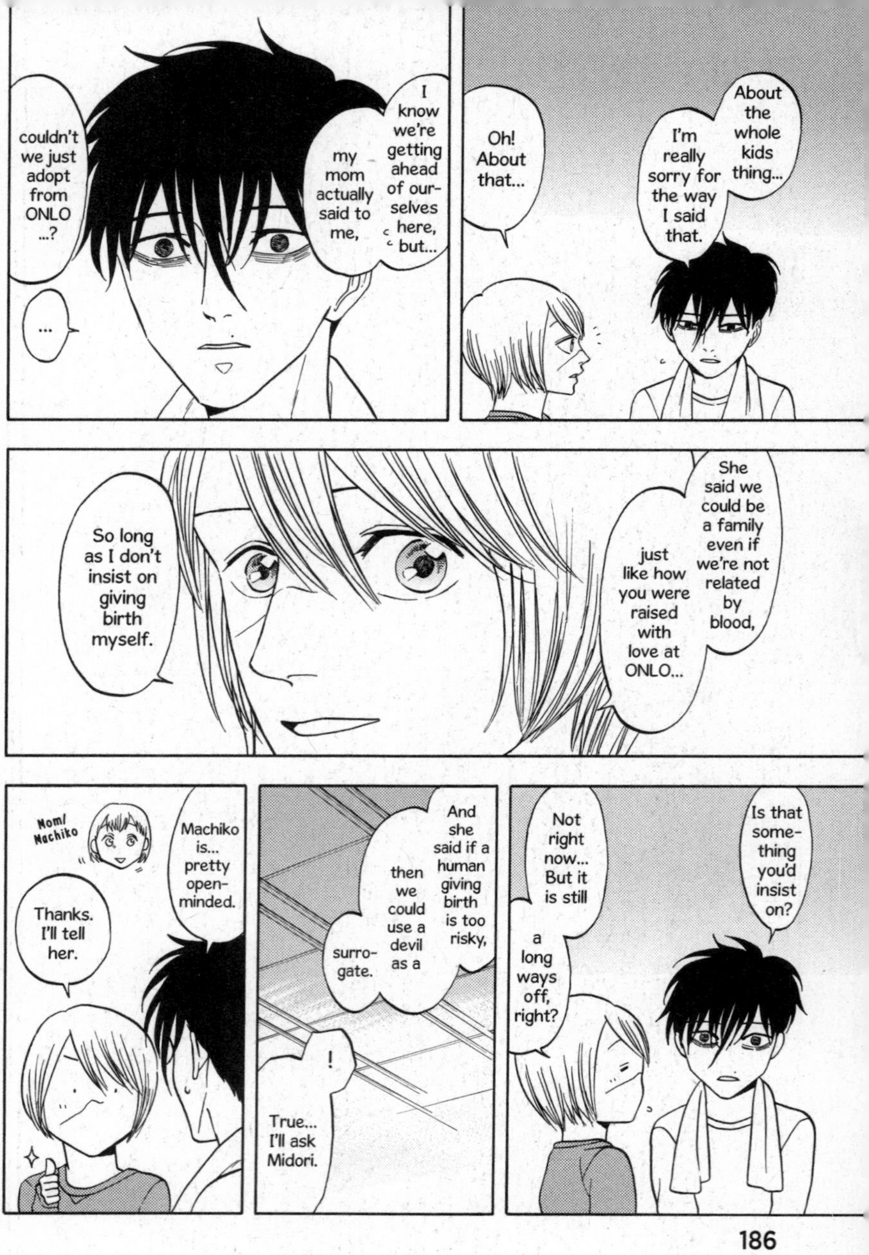
About the whole kids thing...
I'm really sorry for the way I said that.
Oh! About that...
I know we're getting ahead of ourselves here, but...
my mom actually said to me,
couldn't we just adopt from ONLO ...?
...
She said we could be a family even if we're not related by blood,
just like how you were raised with love at ONLO...
So long as I don't insist on giving birth myself.
Is that something you'd insist on?
Not right now... But it is still
a long ways off, right?
And she said if a human giving birth is too risky,
then we could use a devil as a
surrogate.
!
True... I'll ask Midori.
Machiko is... pretty open-minded.
Mom/ Machiko
Thanks. I'll tell her.

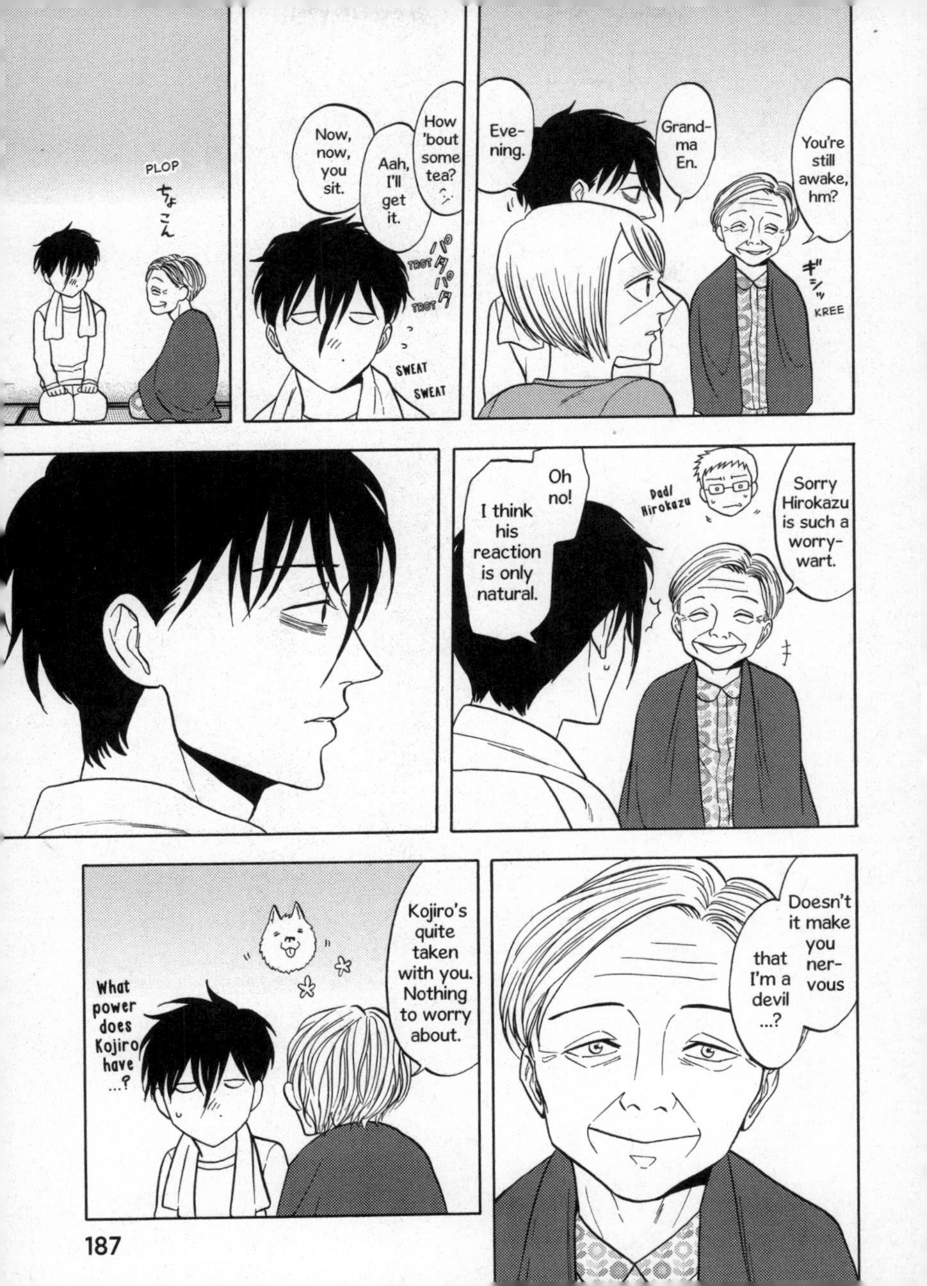
You're still awake, hm?
Grand-ma En.
Eve-ning.
ギシッ
KREE
How 'bout some tea?
Aah, I'll get it.
Now, now, you sit.
パタパタ
TROT TROT
SWEAT SWEAT
PLOP
ちょこん
Sorry Hirokazu is such a worry-wart.
Dad/ Hirokazu
Oh no!
I think his reaction is only natural.
Doesn't it make you nervous
that I'm a devil ...?
Kojiro's quite taken with you. Nothing to worry about.
What power does Kojiro have ...?

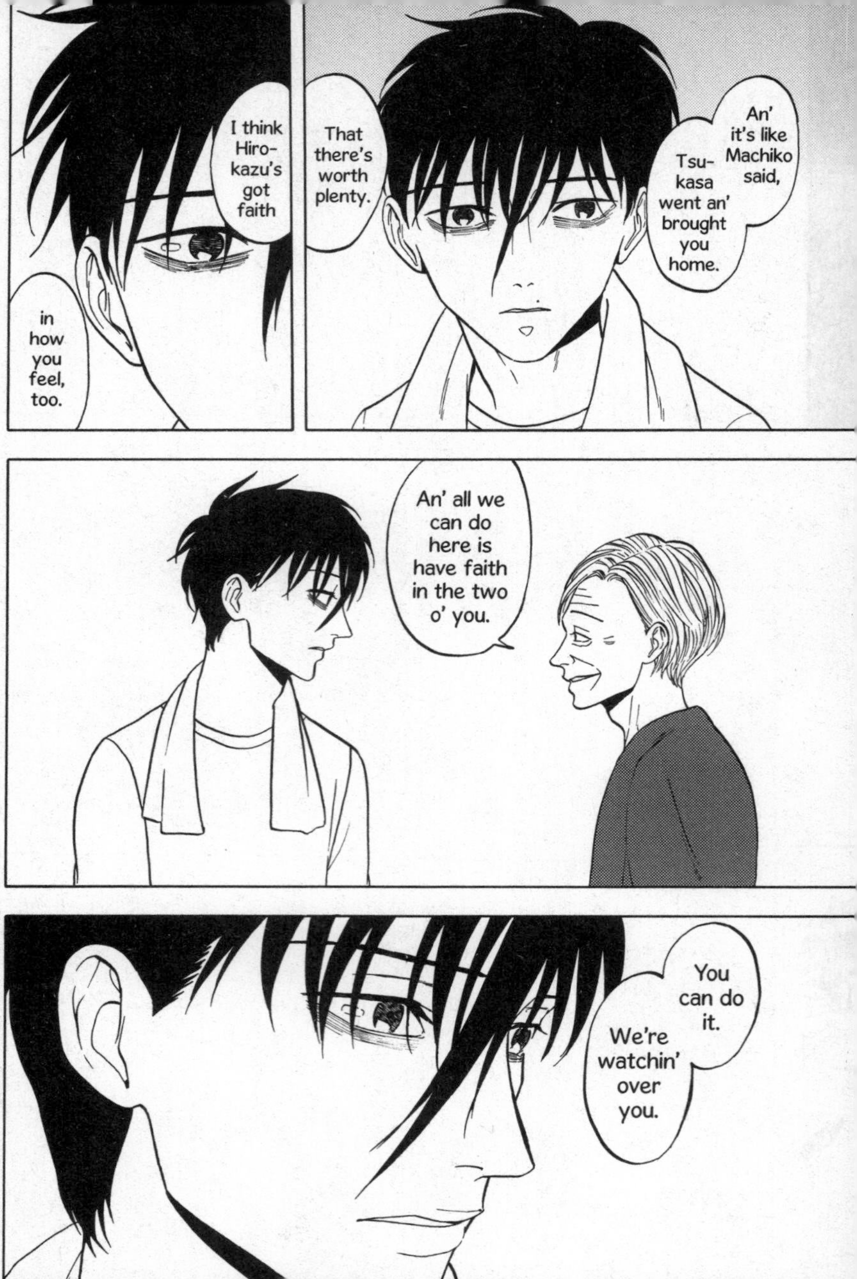
An' it's like Machiko said,
Tsu-kasa went an' brought you home.
That there's worth plenty.
I think Hiro-kazu's got faith
in how you feel, too.
An' all we can do here is have faith in the two o' you.
You can do it.
We're watchin' over you.

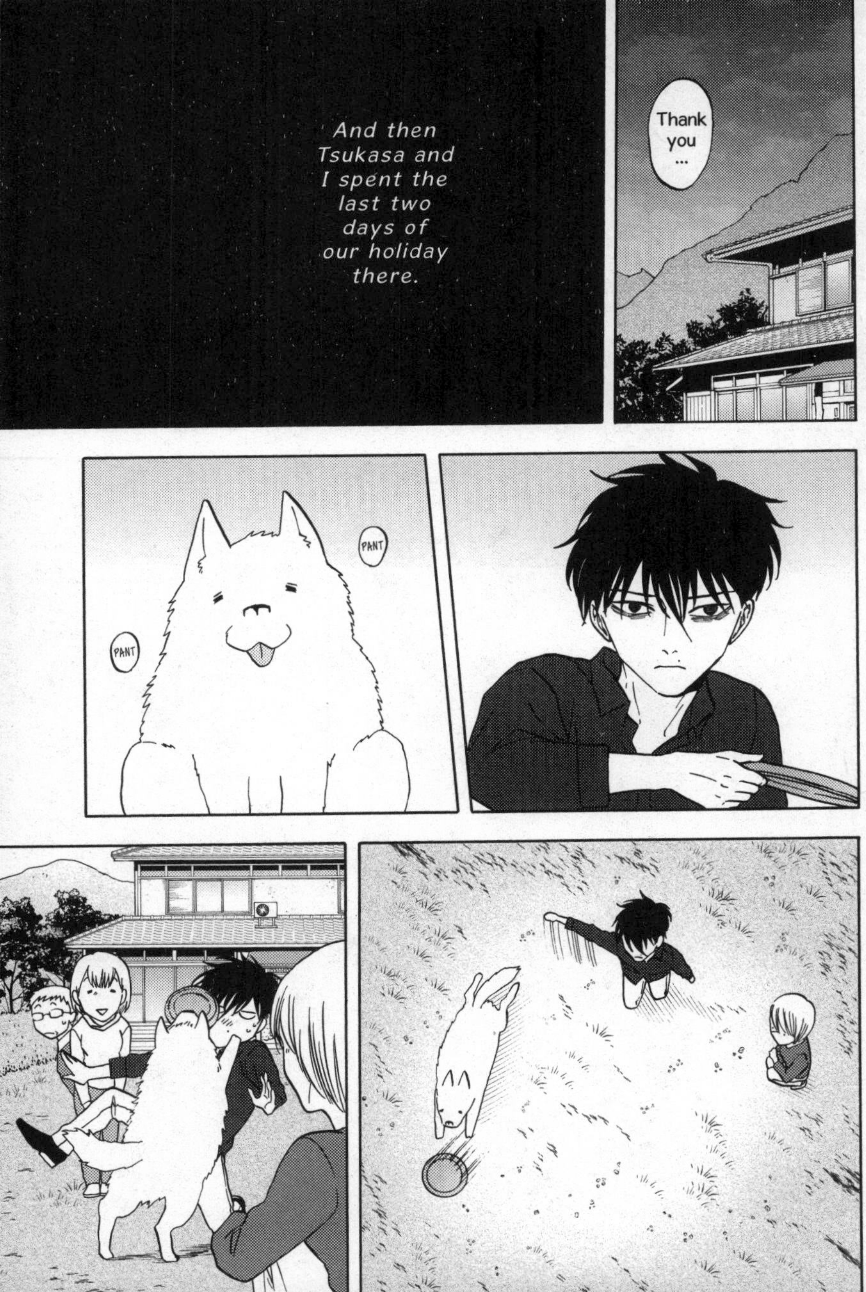
Thank you ...
And then Tsukasa and I spent the last two days of our holiday there.
PANT
PANT

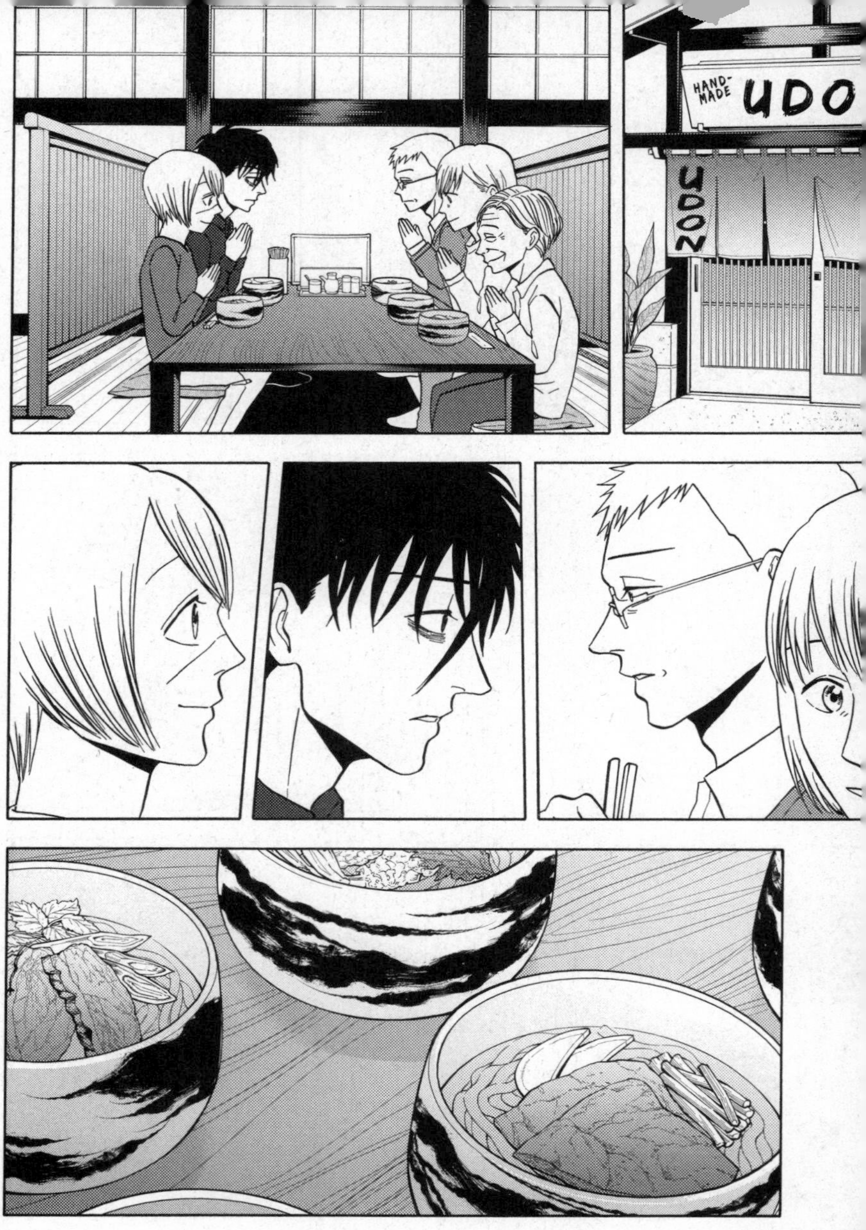
HAND-MADE
UDO
UDON

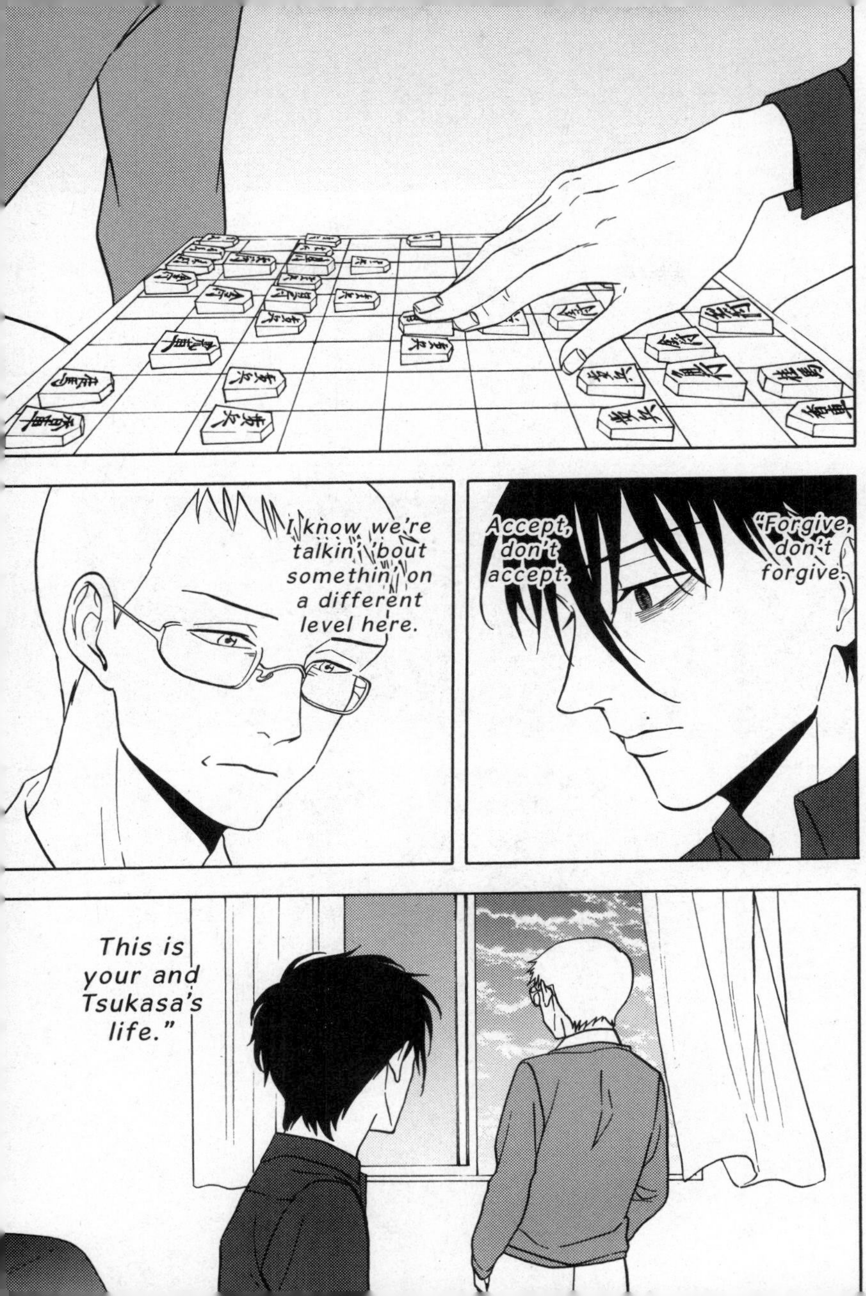
"Forgive, don't forgive.
Accept, don't accept.
I know we're talkin' 'bout somethin' on a different level here.
This is your and Tsukasa's life."

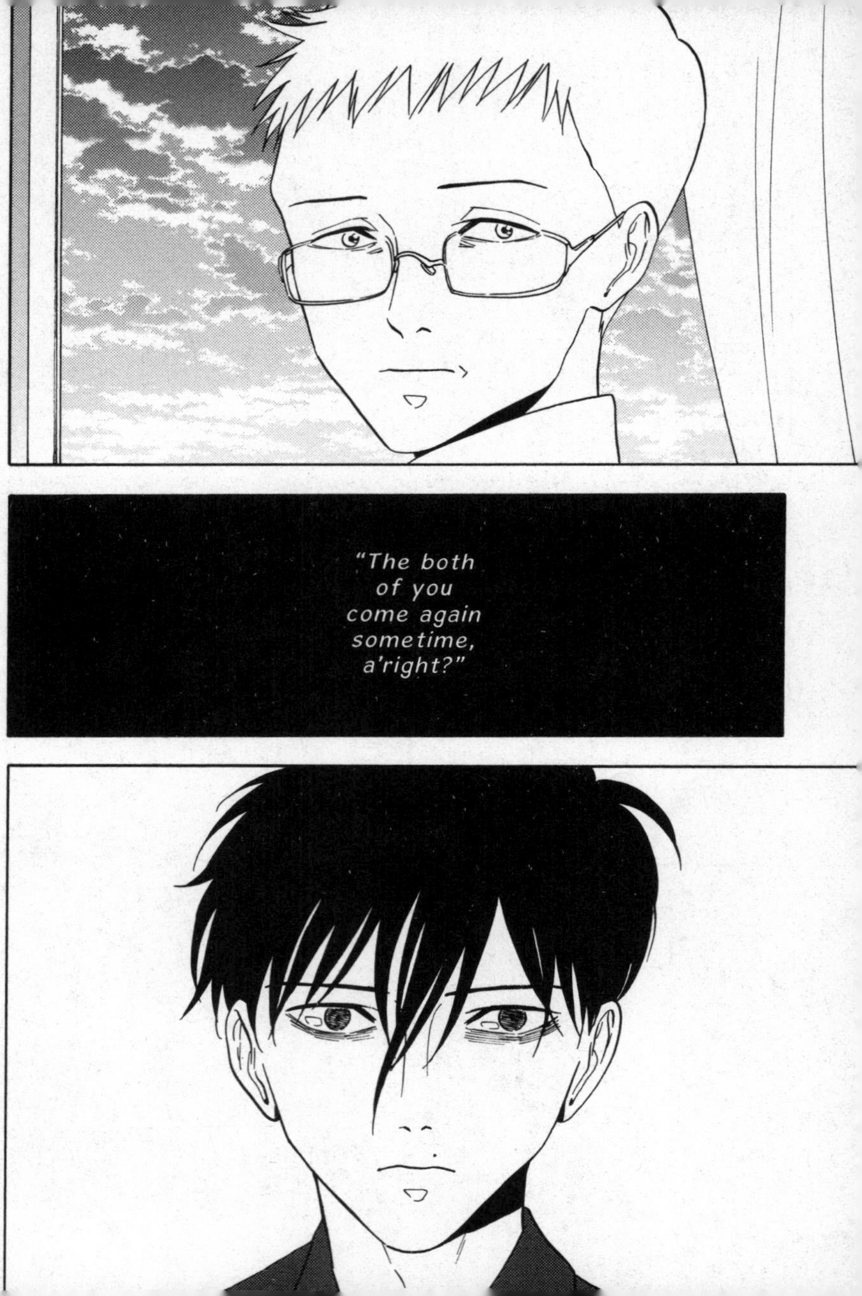
"The both of you come again sometime, a'right?"

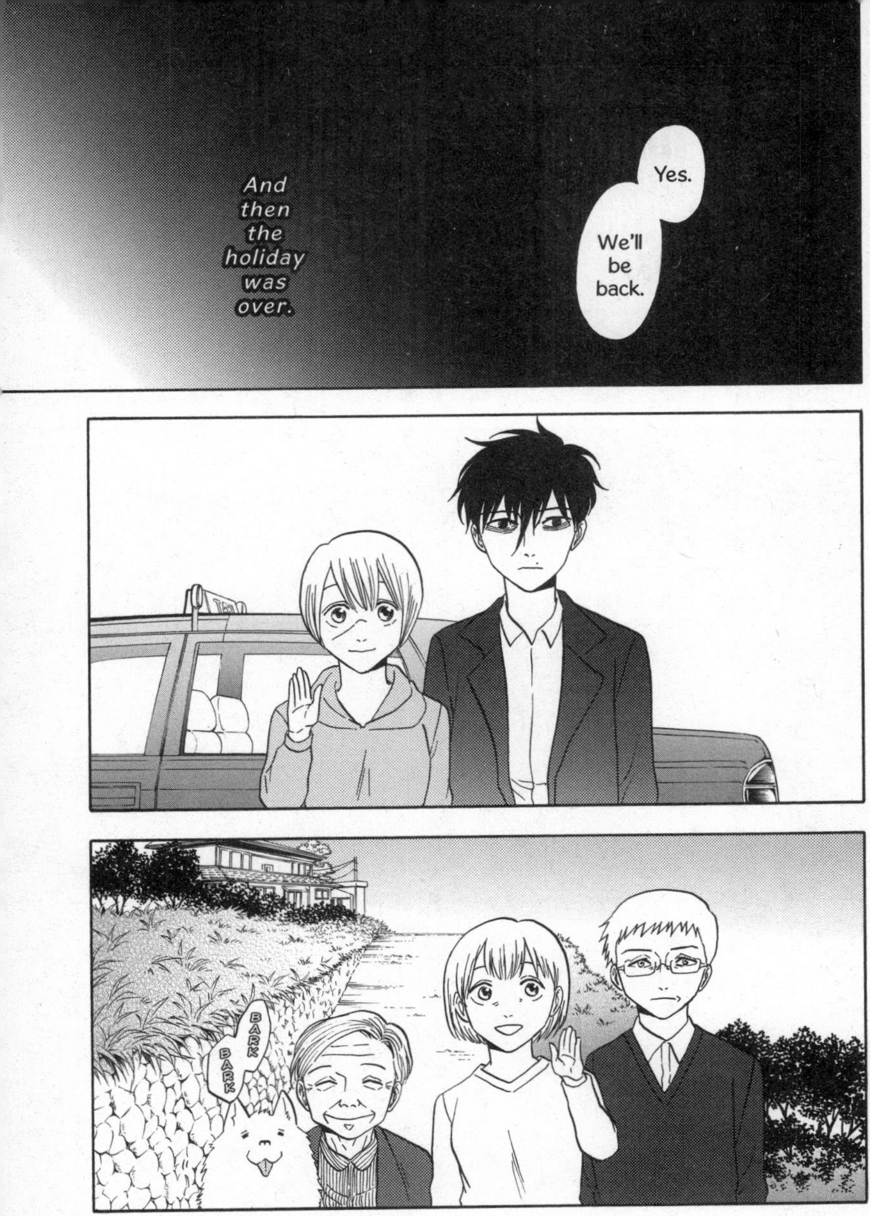
Yes.
We'll be back.
And then the holiday was over.
BARK BARK

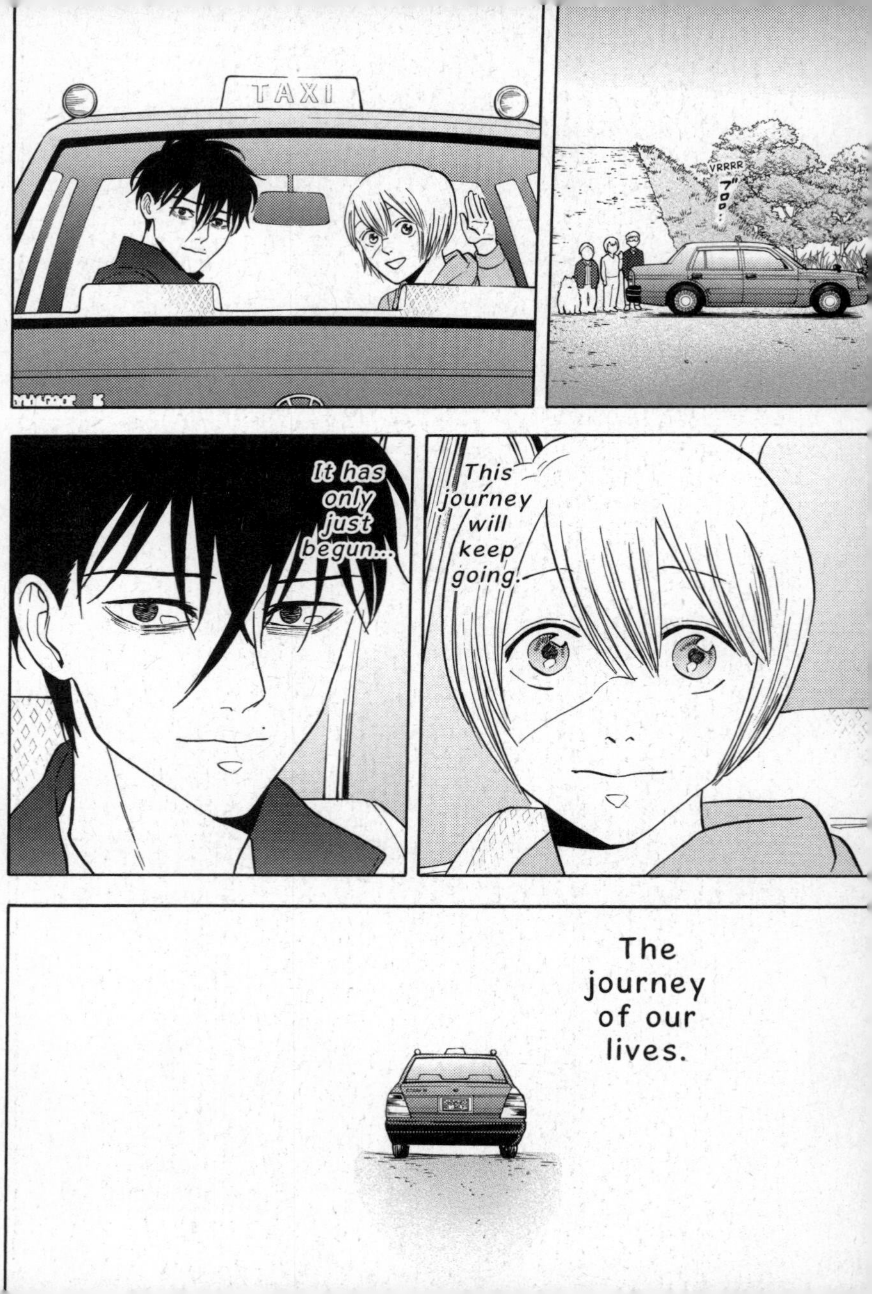
VRRRR
ブロロ…
TAXI
This journey will keep going.
It has only just begun...
The journey of our lives.

Previously unpublished Line X
Tokyo Branch Jail Experience Course No. 1

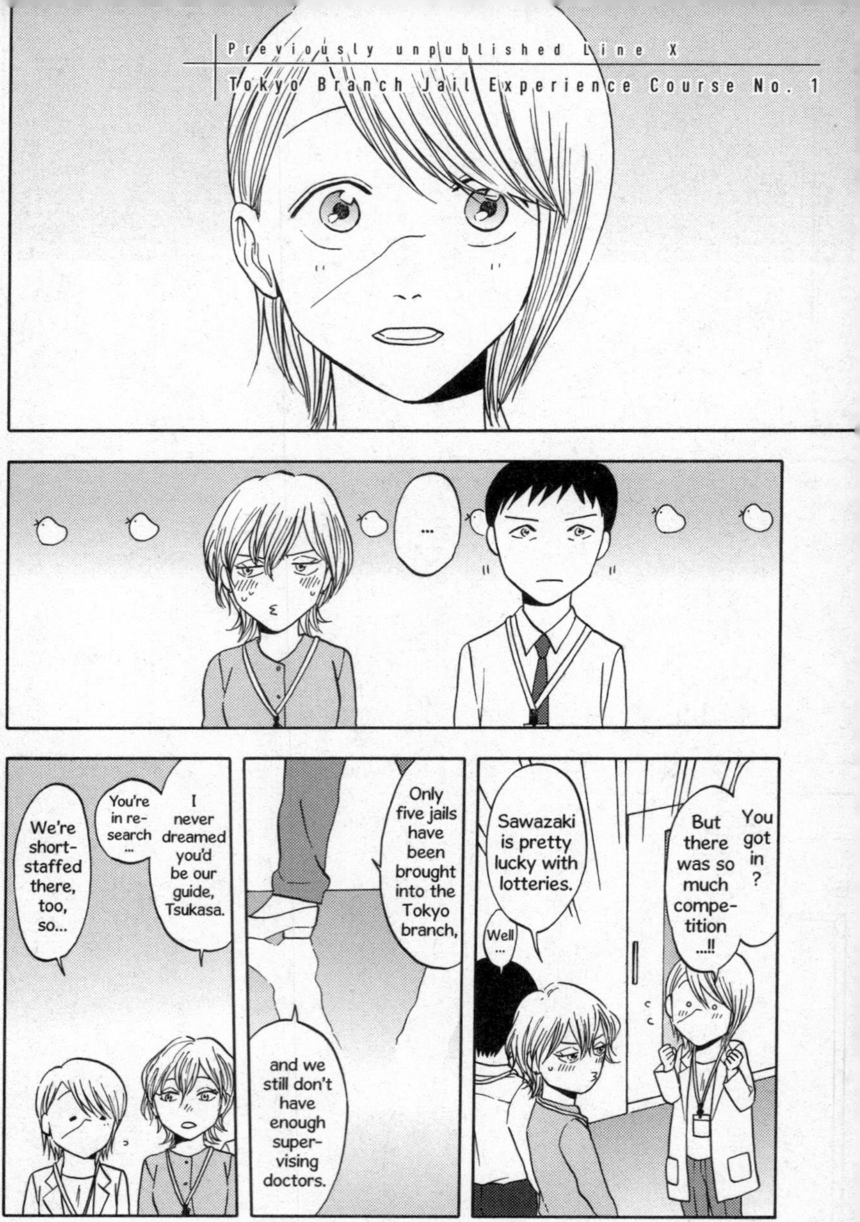
…
You got in?
But there was so much competition …!!
Sawazaki is pretty lucky with lotteries.
Well…
Only five jails have been brought into the Tokyo branch,
and we still don't have enough supervising doctors.
I never dreamed you'd be our guide, Tsukasa.
You're in research…
We're short-staffed there, too, so…

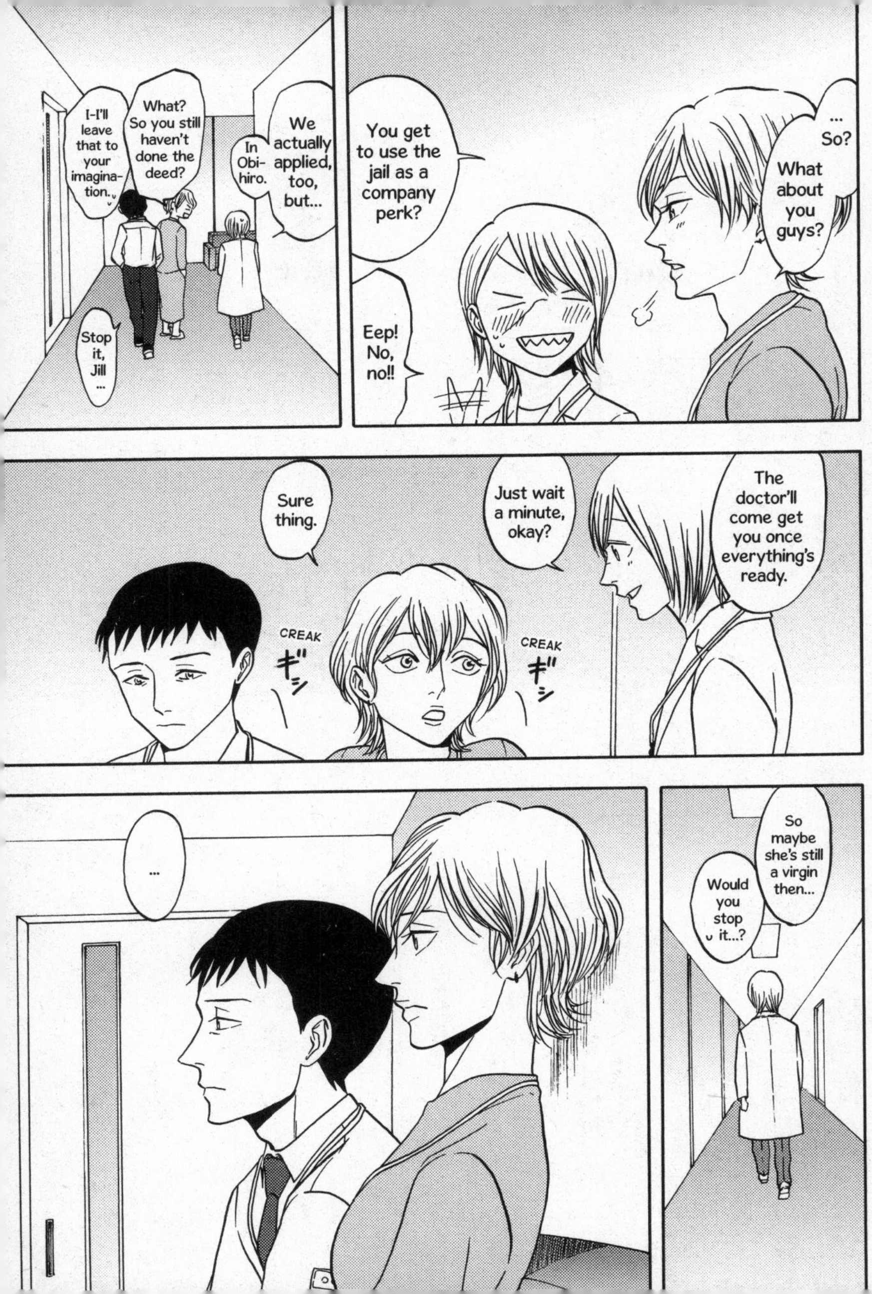
... So?
What about you guys?
You get to use the jail as a company perk?
Eep! No, no!!
We actually applied, too, but...
In Obi-hiro.
What? So you still haven't done the deed?
I-I'll leave that to your imagination..
Stop it, Jill ...
The doctor'll come get you once everything's ready.
Just wait a minute, okay?
Sure thing.
CREAK
ギシ
CREAK
ギシ
So maybe she's still a virgin then...
Would you stop it...?
...

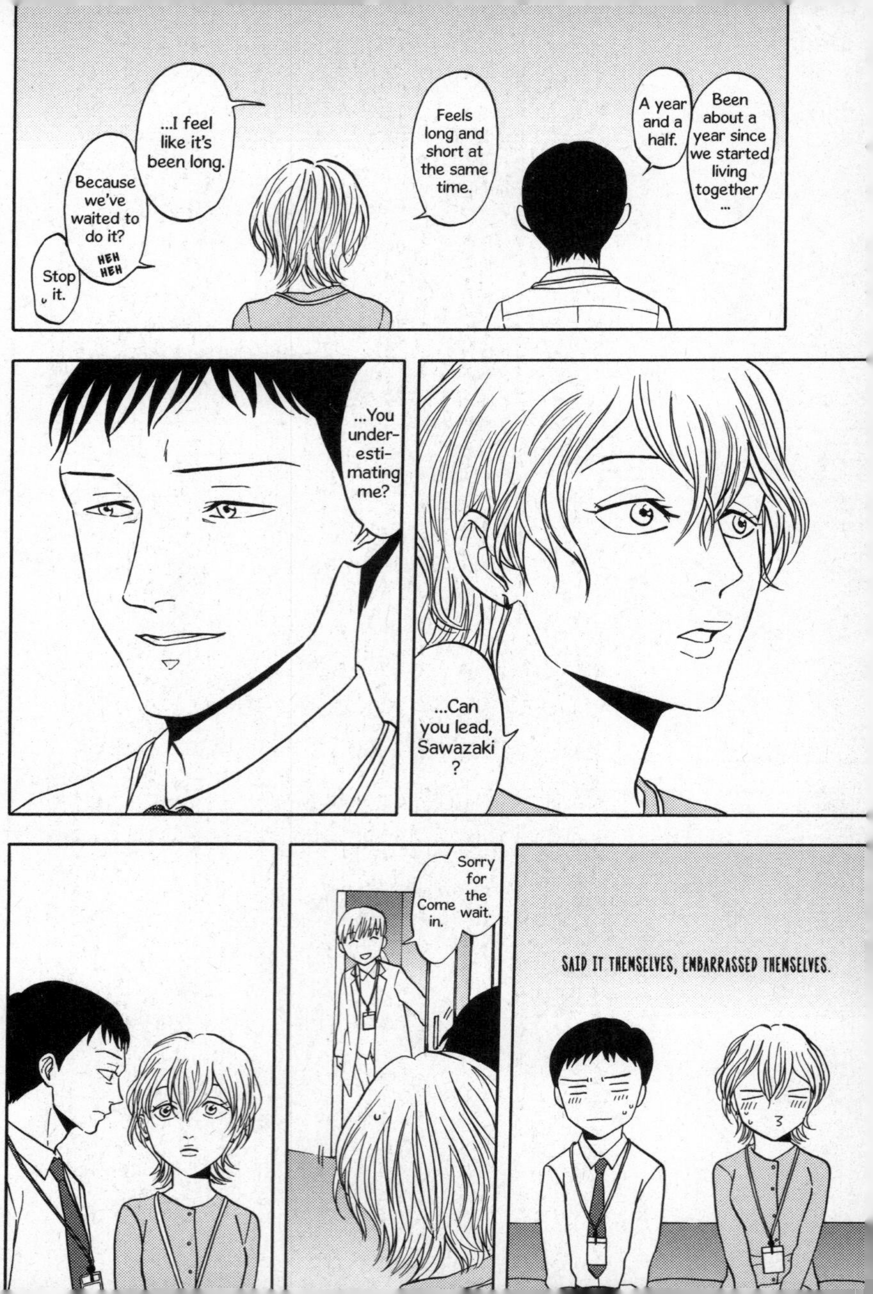
Been about a year since we started living together ...
A year and a half.
Feels long and short at the same time.
...I feel like it's been long.
Because we've waited to do it?
HEH HEH
Stop it.
...Can you lead, Sawazaki?
...You under-estimating me?
SAID IT THEMSELVES, EMBARRASSED THEMSELVES.
Sorry for the wait.
Come in.

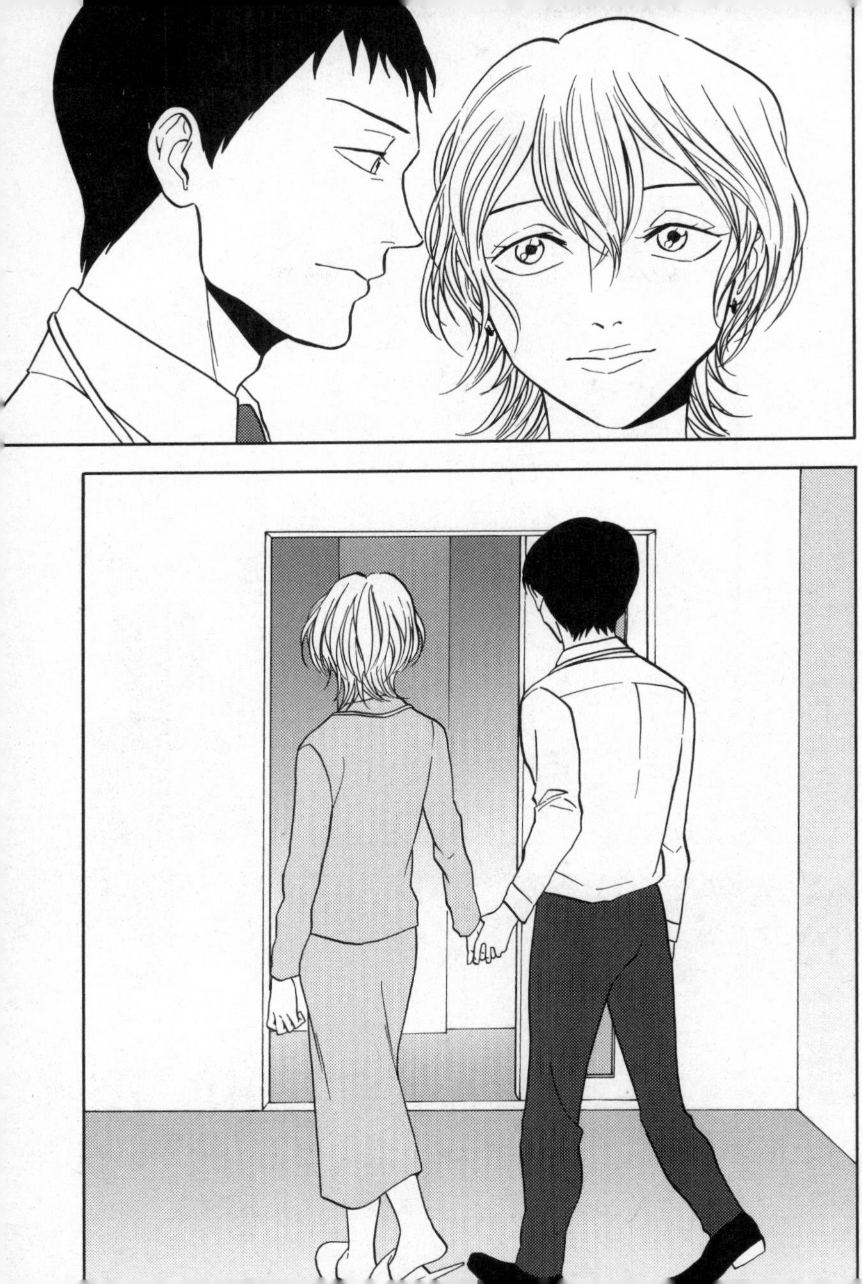

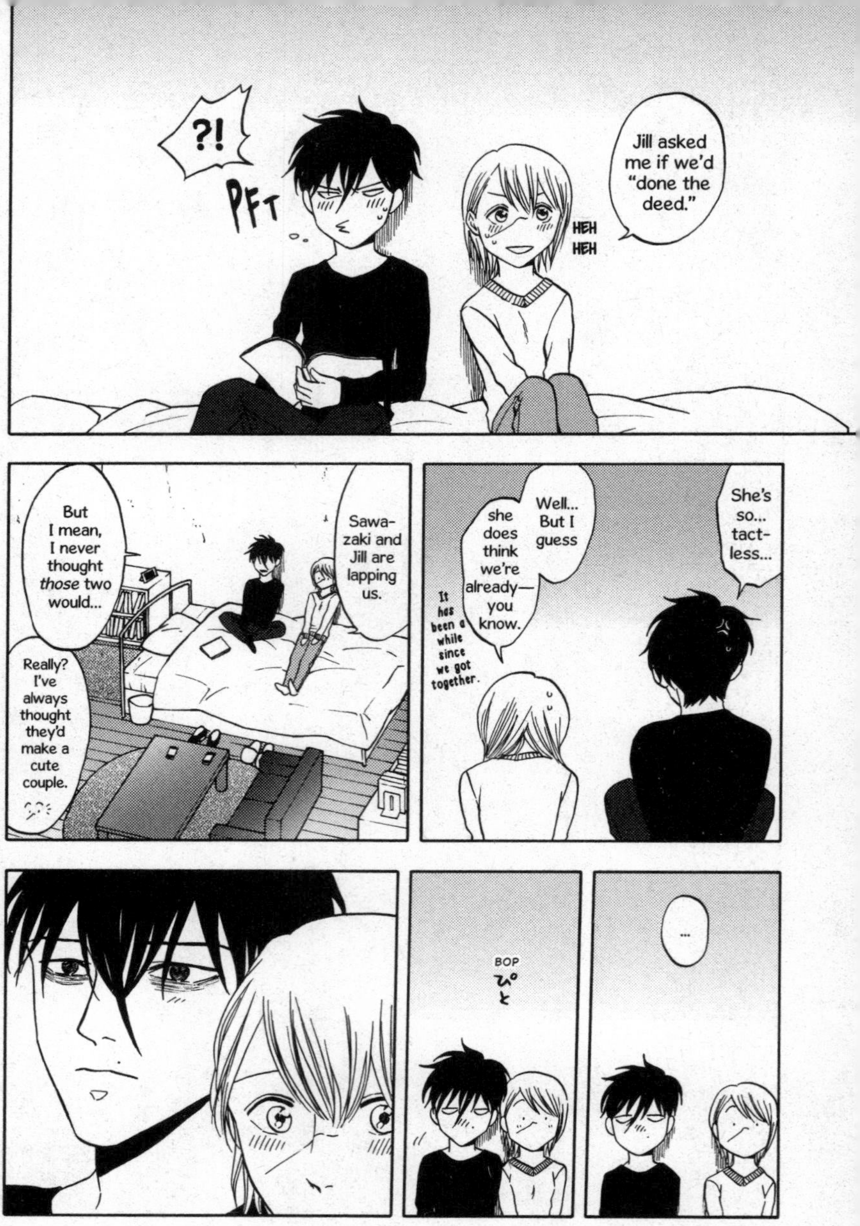
Jill asked me if we'd "done the deed."
HEH HEH
?!
PFT
She's so... tact-less...
Well... But I guess
she does think we're already—you know.
It has been a while since we got together.
Sawa-zaki and Jill are lapping us.
But I mean, I never thought *those* two would...
Really? I've always thought they'd make a cute couple.
...
BOP
ぴと

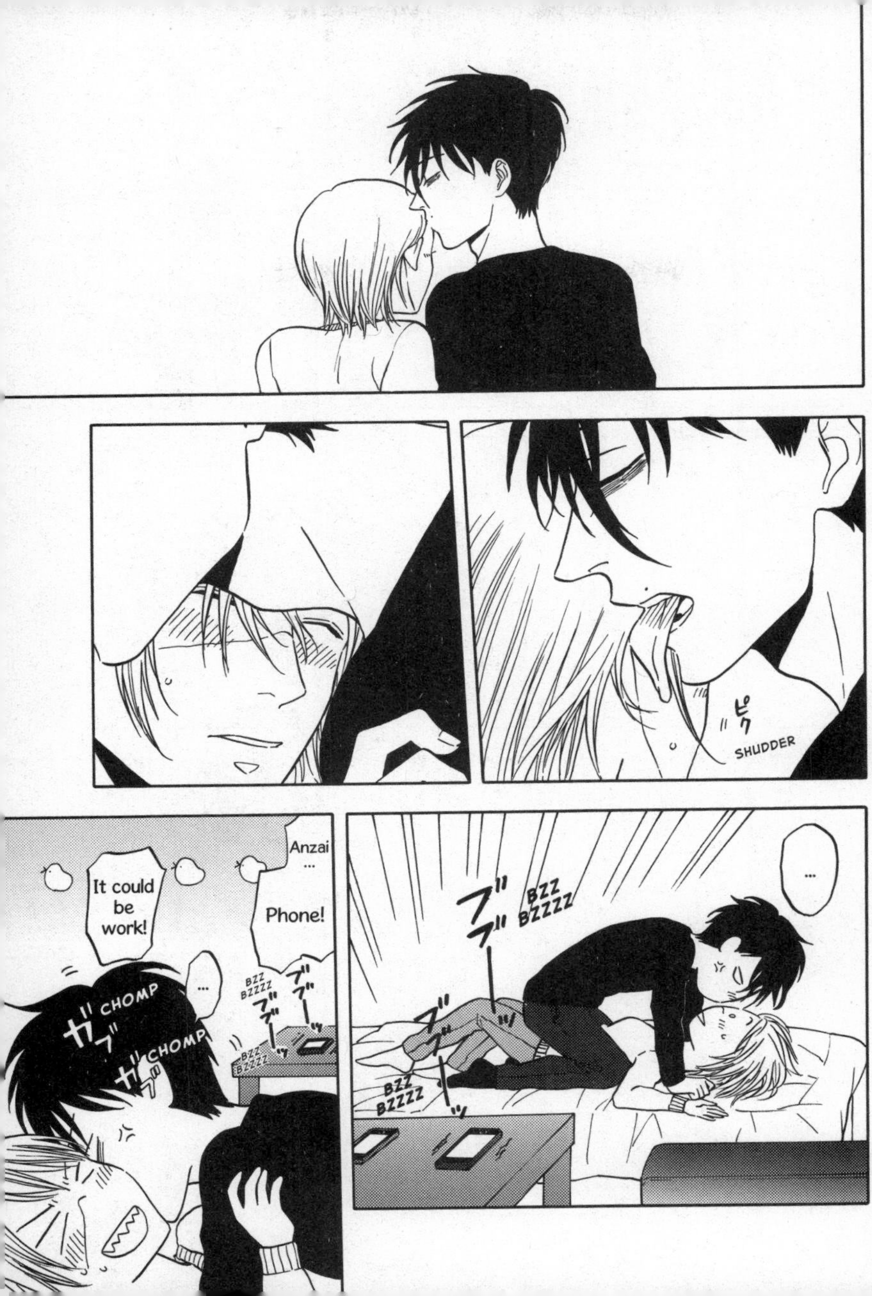
ピク
SHUDDER
...
BZZ BZZZZ
BZZ BZZZZ
Anzai ...
Phone!
It could be work!
...
BZZ BZZZZ
CHOMP
CHOMP
BZZ BZZZZ

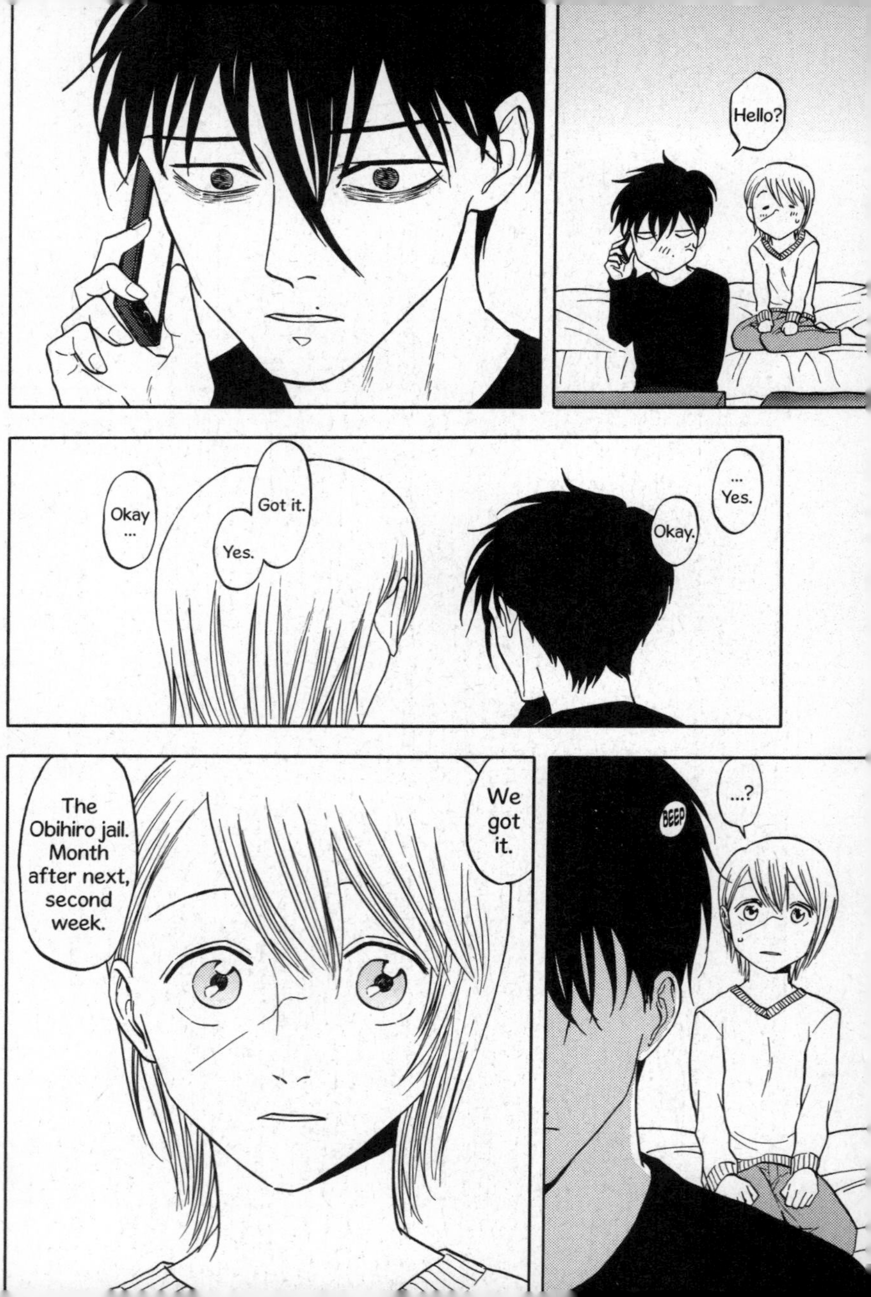
Hello?
... Yes.
Okay.
Got it.
Yes.
Okay ...
...?
BEEP
We got it.
The Obihiro jail. Month after next, second week.

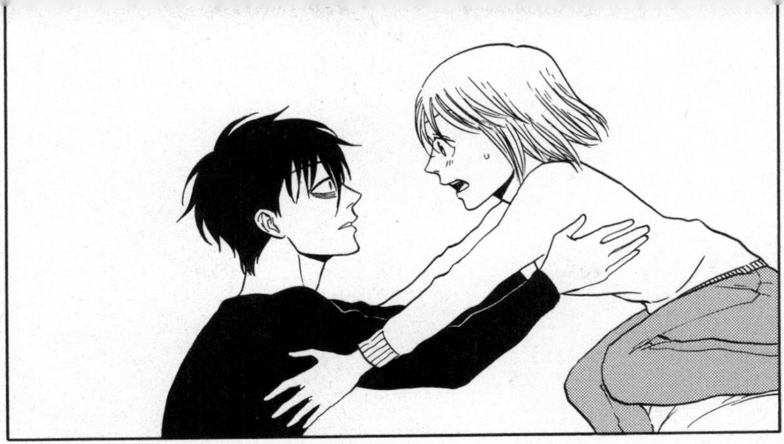

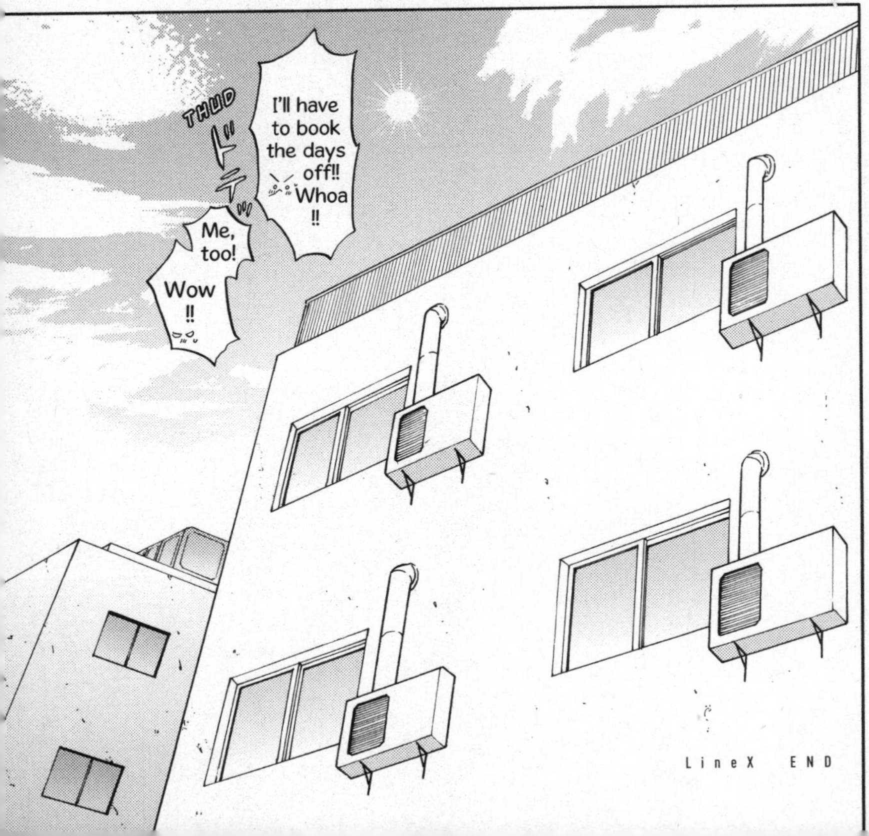
I'll have to book the days off!!
Whoa!!
THUD
ドテッ
Me, too!
Wow!!
LineX END

I would
like to offer
my sincerest
gratitude to
everyone
involved in
Devils' Line.

Editor   J-ko
Initial editor M-mura
Design   Hisamochi
Main assistant Chiguro Tsukishima
Assistant   Tani-H
Aomori photography
/Tsugaru dialect assistance W.A.
Private home photography studio mon
assistance   Oyamadai Studio
                /People in the neighborhood
Kagawa dialect assistance editor S-hara

And you, dear reader

EARLY GROUP WRAP PICTURE

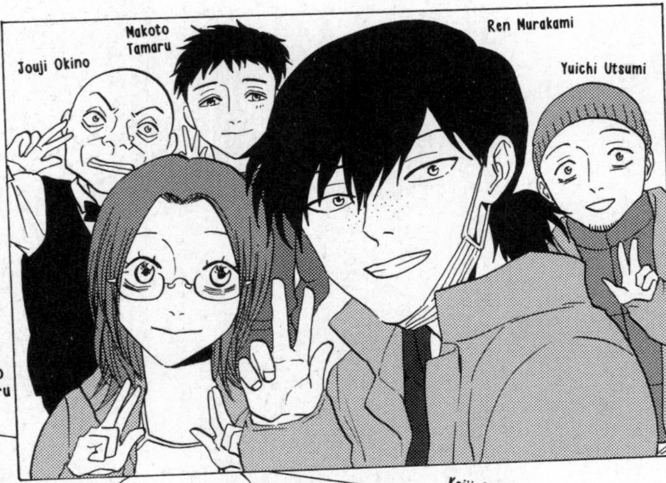
Ren Murakami
Yuichi Utsumi
Makoto Tamaru
Jouji Okino
Yuuko Tamaru

GROUP THAT THOUGHT THEY WERE IN THE EARLY WRAP BUT WEREN'T

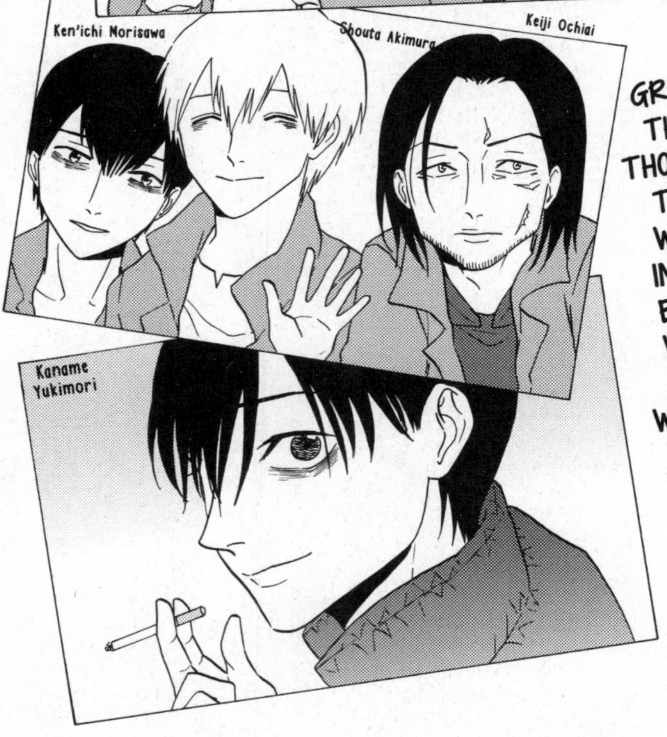
Keiji Ochiai
Shouta Akimura
Ken'ichi Morisawa
Kaname Yukimori

MAIN CAST

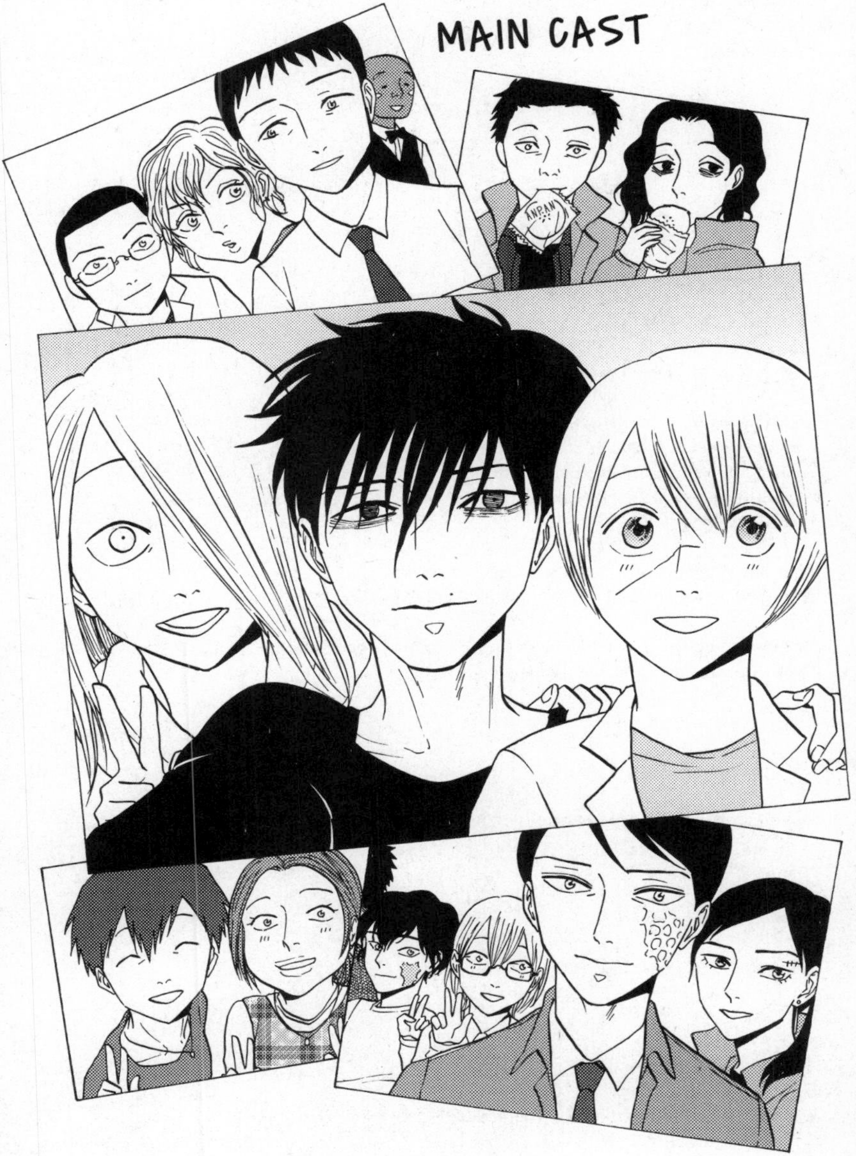
ANPAN

DEVILS' LINE 14

A Vertical Comics Edition

Translation: Jocelyne Allen
Production: Risa Cho
        Lorina Mapa

© 2019 Ryo Hanada. All rights reserved.
First published in Japan in 2019 by Kodansha, Ltd., Tokyo
Publication rights for this English edition arranged through Kodansha, Ltd., Tokyo
English language version produced by Vertical Comics, an imprint of Kodansha
USA Publishing, LLC

Translation provided by Vertical Comics, 2020
Published by Kodansha USA Publishing, LLC, New York

Originally published in Japanese as *Debiruzurain 14* by Kodansha, Ltd., 2019
Debiruzurain first serialized in *Morning two*, Kodansha, Ltd., 2013-2019

This is a work of fiction.

ISBN: 978-1-947194-87-8

Manufactured in the United States of America

First Edition

Second Printing

Kodansha USA Publishing, LLC
451 Park Avenue South
7th Floor
New York, NY 10016
www.kodansha.us

Vertical books are distributed through Penguin-Random House Publisher Services.